INSIDERS' GUIDE® TO
OKLAHOMA CITY

HELP US KEEP THIS GUIDE UP TO DATE

We would love to hear from you concerning your experiences with this guide and how you feel it could be improved and kept up to date. Please send your comments and suggestions to:

editorial@GlobePequot.com

Thanks for your input, and happy travels!

INSIDERS' GUIDE® SERIES

INSIDERS' GUIDE® TO

OKLAHOMA CITY

DEBORAH BOUZIDEN

INSIDERS' GUIDE

GUILFORD, CONNECTICUT
AN IMPRINT OF GLOBE PEQUOT PRESS

All the information in this guidebook is subject to change. We recommend that you call ahead to obtain current information before traveling.

To buy books in quantity for corporate use or incentives, call **(800) 962–0973** or e-mail **premiums@GlobePequot.com.**

INSIDERS' GUIDE®

Project editor: Ellen Urban
Layout artist: Kevin Mak
Text design by Sheryl Kober
Maps by Trailhead Graphics, © Morris Book Publishing, LLC

ISBN 978-0-7627-5345-1

Printed in the United States of America
10 9 8 7 6 5 4 3 2 1

CONTENTS

Directory of Maps

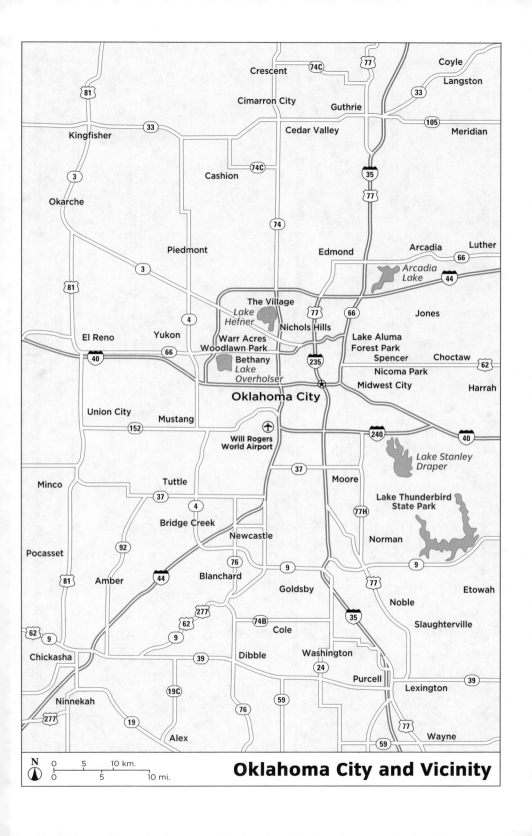

Oklahoma City and Vicinity

Edmond

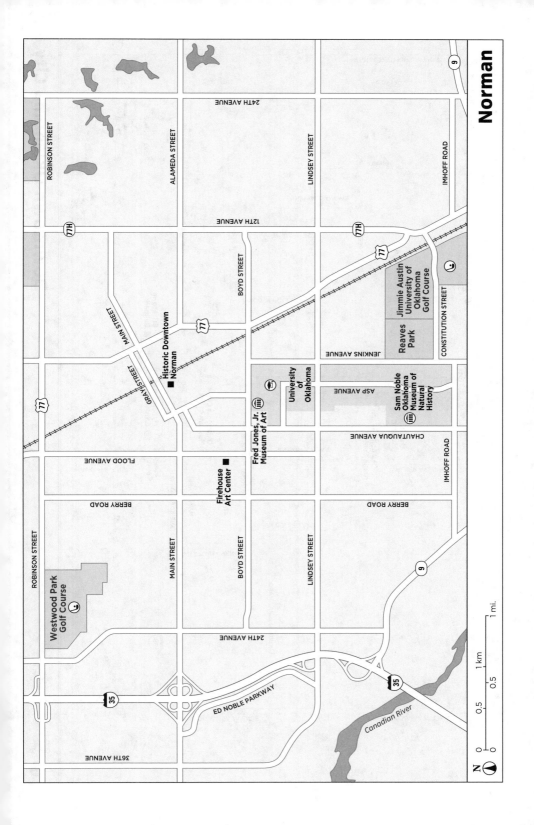

Norman

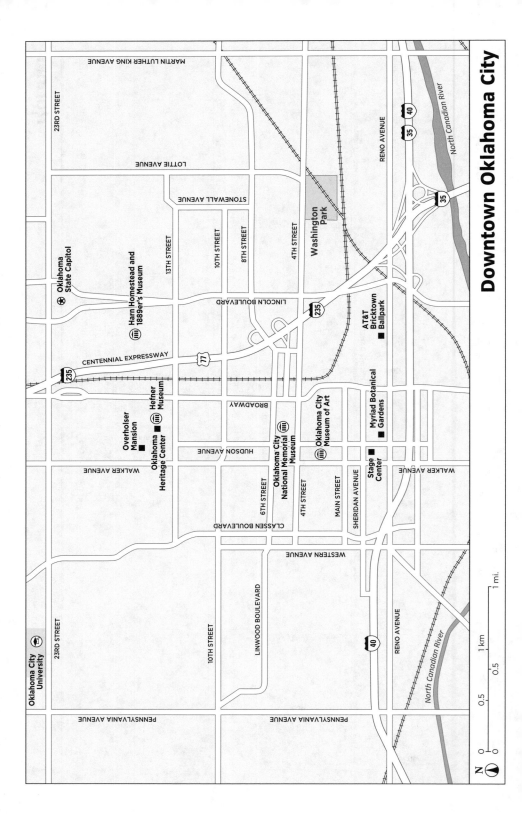

Downtown Oklahoma City

PREFACE

Welcome to beautiful Oklahoma City! Located in the heart of Oklahoma, Oklahoma City has something to offer everyone be they young or young at heart, male or female, newcomer or long-time resident. From family restaurants to fine dining, to shopping, to exploring a museum, readers will find it worthwhile and fun to spend a great deal of time exploring the area.

When I started writing this book, I wanted to give readers the flavor of what it is like to visit or live in Oklahoma City. I wanted to show readers that whoever you are, whatever you do, or wherever you are from, Oklahoma City is a little like discovering a treasure mine. There were places I knew about and frequented when I began, but as the book progressed and I talked to more and more people, I discovered new places that I wanted to visit.

While the interstates run north and south, east and west through and around the city, it's only when you jump off the fast lane and drive down smaller streets and side roads that you can appreciate Oklahoma City's charm. Bricktown sits just to the east of downtown Oklahoma City and is a great place to kick back, do some dancing, watch a ballgame, and generally have a good time. Stockyards City, located to the southwest of downtown, welcomes cowboys and cowgirls of all ages. Shoot, they'll even let those who are just interested in what goes on down there come visit! Museums and art galleries dot Oklahoma City, giving even the heartiest knowledge seeker and art lover places to visit.

The people of Oklahoma City are a friendly bunch. They like Mexican food, football and basketball games, rodeo, shopping, museums, and more. They have big hearts and welcome you into their homes and businesses. When they ask you how you are doing, they really want to know, and when you ask for advice, be it about politics or the best place to eat in town, they will give you their honest opinion.

The Insider's Guide to Oklahoma City was written to help you explore and find your way around this fascinating and unique city. If you are coming for a visit, whether business or pleasure, this book will point out places to stay, activities to enjoy, and events taking place in the month of your visit. If you live here and want to get away for a day or for the weekend, there is a chapter for you, too. Looking to move here? The book has overviews of education, health services, churches, and media in the Oklahoma City area. If you have lived here for a while, this book may help you find a new restaurant, a new event to attend, or simply remind you of places you haven't been to for a while.

There are special treasures hidden all around Oklahoma City. My hope is that through this book you will find places to visit and treasures of your own.

ACKNOWLEDGMENTS

Putting together a book of this size and type is never easy. It takes a lot of people sharing information and pointing the author in the right direction. I would like to thank all the people who took the time to write or speak to me about our fair city. I especially love those of you who got back to me within hours or the following day. It saved me time and huge amounts of frustration. Special thanks goes to Jennifer McClintock, who went above and beyond the call of duty, staying late and working on her days off to make sure I had the information I needed, and to Ron Watkins, owner of Avalon Seafood, who contacted restaurants and other businesses along May Avenue for me.

Gratitude goes to my daughter, Yolanda, who cleaned, cooked, brought food to my desk, and did basic research in the early stages of the book. And to my friends, thank you all for understanding when I didn't call you back or couldn't meet up with you for a cup of coffee. To all those who said prayers, know that I felt your strength on the days the interviewing went well and words flowed. In the end, when this was finished, we did get our sea-splitting size miracle.

I would be remiss if I didn't thank my editor, Amy Lyons at Globe Pequot Press. Her guidance, support, pep talks, and encouragement made it possible for me to continue. You have no idea how many times a day I wanted to give up.

Thank you all. This is as much your book as it is mine.

HOW TO USE THIS BOOK

Want to know where to go to get the best Mexican food in town? Shopping for kibbe, a diamond ring, or a unique gift for Mom? Want to take the kids to a place where they will have an interactive experience? Look no further than in the pages of this book. Consider the *Insiders' Guide to Oklahoma City* your handheld encyclopedia to everything you want and need to know about Oklahoma City.

This book is organized by chapter to make the search for anything you're looking for easier. If you're new to town and need to know which highway will take you from the north side of the city to the south side quickly, check the "Getting Here, Getting Around" chapter. If you're here for a vacation or on business, you will find the "Accommodations" chapter helpful.

If you're curious about the cuisine that Oklahoma City offers, see the "Restaurants" chapter. In addition to information about location, menu, and prices, sometimes the history of the restaurant is included. For instance, in the early 20th century, County Line BBQ was a speakeasy. That ambience still lingers today.

At least one "Close-Up" box is featured in each chapter. These provide you with a closeup look at various subjects. "Insiders' Tips" (indicated by 🛈) are also in every chapter to give you hints on how to find information. For instance, where can you go online for tornado safety information? An Insiders' Tip in the "Area Overview" chapter will tell you.

If you are a longtime resident of the Oklahoma City area, you will find the "Nightlife," "Attractions," and "Annual events" chapters helpful. Perhaps you will find an event that you weren't aware of. This may be your time to step out and try something new. Most entries have Web sites, so if you're not quite sure, hop on the World Wide Web and take an electronic peek before you go in person.

What about a little adventure outside the city? The "Day Trips and Weekend Getaways" chapter will give you ideas for where to go during the day and have you back home in your own bed at night.

If you're new to the area, same rule applies, but in your case, a visit to some of our local museums and/or attractions might be just the thing. You can discover some of our local artists in the Paseo District or visit the Oklahoma Heritage Center to learn more about Oklahoma's history. If you have children, check the "Kidstuff" chapter. Several attractions like the Omniplex and the City Arts Center have summer camps or ongoing programs for children of all ages.

If you are considering moving to the area, check out the "Relocation," "Education," and "Retirement" chapters. These chapters are filled with tips on how to make your transition to life in the city as smooth as possible. You will find out how to register to vote, what schools are in the area, and how to receive a relocation packet.

In some chapters, you will notice an entry repeated. The Oklahoma City Zoo is one example. It is listed in the "Attractions" chapter because it is one of Oklahoma City's premiere places to visit. It is also listed in the "Annual Events" chapter because it holds several special annual events each year. Since the zoo also has special programs for children, it is listed in the "Kidstuff" chapter as well.

As with any printed material, I've tried to include up-to-date, accurate information, but in our world, things change quickly. Be your own best advocate. Be cautious, not only with your children, but also with yourself. Call venues before heading out to make sure events are still scheduled. Call attractions and restaurants to confirm hours. If you go to a nightspot and it doesn't look or feel right, don't enter. Know that prices change and sometimes they change quickly. Businesses also come and go. Talk to those around you; get the opinions of others about where to go, what to do, and when to do it. Summers are hot in Oklahoma and in spring, thunderstorms can pop up anywhere at anytime, so be prepared for those weather changes.

We love to hear from our readers and if you'd like to comment on some of the sights mentioned in this book, please contact us. If you catch an error or know of a particular restaurant, bar, store, or other spot that should be included in a future edition, please let us know. *Insiders' Guide to Oklahoma City* will be updated periodically and your feedback would benefit the next edition. Please write to us at Insiders' Guide to Oklahoma City, GPP, PO Box 480, Guilford, CT 06437-0480 or at editorial@globepequot.com.

AREA OVERVIEW

Welcome to Oklahoma City. At first glance, it may seem like any other metropolitan area, but those who have been around for awhile, know that Oklahoma City is unique. It had an exciting beginning that has never been forgotten. It is a growing and expanding city, one that residents encourage by voting to support expansion. A one-cent sales tax for the Metropolitan Area Projects (MAPS) first began in Dec 1993. It has afforded improvements to downtown Oklahoma City areas, like Bricktown, the Cox Center, and the Ford Center. Voters approved to continue the temporary one-cent sales tax in 2009. This paves the way for more city improvements under the MAPS 3 project.

The people who live here are a resilient bunch. Oklahoma City's forefathers survived the dust bowl and the Great Depression. More recently, in 1995, residents came together to respond to, what was at the time, the deadliest terrorist attack in U.S. history. Oklahoma residents are a friendly bunch as well, welcoming visitors not only into their culture, but also into their hearts. They are happy to offer directions or recommend personal favorite places to eat or things to do if you ask. Residents here are the type of people who wave as they pass or stop to say hello and see how you are doing. When a neighbor is in trouble, they lend a helping hand where and when they can even if their own misfortunes are great.

Oklahoma City is family-friendly, which is evident by all the things there are for families to do around the area. It has an employment rate that's better than the national average. In Feb 2009, according to *Fortune* magazine, three of the 100 best companies to work for are located here—Chesapeake Energy, Devon Energy, and American Fidelity Assurance. *Forbes* called Oklahoma City a recession-proof city and while part of its success comes from its connection with the oil and gas industry, its economy base is diversified, making it resilient to economic down times. In Nov 2008, CNN listed Oklahoma City as one of the "30 Best Cities to Find a Job." Oklahoma City was the largest city on that list.

Oklahoma City has made its mark not only here but also across the country and the world. Its future looks bright and with the commitment of the community and its leaders, Oklahoma City will continue to grow and thrive. It is a city on the move and that move is upward.

LOCATION, LOCATION, LOCATION

To really understand the importance of Oklahoma City, you must learn to appreciate its geographical location. Oklahoma City is located in the very heart of the State of Oklahoma. It is the centerpiece of everything that happens here. I-35, I-40, and I-44 pass through it and bring commerce and travelers from the north, south, east, and west.

People from all over the state come here to enjoy the fair, go to school, attend business meet-

ings, or just play a game of golf. Because of its central location, the city is about two to three hours from anywhere in the state. You can travel to Tulsa in 90 minutes; make it to Wichita, Kansas, in three hours; and Dallas, Texas, in about four to five hours.

Roughly to the east of I-35 is a geographical line known as the Crosstimbers. It has trees and rolling hills. To the west are Oklahoma's flat plains where you can see from one town to another and where American bison used to roam.

The city is divided by Reno Avenue. On the north side, you will find Integris Hospital, the

Oklahoma City Zoo, Quail Springs Mall, Warr Acres, the Village, and Edmond. On the south side, you will find Stockyards City, Will Rogers World Airport, the Warren Theatre, Crossroads Mall, Moore, and Norman. Traveling from one side of the city to the other can take as little as 10 minutes or as long as 45 minutes depending on which streets or highways you choose and where you are going.

OKLAHOMA CITY STATS

Oklahoma City is the most populous city in the State of Oklahoma. It is home to the state capitol and county seat. Oklahoma City is the 29th largest city in the United States and its Metropolitan Statistical Area (MSA) is the 47th largest metropolitan area in the United States. Seven counties included in that MSA are Oklahoma, Canadian, Cleveland, Grady, Lincoln, Logan, and McClain. While Oklahoma City's population is 534,000, its MSA population is 1.2 million. The city covers 621.2 square miles: 607 square miles of land and 14.2 square miles of water.

In Jan 2009, Oklahoma City was listed among Forbes "America's 25 Strongest Housing Markets." The Milken Institute named the city to its list of Best Performing Cities 2008: Where America's Jobs Are Created and Sustained. It continues to rank high in city innovation, housing affordability, air and tap water quality, and water supply.

Encompassing and surrounding Oklahoma City are communities that thrive and support the county seat. While there are 28 communities covered in the MSA, there are 10 that sit within, are closest to, or back up to Oklahoma City. They are Bethany, Del City, Edmond, Midwest City, Moore, Nichols Hills, Norman, the Village, Warr Acres, and Yukon. The city also has three unique areas: the Historical Preservation Districts, Bricktown, and Stockyards City.

SKYLINE

Oklahoma City has one of the most beautiful skylines in the country. Because of its flat geographical location, the city can be seen from its interstates. At night, the lights of downtown reflect the hopes of its people. From I-235 and I-40, one can see the hustle and bustle of Bricktown, the skyscrapers of downtown, and looking back to the north, the dome of the capitol building. While the downtown skyline did change when the Alfred P. Murrah Federal Building was bombed in 1995, it has recovered nicely with the addition of the Oklahoma City National Memorial & Museum. Driving farther west on I-40, you can see Stockyards City as you pass Pennsylvania and the State Fair Park as I-40 intersects with I-44.

Oklahoma City sits in the Bible Belt and one can see steeples of churches poking up through the skyline. Some say there is a church on every corner and while that is not completely true, Oklahoma City and all its surrounding communities do have their fair share of places to worship.

Driving up Lake Hefner Parkway, you can get a clear view of Lake Hefner to the west. But the best view of all of Oklahoma City is located at Portland Avenue and the Northwest Expressway. This location is the highest point in Oklahoma City. From here looking toward the southeast, you will see the downtown skyscrapers and the capitol. Looking toward the northwest you can see Lake Hefner and on a good day Mercy Health Center. Traveling I-40 east, past Del City and to the south, you will see Tinker Air Force Base and on I-44 south, look to the west and Will Rogers World Airport will be to your right.

i For more information about Oklahoma City, check out these Web sites: www.okcchamber.com (Oklahoma City Chamber); www.visitokc.com (Oklahoma City Convention and Visitors Bureau); www .travelok.com (Oklahoma Tourism and Recreation Department); and www.newsok.com (the Oklahoman, Oklahoma City's official newspaper).

THINGS TO DO

While Oklahoma City may not be known as a huge tourist destination yet, there are a lot of things to do here that will keep even the heartiest investigative soul busy for days. If you like art, there are a number of galleries in the city. Istvan Gallery, the Oklahoma City Museum of Art, and the City Arts Center should be first on your list. Be sure to check out the Paseo Art District, as this is where a number of artists live and work. There are several art festivals held throughout the year where you can appreciate many different art forms and buy something to take home.

If shopping is your cup of soup, you will find everything from cowboy hats to business suits in the area. Cowboys and cowgirls head down to Stockyards City. There are numerous stores that cater to those who like boots, jeans, and 10-gallon hats. For those seeking a different type of fashion, there are numerous boutiques and malls. Crossroads is located on the southeast side of the city, while Penn Square and 50 Penn Place sit along the Northwest Expressway, and if you live north or are traveling north, Quail Springs will be just right for you.

Ready to party hearty, kick up your heels, and have some fun? Head down to Bricktown. There are numerous restaurants and clubs here. Don't forget about north Western either. Between 36th and 50th, you'll find Musashi's, Sushi Neko's, and VZD's.

History buffs will find lots to discover in and around the city. There are several museums you can immerse yourself in, like the National Cowboy Hall of Fame and Western Heritage Center, 45th Infantry Museum, and the Gaylord Pickens Oklahoma Heritage Museum. If you are interested in researching your family history or just learning more about Oklahoma firsthand, there's no better place to go than the Oklahoma History Center. It houses a huge library and archives for those seeking information. Indian rolls, out-of-print history books, and some of the first printed city newspapers can all be found here.

OKLAHOMA CITY WEATHER

Oklahoma is home to fast weather changes and with Oklahoma City sitting in the middle of the state, it sees it all. From snow to ice, rain, and hail,

you will experience it all if you stay in Oklahoma City for an extended period of time. The average rainfall is 35.97 inches. The temperature can reach as high as 113 degrees Fahrenheit, as it did on Aug 11, 1936, and as low as -17 degrees Fahrenheit, as it did on Feb 12, 1899. But on average the high is 71.2 degrees Fahrenheit and average low is 49.2 degrees Fahrenheit. Oklahoma City sees the sun 68 percent of the year, or 248 days a year.

In the winter, the greatest threat is ice. When ice hits the city, electrical lines often get pulled down by the weight of the ice. Residents prepare by having flashlights, water, and extra food. In some cases, a generator is a good item to have as well. Utility companies will work overtime to get power restored, but outages can last anywhere from a few hours to several days depending on the intensity of the storm.

Flooding is an issue during spring storms. While the city works diligently at maintaining run-off systems, sometimes when torrential rains come, water floods roadways and neighborhoods. Television and radio stations warn when flooding is a possibility. Be prepared. Do not let your children play in flood-prone areas and never drive through standing water. Many times people in cars have been washed away because currents are high or roads are washed out. Turn around and find another route.

Thunderstorms with hail, high winds, and tornadoes are also part of Oklahoma City's climatic landscape. Tornado season typically runs from Mar through May, but Oklahoma City can experience tornadoes at any time of the year. If storms are threatening, television and radio stations play a big part in alerting citizens of danger. If you are visitor staying in a hotel during a storm, stay away from windows and go down to the lowest level of your hotel when and if you hear sirens.

If you are living here, make plans ahead of time. Know what you will do and where you will go if a tornado is heading toward your location. Warnings will be given and it is important that you heed those warnings.

ℹ️ To get tornado safety information, visit www.news9.com. Click on "Weather Safety."

LANGUAGE

English is the official language of Oklahoma City, but Spanish and Chinese can be heard frequently on the streets and in stores. Along Northwest 23rd Street from Meridian to MacArthur is a high concentration of Latinos who speak Spanish more often than English. The same can be said for the Asian influence along Classen and 23rd.

GOVERNMENT

Oklahoma City has an elected mayor and eight elected city council members, one for each of the eight wards of the city. The mayor and the council are elected to four-year terms. The council members, however, are elected on alternating four years. This means that wards 2, 5, 6, and 8 will be up for election in 2011 and wards 1, 4, 5, and 7 will be up for reelection in 2013.

Oklahoma City has a council-manager form of government, which was established in 1927 by a city charter amendment. In this system, the mayor and city council set the policy and conduct city business. The mayor and council appoint a city manager, who carries out the day-to-day operation of the city.

UNIQUE CITY AREAS

Oklahoma City was settled back in 1889. From that time forward there were areas of the city that grew, flourished, diminished, and then with community help came back to life. Bricktown was one such area. Stockyards City, however, has always been a strong city area because of the cattle industry business located there. Then there are the Historic Preservation Districts. These are areas located around the capitol and north of downtown Oklahoma City. They are communities that were established between 1900 and 1949. Today, visitors can see stately mansion in some neighborhoods and structures that need restoration in others.

Oklahoma City Resources Online

For information about what's happening in and around Oklahoma City—its restaurants, sporting events, social scene—visit these Web sites:

www.bricktownokc.org
www.oktourism.com
www.eataroundokc.com
www.oklatravelnet.com
www.okgazette.com

Bricktown

Bricktown, once a decaying part of Oklahoma City, has been renewed to an economic, cultural, and commercially viable community embracing its history and expanding its future. Two years before the 1889 Land Run, the Santa Fe Railroad built its tracks here. Rock Island, Frisco, and the Katy soon followed. Large freight operations shipped out cotton, cattle, horses, fruit, mules, wheat, corn, produce, and other products from its docks. Arriving were manufactured goods, like radios, farm machinery, hardware, automobiles, and Sears ready-to-assemble homes. After oil was discovered in Oklahoma City's oil fields, it, too, was shipped from here by rail. Coming and going on the trains were residents and salesmen.

To accommodate commerce and passenger traffic, the city's early residents began constructing redbrick buildings here. From 1898 to 1930 there was a building boom and then when the Great Depression hit, constuction stopped. After World War II, suburban sprawl began and new industrial parks grew away from this commercial center because of cheap land and the trucking industry.

By 1980 the area had become a virtual graveyard of brick buildings. Enter Oklahoma City and its MAPS program. With vision, leadership, and a plan to revitalize the area, Bricktown came back to life.

Today, one can shop, eat, attend a sporting event, watch a movie, visit a museum, or spend the night in one of the nearby hotels. Events happen here year-round and are attended by thousands. On the far east side of Bricktown, apartments are being built so that those who wish to can live in the area too.

Stockyards City

Located to the southwest of downtown Oklahoma City, Stockyards City was the first urban district established in Oklahoma. It is geared toward the authentic working cowboy. Historic Stockyards City started up at the same time the stockyards themselves opened and was originally known as Packingtown. It served as a mercantile district for the stockyards. In the early days you could find a hay market, cotton gin, cotton compress, wagon factory, and harness factory here. Today, it is an historic district with food, entertainment, and shopping.

It is listed on the National Register of Historic Places and in the book, *1,000 Places to See Before You Die*.

Historical Preservation Districts

Oklahoma City has 19 registered historic districts on the National Register of Historic Places. While they are all important to Oklahoma City's history, we will concentrate here on the six that sit closest to downtown Oklahoma City. These were built during the city's early days and its expansion outward from 1900 to 1949.

The Capitol–Lincoln Terrace Historic District is bounded by 13th Street on the south, 23rd Street on the north, Lincoln Boulevard on west, and roughly Kelley Avenue on the east. The district encompasses 741 acres and includes 153 buildings. The architectural styles are Tudor revival, Mission revival and Spanish revival, and colonial revival. This district is located near the capitol, the Governor's Mansion, and the Oklahoma History Center.

The Carey Place Historic District was added to the National Register in 1998. Near Oklahoma City University and Shepherd Mall, this District covers 55 acres and has 32 buildings in its area. Its boundaries run from the 1800 block to the 2100 block of Carey Place. The architectural styles are Mission and Spanish revival, and colonial revival.

The period of significance for the Edgemere Park Historic District was between 1900 and 1924 and 1925 to 1949. Its boundaries are Northwest 30th on the south, Northwest 36th to the north, Robinson to the east and Walker to the west. The domestic architectural style is bungalow and craftsman. It covers 1,150 acres and has 322 buildings. It sits closest to the Paseo Art District.

Heritage Hills Historic and Architectural District is only minutes from downtown. It was added to the National Register in 1979. Its boundaries are roughly from Robinson to Walker Avenue to Classen Boulevard, 14th and 15th Streets to 21st Street. It covers 1,875 acres and has 351 buildings. Its architectural style included Mission and Spanish revival, late-19th and early-20th-century American movements, and Colonial revival.

In 1903, Henry Overholser, one of Oklahoma City's founding fathers, built his grand mansion here. Soon, other city and state leaders, like Charles Colcord and Frank Johnson were attracted to the area and built their homes here as well. Today the Overholser Mansion is a museum in the Heritage Hills historic district. It still contains all of the original family furnishings and belongings.

Every Oct, the Heritage Hills historic district offers a home and garden tour. Residents open their homes and guests are invited to tour the homes and their gardens. Please check the Heritage Hills Historical Preservation Web site at www.heritagehills.org for more information.

The Maney Historic District is located at 725 NW 11th St., 1200 and 1224 North Shartel Ave. It covers 15 acres and has three buildings, including the Grandison Inn at Maney Park. This Victorian mansion was built in 1904 by J. W. Maney. He came to Oklahoma City in the Land Run of 1889 and stayed. Wanting to move to the country, he moved the house from 917 North Robinson to where it is today at Northwest 11th and Shartel. Today, guests can spend the night and step back in history.

Putnam Heights Historic Preservation District covers 510 acres and has 97 domestic single dwellings. It was added to the National Register in 1982. The district is located between Georgia and McKinley Boulevards and 35th, 37th, and 38th Streets, and the architectural style ranges from bungalow craftsman to late-19th- and 20th-century revivals. This district sits on the west side of Classen and is minutes from Penn Square Mall.

CITIES IN AND AROUND OKLAHOMA CITY

The following cities either surround or are located within Oklahoma City. Communities, like Capitol Hill, Forest Park, and Valley Brook, and cities, like Shawnee, Tecumseh, and Noble are included in Oklahoma City's MSA and are important to the continued economic growth of Oklahoma City, but have either merged with the city, are extremely small, or are too far away to include for purposes here.

Bethany

CITY OF BETHANY
6700 NW 36th St.
(405) 789-5005
www.cityofbethany.org
Bethany sits on the western edge of Oklahoma City's metropolitan statistical area. According to the census, its population in 2000 was 20,307. The estimated median household income in 2007 was approximately $51,000. The city covers 5.2 miles and the jagged borders run along Northwest 16th to the south, 63rd Street to the north, MacArthur on the east, and a little farther than Council Road on the western edge. Lake Overholser, the metro's oldest lake, sits to the immediate west of Bethany.

Schools are located in either the Bethany School District or the Putnam City School District. There is one hospital, Deaconess Hospital, and three colleges: Bethany Beauty College, Oklahoma Baptist College, and Southern Nazarene University. Bethany is governed by a mayor, eight council members, and a city manager. The tax rate is 4 percent and the only zip code is 73008.

This city is a town with a big heart. The town was platted in the summer of 1909. It took a while for the town to grow into more than a tent city because supplies had to be transported by wagon from Oklahoma City, a journey that took an entire day. Bethany was finally incorporated as a town in 1910.

Del City

CITY OF DEL CITY
4517 SE 29th St.
(405) 677-5741
www.cityofdelcity.com
Del City is located to the east of downtown Oklahoma City. It covers 8 square miles and has a population of 23,000. It was established in 1948. The city was founded by George Epperly and named after his daughter, Delphinia. Located near I-35 and I-40, it is an easy commute to Oklahoma City. Its affordable housing and community organizations make it an ideal place for young families. Recreational facilities, like Ray Trent Park, Eagle Lake, Wiggly Field Dog Park, and the Eagle Harbor Aquatics Center, draw visitors not only from the immediate area but also from other parts of Oklahoma City as well.

Del City is known for its annual Armed Forced Day & Shriners Parade held in May, maintaining and strengthening its strong link with the military. Many of the city's residents work or are retired from Tinker Air Force Base. One of Del City's sons is a two-time Olympic gold medalist. John Smith, who grew up in Del City and attended Del City High School, won the gold in 1988 and again in 1992 for wrestling. Today Smith is the head wrestling coach at Oklahoma State University.

Del City is governed by a mayor and four council members. The average income is $36,000 and the tax rate is 3.5 percent. There are six schools, including two private schools, in the district. One technology school, Mid-Del Technology and Training Center, within the city limits. Rose State Junior College and Midwest Regional Hospital are less than 5 miles from Del City.

Zip codes for this area are 73115, 73135, and 73165.

Edmond
EDMOND CHAMBER OF COMMERCE
825 E. Second St. #100
(405) 341-2808
www.edmondchamber.com
Edmond's motto is "A Great Place to Grow." Ask any of its residents and they will agree. Located 15 minutes north of downtown Oklahoma City via the Broadway Extension, its population is over 83,000. It covers 90 square miles and the Edmond Public School District is 130 square miles.

Edmond has a long history in the area. It was originally explored by Washington Irving in 1832 and noted in his publication, *A Tour on the Prairies*. In 1867, with the opening of the Chisholm Cattle Trail, located a few miles north of the town site, the area became a haven for cattle ranchers and ranch hands. In 1886 the Santa Fe Railroad surveyed a route through the area and in 1887, the Santa Fe filed an official request to call mile 103 Edmond. Edmond was an important stop on the line because it was possible to get food there. On Apr 22, 1889, the first of the Oklahoma land runs began. Several railroad workers were among the first to make their runs and stake their claims. At 12:05 p.m. a crew of surveyors began laying out a town site. This began a series of firsts in Oklahoma Territory: first public schoolhouse, first church, first library, and first public institution of higher education.

Edmond is governed by a mayor and four council members. The average income is $90,000. Residents in other Oklahoma City suburbs sometimes refer to Edmond as "that town." Edmond is considered a "new money" place to live meaning that those who have made their wealth at the end of the 20th century moved here. The tax rate is 3.25 percent. There are 3 high schools, 5 middle schools, and 15 elementary schools. Two colleges make their home here, Oklahoma Christian University and the University of Central Oklahoma. Edmond Medical Center has been the only hospital for a number of years, but Integris

Health Center is building a new hospital located on the east side of I–35 between 2nd and 15th Sts. Groundbreaking was held in Oct 2009. The three largest employers here are the Edmond Public School System, the University of Central Oklahoma, and the City of Edmond.

Zip codes are 73003, 73013, 73034, and 73083.

Midwest City
MIDWEST CITY CHAMBER OF COMMERCE
5905 Trosper Rd.
(405) 733-3801
www.midwestcityok.com
North of I-40 on the east side of Oklahoma City is the 25-square-mile town of Midwest City. It was founded in 1942 by W. P. "Bill" Atkinson, a prominent businessman and builder in Oklahoma City. Midwest City gets its name from Tinker Air Force Base, which used to be called Midwest Air Depot.

Tinker Air Force Base plays a large role in Midwest City's economy and cultural attitude. The city's southern boundary runs adjacent to the base and many military families make their homes here. Population is right around 55,000 and the estimated median income runs about $41,000 a year.

In May 3, 1999, Midwest City was hit by an F5 tornado. As a result, the city had to rebuild some of its economic structure as well as homes. Today, there is still middle-class, post-war housing, but there is also newer, upscale housing. The east side of town has many new housing additions. The city also has a variety of recreational facilities available, such as 33 public parks, Lake Stanley Draper, a soccer complex, a bowling center, two golf courses, and a million-dollar water park.

In 1951 Midwest City was called "America's Model City." Today, it is designated "Tree City USA" and "Certified City."

Midwest City's government is run by a mayor and six council persons representing the six wards of the city. The council and mayor are elected officials. The mayor appoints a city manager, board members, and committee members.

Zip codes are 73110, 73130, 73140, and 73145.

Moore

MOORE CHAMBER OF COMMERCE
305 W. Main St.
(405) 794-3400
www.moorechamber.com
Moore is 20 minutes south of Oklahoma City. It can be reached by driving south on I-35. This city was established in 1893 and is named after a Santa Fe Railroad employee. It covers 22 square miles and has a population of more than 52,000. The governing body consists of a mayor and seven council members. The city sales tax rate is 3.5 percent. Moore has 3 high schools, 5 junior high schools, and 21 elementary schools. There is one college, the Hillsdale Free Will Baptist College, and one hospital, the Moore Medical Center.

The city is famous for being the home of country-music singer Toby Keith. It is also known for its friendly people and new business growth. On May 3, 1999, Moore was almost destroyed by an F5 tornado, but the residents cleaned up and rebuilt their lives and their city. Today, the residents and the city continue to thrive and grow. Along the interstate on South 19th St. there is a large amount of commercial development underway. Residential additions are spreading out along the east and west sides with development continuing south toward Norman and north toward Oklahoma City.

Zip codes are 73153, 73160 and 73170.

Nichols Hills

CITY OF NICHOLS HILLS
6407 Avondale Dr.
(405) 843-6637
www.nicholshills.net
In 1929, Dr. G. A. Nichols wanted to build a community near Oklahoma City where families could live without the hustle and bustle of a metropolitan area. He bought 2,700 acres north of Oklahoma City, paid engineers to plat streets from Kansas City, and planted 5,600 large shade trees and 35,000 smaller ones. He placed the entrance to his community at Northwest 63rd and Western. In 1931, the town was named after its founder.

In the beginning, the town was out in the country. Today, Oklahoma City surrounds this 2-square-mile city. Ask the approximately 5,000 residents if they feel they are living in a metroplex and they will say no. Large trees and huge lots add even more character to this area of historic homes, upscale stores, and restaurants. While Edmond is known for "new money," Nichols Hills is known for "old money." Take a drive up Western from 63rd on its winding streets and you will see why.

Nichols Hills is governed a city manager and three councilpersons, one for each ward. The councilpersons serve a three-year term and are elected in a nonpartisan general election.

Zip codes are 73116 and 73120.

Norman

NORMAN CHAMBER OF COMMERCE
115 E. Gray St.
(405) 321-7260
www.normanok.org
Norman is 17 miles south of Oklahoma City. The best and quickest way to reach this city is by taking I-35 south. Norman is named after Abner E. Norman, a young surveyor sent to survey the area by the U.S. Land Office in 1870. The town was incorporated on May 13, 1891, and the charter adopted in 1919.

Norman covers nearly 200 square miles and has an estimated 111,000 residents, making it the third largest city in Oklahoma. There are 2 high schools, 4 middle schools, 15 elementary schools, and 1 alternative school in the Norman Public School System. The city is governed by a mayor, eight council members, and a city manager. The estimated median household income in 2007 was $62,000.

Education, manufacturing, and government agencies are Norman's economic base. The University of Oklahoma and the National Oceanic and Atmospheric Administration's (NOAA) National Severe Storms Laboratory is located here. Movie star James Garner and country music star Vince Gill claim Norman as their hometown.

Zip codes for Norman are 73019, 73026, 73069, 73070, 73071, and 73073.

The Village

CITY OF THE VILLAGE
2304 Manchester Dr.
(405) 751-8861
www.thevillageok.org

The Village was established in 1950 and was named for the Village Store, a local hangout for developers in the late 1940s, early 1950s. It covers a 2.6-square-mile area. Its population is 10,157 and the estimated median household income is approximately $44,000 a year. The governing body of the city consists of a mayor and four council members. The tax rate is 4 percent. There are three public and two private schools and the only zip code is 73120.

The Village is known as a city of character. As a middle-class, post–World War II city, its property continues to increase in value. Wiley Post Airport, formerly Curtis Wright Airfield, is located here. The city's boundaries are Waverly Avenue on the east, Lake Hefner Parkway on the west, the center of Hefner Road on the north, and the south zigzags from Andover to Brighton to Westchester.

Warr Acres

CITY OF WARR ACRES
5930 NW 49th St.
(405) 789-2892
www.cityofwarracres.com

Located to the northeast of Bethany and surrounded by Oklahoma City is this 3.5-square-mile city. City boundaries for Warr Acres are Wilshire Boulevard to the north, Northwest 36th to the south, Ann Arbor to the east and Mueller to the west. It has a population of 9,735 and the estimated median household income is around $43,000. In 2008, the city celebrated its 60th anniversary having been established in 1948. The tax rate is 4 percent, one of the metro's more competitive rates. The governing body is an elected mayor and eight council members for four wards. Their terms are served for two years and staggered. Warr Acres is proud that one half mile of historic Route 66 is along the city's southern border. Today the city continues to grow and expand in population.

Zip codes are 73122, 73123, and 73132.

Yukon

YUKON CHAMBER OF COMMERCE
510 Elm St.
(405) 354-3567
www.yukoncc.com

Yukon is located to the west of Oklahoma City with easy access to I-40 and the John Kilpatrick Turnpike. Route 66 runs through the heart of town. Yukon was established in 1891 when A. N. Spencer, a cattleman turned railroad builder, was building a rail line from El Reno, Oklahoma, to Arkansas. There were no towns between El Reno and Oklahoma City, so Spencer bought some land and with his brother, L .M. Spencer, who owned a real estate agency, they starting developing the area.

Today, Yukon has a population of 25,000 and covers an area of 26 square miles. Its boundaries run from Wilshire on the north side, to Northwest 10th on the south, Sara Road on the east, and Gregory Road on the west. Yukon is the home of country-music-superstar Garth Brooks, actor Dale Robertson, and the Oklahoma Czech Capital. Every year in Oct hundreds of people of Czechoslovakian descent come to Yukon to celebrate their customs, heritage, and culture.

Today the town is experiencing an economic upturn. New businesses are coming to the area. The average income is around $58,000. The city tax rate of 4.35 percent plus Oklahoma state tax of 4.5 percent makes the total rate 8.85 percent. The governing body consists of a mayor and five council members.

Yukon has seven grade schools, two middle schools, two high schools, two private schools, and one college, the Canadian Valley Technology Center. The largest businesses are Integris Canadian Valley Regional Hospital, Kohl's department store, Ranchwood Nursing Center, and Santa Fe Cattle Company.

Zip codes are 73099 and 73085.

Vital Statistics

Mayor: Mick Cornett

Governor: Brad Henry

State capital: Oklahoma City

Area cities: Bethany, Del City, Edmond, Midwest City, Moore, Norman, Nichols Hills, the Village, Warr Acres, Yukon

City of Oklahoma population: 534,000

Oklahoma city metropolitan statistical area: 1,308,537

Area: 622.5 square miles

Elevation: 1,285 feet above sea level

Nickname: The City

Average temperatures: Annual daily average is 60.2 degrees Fahrenheit; average daily high is 71.2 degrees Fahrenheit; average daily low is 49.2 degrees Fahrenheit. Record high was 113 degrees Fahrenheit on Aug 11, 1936, and the record low was −17 degrees Fahrenheit on Feb 12, 1899.

Average rainfall: 35.97 inches

Average days of sunshine: 248 days

Months of most active severe weather: Mar, Apr, May, and June

City founded: Apr 22, 1889

State founded: Nov 16, 1907. Oklahoma was the 46th state to join the United States.

State wildflower: Indian blanket

State bird: scissor-tailed flycatcher

State tree: redbud

Major universities: University of Central Oklahoma, Oklahoma City University, Southern Nazarene University, University of Oklahoma, OU Health Science Center, OSU-Oklahoma City, Oklahoma City Community College, Rose State College, Mid-America Christian University, Oklahoma Christian University, Hillsdale Free Will Baptist College, and Southwestern Christian University

Time zone: Central standard time; observes daylight saving time

Dress codes: Dress is casual and comfortable. From late Nov to late Apr, have a light jacket or sweater handy. Carry a raincoat and/or umbrella with you from Mar into early June.

Major area industries: aviation/aerospace, biotechnology, business services, energy, government, health care, hospitality and entertainment, telecommunications, transportation and logistics, and weather

Sports: Oklahoma City Thunder, Oklahoma City Blazers, Redhawks, Oklahoma City Yard Dawgz, Oklahoma Sooners, and the Oklahoma State Cowboys

Famous sons and daughters: Garth Brooks (singer), Wiley Post (aviator), Toby Keith (singer), Mickey Mantle (athlete), Bart Conner (gymnast), Shannon Miller (gymnast), James Garner (actor), Sean O'Grady (athlete), Ron Howard (actor/director), Brad Pitt (actor), Vince Gill (singer), Lon Chaney Jr. (actor), Megan Mullally (actress), Louis L'Amour (author), Edward Ruscha (artist).

State and city holidays: Jan 1 (New Year's Day), 3rd Mon in Jan (Martin Luther King Day), 3rd Mon in Feb (Presidents' Day), May 25 (Memorial Day), July 4 (Independence Day), 1st Mon in Sept (Labor Day), Nov 11 (Veterans Day), 4th Thurs in Nov (Thanksgiving), Dec 25 (Christmas Day).

Chamber of commerce: Greater Oklahoma City Chamber of Commerce (405-297-8900; www.okc chamber.com), 123 Park Ave.

City Web site: www.okc.gov

Major airports: Will Rogers World Airport, Wiley Post Airport

Public transportation: Central Oklahoma Transportation and Parking Authority (COTPA; 405-235-RIDE; www.gometro.org)

Military bases: Tinker Air Force Base

Driving laws: Seat belts are required for all passengers. Maximum speed limit on interstates outside city limits is 70 miles per hour. Inside city limits the speed limit is 60 miles per hour. Most turnpikes allow for 75 miles per hour.

Alcohol law: Oklahoma County offers liquor by the drink. You must be 21 years old to purchase alcoholic beverages. Approved licensed premises can sell beer, wine, and mixed drinks until 2 a.m.

Tobacco laws: Oklahoma state law regulates smoking and nonsmoking areas. Smoking is prohibited in any indoor workplaces—including restaurants and hotels—unless a separate ventilation system under negative pressure is installed for ventilating the smoking area. Smoking is permitted without limitation in bars, private clubs, bingo halls, retail tobacco stores, small family-owned workplaces, workplaces occupied exclusively by smokers, veterans' halls, and designated employee smoking areas. Oklahoma state law expressly preempts any local jurisdiction from enacting local smoking regulations which are more stringent than state law and mandates that any local smoking regulations be exactly the same as the state regulations.

Daily newspapers: *The Daily Oklahoman,* the *Journal Record,* and the *Edmond Sun*

City sales tax: 3.875 percent

State sales tax: 4.5 percent

Visitor centers: 1) North of Oklahoma City, located west of I-35 on the south side of 122nd Street, near the intersections of I-40, I-44, and I-35, (405-478-4637). 2) In Midwest City at 7200 Southeast 29th (405-739-8232), and 3) at the capitol in Oklahoma City, Northeast 23rd and Lincoln Boulevard in the first floor rotunda (405-521-3356).

Time and temperature: (405) 599-1234

GETTING HERE AND GETTING AROUND

Oklahoma City is located in the heart of the state. It is well connected by highways and even though the city has only one major airport, Will Rogers World Airport, visitors come and go with ease. Once here, unless you are staying downtown, you'll want to have a car of your own, especially if you are staying for an extended visit. Oklahoma City does have METRO Transit (www.gometro.org), which consists of buses and trolleys, but a vehicle will allow you to get around quickly and more easily.

To get your bearings, there are a few things you must know. First, the city is laid out in named streets and numbered streets. Major named streets run north and south. Numbered streets run east and west. Second, the north and south sides of the city are divided by Reno Avenue. Everything north of Reno will be called north and then the name or number of the street. Everything south will be called south and the name or number of the street. Third, east and west is divided by Broadway and Santa Fe. Which means everything west of Santa Fe, will be west in the address and vice versa for the east side. This divides the city into four pieces of a pie. There are exceptions to these rules, but for the most part, remember the divisions and you can find your way around easily.

When driving around town, you will find that because of the city's expansive interstate system, you can get from one side of the city to the other in about 35 to 45 minutes, unless it is rush hour. Highways and streets get crowded from about 6:30 to 9 a.m. and from 4:30 to 6:30 p.m. Turn on your radio and relax. Unless there is a major accident on the highway you're on, traffic will still flow at a nominal speed even though it may be quite thick. Residents here have learned to add 10 to 15 minutes to their drive time during these busy hours. If you get lost or need assistance, don't hesitate to ask someone for directions or help. Okies, as Oklahomans are called, are a friendly bunch and will be happy to assist you in any way they can.

Driving in Oklahoma City weather can become tricky, particularly during tornado season, which is generally Mar through Aug, although tornadoes can happen any time of the year. Storms tend to move from west to east. When dark clouds gather in the west, be it north or south, drivers should tune their radio to any number of the local radio stations, although KOMA-FM92.5, seems to be the station of choice because Gary England, a native Oklahoman and local weatherman, warns locals from this station. When storms start building, the stations begin broadcasting information about where the storms are, how severe they are, and where they are headed. A tornado watch means conditions are favorable for a tornado to form. A tornado warning means a tornado has formed or is on the ground.

Famous for its severe weather, the city has built an early warning system for its residents in the form of loud sirens. They are located throughout the city and when the National Weather Service sees a tornado on its radar in the area, the sirens go off.

If you are driving and a tornado is imminent and you see it or debris or hear sirens, do not try to outrun a tornado. Tornadoes have a tendency to twist and turn in location at will. Lives have been lost by drivers trying to outrun a tornado and actually driving in to it. Leave your vehicle immediately. Cars and pickups offer no protection. People are actually safer outside as tornadoes have been known to pick up vehicles and toss them around like toys. Seek shelter.

If you are downtown, public and civic buildings have underground shelters. If you are in a business location, go to an inside hallway at the lowest level of the building. Avoid places with wide-span roofs such as auditoriums, cafeterias, large hallways, or shopping malls. Get under heavy pieces of furniture and use your arms to protect your head and neck. If shelter is not available or there is no time to go indoors, find a ditch, ravine, or low-lying area and lie as flat as you can. Once again use your arms to protect your head and neck. Avoid overpasses and underpasses. While many may think an underpass is a safe place to be during a storm, it can expose people to flying debris and in some cases individuals have been sucked up in tornadoes while thinking they are safe up under an underpass.

During storms in Oklahoma, be aware of the potential for flash flooding. These storms can dump inches of rain in a matter of minutes. Never drive into water covering the roadways. Flood-related drownings occur because of vehicles driving into flood waters. The safest thing to do if you see water covering the road is to turn around and find an alternative route.

GETTING HERE

By Air

WILL ROGERS WORLD AIRPORT (OKLAHOMA CITY'S PRIMARY AIRPORT)
7100 Terminal Dr.
(405) 680-3200
www.flyokc.com

WILEY POST AIRPORT
5915 Phillip J. Rhoads Ave.
(405) 789-4061
www.wileypostairport.com

Oklahoma City has two airports, Wiley Post Airport located in Bethany and Will Rogers World Airport in southern Oklahoma City.

Wiley Post Airport is a haven for business, corporate, and general-aviation travelers. It is home base for nearly 400 aircraft, ranging in size from single-engine planes to corporate jets. Over 80,000 flight operations were logged here in 2008. Owned and operated by the Oklahoma City Department of Airports, this airport is designated as a reliever for Will Rogers World Airport. Large commercial airlines do not fly in or out of Wiley Post, so it is less known to travelers than the larger Will Rogers World Airport.

Will Rogers World Airport is the way most commercial-flying visitors arrive in Oklahoma City. Named after the famous humorist and Oklahoma native, Will Rogers, this terminal sits on a little over 8,000 acres. Dedicated in 1966, it services over 1.9 million passengers per year. In 2000, an expansion project began that was completed in 2006 at an estimated cost of $110 million. This expansion increased the size and functional area of the terminal. The expansion went east, west, north, south, and up. It increased the lobby, gate hold area, and common use area; updated concessions; and improved passenger circulation.

Not as big as O'Hare International Airport in Chicago or even Dallas Love Field, the Will Rogers terminal has two levels. On Level 1, travelers will find airline baggage claim and rental cars. More on rental cars later. On Level 2, visitors will find ticket counters and airline gates.

There are escalators, stairs, and elevators that carry travelers between floors. Level 2 has a smoking lounge, coffee shop, bar, a place to purchase snacks, and retail areas. A vending area is located on the east end of Level 1. Restrooms are located throughout, with two on Level 1 and four on Level 2.

The airport is serviced by six airlines: American, Delta, Continental, Frontier, Southwest, and United. Approximately 80 flights go out per day. They fly nonstop to 20 destinations, most with major connecting hub airports like Denver, Dallas, and Las Vegas.

When you fly out of Will Rogers, it is usually a good idea to arrive early, at least an hour and a half, so there's plenty of time to check in and make it through security. Contact your airline to find out what it recommends. Some airlines may move faster than others. Some days and times may be better. The wait at airport security checkpoints can vary quite a bit depending on all these factors. Just because you made it through in 10 minutes one day, does not mean that it will take 10 minutes next time.

If you are driving to the airport, you need to know that no vehicle can be left unattended within 300 feet of the terminal and any vehicle left so will be ticketed and towed. Drivers also cannot park at the curb to wait for arriving passengers. If the passenger is not at curb yet, drivers need to loop around and come back or take advantage of the one hour of free parking in the parking garage. After the free hour has passed, the charge is $1 per hour, or $23 a day.

If visitors need to park long-term, they can choose from the five-level garage just north of the terminal, semicovered shuttle parking, or shuttle parking. The fee for the garage and semi-covered shuttle parking is $5 a day, or $25 a week. Long-term shuttle parking is $4 a day, or $20 a week. All garages are clearly marked and navigating is fairly simple as long as visitors follow signs.

Getting from the Airport to the City

There are many ways to depart from the airport. Taxis, shuttles, and van transportation are located on the north side of the Garden Plaza pickup/drop off area outside the Level 1 exits. If you are renting a car or using your hotel's shuttle service, there are courtesy phones at the Travelers Aid stations on both levels.

Car Rental

If you haven't made arrangements to rent a car yet, you're in luck. Six car rental agencies have locations inside the airport terminal on Level 1. If you have made arrangements, you can proceed to your preferred car rental agency and pick up the keys to your car. Returning your car is just as easy. You park your rental in the Rental Car Parking on the north side of the terminal and leave the keys at the Car Rental Agency counter.

Airlines Serving Oklahoma City

American Airlines
(800) 433-7300,
www.aa.com
American offers daily nonstop departures to Dallas/Ft. Worth, Chicago, and St. Louis.

Continental Airlines
(800) 525-0280,
www.continental.com
Continental offers daily nonstop departures to Houston Intercontinental and New York Newark.

Delta Airlines
(800) 221-1212,
www.delta-air.com
Delta offers daily nonstop departures to Atlanta.

Frontier Airlines
(800) 432-1359,
www.flyfrontier.com
Frontier offers daily nonstop departures to Denver.

Southwest Airlines
(800) 435-9792,
www.southwest.com
Southwest offers daily nonstop departures to Dallas Love Field, Houston Hobby, Kansas City, St. Louis, Las Vegas, and Phoenix.

United
(800) 824-6200,
www.united.com
United offers daily nonstop departures to Chicago, Denver, and Los Angeles.

Avis (800) 831-2847
Budget (800) 527-0700
Dollar (405) 681-0151
Enterprise (800) 261-7331
Hertz (800) 654-3131
Thrifty (405) 685-7727

Other Means of Transportation

If you don't need to rent a car, there are other ways to reach downtown Oklahoma City. METRO Transit (www.gometro.org), provides daily service to and from the airport. The route travels up Meridian Avenue and connects to downtown. Travelers can board at the Transportation Plaza at the baggage level of the terminal. Schedules and rates can be found at the METRO Transit Web site.

Perhaps you want to take a taxi. The average fare from the airport to downtown is $20. Taxis can be found outside Level 1 just north of the Garden or Transportation Plaza. Rates are posted on the cabs, can be obtained from the cab driver, or you can find them ahead of time by calling the cab company. Don't forget to include a tip.

A-1 Taxi Service (405-321-3111) charges $3 to load and $2.25 a mile. The average fare to downtown runs $20. Checker Cab Company (405-236-5551) and Yellow Cab Company (405-619-3434) both charge $2 to load and $1.80 a mile. The average fare to downtown Oklahoma City is $22.

If you would prefer to travel in style, contact the Royal Limousine Service (405-789-9500; www.RoyalLimoUSA.com). This company provides luxury transportation. Prices start at $50 for transportation around Oklahoma City.

Another option is to catch a public van. These vans transport passengers to and from the airport. Several hotels in the area offer shuttles to their guests. Ask when you make your reservation if a hotel shuttle is available and if it's complimentary. Even if a small fee is charged, it is usually cheaper than a taxi.

If a hotel shuttle isn't available, there are a few shuttle companies that will accommodate you. Airport Express (405-681-3311 www.taxivan.com), is the better known. The average fare for this ride from the airport to downtown is $20.

Check the Web site or call to confirm the rate for the time of your visit. Metro Express (405-681-3311) is another option.

Travelers in wheelchairs or who have other physical limitations might want to consider Medride Assisted Transport. Drivers assist passengers in and out of the vehicle. The Medride are easy to spot in the loading lane. They are blue. To find out current rates and make a reservation call (405) 685-8267.

By Train

Oklahoma City currently has one train, the Heartland Flyer (www.heartlandflyer.com). It leaves Oklahoma City and travels south, making stops in Norman, Purcell, Pauls Valley, Ardmore, Gainesville, and finally Fort Worth. Visitors can ride up to Oklahoma City from Fort Worth, Texas, or ride down to Fort Worth and catch the Texas Eagle at the station where the Heartland Flyer stops.

The Heartland Flyer operates seven days a week. It leaves the Oklahoma City train station at 8:25 a.m. and arrives in Fort Worth at 2:06 p.m. At 5:25 p.m., the train pulls out of the Fort Worth station and is back in Oklahoma City by 9:39 p.m.

Call (800) USA-RAIL for current fares. Amtrak periodically runs special promotions and rates may vary.

By Bus

If you'd rather travel by bus, the Union Bus Station (405-235-6425), located downtown on West Sheridan Avenue, can make sure you get on the right one for your destination. Built in 1941, the station has not changed much. Greyhound Bus Lines (800-231-2222; www.greyhound.com), operates out of this station, as well as Jefferson Lines.

By Car

Understanding Oklahoma City's highway system is half the battle of driving here. You can get from one side of the city to the other quickly using several of the major streets, highways, interstates, or turnpike systems.

I-35

I-35 divides the state in half (east and west) and connects the city to Wichita, Kansas, to the North and Dallas, Texas, to the South. Traveling south from the north the interstate passes along the eastern side of Edmond and becomes the Shannon Miller Parkway for approximately 4 miles and then runs along the east side of Oklahoma City. It picks up I-44, or the Turner Turnpike, on the northeast side of Oklahoma City and drivers can exit here to get on the Kilpatrick heading west. As you stay on I-35, you will pass I-44. The I-44 interchange cuts through the north side of Oklahoma City. As you stay on I-35 and get closer to the city, it curves and connects with I-40. About a mile heading west, drivers pick up I-35 again as they head south to Moore, Norman, Ardmore, and eventually Dallas. This is not a toll road.

I-40

I-40 divides the state in half (north and south) and connects the city to Fort Smith, Arkansas, to the East and Amarillo, Texas, to the West. It is also known as the Stanley Draper Expressway, but most locals refer to it as I-40. Traveling from east to west, drivers can exit south on I-35 and head to Norman or exit north on to the Centennial Expressway and head to the capitol area or Edmond. If you stay on I-40, you will pass through the heart of downtown Oklahoma City. Bricktown sits on the north side of the interstate and Stockyards City to the south. As you keep traveling west, you will come to the I-44 junction where you can exit north or south. On the northeast corner sits the State Fair Park. Staying on I-44, you will travel west past the southern edge of Yukon, Weatherford, Clinton, Elk City, and eventually Amarillo, Texas. This is not a toll road.

I-44

I-44 enters Oklahoma in the far northeastern corner of the state at Miami, Oklahoma. It becomes the Turner Turnpike on the southwest side of Tulsa and is a toll road until it joins I-35. The fare is $3.50 for cars. The two interstates are joined for about 4 miles when I-44 breaks off and heads west. Drivers will pass Remington Park on the

south and the National Cowboy Hall of Fame and Western Heritage Museum on the north. The interstate curves past Lincoln Boulevard, where the capitol is located on the south side; past the Broadway Extension heading north and the Centennial Expressway (also known as I-235) heading south; past Northwest Expressway, where Penn Square Mall and 50 Penn Place are located; then past May Avenue, eventually curving and joining Lake Hefner Parkway becoming North Grand Boulevard until it crosses I-40, at which time it also becomes known as the Southwest Expressway.

As you keep traveling south, you can exit off to head southwest at which time the interstate becomes I-44 again and H. E. Bailey Turnpike. Toll for cars to Chickasha is $1.25. Stay on the turnpike and you will come to Lawton and eventually Wichita Falls, Texas.

I-240

This interstate runs east and west from the east side of Tinker Air Force Base to the I-44 junction near Will Rogers World Airport along the south side of the city. Lake Stanley Draper, Crossroads Mall, strip malls, churches, and car dealerships sit on either side of this interstate. Just west of Crossroads Mall is I-35. I-240 runs over the top of it and drivers can exit to catch I-35 north or south. Traffic can get thick and bogged down here during morning and afternoon rush hours. Use caution. There is no charge for this interstate.

I-235 or the Centennial Expressway

I-235 is also known as the Centennial Expressway and runs north and south. It starts at the I-44 junction and runs south downtown. If you exit and go north, you will be on the Broadway Extension. Going south, drivers will pass train cars, the capitol, and state offices on the left, or east side, of the Interstate. On the right, or west side, drivers will see the downtown area. This interstate eventually crosses I-40 and merges with I-35.

Broadway Extension or OK 77

This highway gets a lot of traffic from people traveling in and out of Edmond and those going to the north side of the city. It runs north and south.

Drivers exit off north at the I-44 junction. As they travel north, they will pass the Daily Oklahoman newspaper offices on the east side, and eventually come to the Kilpatrick Turnpike. Here they can exit east and west. Going east will take them to I-35 and the Turner Turnpike. Going west will take them to the Quail Springs Mall area. Continuing north will take drivers to 2nd St. in downtown Edmond. Even though it is OK 77, most of the locals refer to it as the Broadway Extension.

Kilpatrick Turnpike

Running east and west, this turnpike begins on the east side at I-35 and runs west, looping south to meet I-40 on the west side of the city. It passes the Quail Springs Mall area and Barnes and Noble on the north side and Lowes and Office Depot on the south side. Drivers can exit to loop onto the Lake Hefner Parkway heading south or north on Portland a mile west of the mall. If you stay on the turnpike, you will pass Mercy Hospital and Martin Nature Park on the south side. Continuing west, you will pass exits to Bethany and Yukon, eventually ending up at I-40 where you can go east back into the city or west, another exit to Yukon. There is a charge for travel on this highway. Toll rates range from $.30 to $9.50 depending on where you enter and exit. Make sure you have the correct change when exiting. The toll road is heavily monitored by cameras, highway patrol, and Edmond police.

Memorial Road

If you prefer not to pay toll, you can travel Memorial Road. It runs east and west and runs along the north side of the Kilpatrick. JYou can exit off I-35, just north of the Kilpatrick Turnpike, and go east or west on Memorial. Before the Kilpatrick was built here, Memorial was the main thoroughfare. It will take a little more time of course because of the stoplights, but it is free and an option.

Lake Hefner Parkway

Also known as OK 74, it runs north and south from Memorial Avenue to I-44. Traveling south from Memorial, you will pass Lake Hefner on the right, or west, 2 or 3 miles into your trip. Four miles farther south and you will pass Integris

Baptist Medical Center on the south side of the Northwest Expressway and east, or left, of where you are. To the right, you will see office buildings. This is reportedly the highest point in Oklahoma City. If you exit here and go west, turn into the office buildings and look southeast, you will see the State Fair Park, the capitol area, and the skyscrapers of downtown Oklahoma City. This is a free roadway.

Northwest Expressway

Some may know this highway as OK 3. Ask the locals to direct you to OK 3 and they won't know what you're talking about. To them it is the Northwest Expressway. It runs southeast from an exit off I-44 northwest to the OK 81 junction near Okarche, northwest of the city. The Northwest Expressway is a highly commercial thoroughfare. As you immediately exit off I-44, Penn Square Mall sits on the right, or north, side and 50 Penn Place sits on the left, or south side. Traveling west you will pass Integris Baptist Medical Center on the south and go over Lake Hefner Parkway and multiple other businesses until you hit County Line Road. Here businesses give way to housing additions and fields. On this farthest west side, you can exit to the Kilpatrick Turnpike or go under it and continue west.

SR 66

The Mother Road cuts and weaves its way through the city alongside interstates and main thoroughfares. It runs along the north side of the Turner Turnpike; goes through Arcadia, east of Edmond; then hooks into I-35; travels and connects to I-44 heading west; and then at the 39th Expressway connects with its original path eventually running through Bethany. Some say the path runs through Edmond, but maps show it as stated above. Special SR 66 road signs used to mark the path, but they have been stolen or lost to the weather or accidents. To be sure you are traveling through the city on SR 66 you must use a specifically prepared map, such as the Oklahoma Route 66 Association Official Trip Guide. You can purchase your map from the Oklahoma Route 66 Association at www.oklahomaroute66.com.

Pike Pass

The easiest way to get around on the city toll roads is to purchase a PIKEPASS. This device is a little white square box that you mount on your windshield. When you exit or enter a toll road, the device sends a signal that deducts the appropriate toll amount from your already funded account. Rates vary according to the type of vehicle you drive and the turnpike you travel. To get a PIKEPASS, you need to open a PIKEPASS account at the PIKEPASS store at 4401 West Memorial Rd., Suite 130. Be sure you take your driver's license, a valid credit or debit card, and the license plate number of your vehicle. If you intend to sign up more than one vehicle, have the license plate numbers of all the cars with you. If you do not have a credit or debit card, or would like to get your PIKEPASS by mail, call (800) 745-3727 for assistance. If you would like to investigate the tolls or learn more about PIKEPASS, visit the Web site at www.pikepass.com.

Children and Vehicles

In 2006, Oklahoma City tightened the law regarding child safety seats in vehicles. Oklahoma statutes state, "Every driver when transporting a child under 6 years of age in a motor vehicle operated on the roadways, streets, or highways of this state, shall provide for the protection of said child by using a child passenger restraint system. Children at least 6 years of age but younger than 13 years of age shall be protected by use of a child passenger restraint system or a seat belt."

There are exceptions to this law, like passenger cars manufactured before 1967 and pickups, vans, and SUVs manufactured prior to 1971 that were not required to have seat belts. Also, school buses; taxis; and many commercial transport vehicles, like vans and shuttles which carry more than 10 passengers, are not required to have seat belts and are exempt from the law. But if you have a vehicle that has seat belts and a child, make sure he or she is properly secured in a car seat or buckled up. Properly is the key word here. You can read in-depth about how to properly secure a child on the Oklahoma Highway Safety Office's Web site at www.ok.gov/ohso. You should know that if it appears that a driver has not properly secured a child, a law enforcement officer is authorized to stop the vehicle. If you are ticketed, the fine is $50.

Parking

For the most part, parking is free across Oklahoma City with the exception of downtown. There are metered spaces on the streets, but they tend to be snatched up quickly. Sometimes driving around the block will afford you a parking opportunity, but when that fails, check out the parking garages. There are seven lots regulated by the Central Oklahoma Transportation and Parking Authority (COPTA; 405-235-PARK; www.parkingokc.com). Rates average $2 for the first hour and $1 for each hour thereafter. The maximum all-day fee is $7. These rates usually do not apply for special events. Fees run from $5 to $6 when events with more than 10,000 people in attendance are occurring.

By Public Transportation

The bus service, METRO Transit (www.gometro.org) is a good way to get around Oklahoma City. Bus service operates Mon through Fri from 5:30 a.m. to 7:30 p.m. The service has over 25 interconnecting routes, including three express routes that take passengers all over the metro area. You will need to check each route for exact times buses will come by your location. You can download a schedule and time map from the METRO Transit Web site, e-mail the service at metrotransitcustomerservice@okc.gov, or call (405) 235-RIDE.

Buses do not run on certain holidays, so check ahead. Oklahoma City regular local fares cost $1.25. Unlimited 30-day passes for regular service cost $40. Express service costs $2.25. A 30-Day Express Pass is $50. Discounts fares and passes are available for seniors, ages 60 and up, disabled persons (valid ID required), Medicare members, and children ages 6 to 17.

Individuals can purchase passes from the Downtown Transit Center at 420 NW 5th St.; Buy For Less grocery stores, in person only, at 2500 North Pennsylvania, 2121 West Hefner, Southeast

44th and I-35, 3501 NW Expressway; or by mail from Union Station, 300 Southwest 7th, Oklahoma City, OK 73109.

When you park in one of COPTA's lots you can take an Oklahoma Spirit Trolley to your Oklahoma City downtown destination for free. You will be required to show your parking pass or stub to the trolley operator so hang on to it. The Oklahoma Spirit Trolley System has three lines. The Blue and Red Lines travel throughout the downtown area. The Orange Line goes up and down the I-40 and Meridian Avenue corridor.

If you do not have a car to park, you can still ride the trolley. The Red and Blue Lines charge $0.25 and the Orange Line charges $1.00. A one-day pass, which is good on all trolley lines, costs $2.00 and a three-day pass is $3.00. Please bring exact fare. Drivers cannot make change. Children under six can ride free when accompanied by a paying passenger.

HISTORY

Oklahoma City had an exciting and somewhat unusual beginning. Since its settlement in 1889, it has been referred to as a city "born grown" because its population went from about three to approximately 10,000 in one day. Many of those early settlers left within a few days, but those who stayed started building and planning for the city's future.

The city has seen growth spurts, decline, wealth, disasters, revitalization, tragedy, and triumph. Men of foresight and vision, like Henry Overholser, William Fremont Harn, John Shartel, and Anton Classen, contributed to the success of Oklahoma City and their names are memorialized today by lakes, streets, and museums named after them.

With so much history and change, it would be impossible to cover everything in the space allotted here. Therefore, in this chapter, you will be reading the highlights, an overview of the events that caused major change to Oklahoma City from before its existence to its latest natural disaster.

If you find your interest peaked and you want to read more, head down to the Oklahoma History Center at 2401 North Laird. The building sits across from the capitol on the northeast corner of North Lincoln Boulevard and Northeast 23rd Street. In the history center's library and archives collection, you will discover pictures, old newspapers, land records, and books. Some of the books I found invaluable while doing my research for this chapter are *Born Grown: An Oklahoma City History* by Roy P. Stewart, *Historic Oklahoma County* by Pendleton Woods, and *Heart of the Promised Land: Oklahoma County* by Bob L. Blackburn. If you like pictures with your history, pick up the Oklahoma City series from the Images of America book series by Terry L. Griffith. Some sources, like *Oklahoma City: From Public Land to Private Property* by Berlin B. Chapman, *The First 8 Months of Oklahoma City* by "Bunky" Irving Geffs, and *Land Sales: Oklahoma County Land Sales and Land Contests 1889–1994* by LaFonda Owens Manley, can only be found in the archives at the Oklahoma History Center. Take a pencil and a notepad and quarters if you want copies and plan to spend a lot of time. The Oklahoma History Center is not a place you want to hurry through.

Early explorers saw the middle of Indian Territory as a place of promise. Those who wanted to settle the area agreed. It sat along the North Canadian River so there was water and it was centrally located with a means of transportation running through it—the railroad. It was just a matter of time before something big started growing here and when it did, the area changed forever.

PRESETTLEMENT

Before Oklahoma City became a thriving metropolis, it was a lot of things to a number of different people. Stone Age nomads wandered through in search of wooly mammoth. This gave way to nomadic tribes, who followed the water, looking for buffalo and other game for food and clothes.

Oklahoma wildlife was varied and plentiful in earlier times. The first Americans discovered all types of wildlife, like antelope, elk, wolf, badger, otter, and bear. Hard to imagine now, but it is reported that on one hunting trip a group of mountain men claimed to have killed 20 bears along the North Canadian River. And while bear were impressive, nothing compared to the American bison, or buffalo, that roamed here.

Indian tribes, like the Caddo, Wichita, Pawnee, Osage, and Apache, lived and hunted here in 1540 when Francisco Vásquez de Coronado marched his men northward from New Spain. In time, both Spain and France would lay claim to the Oklahoma area until 1803 when France sold a vast area of land to the United States in the Louisiana Purchase. This land included what is now Oklahoma.

i Check out more of Oklahoma City's history on www.theus50.com/oklahoma, http://dougdawg.blogspot.com, and www.okhistorycenter.org.

To see what lay beyond the Mississippi River in the new territory that the United States purchased, President Thomas Jefferson formed expeditions and sent explorers into this newly acquired land. Thirteen explorers traversed the lands of Oklahoma, five coming all the way into the central part of the state.

Thomas James was the first explorer. He came hoping to trade guns and blankets for buffalo robes and beaver pelts from the Comanche. What he found was a "beautiful, rich, and fertile land filled with promise."

Washington Irving, the well-known American author, came next. In 1832, he spent seven days in the Oklahoma county area, hunting bear, buffalo, and turkey. On this trip, he met a band of Osage warriors. They were on a hunting excursion themselves. Irving wrote about his adventure in a book published in 1835 titled, *A Tour on the Prairies*.

Some years after Irving, the United States began using Oklahoma as an Indian reservation. The area became known as Indian Territory, a place where Indian tribes from the lands east of the Mississippi River could be relocated. The Five Civilized Tribes—Cherokee, Choctaw, Chickasaw, Creek, and Seminole—came here via the Trail of Tears. They settled in the eastern part of the state with the Cherokee inhabiting the north, the Choctaw and Chickasaw in south, and the Creek and Seminole in the middle, an area which would later become Oklahoma County.

By 1860, the tribes were beginning to prosper. They developed politically and built schools, factories, and towns. They had settled in to their new homes as best they could when the Civil War broke out between the states. This would change Indian Territory and start a chain of events that would lead to settlement and later statehood.

When the Civil War started, many Indian tribes sided with the Confederacy because of the geographical location of the territory. The Creek and Seminole Nations were two that would pay heavily for that loyalty. After the North won, the Creek and Seminole Nations were required to sell back more than two million acres to the U.S. government at a price of $2 an acre as punishment. This land became the Unassigned Lands with present-day Oklahoma County as part of those lands.

Under the Reconstruction Treaties of 1866, the U.S. government could assign the land to other Indian tribes and give rights-of-way through Indian Territory to railroad companies. By 1888, rail lines ribboned Oklahoma. The first track into the area was laid by the Southern Kansas Railway Company. It was determined by surveyors that the best route was through the Unassigned Lands. In 1886 tracks began being laid from southern Kansas at the rate of one and half mile per day. By Feb 1887, the tracks made it into Oklahoma County.

Two locations were designated for coal stations and water wells by surveyors who plotted the route. Edmond, originally known as Summit, was chosen because of its elevation and available spring water. The next watering point would be Oklahoma Station because of its location along the north bank of the North Canadian River. After the tracks were finished, one freight train and one passenger train passed along the tracks every day.

Except for the stops at Summit and Oklahoma Station, the trains traveled through undeveloped and unsettled areas, and this did not make the railroad companies much money. Railroad officials and its stockholders, therefore, saw settlement along the tracks as the only way they could generate business and make a profit.

Others agreed that the area should be settled. Men like C. C. Rutherford, David Payne, and William L. Couch attempted in various ways to settle the Unassigned Lands, but were always removed by calvary soldiers. These settlers became known as "Boomers."

RUN OF 1889

Even though Indian tribes bordered all sides of the Unassigned Lands, there was so much interest in settling the area that it didn't take the federal government long to hear the cries of the people and do something about it. With the land not being used for anything except railroad tracks, it was the perfect location and opportunity for homesteading.

So on Mar 23, 1889, in his third week in office, President Benjamin Harris signed a proclamation calling for opening the Unassigned Lands on Mon, Apr 22, 1889. It was to be a race and the first person to reach an area of land and stake a claim would be owner of that particular property. There were other rules to be followed, however.

First, boundaries were set where hopefuls could line up and wait for the starting gunshot. These boundaries were the southern line of the Cherokee Outlet on the north; the Indian Meridian (96th Meridian) on the east; the Southern Canadian River on the south; and the Cheyenne-Arapaho country on the west, roughly where US Highway 81 is located now.

Second, to be qualified for the run and to stake a claim, a man had to be 21 years of age or older and a woman had to be unmarried, legally divorced, or widowed and 21 years of age or older. Also qualified were individuals from other countries who had declared their intent to become naturalized citizens of the United States. Their reward would be a 160-acre homestead.

Three days prior to the run, people were allowed to travel across the area to get into position for their dash to the land they wanted. This allowed many an opportunity to slip into their area early and hide out in creek beds, under bushes, and in any other place where they wouldn't be seen, so they could stake their claim ahead of time while looking like they came in with the run. These "early birds" became known as "Sooners."

Those who waited legitimately at the boundaries sat on horses or in wagons or were on foot . There is no official count as to how many made the 1889 Run. Estimates vary from 25,000 to 50,000.

At the time of the run, there were only six buildings located at Oklahoma Station—a depot, the home of the stationmaster, a section house, a shack that served as post office, a government office structure, and the stage lines stockade. While there were no county lines or a town site designated yet, many considered Oklahoma Station a natural choice because it had water from the North Canadian River and the railroad already available. So when homesteaders stepped, or in some cases jumped, from the train, they began placing their claims.

Also, from the train came two survey companies—the Oklahoma Colony Company and the Seminole Land and Improvement Company. They immediately began surveying and platting the town. The new boundaries of Oklahoma Station were the Santa Fe Railway, Northwest 7th Street, Walker, and Southwest 7th Street. For those who had staked their claim within this boundary, they were called upon to pay $25 a lot. They wasted no time in paying the amount. They knew if they didn't pay, someone else would. In retrospect $25 was a bargain, considering that 52 days later, lots on Main Street ranged from $100 to $1,000.

Three weeks later, on June 14, 1889, the population of Oklahoma Station was 2,685 men, 721 women, and 736 children for a total of 4,138 people. Businesses included 34 grocery stores, 37 restaurants, 10 hotels, 20 boardinghouses, 5 newspapers, 6 livery stables, 4 banks, and 7 ice cream parlors.

The initial population was higher the day following the run, but many people decided within a week or two to leave. Conditions were too difficult, their claim was jumped, or they were run off their claim, as was the case of Robe Carl White.

A 19-year-old young man from Kansas, White had staked a claim on Main Street. That evening, he watched as two men came toward his lot. They carried guns and a tent. When they got to White's lot, they began setting up their tent. A heated discussion followed. After a confrontation, White compromised and left with his life.

While White was under age and legally couldn't stake a claim, there were those who met the qualifications and were still run off their claims. Some, like White, were lucky. They escaped with their lives. Others left in a pine box.

It would take years for some claims to be settled.

ℹ️ **The Oklahoma Historical Society is always interested in welcoming new members and those who just want to know more about Oklahoma. Call (405) 521-2491 or visit their Web site at www.okhistory.org.**

LAW AND ORDER

There were several attempts at forming a city government. Mayors and other city officials were elected and then they resigned. Oklahoma Station became known as a "wide open town." In those early days, there was no formal law, no courts, and no organized enforcement code. The only thing that kept the newly formed city from imploding was a pair of deputy U.S. marshals and a calvary infantry company.

On May 2, 1890, the Organic Act for Oklahoma Territory was passed. This act created seven counties, Canadian, Cleveland, Kingfisher, Logan, Oklahoma, and Payne, and applied the laws of Nebraska to the area until a territorial assembly could enact its own. The act designated Guthrie as territorial capital. It was also during this time that a petition was gathered with 647 signatures that allowed Oklahoma Station to become Oklahoma City.

STATE CAPITAL

Oklahoma became a state on Nov 16, 1907. Oklahoma City's economy and physical growth picked up steam as statehood took away a lot of the legal and political problems of being a territory. A new problem was deciding on a permanent location for the state capital. Several towns wanted to be the state capital, Oklahoma City and Guthrie being the most outspoken about it. So heated were the debates during territorial legislative sessions that pistols were drawn, fists flew, and more shouting about the capital's location was heard on the floor than about other state business matters.

Cities started holding secret meetings with one another, or so the rumors go. Kingfisher residents so badly didn't want Guthrie to be the capital that they told Oklahoma City officials they would throw their support and money behind them if it looked like Guthrie was going to win. However, the two cities had a falling out and no one to this day can confirm whether the incident really happened or not.

While officials continued to bicker, the decision was put to a vote of the people on June 11, 1910. Oklahoma City won handily with 96,261 votes as opposed to Guthrie's 31,301 and Shawnee's 8,382 votes. Now with the election results in, Governor Charles Haskell ordered the official state seal moved to Oklahoma City. He telephoned his private secretary, W. B. Anthony, and told him to go get the seal and bring it to Oklahoma City. When Anthony arrived at the secretary of state's office, he was met by Earl Keyes, a clerk at the Logan County Courthouse. Keyes gave Anthony the seal wrapped in a brown paper bag. Keyes had received a note from Bill Cross, the secretary of state, telling him to give Anthony the seal. The next day, the governor proclaimed Oklahoma City the official capital.

Those who wanted Guthrie as state capital accused Oklahoma City of stealing the seal under darkness and absconding with it. Reports were that someone went through a window. Another report was circulated that the seal was smuggled out in a bundle of dirty laundry. Lawsuits followed, but nothing ever came of them. After 100 years, there are rumors that some in Guthrie still hold ill will over the matter and every now and then the topic of seal thievery will make it in to local conversation.

With Oklahoma City secure as the capital, thoughts naturally turned to a location for the capitol. I. M. Putnam and John Shartel wanted the capitol to be located on their land northwest of the city, in an area which is now Putnam City. To secure the deal, they offered the state 1,600 acres of land and $1.7 million in cash.

Another offer, however, was extended by William Fremont Harn and J. J. Culbertson. They owned land northeast of the city between Northeast 13th and Northeast 23rd Street. Harn offered 40 acres to the state for free and Culbertson offered a matching land gift. A selection committee finally chose the Harn-Culbertson offer because it was minutes from the downtown business district. Putnam and Shartel's land was 20 minutes away.

Seven years later at a price of $1.5 million the Oklahoma capitol was complete.

THE FLOOD OF 1923

During Oklahoma City's boom time, multistory brick buildings were erected, schools and hospitals built, and a trolley line established. Even though Oklahoma City had seen some tough economic times in the 1890s, with statehood and the location of the capitol decided, the city and its people were once again on the move.

Then 1923 arrived. Floodwaters caused havoc more than once that year. Spring rains into June had been heavy, but in Oct the water was so abundant, it caused major city damage. For three days, from Oct 13 to 16, torrential rains fell in the Canadian River's northwestern watershed. Overholser Lake, the city's water reservoir, could not hold all the water and floodwaters breached the reservoirs earthen embankments. In the past to prevent the dam from breaking, the floodgates had been opened. This time, millions of gallons of water flowed over the dam into the swollen North Canadian River. Other embankments, which would normally permit the water to pass through were not large enough to allow the huge volume of water to flow on down river.

Therefore, it came in to the city. No one could have anticipated the amount of damage that followed.

Water traveled down the south side of Main Street onto Hudson; then east of Robinson, from Grand Avenue to the corner of Broadway; east to the railroad lines; and continued east to what is now Bricktown. Floodwaters were photographed all the way back to May Avenue on Main. The destruction was measureable. The water lifted buildings from their foundations; twisted 132-pound railroad tracks; destroyed homes, businesses, and bridges; and split Wheeler Park, Oklahoma City's first zoo, in half, killing most of the animals and destroying its remaining property.

Damages cost the capital city over $15 million in 1923 prices. As a result of the flood, lawsuits were filed and many businesses relocated, one of which was the zoo. Wheeler Park became the Oklahoma City Zoo. Its new location was Northeast 50th where it is still located today.

OIL AND MORE

The 1930s were marked by Americans struggling to survive the Great Depression and for Oklahoma citizens it was no different. However, there were three things that brightened the horizon for Oklahoma City. First, Oklahoma City had four years of more than $1 million per month in building permits collected. Second, Rock Island and Santa Fe railroad tracks were being removed from downtown and four civic buildings were to be constructed in the area vacated. Third, oil was discoved in the Oklahoma City Field on Dec 4, 1928.

For years, people had dreams of finding oil in and around Oklahoma City. As early as 1890, an unknown wildcatter ran a test at Northeast Fourth Street and the Santa Fe tracks. When nothing looked promising, he moved to other areas. Geologists searched for years to find places where oil could be with no luck, but they kept searching. In 1925, only traces of oil were found in a well dug to a depth of 4,480 feet.

Experimental drilling continued, however, and at 3 p.m. on Tues, Dec 4, 1928, on a piece of property located near present-day Southeast 59th St. and Bryant, the mother lode of "black gold" was tapped. The Foster Petroleum Corporation of Bartlesville and the Indian Territory Illuminating Oil Company had been digging this well since June and when the flow of oil was brought to the top, 4,909 barrels of oil were produced in the first 20 hours. Ten days later the well was dug deeper and in its first month, the Oklahoma City Number One well produced 110,496 barrels of oil at a price of $1.56 per barrel. Drilling costs of this first well was $57,000.

News of the oil discovery bought people to the area from all over the country. By Sept 1929, there were 15 wells in the Oklahoma City Field, producing 15,000 barrels daily with 19 more wells being drilled. New wells were being drilled so quickly that the amount of oil coming out of the ground caused a glut and prices nosedived. Regulations were then established as to where oil wells could be dug and how much oil each well could produce.

While many wild wells caused excitement, there is one that is remembered best. On Mar 26, 1930, the "Wild Mary Sudik" blew a plume of oil from the ground. Strong winds sent an oil film south as far as Norman. Wild Mary produced 20,000 barrels of oil a day with about 200 million cubic feet of gas.

The oil boom continued with new wells being drilled throughout the city, some even being placed on capitol grounds as is still evident today. Black gold helped Oklahoma City grow and prosper.

Between oil and the federal New Deal programs of the 1930s, like the Works Progress Administration (WPA), the Public Works Administration (PWA), and the Civilian Conservation Corps (CCC), Oklahoma City was on a path of recovery and was growing again. A municipal auditorium, the Oklahoma City National Guard Armory, and amphitheaters at several parks were constructed during this time. Through the years, businesses, like TG&Y stores, Anthony stores, and OTASCO, put down roots in Oklahoma City, as did Sonic and Braum's Ice Cream and Dairy stores.

In 1982, Oklahoma City saw hard economic times again. When oil prices dropped to 10 cents a barrel, this "oil bust" caused problems for certain banks in the area. Penn Square Bank, one of the largest in the city, was only one of the banks declared insolvent and forced to close. Practices here caused a domino effect on other banks across the nation and subsequently resulted in banking laws being scrutinized and revised.

i To find information on someone in Oklahoma's past, perhaps a relative or an early pioneer, contact the Oklahoma Genealogy Society (405-637-1907; www .okgensoc.org). They may be able to help.

BIG CHANGES AGAIN

With the dawn of the 1990s, the city was picking up the pieces of the 1980s and moving on. The next decade however, would bring three new major changes to Oklahoma City, changes that would affect the downtown skyline and suburban areas. One was an exciting change brought about by leaders and a vote of the people. The other two were forced upon Oklahoma City and they changed the city and its people forever.

The Good

In the late 1980s and early 1990s, city leaders began looking at the downtown city area and noting its decline. People didn't come downtown anymore. There was nothing to do and the old brick buildings east of downtown were dilapidated and beginning to crumble from old age and lack of use.

Elected officials came together and devised a plan to save downtown. The plan was called Metropolitan Area Projects, or MAPS as most Oklahoma City residents call it. It was a visionary capital improvement program that would upgrade certain facilities and build new ones. To pay for the projects, a temporary one-cent sales tax would be collected. City voters approved this tax on Dec 14, 1993.

Work began immediately. During the 60 months the tax was in effect, over $309 million was collected. Improvements were made to the state fairgrounds, the North Canadian River, Civic Center Music Hall, and the Myriad (now called the Cox Business Services Convention Center). The Ford Center, a new library/learning center, AT&T Bricktown Ballpark, and more were constructed because of the temporary tax. Projects were completed on Aug 17, 2004. MAPS was so successful in creating jobs and bringing businesses to the downtown area, however, that city voters approved two more temporary sales taxes. MAPS 2 saw more improvements to the city and MAPS 3 is well underway with a new convention center being discussed for downtown.

The Bad

The citizens of Oklahoma City woke to a bright, sunny day on Apr 19, 1995. Fathers and mothers went to work. Children went to day care or school. The business of Oklahoma City started as usual, with prayer breakfasts, people rushing in and out of buildings delivering packages, paying bills, and discussing the spring storm season. That is until 9:02 a.m.

At 9:02 a.m. the earth shook, glass broke, and concrete walls shattered and fell. People from as far away as Guthrie and Norman knew something unusual had happened. Those who weren't in the immediate area thought maybe it was an earthquake. Those who were downtown went screaming and running for their lives.

An ammonium nitrate and fuel oil bomb delivered in a Ryder truck had exploded in front of the Alfred P. Murrah Federal Building, shearing off the front face of the building. The Murrah building was home to many offices, including those of the Bureau of Alcohol, Tobacco, and Firearms; the Social Security Administration; Housing and Urban Development; U.S. Department of Veterans Affairs; the Secret Service; and the Drug Enforcement Administration. A day care also operated there.

As news spread of what happened via radio, television, and word of mouth, rescue workers raced to the area. Government offices and businesses downtown closed. Parents were urged to pick up their children from school. Residents complied and returned home to watch coverage of the recovery effort on television. Most suffered from shock as they tried to comprehend what happened. For those who went downtown during those early days after the explosion, one thing will stay with them forever—the heavy silence that permeated the air. Lines of people waited to find where they would be assigned to work in the recovery and clean-up process, yet no one spoke. It was as if the entire city attended a funeral.

A week later, the official body count was 168 with over 800 injured. Nineteen of of the dead were children who had been in the day care. Damages totaled upwards of $652 million. A little over a month later, on May 23, 1995, what was left of the Alfred P. Murrah Federal Building was demolished.

The survivors received no major federal funding assistance. The Murrah Fund, created by the state legislature, collected over $300,000 in federal grants and $40 million in donations. These funds were used, and are still being used, to aid survivors and those who lost loved ones in the blast.

Oklahoma City slowly came out of its shock. Books were written a few months later about the event, heroic rescuers, survivors, and those who did not survive. Five years later, on Apr 20, 2000, the Oklahoma City National Memorial was dedicated. The memorial is located where the Murrah building once stood and is a place where people can go to remember those who died and celebrate those who lived.

After that horrific day, Oklahoma City residents promised themselves that they would become stronger and show the rest of the world that they could take care of their own and recover. And they did.

And the Ugly

Anyone who lives in and around Oklahoma City knows the danger from spring storms, mainly hail, damaging winds, and tornadoes. Television and radio stations begin preparing residents in Jan for what they need to do in case of a tornado. Residents take watches, advisories, and warnings seriously. However much they prepared though, no one was ready for the devastation that came on May 3, 1999.

The weekend was over. People had gone back to work. It had stormed on Fri and Sat, bringing rain and some hail but Sun hadn't been bad. Mon looked even better with the sun shining, but weather forecasters warned of severe weather building in the afternoon.

As the day heated and the humidity rose, many commented that a storm was sure to come. Storm chasers, men and women who drive toward storms to gather information and report to stations, were deployed. About 4 p.m. the first reports of a severe storm building was reported by newscasters on television and radio. At that time, it was too far to the west to cause great concern in Oklahoma City. Storms are known to build and collapse within minutes. Residents continued to watch, but went about their business.

By 5 p.m., people were heading home from work. Weather forecasters had picked up the frequency of their reporting as the storm out west had intensified and was moving toward the city. The stormchasers were reporting the storm's movement and the damage it was leaving behind. At 6:30 p.m. from Chickasha, across the Bailey Turnpike, to Newcastle the tornado had grown and was destroying everything in its path. Baseball-size hail was being reported and the tornado had spread to a mile wide in size.

Television and radio station programming gave itself over to weather reporting and local meteorologists. They had calculated the path of the storm and it was headed for the south side of Oklahoma City.

"This is not a drill," Gary England, KWTV News 9 weatherman said about 7 p.m. "You must take cover immediately. If you're in a mobile home get out. Get below ground if possible. If you can't, move away from windows, go to the lowest part, center of your house. This is a very dangerous situation. Take cover now."

All cameras, storm chasers, and meteorologists were focused on the tornado and where it was headed. Residents of Oklahoma City who didn't need to take cover were glued to their television sets. Some had just come from the area that was in imminent danger.

The mile-wide tornado with winds in excess of 318 miles per hour roared into the west side of Moore, a south Oklahoma City suburb. The black sky whirled as debris from homes and businesses were literally being blown away. It took about 30 minutes for the tornado to move from the west side of Moore through the southeast side of Oklahoma City, Del City, Midwest City, and head toward Choctaw.

The F5, supercell tornado cut a 50-mile-long path seven miles south of downtown Oklahoma City. Forty-four people died, 750 were injured, and 10,000 homes were destroyed. The total damage estimate was $1.2 billion.

Within minutes of the storm's passing, rescue workers moved into the area and the American Red Cross arrived on the scene. Already on-site, storm chasers and their cameramen gave viewers the first images of damage. Piles of rubble were everywhere. Treetops were sheared off. Concrete slabs where homes once stood were swept clean as if nothing had existed there before the storm. The area that had held homes, churches, schools, and businesses now looked as if a bomb had exploded.

The recovery and rebuilding process began immdiately. Ten years later, Moore, Del City, and Midwest City are larger and stronger than they were before that Mon evening on May 3, 1999.

All of Oklahoma City and its surrounding areas are stronger.

LOOKING AHEAD

Even though Oklahoma City has faced many challenges, it has risen to those challenges. Being in the center of the state, Oklahoma City is watched by cities and towns around the region. Those cities and towns have seen the way Oklahoma City responds to crises and they know their capital city will survive. Oklahomans are strong. They see the future and embrace it, no matter what happens.

From Oklahoma City's beginning when strong people came and settled here to its future and its legacy, Oklahoma City will continue growing and expanding. Its residents laugh and play together, cry and mourn together, build and celebrate together. It is a city on the move and its people will make sure that the movement is continually forward.

ACCOMMODATIONS

It used to be a challenge to find a place to spend the night in Oklahoma City, but not anymore. Since the early 2000s, there has been a hotel building boom and now one can find a place fairly easily. The exception is downtown when events are in progress, like championship games, concerts, or the Opening Night celebration. With the interstate system, however, that doesn't need to be a problem either as one can find a place within 15 or 20 minutes of downtown.

This chapter includes many hotels around the area, but as construction continues, there is no way to cover them all. For instance, while the Kilpatrick Turnpike/Memorial Road area currently has 13 hotels, three more are scheduled to open by the end of 2009. The metro continues expanding outward and more hotels will surely be added in the future to accommodate the visitors Oklahoma City plans to draw.

Like in other metropolitan areas, hotels and motels in Oklahoma City tend to exist in clusters. The downtown cluster includes the Bricktown Hotel and Convention Center and the newly refurbished historical Skirvin. Down Meridian toward the airport, you'll find the Embassy Suites and a little farther north, you'll find the Biltmore. Near Penn Square Mall, along Classen and I-44, is another cluster. North of the city, along the Kilpatrick Turnpike, near Quail Springs Mall are 13 to 15 hotels. North toward Edmond, along I-35 and Second Street, you'll find a cluster and south of the city toward Norman along I-35, you'll find even more accommodations. Going west to Yukon along I-40 are more hotels as well as east toward Midwest City.

Besides hotel and motels, I have included bed-and-breakfasts in this chapter. Oklahoma City has several quaint and charming bed-and-breakfasts in the area. The Grandison is downtown, but has a secluded feel to it. Visitors will enjoy quiet evenings in a comfortable atmosphere with the convenience of being downtown.

While Oklahoma City isn't a tourist town per se, we do have different tourist seasons that are typically related to events. For instance, when the fair opens in Sept, people from across the state flood in and rooms can fill up fast. As with any travel, as soon as you know you will be coming to the area, call and make your reservation.

All bed-and-breakfasts and most hotels are nonsmoking. When making your reservation, be sure to ask if you want a location that allows smoking. Most offer wheelchair accessible rooms as well. Cable or satellite TV is standard with in-room movies available for a small fee. In many cases, small children can stay for free in the same room as a parent. To make guests feel more at home, many rooms include in-room coffee, hair dryers, and irons. For extended stays, dry cleaning services may be available. Almost all hotels have high-speed or wireless Internet access available either for free or for a small fee. Many hotels have continental breakfasts available or a restaurant offering room service. This information is included in the listings below. Ask about pets when making reservations as most accommodations do not allow pets, with the exception of service animals. Also check about phone charges. Most hotels charge for local or long distance phone calls. So keep your cell phone handy or use the lobby pay phones so you'll know how many quarters are dropped in.

All accommodations listed accept major credit cards. Prices vary from season to season. Off-season runs typically from Oct to Apr and weekends are busier than midweek, so prices may be higher then. Check the Web sites for special prices and don't forget Expedia and Travelocity when checking for deals.

Price Codes

All listings in this chapter include a price code. This code ranges from one to four dollar signs and represents the lowest price in off-season to the highest price in-season for a one-night stay. Rates do not include tax or any extras.

$................ Less than $100
$$ ....$100–$150
$$$ ....$151–$200
$$$$ ....$201–$251 +

HOTELS

Oklahoma City

BILTMORE HOTEL $-$$
401 S. Meridian
(405) 947-7681
www.biltmoreokc.com

Just off I-40 at Meridian, visitors will find the Biltmore a welcome site. Built in 1972, the hotel sits on four and a half acres. With its 509 pet-friendly rooms and free parking, this hotel offers a nice place to stay after a long trip. Wheelchair-accessible rooms are available as well as free local phone calls, free wireless Internet, voice mail, valet cleaning services, and safety deposit boxes. The hotel has three outdoor pools, a heated indoor pool, an indoor sauna and hot tub, a fitness room, a business center, lighted tennis courts, and 24-hour security. Upon request, visitors can get microwaves in their rooms for a small fee. Cribs and rollaways are complimentary. Rooms are furnished with hair dryers, irons and ironing boards, coffee makers and most have small refrigerators. For guests attending events in the city, there is a complimentary shuttle service to downtown and fairground activities for hotel guests.

The Biltmore offers two restaurants and two clubs. The Brandywine Room gives guests a full-service dining experience with a full-service bar. It serves steak, chicken, and vegetarian meals. If you are staying over the weekend, be sure to check out the Sun brunch buffett.

The Casa Café serves breakfasts, everything from continental to omelets to steak and eggs.

It is open for lunch, serving soups, salads, sandwiches, and other entrees.

The Chisholm Club, located in the west building of the complex, offers free dance lessons. It has a live deejay on Fri and Sat. Offering a full-service menu, pool tables, shuffleboard, and darts, guests can eat and play under the same roof.

The Sports Page Club, located in the main building, is Oklahoma City's number-one offtrack betting facility for thoroughbred and quarter-horse racing. Races are simulcast on televisions around the room. A full-service bar and restaurant can also be found here.

BRICKTOWN HOTEL AND CONVENTION $-$$
2001 E. Reno Ave.
(405) 235-1647
www.bricktown-hotel.com

If you want to be close to downtown without being downtown, this may be the hotel for you. Located, 1.5 miles from downtown in Oklahoma City's historic Bricktown District, the newly remodeled Bricktown Hotel has all the amenities a traveler looks for. Airport shuttle service is available for a $15 fee, which is cheaper than cab service. The hotel also offers free shuttle van service to Bricktown. All rooms have Serta mattresses, refrigerators, microwaves, hair dryers, irons and ironing boards, coffeemakers, digital cable television, desks with lots of plug ins, and free wireless Internet. While the hotel offers an expanded continental breakfast, there is no on-site restaurant. The Bricktown Hotel is pet friendly and pets receive a goody bag at check-in.

CANDLEWOOD SUITES $-$$
1701 N. Moore Ave., Moore
(405) 735-5151
www.candlewoodsuites.com

Located in Moore, these hotel rooms are large, built for a comfortable stay. Each suite has a full kitchen, complete with a microwave and a full-size refrigerator. For the business executive, there is an oversize executive desk with two separate phone lines. A CD/DVD player is available in every room and the hotel has a DVD and CD library. A fitness center is available. Pets are allowed with a nonrefundable fee based on length of stay. Pet must weigh less than 80 pounds. Queen and full beds are in the 61 rooms available. This hotel is owned and operated by Kusum Hospitality.

Moore is located on the south side of Oklahoma City. From this hotel, you are minutes from Crossroads Mall, Bricktown, and Will Rogers World Airport. There are plenty of restaurants in the area as well.

COLCORD HOTEL $$$–$$$$
15 N. Robinson Ave.
(405) 601-4300
www.colcordhotel.com

Opened in the fall of 2006, this 12-floor, 108-room, $16-million renovated hotel is the first boutique hotel in Oklahoma City. That's not its only first, however. The building has the distinction of being the first skyscraper in the city and the first to have an elevator. The hotel is a member of Historic Hotels of America and is listed on the National Register of Historic Places. Modernized now, it is a sophisticated and upscale hotel, featuring a state-of-the-art fitness center. Each guest room offers complimentary wireless Internet access, iPod docking stations, and flatscreen televisions. Convenient parking is available downtown.

An upscale restaurant, La Baguette Restaurant,, with its stylish furnishings, handblown glass lighting, warm ambience, and modern French flair serves fresh seafood and offers an extensive wine list.

COURTYARD DOWNTOWN $$–$$$
2 W. Reno Ave.
(800) 217-9905
www.marriott.com

With 225 smoke-free rooms, the Courtyard Downtown may be what you are looking for. It has a stylish modern lobby, spacious guest rooms, and 5,000 square feet of space and an outdoor courtyard. There is a full-service business center, deluxe fitness center, indoor heated pool, and whirlpool. The guest rooms offer wired high-speed Inter-net access, hair dryers, irons, in-room coffee service, and microwaves, but no refrigerators. Some deluxe rooms offer in-room whirlpools. On-site parking is $12 a day. Pets are allowed with a $100 nonrefundable sanitation fee.

The Courtyard Grille, the hotel's restaurant, serves breakfast and dinner. Enjoy the fresh breakfast buffet while reading your complimentary weekday newspaper.

This hotel is located downtown and is minutes from Bricktown.

EMBASSY SUITES OKLAHOMA CITY AIRPORT $$–$$$
1815 S. Meridian
(405) 682-6000
www.embassysuites.com

Located 10 to 15 minutes north of Will Rogers Airport on Meridian, weary travelers will not do any better than the Embassy Suites. With 236 two-room suites, there is plenty of space to stretch out and relax. There is an indoor swimming pool, workout area with state-of-the-art equipment, a business center, and a game room. There is ample free parking, and the hotel offers complimentary airport shuttle service. This hotel was renovated in 2005, has lots of meeting space, and wireless Internet. The Atrium restaurant serves complimentary breakfast, and a manager's reception is held in the early evening with light hors d'oeuvres served in the same area. The Landing restaurant serves American lunch and dinner cuisine. It smokes prime rib at the back of the hotel and serves a Southwest grilled chicken salad that you will remember long after your visit is over.

HAMPTON INN $$–$$$
1833 Center Dr., Midwest City
(405) 732-5500
www.hamptoninn.com

Located in Midwest City, 5.62 miles from the center of Oklahoma City, this hotel put you minutes from downtown events. Owned and operated by Kusum Hospitality, the hotel's goal is to give you a clean, comfortable hotel room during your stay. One hundred rooms are available. Some have king beds with a whirlpool and some rooms are available with queen beds. Smoking and nonsmoking rooms are available. Connecting rooms are also available. Irons and ironing boards and alarm clocks are in every room. High-speed Internet access is available. This hotel does not have a restaurant, but there are plenty of chain restaurants in the area.

Located nearby are Remington Park, the Oklahoma Firefighters Museum, and the Science Museum.

HAMPTON INN & SUITES $$–$$$
300 E. Sheridan
(405) 232-3600
www.hampton.com

Nine floors welcome you to this hotel. This downtown hotel is a nonsmoking establishment and offers one or two beds, king or queen. Guest rooms are equipped with coffeemakers, irons, ironing boards, minifridges, nightlights, lap desks, free high-speed Internet, a and a newspaper Mon through Fri. A complimentary hot breakfast is offered. Served in the dining room or get an "on the run breakfast bag" when you don't have the time to sit and eat. In the suites, you will find a sofa bed and wet bar. Some suites have in-room whirlpools. Self-parking is $6 a day. This hotel is located near Bricktown and 10 minutes from museums and the Oklahoma City Zoo. If your intent is to have fun, you'll find plenty to get to from here.

i To learn about even more hotels in the area, contact the Oklahoma City Convention and Visitors Bureau (405-297-8912; www.okccvb.org), the Edmond Convention and Visitors Bureau (405-341-4344; www.visitedmondok.com), and the Norman Convention and Visitors Bureau, (405-366-8095; www.visitnorman.com).

RENAISSANCE OKLAHOMA CITY
CONVENTION CENTER HOTEL
AND SPA $$$–$$$$
10 N. Broadway Ave.
(405) 228-8000
www.renaissanceoklahomacity.com

Located in the heart of downtown Oklahoma City, this 15-floor, 311-room hotel is a place of class and style. With newly renovated guest rooms and public space, this hotel has achieved four-diamond status. Amenities include a full-service business center; full spa (The Spa at 10 North); an indoor pool and whirlpool; fitness facilities; Caffeina's Marketplace featuring Starbucks; 24-hour room service, and a restaurant, 10 North Grille, with a world-class executive chef. This hotel is smoke free. Guest rooms offer hair dryers, bathrobes, irons and ironing boards, coffeemakers/tea service, Internet browser/Web TVs, color televisions, and electrical adapters. Some rooms have a minibar or wet bar, microwave and refrigerator. If you need a crib, rollaway bed, or pull-out sofa bed, ask the front desk. These amenities are available in some rooms as well.

SHERATON HOTEL $$$–$$$$
1 N. Broadway
(405) 235-2780
www.sheratonokc.com

If your business or vacation is all about downtown, then you will want to stay at the Sheraton. Located within steps of the Cox Convention Center, across from the Ford Center Arena, and blocks away from the Historic Bricktown area, you will be in the middle of all Oklahoma City has to offer. An underground concourse connects the hotel to most of downtown. The Sheraton is a smoke-free environment. They have a 24-hour business center, outdoor pool with sundeck, exercise facility, 24-hour room service, and a full restaurant and bar. The rooms are spacious and offer executive desks with Wi-Fi.

Besides the regular amenities, the traditional guest rooms also offer a complimentary breakfast, afternoon hors d'oeuvres, two complimentary drinks per room, a variety of beverage options, and an evening cash bar. In addition to the amenties of the traditional rooms, the Executive Club rooms also include bottled water supplied daily and plush bathrobes. On the same floor as the Executive Club rooms, the Sheraton offers two presidential suites. They include a wet bar, seating area, dining room, and an extra-large bathroom with Jacuzzi tub.

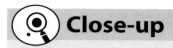 **Close-up**

Skirvin Hilton

The Skirvin (1 Park Ave., 405-291-0013, www.skirvinhilton.com, $$$–$$$$) has a long history in Oklahoma City and now is the jewel it was meant to be. Built by William B. Skirvin in 1911, it opened on Sept 26 of that year with two bays and 10 stories. Skirvin decided on its location because it was a mile from the train station and he could attract guests as they disembarked. As the city grew, more people arrived, and businesses started thriving in the area. Skirvin added another bay and four more floors, resulting in a grand total of 500 rooms.

At one time, there was another hotel across the street called the Skirvin Tower. It also had 500 rooms and Skirvin connected the two by an underground tunnel. Guests would check in at the Skirvin and then be led underground to the tower where their rooms were. Today, the Skirvin Tower is an office building.

Some years after William B. Skirvin died in a car wreck, his children sold the hotel to Dan James, who owned several other hotels. James owned the hotel until the 1960s when he decided it was a good time to get out of the hotel business and sold all his holdings.

In 1988, times were so hard for the Skirvin that it had to close. It had become too expensive to operate. Its glory days were over. The hotel that had entertained guests like Dean Martin, Jerry Lewis, Bob Hope, and President Eisenhower was boarded up and a chain link fence was erected around it.

When Oklahoma City proposed the Metropolitan Area Projects (MAPS) and it became a reality, discussions began about what to do with the Skirvin. City officials didn't want to destroy it because of its historical significance. After all, it was built just four years after Oklahoma became a state.

Enter John Weeman. Being a developer and having a long history in the hotel business, he saw the Skirvin's potential, but knew he could not do it alone. He approached Marcus Hotel and Resorts, a company that had been in the hotel business about 74 years. The company understood old iconic hotels and what they meant to their communities. A partnership was formed and plans to refurbish the Skirvin were put into action.

Financed with state and federal funds and using historic tax credits, this $56-million-dollar renovation has turned an old dilapidated building into a downtown jewel. Every pipe, wire, and valve was replaced and the guest rooms were expanded, making the hotel's capacity 225 rooms as opposed to the 500 rooms it originally had.

The new Skirvin opened its doors on Feb 27, 2007, and it is rated a 4 diamond hotel by AAA. You will find all the amenities available at other hotels along with a few surprises.

There is a business center, swimming pool, whirlpool, and 1,200-square-foot gym available to guests. The Park Avenue Grill, the on-site restaurant, is ranked as one of the top three in the market and is very popular. If you like live entertainment, look no further than Red Piano Bar. It has become the downtown destination to be and is open six nights a week.

The Skirvin is 100 percent nonsmoking. Guests will find coffeemakers, hair dryers, irons, ironing boards, flatscreen televisions, and comfortable full-size or king-size beds to relax on. The cloth throw at the bottom of each bed is called "Bedtime Story." It tells the history of the Skirvin and is unique to this hotel. Custom furniture decorates each room and the bathrooms have heated mirrors. Closets have lights and guests will find a can of spray starch in each one. High-speed wireless Internet is available for $9.95 a day.

Guests may park their own cars or have them valet parked. The Skirvin accepts all major credit cards and is wheelchair accessible. Pets are welcome but there is a nonrefundable cleaning fee. There is no charge for extra people in a room.

The Aria Grill serves breakfast, lunch, and dinner. The menu includes made-from-scratch pastries, a pasta and potato bar, and hand-tossed pizza. The lounge opens at 4:30 p.m.

BED-AND-BREAKFASTS

GRANDISON INN AT MANEY PARK $$-$$$
1200 N. Shartel
(405) 232-8778
www.grandisoninn.com

Want to get away from it all, yet still be close to downtown? Look no further than the Grandison. Built in 1907, this three-story 7,000-square-foot bed-and-breakfast is one of the finest examples of Victorian architecture in Oklahoma. Through its 100-plus-year history, it has been a private home, law offices, and two restaurants, and in 1985 it was home to the *Oklahoma Gazette* newspaper. In Jan 1997 it opened as the Grandison Inn at Maney Park. Guests will enjoy the maple hardwood floors, stained glass windows, mahogany woodwork, and original stained-glass windows. Eight rooms are available, each with its own theme and history. Given such names as the Treehouse Hideaway, Hunter and Hound, Royal Retreat, and Memory Cove, what potential visitor wouldn't be intrigued by the rooms? Each room has its own private bath with whirlpool and/or shower. Television, cable, and a DVD player are standard in each room. Visitors can bring their own DVD movies or check out the titles in the Grandison movie library.

A Butler's Pantry on the second floor is stocked 24 hours a day with complimentary snacks, drinks, and a home-baked dessert every night. A continental breakfast is served in the pantry on weekdays and features in-season fruits, cereal, and pastries served from early morning to noon. On the weekends a hot breakfast is served for guests in the first floor dining room from 9 to 10:30 a.m.

The Grandison is listed on the National Register of Historic Places and won the 1997 Historic Preservation Award. The Grandison has also been named one of the top 15 inns in the United States for honeymoons and anniversaries by *Arrington's Inn Traveler* magazine.

JUDY'S LAMPLIGHT INN $-$$
1225 NW 37th St.
(405) 524-5453
www.bbonline.com/ok/lamplight

This quiet Inn offers guests a home away from home. Built in 1910, this historic American four-square home opened as a bed-and-breakfast in 1998. Antiques and an oil lamp collection decorate the inn. The home has its original oak woodwork. A spacious living room, dining room, library, and backyard deck and flagstone patio with a small waterfall give guests the peace and relaxing atmosphere they seek.

Three rooms are available for rent. They each have ceiling fans, telephones, and televisions with cable. The Evening Shade has a queen bed and is decorated in warm colors and accented with toys from the past. It has its own private bath with shower. The Morning Side Room has a double bed with private bath and tub. It is a Victorian room decorated in rose colors with antique furniture. Amber's Nook has a double bed and a shared bath. It is a little room and has an antique iron bed as its centerpiece.

The inn has been home to the Renteria family for 30 years. The innkeeper, Judy Renteria, is always delighted to welcome guests to her home. Specializing in gourmet, Mexican, and home-style cooking, her kitchen creations are sure to please even the pickiest eater. You may come in as a stranger, but you'll leave as part of the family.

RED STONE INN $$-$$$
3101 NE 50th St.
(405) 427-0383
www.redstoneinnokc.com

Originally built in the 1930s of native red stone, this lovely home fell into disrepair until it was rescued in 1997. Today the home sits surrounded by 7.5 acres of wooded sloping acres and koi ponds. Ten minutes from Bricktown and mall and antiques shopping, this inn gives visitors the perfect place to relax and get away from it all, while keeping you in the middle of things. The inn has four guest rooms, three of which are suites. Two suites have private balconies and all are decorated with family antiques and have private baths and televisions.

The rooms named after local Oklahoma attractions will draw any visitor. The Belle Isle Suite is named for the Belle Isle District when it had lakes, amusement parks, and trolleys. The Cimarron Suite takes its name from the Cimarron River, which lazily travels through central Oklahoma. The Capitol Suite gets its name from the Oklahoma capitol. This suite, with its Jacuzzi and balcony where one can see the new Oklahoma capitol dome, gives guests a true feel of Oklahoma hospitality. Finally, the Hall of Fame Room is named for the National Cowboy and Western Heritage Museum, which is only minutes away.

Prepared by the innkeepers, Mark and Ann Amme, breakfast in the breakfast room is a delicious hot meal, such as eggs Benedict with andouille sausage, brie soufflé, puffy apple pancakes, or some other wonderful treat. Homemade cookies, fruit, and sodas are always available throughout the day in the breakfast room.

i To find more bed-and-breakfast inns, look online at www.bbonline.com/ok. Many Oklahoma B&B's belong to this organization and are listed here.

RUSTY GABLES GUEST LODGE
AND GALLERY $$$
3800 NE 50th St.
(405) 424-1015
www.rustygablesbb.com

In northeast Oklahoma City, located on a 30-acre ranch called the N Triangle P Ranch, five minutes from downtown, this B&B is flowing with Old West charm. The pine lodge welcomes visitors with wagon wheels, wicker chairs on the front porch, and a larger-than- life horseshoe hanging over the entrance. The house was constructed in 2004 by Sam Nicolosi and Don Paul with the express purpose of sharing "ranch life" with visitors.

Visitors will feel pampered, however, as they move into one of the two guest suites. The Emerald Glen Suite is decorated in greens, navy, and burgundy, with a theme reminiscent of Jack

London's *Call of the Wild*. It features an aspen-timber, pillow-top king bed, wilderness decor and artwork, refrigerator, microwave, and multiple sitting areas.

The Western Sunset Suite shows off its 1940 buckaroo cowboy theme in sunset reds and desert tans. It features a king bed and vintage artwork.

Both rooms have private entrances, private baths with showers and oversize Jacuzzi tubs, satellite television and radio, DVD/VCR, self-controlled heat and air conditioning, rock fireplaces, robes, afternoon treats, and bathroom amenities.

Spa services are available for a fee. The services featured are full-body and chair massage, reflexology, salt glows, herbal clay or seaweed wraps, and facials. Packages are available.

Guests can roam the ranch's trails on foot or horseback. Guided tours on horseback are offered and you can ride your own horse. A six-stall barn is available for overnight stabling.

On Fri and Sat a full breakfast is served in the gallery. Sun through Thurs an expanded continental breakfast awaits guests.

Don't miss the artwork in the Great Room Art Gallery. This room offers up-and-coming western artists a place to showcase and sell their work.

WHISPERING PINES INN $$–$$$
7820 Easy Highway 9
(405) 447-0202
www.bbonline.com/ok/whisperingpines

Built in 1994, this two-story Victorian inn has seven guest rooms and a great many surprises. Located in Norman, 10 minutes from the University of Oklahoma, it is surrounded by 20 acres of beautiful trees and rolling pastures. The house has a wraparound porch, gazebo, grand staircase, and antiques in abundance.

The seven guest rooms have private baths with whirlpools or Jacuzzis; televisions with VCR; robes; dining areas; kitchenettes; and complimentary sodas, popcorn, and snacks. A private breakfast for two is delivered to your room at no extra charge. You can order off a menu consisting of six choices. Guests also have access to full movie library.

The Emerald Dream Cottage Suite features a stylish European-like canopy that drapes a four-poster king-size cherry wood bed. The suite also has a lush loveseat, fireplace, and overlooks the pavilion and pond.

The Secret Rose Suite is decorated in a royal theme. Its colors are red with a tint of gold. It features a canopied king-size bed and fireplace.

The Pine Cone Cottage has a rustic mountain look with a king-size poster bed made of aspen logs. This cottage has a living room, kitchen area, bedroom, and private bath with corner double whirlpool tub. Breakfast is delivered hot to the door each morning.

The Satin Splendor Room has satin bedding, a sitting area in front of the fireplaces, a quiet dining table for two, and a large den with kitchenette. The balcony view overlooks the pond and trees below.

Ready for a private hideaway? Stay in the Stardust room. Decorated in dusty soft pink and dark brown, this room features a king-size four poster bed with a brown canopy. The kitchenette in this room has a microwave and mini refrigerator.

The Lavender and Lace Suite is decorated in lavender and white lace. Elegant, yet comfortable, this room has a king-size, lace canopy bed. The strong male will feel comfortable here with the love of his life.

The last room, the English Hunt Room, is decorated in English fox-and-hound-era decor with dark browns and deep greens. It has a queen-size bed and a separate dining area.

Located in the main house is a restaurant, which serves French continental fare and a full-service bar with a selection of 100 wines. The restaurant menu consists of pork tenderloin, salmon, duck, lamb, fresh seafood, wild game, and Angus beef. The dress code is business casual. It is open Mon through Sat, from 6 p.m. until the last guest leaves.

all across the country. The grounds have almost three wooded acres filled with gardens, two koi ponds, a gazebo, and sitting areas. The innkeepers, Lionel and Johnita Turner, have turned the English Tudor country mansion into a peaceful getaway.

Guests have four accommodations to choose from, each special in its own right. In the upstairs north wing is Arthur's Place. It features a hand-carved, mahogany, king-size bed; a fireplace; a sitting area; and a writing desk. The bathroom is a pavilion surrounded by an inspiring stained-glass wall, glass shower for two, and a king-size jetted whirlpool.

In the upstairs south wing, Eleanor's Suite is decorated in soft garden colors and features a queen-size bed. The bedchamber opens onto the balcony of the conservatory with a king-size jetted tub for two and a sitting area for morning coffee. The master bath includes a shower and double sinks. An adjoining bedroom is available with this suite.

The Fox Run is a favorite with travelers. It has a double bed, workspace for business guests, and an adjoining bath in the hall.

For a truly one-of-a-kind, fairy-tale experience, guests will want to stay in the Pleasant Under Glass room. Located in the gardens, the greenhouse cottage encloses a king-size jetted tub for two under glass for moonlight nights, yet with floral screening for privacy. A hand-carved and painted queen-size bed, fireplace, and private bath and shower, add to the elegance of the stay. This room is the ultimate in fantasy and privacy.

Breakfast has an elegant English touch with the cook's specialty of scones and fruit compote. It is served in the great hall overlooking the ponds and a bird feeding station.

The Mansion is a nonsmoking location.

WILLOW WAY BED & BREAKFAST $$–$$$
27 Oakwood Dr.
(405) 427-2133
www.willowwaybb.com
Located in the Forest Park neighborhood, this wooded country retreat welcomes visitors from

Edmond

ARCADIAN INN $$$–$$$$
328 E. First St., Edmond
(405) 348-6347
www.arcadianinn.com

Located west, across the street from the University of Central Oklahoma campus in Edmond, this inn is known for its personal attention to service and romantic detail. It has been voted one of Oklahoma's top five bed-and-breakfasts for the last 15 years and named the "#1 Bed & Breakfast" by Edmond *Leisure Life* readers. Eight rooms are available here.

The Crown Jewel Villa is a private room carriage house suite, decorated in blue art deco. It features a canopied king bed, a Jacuzzi for two, a gas log fireplace, a wet bar with fridge and microwave, a television with DVD and VCR, a European shower for two with multiple shower heads, and a private candlelight breakfast.

The Magnolia Suite offers an elegant southern plantation ambience. It has a private entrance; a custom-built, canopied king bed; a gas log fireplace; a European shower; and a Jacuzzi tub for two. This suite also has a refrigerator and a microwave.

The Royal Master Suite, decorated in golds and purples, give guests the royal treatment. It has a private entrance, a canopied king bed, and a gas log fireplace. Breakfast can be served in bed.

The Captain's Quarters has an elevated king bed, surrounded by gauze drapes. The room features a roaring fireplace and a private entrance. Breakfast is served in the room.

Remembrances is decorated in reds and gold and feels like Camelot. It has a fireplace, a sitting area, and a canopied king bed. A private candlelit breakfast is served.

M'Lord's Chambers is a getaway for the guys. This gentleman's retreat offers a king bed, a private sunroom, a balcony, and a gas log fireplace.

Emerald Nights and the Garden Room have canopied queen beds, Jacuzzis for two, and breakfast served by candlelight.

All rooms have LCD televisions, DVDs, VCRs, and CD players, small refrigerators and coffee and tea makers.

HOLIDAY INN EXPRESS $
3840 E. Second St., Edmond
(405) 844-3700
www.holidayinnexpress.com

Located at I-35 and Second Street, this hotel, owned and operated by Kusum Hospitality, is a warm and friendly stop. Renovated every few years, it offers an indoor pool, a whirlpool, on-site laundry facilities, and a health and fitness center. Business services are available and include copying and wireless Internet and fax services. Rooms come with hairdryers, coffeemakers, and irons and ironing boards. Complimentary breakfast is available and kids eat free. Eighty-one rooms are available. With this hotel's location, you have easy access to city events and activities. Within 15 minutes you can be at Remington Park, the Oklahoma City Zoo, or the Science Museum.

i To find hotels by type or location, go to www.oklahomacity.com. Here you can search by price, most popular, or pet friendly. This site lets you find the perfect hotel for you.

TWO HEARTS INN $$$–$$$$
2118 W. Edmond Rd., Edmond
(405) 715-2525
www.twoheartsinn.com

On the west side of Edmond, behind the Inspirations Tea Room, sits this Inn. Larry and Tamara Rhodes started this bed-and-breakfast as a retreat for couples and to help them nurture their own relationship. Located just a 20-minute drive from the heart of Oklahoma City, Two Hearts Inn is an upscale, luxurious, and romantic environment with beautiful grounds and suites where couples can get away without going away. Six suites are available.

Suite Hearts, Suite Tuscany, and Suite Venetian are the largest of the six suites and are the most luxurious. All three feature a king-size bed, sitting and dining areas, private deck, and a large, flatscreen television. Suite Hearts is decorated ingolds and burgundy. It is over 500 square feet, with granite countertops, 12 feet of windows, a private entrance with walk-out deck, and a great view of a wooded area. The Suite Tuscany features an ornate stone fireplace, a travertine stone floor, granite countertops, a bar sink, a refrigerator and windows as well. Suite Venetian has carpeting and a view of a creek meandering through a small wooded area.

Suite Chic has over 300 square feet, a stone tile floor, built-in fireplace, a beautiful black bed with hand-carved ornate roses, above-counter bowl sinks, a bar sink, and a refrigerator.

Step into Suite Island and you will feel transported to your own personal island. It is the innkeepers attempt at an escape to a faraway place, where the pace is slower and there is time to enjoy the beauty of life. This room accomplishes that goal and more. Golds and greens decorate this over 300-square-foot unit. It has a bamboo floor with a 6-foot-tall Feng Shui water fountain. Relax in an island bed with pineapple finials. To top off the decor, a palm tree column and pineapple light sconces accent the space.

Think of visiting the West? Look no further than Suite Santa Fe. This is the Rhodes's answer to a classic New Mexico–style suite with terra-cotta floors and kiva fireplace. This suite is over 300 square feet, has travertine stone floors, a two-person Jacuzzi with a 40-inch fireplace above it, a custom-made ornate wardrobe and dressers, and 12 feet of windows.

For all suites, breakfast is delivered to the guest's door to be enjoyed in private and features cuisine prepared by the Tea Room's award-winning cook staff.

Norman

CASA BELLA BED & BREAKFAST $$$
638 E. Brooks St., Norman
(405) 329-2289
www.casabellabedandbreakfast.com

This bed-and-breakfast is a charming Mexican-style small home located in a quiet residential area of Norman. Completely renovated in 2004, the guesthouse feels like a visit to old Mexico. The grounds around the home feature a stone patio with a fountain. Chairs and tables invite guests to stop and sit a spell after a walk around the yard. The quaint waterfall surrounded by lush greenery will transport you to a peaceful place, away from all your stress and worries.

The home, also called a Casita, has two bedrooms. Each room has a queen sized bed. There is a double shower covered with Mexican tiles and a living area. The kitchenette has a serving bar, refrigerator, microwave, and is stocked with its own serving dishes. Other amenities include ceiling fans, a stereo system, satellite television with DVD/VCR. If you must make calls a telephone is provided. Local calls are free. Don't worry about a hair dryer, iron, soaps or lotions. They are already on site.

A continental breakfast is included in the rate.

CUTTING GARDEN BED
& BREAKFAST $–$$
927 W. Boyd St., Norman
(405) 329-4522
www.cuttinggardenbandb.com

Established in 1993, this bed-and-breakfast is Norman's oldest. The three-bedroom home boasts one of the more unique settings for a bed-and-breakfast with an incredible natural backyard complete with flowers, herbs, and 100-year-old pecan trees. The back deck surrounded by greenery is a perfect place to relax, sit back, and enjoy a glass of something cold.

The three guest rooms are the perfect blend of hospitality and coziness. The Flo Room is decorated in raspberry, deep burgundies, and sage green. This room is upstairs and has a wrought-iron queen bed, a private balcony with access to the garden with hot tub, a private bath, digital cable television, air conditioning, and high-speed Internet access.

Also upstairs, the Celestial Room will have you dreaming of the sun, moon, and stars. It is decorated in rich blues and gold; has a sitting room with a wicker loveseat, table and chairs; a private bath with a two-person Jacuzzi tub; digital cable television; high-speed Internet; and garden views.

Located on the ground floor, the Many Room is secluded with its own private bath and views of the garden. Decorated in rustic earth tones, this room will help guests escape the hustle and bustle of daily life.

All guests are greeted by fresh-cut flowers and fresh-baked cookies or brownies in their room when they arrive.

Breakfast is served either in your room or downstairs at the breakfast table until 10 a.m. In addition to coffee, hot tea, and orange juice, guests have their choice of homemade Belgian waffles, oven-baked French toast, or choice of omelets with muffins and scones, all garnished with fresh, edible flowers. Muffins are served with homemade jams and jellies. Because the bed-and-breakfast wants to serve its guests the freshest ingredients, it grows its own herbs, edible flowers, and a variety of vegetables.

If you are looking for an environmentally friendly bed and breakfast, this is the place for you. This inn has been "green" for a number of years. They practice organic gardening techniques, recycle all trash that is recyclable, and compost yard and kitchen waste.

HAMPTON INN $$–$$$
309 Norman Center Court, Norman
(405) 366-2100
www.hamptoninn.com
Owned and operated by Kusum Hospitality, this hotel is 2.88 miles from downtown Norman and has 61 guest rooms. Pets are not allowed. A business center, indoor pool, and exercise and fitness facilities are available here. Guests will also find complimentary high-speed Internet service. A complimentary hot breakfast or the On the Run Breakfast Bag will get you ready for the day. If you are checking out the University of Oklahoma, catching a basketball or football game, or visiting one of the museums in the area, this may be the hotel for you. You will find a large number of restaurants nearby with meals that range in price from $5 to $25 each.

THE MONTFORD INN AND COTTAGES $$–$$$$
322 W. Tonhawa, Norman
(405) 321-2200
www.montfordinn.com
This inn sits a few blocks north of Main Street. The buttery-yellow, 4,000-square-foot inn was designed and built to have the feel of an old house. It comes pretty close to the mark. The inn is owned by bed-and-breakfast pros Phyllis and Ron Murray and their son William. The creature comforts of the guest rooms are unsurpassed in Oklahoma. Each of the 10 antiques-filled rooms in the main house has a private bath, most have gas fireplaces, and all are stocked with coffee makersand gourmet coffee, candles, scented soaps, magazines, and piles of pillows.

Three 1,000-square-foot cottages across the street are as charming and comfortable as the inn, with whirlpool baths and tiny kitchens. Hidden Hollow is a whole house unto itself—the restored bungalow has a full kitchen and a yard and is perfect for families.

The inn is named for one of Phyllis Murray's ancestors, a Chickasaw cattle rancher named Montford Johnson. Johnson's license to operate in Indian Territory is framed and hanging on the wall; a kachina doll collection and University of Oklahoma football memorabilia fill other rooms. (Actress Helen Hunt stayed in the hunting-and-fishing-themed Trophy Room while she was in Oklahoma filming the movie *Twister*.) The Murrays cater to business as well as leisure travelers and provide guests with a photocopying machine, fax, modem hookups, and workouts at a nearby gym.

RESTAURANTS

Look in the yellow pages and you might decide to close your eyes and let your finger do the choosing rather than deciding on your own. Oklahoma City has hundreds of eating options, but not to worry. In this chapter, you will be guided to restaurants that are personal favorites or have been highly recommended by friends or other restaurant goers. When you come to town, don't be shy to ask the locals where they eat. They can point you to small establishments that you might not thought of trying and direct you away from places that may have a lot of glitz and glamour, but really aren't that good.

The *Oklahoma Gazette* (www.oklahomagazette.com) is another good place to look for eating advice. Every year, the paper runs a contest choosing the "Best of." Patrons get to vote on what their favorite restaurants are according to food type. One can be assured of finding new places to eat from reading through the contest list.

This chapter includes not only steak houses but also tearooms. It covers cuisine from French to Mexican and establishments that are casual to dressy and for kids to couples.

Most restaurants feature hearty portions like Ted's, Canton, and the barbecue places, so be prepared to bring your appetite. If you do get full before you finish, ask for a take-out box. In Oklahoma no one frowns at saving some for later.

What you will not find in this chapter are national chains. If you're hungry for the familiar, you'll find Oklahoma City has a hearty list of fast-food and better-known places like Taco Bell, Domino's, Red Lobster, Olive Garden, and of course the ubiquitous McDonald's. I have included a few regional chains, but their food is too special to ignore. As a matter of fact, repeat visitors will go to these restaurants the minute they hit town and visit them several time during their stay.

For some of the local hot spots, be prepared for a considerable wait if you go on a Fri or Sat night. An hour wait at Ted's with people flowing out the front door into the parking lot is not unusual. Most restaurants do not take reservations, but you can call ahead to find out how long the wait is or send a member of your party ahead to get in line. The restaurants that do take reservations are duly noted below.

Most restaurants are open for lunch and serve smaller portions at a lower cost until about 4 p.m. Take-out is always an option if you are pressed for time or just want to get home, kick back, and rest.

Some restaurants have full bars and even those that don't will have a wine list and certain types of beers. If you are interested in wines or beers, do your homework before going or ask for the wine list once you arrive at the restaurant.

Be aware that different types of eating establishment have different hours. Breakfast restaurants, like Beverly's, the Classen Grill, and Jimmy's Egg, are open from 6 a.m. until about 1 or 2 p.m. Tearooms are open from about 11 a.m. to 2 p.m. and some dinner establishments don't open until 4 p.m. Several of the Chinese restaurants are closed from 2 to 5 p.m. If you haven't eaten at a specific restaurant before, it might be wise to call ahead and make sure it is open.

Almost all the restaurants listed in this chapter have a Web site with an online menu. Checking out the online menus is a good way to find the types of food you may be interested in and their prices.

This chapter is organized according to type of cuisine and restaurants are listed alphabetically. Each listing below includes a price code and the codes reflect dinner prices for one entree and does not include appetizers, alcoholic beverages, taxes, or tips. Tipping 20 percent is customary and greatly appreciated by your server. Unless otherwise noted, assume the restaurants listed accept all major credit cards, are wheelchair accessible, and have a children's menu.

Price Codes

The price code for each restaurant listed below is a general guide. It is to give you an idea of the price of a single entree, excluding tax and tip. Prices will vary depending on what you order and whether you have alcoholic beverages, appetizers, or dessert. Prices may fluctuate at each restaurant as well.

$................. Less than $10
$$ .... $10–$20
$$$ .... $21–$35
$$$$ .... $36 and more

OKLAHOMA CITY

American

ANN'S CHICKEN FRY $
4106 NW 39th St.
(405) 943-8915
Alvin Burchett was 23 when he opened this restaurant in 1971. Things have been the same here for 38 years. Burchett is still serving great food, still in the same location, and still using the same meat company. What makes his chicken fry so different is that he uses a mixture of club and cube steak together. Breaded with special spices and fried to a golden brown, the chicken is what keeps diners coming back again and again. As a matter of fact, 90 percent of what comes out of the kitchen is chicken fry.

Besides the food, diners may come to relive days and years gone by. The restaurant is decorated with antiques and memorabilia. Guests will often say, "I had one of those when I was a kid."

Ann's Chicken Fry is open Tues through Sat from 11:00 a.m. to 8:30 p.m. Fri and Sat nights are the busiest, so come early or come on another day. The restaurant only seats 64.

BEVERLY'S CHICKEN IN THE ROUGH $–$$
3135 NW Expressway
(405) 848-5050
Beverly's is an Oklahoma City institution. The first Beverly's opened as a Pancake House on May 19, 1921. Through the years, there have been locations on Lincoln, 23rd, and near Penn. Today, the Northwest Expressway location, Beverly's Chicken in the Rough, is the only one and it is open 24 hours a day, 365 days a year. Original founders Beverly and Rubey Osborne came up with the idea for the chicken restaurant when they were driving to California. At the time, the roads were not paved. They were eating chicken out of a bucket on the bumpy road and decided to add to their Pancake House by having an establishment called Beverly's Chicken in the Rough.

Beverly's still makes pancakes made from scratch, but also serves its famous breaded chicken and Big Bev's Burger. The house salad is topped with a garlicky ranch, and is made on the premises. Rolls and biscuits are made fresh daily and there are also real mashed potatoes; hand-cut, fresh French fries made from real potatoes; and salsa made from fresh ingredients.

CAFÉ NOVA $–$$$
4308 N. Western Ave.
(405) 525-6682
www.cafenovaokc.com
Café Nova is a modern design restaurant. It delivers contemporary American food with urban flair. Photography and artwork are some of the features that enhance the ambience. A full bar is available and the bar menu is served all day. Café Nova also serves brunch, which includes an omelet bar, Belgian waffles, salmon BLTs, fish tacos, cordon bleu sandwiches, and crab cakes Benedict. Lunch includes sandwiches, like

a salmon club or a choriza guacamole burger. Entrees, like shrimp and grits or beef portobello pasta, can also be ordered for lunch. The dinner menu includes appetizers, like calamari, shrimp, and scallop ceviche. Pork porterhouse, airline chicken breast, and citrus ahi tuna are just a few of the dinner entrees that guests can order.

The restaurant is open Mon through Fri from 11:00 a.m. to 9:30 p.m.; Sat 5:00 p.m. to 2:00 a.m.; and Sun from 10:30 a.m. to 3:00 p.m.

CATTLEMAN'S CAFÉ AND
STEAKHOUSE $-$$$
1309 S. Agnew Ave. (Stockyards City)
(405) 236-0416
www.cattlemensrestaurant.com

This restaurant was established in 1910 as Cattleman's Café, a little coffee shop where current cattle prices were posted on a blackboard over the counter so that ranchers and farmers who stopped in didn't miss anything. In 1945 a man named Gene Wade won the cafe in a game of craps by rolling a hard six. Wade kept the original counter, added a dining room, and got serious about the steaks: Cattlemen's ages its own beef and hand cuts it in its butcher shop. The restaurant is filled with old photos that show the area in its heyday. There are also sketches of such locally revered figures as John Wayne and Hopalong Cassidy and a 20-foot photographic mural of Wade and his father, Percy, on horseback in a sea of Herefords.

Wade sold the restaurant, but his rocking chair is still in the old north cafe section, inviting patrons to feel at home. Cattlemen's opens at 6 a.m. for a breakfast of grits, steak, and biscuits, and stays open until 10 p.m., Sun to Thurs, and until midnight on Fri and Sat.

CHEEVER'S $-$$$
2409 N. Hudson Ave.
(405) 525-7007
www.cheeverscafe.com

Serving lunch and dinner, this restaurant has been a local favorite since 2000. For years the historic building housed a family-owned florist. Now, its glass, refrigerated floral cases hold desserts, wines, and beer. A few of the specialties are the Yukon gold-bleu cheese potato chips and the mixed seafood tamales. Sandwiches, soups, salads, pasta, and lunch plates are served for lunch. At dinner, guests can find items like steak and seafood. Don't forget dessert when you start eating. You won't want to leave without trying the Oklahoma peach shortcake or the wild huckleberry parfait.

Cheever's is open at various times through the week. On Mon, the restaurant is open from 11:00 a.m. to 9:00 p.m., Tues through Thurs from 11:00 a.m. to 9:30 p.m., Fri 11:00 a.m. to 10:30 p.m., Sat 5:00 to 10:30 p.m., and Sun from 10:00 a.m. to 3:00 p.m.

CIMARRON STEAKHOUSE $-$$$
201 N. Meridian Ave.
(405) 948-7778
www.cimarronsteakhouse.com

It looks like an old western saloon when you pull into the spacious parking lot, but inside the atmosphere is fun and friendly. The Cimarron has a full-service bar and whether you dance or not, you'll get a kick out of the wood dance floor highlighted in the middle of the dining area. While all the food is good, the specialties are sirloin, rib eye, and salmon. There is also chicken, pork chops, ribs, and seafood. Mesquite grilled is a flavor you won't forget. All entrees come with a potato, vegetable, and salad. The ample portions will fill you up for sure.

The Steakhouse is open Sun through Thurs 11:00 a.m. to 10:00 p.m. and Fri and Sat from 11:00 a.m. to 11:00 p.m. From 6:00 p.m. until close the restaurant is very busy so plan accordingly.

THE COACH HOUSE $$-$$$$
6437 Avondale Dr.
(405) 842-1000
www.thecoachhouseokc.com

If an intimate, quiet dinner is what you have in mind, go to this restaurant. Since 1985, it has been considered Oklahoma City's finest upscale restaurant. It serves regional American cuisine. Under the experienced hand of Chef Kurt

Fleischfresser, also the owner, the Coach House offers an ever-changing seasonal cuisine, highlighting the best local produce and regional specialties, prepared with classical perfection. Some of the specialties include smoked salmon croque madame with fried quail egg, grand mariner soufflé with raspberry sauce, and chocolate fauvet with raspberry sauce.

A full bar and a *Wine Spectator* Award–winning wine list are available to enhance your dining experience. In addition to outstanding food and drink, the experienced staff offers thoughtful, personalized service.

The restaurant is wheelchair accessible and parking is ample in their private lot. Reservations are accepted. Guests can call or make reservations online via the Web site.

COCO FLOW $
100 East Main
(405) 524-9500
www.cocoflow.com

Do you love chocolate? If so, then look no further than Coco Flow. This café, located down in Bricktown in the Mercantile, is the chocolate lover's paradise. Here you will find 19 different kinds of truffles, 8 different varieties of pralines, and 7 different flavors of bon bons. There are chocolate-dipped strawberries, dipped dried pineapple, and dipped fruit or nut clusters. You can also choose from éclairs, peanut butter cups, a slice of red velvet cake or cupcake, gelatos, coffees, hot chocolates, and signature coffee drinks. Besides chocolate goodies, crepes, Panini sandwiches, quiches, and salads are served. Box lunches are also available for take-out.

EDNA'S $–$$
5137 N. Classen
(405) 840-3339
www.ednasokc.com

This restaurant is a local neighborhood favorite. People from all walks of life come through the doors. The building was just renovated and a nice, new patio was added out front. The inside walls are filled with dollar bills from patrons leaving their mark on Edna's for the last 20 years.

Edna's serves a full menu with everything from cheese fries to patty melts, but is best known for the lunchbox, a specialty drink made with herbs, fruit, Coors Light, orange juice, and a little something extra. Since keeping track, Edna's has sold 324,585 specials. The restaurant is open year-round. So whether you're hungry for a great burger, thirsty for a lunchbox, or want to pick up a T-shirt for a friend's birthday, you're sure to have a great time at this little hole-in-the-wall.

Edna's is open Mon through Sat from 10:00 a.m. to 2:00 p.m. and Sun from 11:00 a.m. to 2:00 p.m.

FLORENCE'S RESTAURANT $–$$
1437 NE 23rd St.
(405) 424-8336

Florence is from Boley, Oklahoma. She grew up on a farm in the small country town, so country cookin' is what she does in her kitchen. Opening on Fourth Street in 1952, Florence moved her restaurant to its current location in 1969. There is a saying around here that she opened her restaurant on a wing and a prayer. Her prayers paid off.

The atmosphere of the restaurant is casual homey. Its stark white appearance is accented with art, depicting kitchen activities, cooking utensils, and pictures of Florence herself.

Guests here are a diverse group. Many locals eat here, but some come just because they've heard about the restaurant. Florence makes no bones about the restaurant's staying power and is just proud she has been in business so long.

Even though the restaurant sits right across the street from a fried chicken eating establishment, the most popular item here is fried chicken. Florence believes in variety, so each day of the week, she has a special item. Tues is chicken and dressing. Wed is meatloaf and other days, she serves smothered steak, smothered chicken, or beef livers.

There is no alcohol served here. There is no children's menu either, but parents can order half orders of anything on the menu. Parking is ample here. The facility is wheelchair accessible in spite of the small step out front. Whenever Florence or her daughter sees a guest coming in a wheelchairs, they'll go help him or her in.

The restaurant is open Mon through Fri from 7 a.m. to 6 p.m. Don't even think about pulling plastic on Florence. She only takes cash.

ℹ️ **Interested in knowing what kind of beef Oklahoma ranchers raise and sell? Contact the Oklahoma Beef Council (800-235-5403; www.oklabeef.org).**

GRATEFUL BEAN CAFÉ $
1039 N. Walker Ave.
(405) 239-6800
www.gratefulbean.com
Located in the historic Kaiser's Old Fashioned Ice Cream Parlor location, the Grateful Bean carries on the Kaiser legacy. Up until about 1990, when Kaiser's closed, the parlor was the oldest continuously open place to eat in Oklahoma. It was famous not only for its ice cream, but also for its soda fountain. In 1978, the parlor was added to the National Register of Historic Places. Today, guests can still see the original 1917 soda fountain counter bar with its earth-tone ceramic tile and order milkshakes, malts, ice cream sodas, ice cream sundaes, and ice cream cones. Besides ice cream items, the restaurant serves soups, salads, sandwiches, hamburgers, rock-salt baked potatoes, and Indian tacos. For an authentic view of Oklahoma City past, be sure to visit here. It is open Mon through Fri from 11 a.m. to 6 p.m. On Sat and holidays, it is open from 11 a.m. to 4 p.m. Grateful Bean is closed Sun.

HAUNTED HOUSE RESTAURANT $$-$$$$
7101 Miramar Blvd.
(405) 478-1417
www.hauntedhouserestaurant.com
The building that this restaurant is in has a mysterious and shady past. Before it was a restaurant, it was a private residence. The owner of the house, Martin Carriker, was shot in the head. Many blamed his stepdaughter, but before she could go on trial, his wife, Clara, passed away. Still living in the house, Mrs. Pearson, the stepdaughter, met with more bad news when the house was served a foreclosure notice and the house was sched-

uled to be sold at a sheriff's auction. On Feb 14, the sale was finalized and Mrs. Pearson ordered to get out, but before she could leave she was found dead. Reports suggested a drug overdose.

Enter a new season for the old house. Art Thibault, a Minnesota native, leased it and opened it as a restaurant in 1964. While locals come here to eat the great food, many out-of-towners hear of the restaurant's past and come to check it out. Guests can explore the history of the home from pictures hanging on the wall or ask for an information booklet telling of the building's haunted past.

Because the restaurant seats only about 128, reservations are required. Dinner is served from Mon through Sat at 6 p.m. Items you will find on the menu include appetizers, soups, salads, filet mignon, rack of lamb, shrimp and pasta, and Australian lobster tail.

IRMA'S BURGER SHACK $-$$
1120 Classen Dr.
(405) 235-IRMA
www.irmasburgershack.com
Open every day from 11 a.m. to 9 p.m., Irma's mission is to serve guests the best burger made with the best meat found in Oklahoma. Lots of families come here for the hand-battered onion rings and fries. There are windows all around, so getting a window seat in this old diner–style restaurant is not a problem. Sit at a table or grab one of the six stools at the bar. The most popular burgers are the California burger and the mushroom, bacon, and swiss burger made with all-natural beef from the NoName Ranch in Wynnewood, Oklahoma. If you like beef free of pesticides, hormones, and antibiotics, Irma can sell you NoName Beef on the spot. Just ask.

Irma also sells "Made in Oklahoma" products like nuts, candies, sauces, and more.. The restaurant is handicapped accessible. Parking is somewhat limited.

JIMMY'S EGG $-$$
1616 N. May Ave.
(405) 749-2255
www.jimmysegg.com

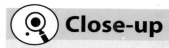

Close-up

Ingrid's Kitchen

Ingrid's (3701 N. Youngs, 405-946-8444, www.ingridskitchen.com) is a bakery, a delicatessen, and a restaurant. Thirty-one years ago, this restaurant opened as a German bakery. It has been under the management of its current owner, Lee Burris, for nine years and is now considered a European and American establishment. It still makes 20 varieties of bagels from scratch in the bakery, but after an expansion, it now produces cakes, pies, cookies, bagels, and 25 different kinds of bread, too. Over 500 items come out of the bakery daily.

For breakfast, guests can choose from omelets, French toast, biscuits and gravy or one of the specialties, like brötchen (German breakfast rolls) or Wiener schnitzel. For lunch, deli sandwiches, German lunchmeat sandwiches, grilled sandwiches, sausage sandwiches, and specialty plates are served. For supper, guests can choose from the bratwurst plate, sauerbraten, or fleisch rouladen.

Dress is casual here. There is a live band from noon to 2 p.m. on Sat and dancing on Sat nights. On Tues, there is live music with dinner. Ingrid's accepts major credit cards, is wheelchair accessible, and has a children's menu. Parking is not a problem no matter how busy it gets.

On Mon Ingrid's is open from 7 a.m. to 6:30 p.m. and does not serve dinner. Tues through Sat it is open from 7 a.m. until 8 p.m. On Sun a brunch buffet is served from 9:30 a.m. to 2 p.m.

Jimmy's Egg has 12 locations in and around Oklahoma City, so one would think it would be easy to find a seat for breakfast. It isn't. This breakfast and lunch restaurant is an institution and has been for the past 20 years. Readers of the *Oklahoman* and the *Oklahoma Gazette* have voted it the restaurant with the best breakfast for the last 10 years. Be prepared to stand in line on the weekends if you don't get to the restaurant minutes after it opens. Breakfast is served until 2 p.m. Guests are tempted with three-egg omelette specialties, like the Wisconsin Omelette, the Meat Lovers Omelette, and Popeye's Revenge Omelette. If you don't like the specialty items, make your own. You can also order eggs Benedict, Belgian waffles, or pancakes.

If lunch is your thing, Jimmy's serves salads, sandwiches, burgers, and lunch specials from 11 a.m. to 2 p.m.

Parking is not a problem. There is a children's menu. Below is a list of some of the other locations around the city:

2132 W. Britton Rd. (the Village), (405) 842-2944

7741 S. Walker, (405) 631-3647

1715 E. 2nd St. (Edmond), (405) 340-6889

6805 SE 15th (Midwest City), (405) 732-6433

3741 NW 39th, (405) 949-5522

JUNIOR'S $$–$$$$
2601 NW Expressway #1W
(405) 848-5597
www.juniorsokc.com

Since 1973, Junior's has been an Oklahoma City landmark. Located on the ground floor of the Oil Center building on the Northwest Expressway, this restaurant offers diners a truly unique experience. Once known as the Oilman's Oasis, it is where oil men came to finalize some of their biggest deals during the oil boom and bust of the 1970s and 1980s.

Junior's offers a fully enclosed smoking room and bar, featuring state-of-the-art ventilation systems, but it also has a complete nonsmoking dining area. On Wed evening, guests can enjoy live music performances and on Mon through Sat nights, a lively piano bar.

This is a fine-dining establishment. The menu includes hand-cut certified Angus steaks, Australian lobster, Caesar salad, shrimp, and Alaskan king crab.

Reservations are required here. A full bar is available. Junior's is open for lunch from 11 a.m. to 2 p.m. and for dinner from 5:30 p.m. to 10 p.m. The bar is open from 11 a.m. to 1 a.m. Mon through Thurs and 11 a.m. to 2 p.m. Fri and Sat. Both the bar and restaurant are closed on Sun.

LUNCH BOX $–$$
413 W. Sheridan Ave.
(405) 232-9409

This restaurant has been operating since 1946. It seats about 180 people in its booths and tables. Casual is the name of the game here even though lawyers, doctors, and judges frequent the place. Today, parents who grew up coming here bring their kids and grandkids. It is a family-friendly place to eat.

Food is cooked fresh and served all day cafeteria style. Guests will find five soups or stews, 10 different kinds of vegetables (fresh or frozen), five different kinds of meat, and five to nine varieties of pie to choose from. You can also order charbroiled burgers, salads, hot links, or the Lunch Box's famous New York–style corned beef cooked fresh every day. The restaurant serves between 100 and 150 pieces of pie per day. Those pies include pecan, cherry, coconut cream, and chocolate.

There are 18 parking spots available plus parking in the street, but not to worry, customers move through fairly quickly. And, most customers are on foot from local businesses in the area. The Lunch Box is wheelchair accessible and will take reservations for parties of 10 or more. The Lunch Box is open Mon through Fri from 10:30 a.m. to 3 p.m. and closed Sat and Sun. No alcohol is served here, just great food for great people.

McNELLIE'S OKC $–$$
1100 Classen Dr.
(405) 601-7468
www.mcnelliesokc.com

Owner James McNellie built McNellie's to be like the pubs he visited in Dublin, Ireland, years ago. He wanted to feature reasonably priced food and an atmosphere ideal for not only singles, but also families with young children Oklahoma City thinks he succeeded. Every Wed, from 5 to 11 p.m. is $3 Burger Night. Sun brunch from 11 a.m. to 2 p.m. features a Bloody Mary bar, which some say is the best in the city. Besides burgers, the restaurant serves a St. Patty's melt, fish and chips, and Landlord's Cottage Pie. If you are thirsty and want a pint, look no further than McNellie's. The pub has a great selection of hard-to-find draft and bottled beers (350 at last count), plus a large selection of single-malt scotches. You can review the list on the pub's Web site.

No reservation is needed here, but Fri and Sat nights can get crowded. Parking is not a problem. The pub is open seven days a week from 11 a.m. to 2 a.m.

MICKEY MANTLE'S STEAKHOUSE $$–$$$$
7 Mickey Mantle Dr.
(405) 272-0777
www.mickeymantlesteakhouse.com

Mickey Mantle's opened in the fall of 2000. The owners, Monte Hough and Jim Ingram, decided Bricktown was the perfect location for their new steak-house concept. The location couldn't be more perfect as it is directly across the street from the Bricktown Ballpark on Mickey Mantle Drive.

The restaurant is dressed in mahogany and offers comfortable booth seating as well as large tables. The dim lighting and bluesy music offer a relaxing atmosphere. The restaurant walls are filled with pictures of Mickey Mantle. Memorabilia from Mantle's career are displayed in the foyer. All memorabilia was donated by the Mantle family.

Signature dishes include cowboy-cut rib eye, New York strip, and the Roquefort filet. The chef daily features the mesquite-smoked filet served with the restaurant's signature bourbon sweet mash. If you have no room for dessert, go ahead and take home the homemade chocolate cake made with bits of cinnamon.

This is an award-winning restaurant. Ii has received nominations and awards for Best Steakhouse in Oklahoma City, Best Place to Celebrate a Special Event, and Most Romantic Dinner. The most recent award is the Best Place for Pre-Event Dinner in the 2008 *Oklahoma Reader*'s Choice Awards.

Reservations are not required, but highly recommended. Valet parking is available. The restaurant is wheelchair accessible.

Dining room hours are Sun through Thurs from 5 to 10 p.m. and Fri and Sat from 5 to 11 p.m.

MUSEUM OF ART CAFÉ $–$$$$
415 Couch Dr.
(405) 232-6262
www.okcmoa.com

Located on the ground floor of the Oklahoma City Museum of Art, this cafe serves lunch, dinner, and Sun brunch. The cafe's metropolitan ambience, superb cuisine, and exceptional service bring a taste of Chicago, San Francisco, and London to Oklahoma City. The full-service restaurant offers fine dining with a French-fusion menu prepared fresh daily. An accommodating staff welcomes special requests and delights in quality service. Patio tables are available for seasonal dining alfresco along with an array of coffees, teas, espressos, cappuccinos, and a full bar. Cocktails are served at a new black granite bar in an atmosphere unique to the cafe. Classic high tea is served from 3 to 5 p.m. Tues through Sat. Dinner and Sun brunch reservations are suggested.

NONNA'S EURO-AMERICAN RISTORANTE AND BAR $–$$$$
124 E. Sheridan Ave
(405) 235-4410
www.nonnas.com

Starting with her own recipes, Avis Scaramucci opened a bakery in 1995. In 1996, she branched out to lunch and then eventually dinner. Named after Scaramucci's husband's Italian grandmother, the restaurant can be described as fine dining in a casual European atmosphere. It is located in the historic Bricktown District in a 100-year-old brick warehouse, right across from where the Redhawks play. Being the consummate hostess, Scaramucci makes sure there are fresh flowers on each table daily. At lunch, diners are served on bare wooden tables. At night, the restaurant becomes a little dressier as linens cover the tables. But don't think you have to dress up. This is a come as you are place to eat. Lots of families as well as businessmen come here.

Some of the specialties are pastas, quiche, fresh seafood, and steaks. Fresh vegetables, like lettuce, tomatoes, and squash and edible flowers, are grown by Cedar Spring Farms, Scaramucci's greenhouse, and served in the restaurant.

Nonna's is open Mon through Sat. Lunch is served from 11 a.m. to 2 p.m. and dinner from 5 to 10 p.m. There is a bridge menu available from 2 to 5 p.m. The bakery is open from 10 a.m. to 10 p.m. Nonna's is wheelchair accessible, will accept reservations, and has a children's menu.

PARK AVENUE GRILL $–$$$$
Located in the Skirvin Hotel
1 Park Ave.
(405) 702-8444
www.parkavegrill.com

This restaurant opened in 2007, when the newly remodeled Skirvin Hotel reopened. It is located inside the Skirvin Hotel on the first floor. The restaurant interior features the original floor and ceiling tile, which was painstakingly restored. The atmosphere can be described as casual fine dining in a historic 1930s atmosphere.

Clientele here is predominantly locals coming downtown to have a nice dinner, celebrate a special event, or attend a sporting or theater event. There are also a large portion of hotel guests as well. Dress is business casual.

The Park Avenue Grill serves steaks and seafood. Chilean sea bass, bone-in cowboy rib eye, and the weekend prime rib are the most popular items. There is a full-service bar as well as an award-winning wine list.

Something unique is the restaurant's Chef's Table. It is dining in the kitchen and is by reservation only. The table seats from two to six guests and the menu is chef's choice. This experience offers a unique perspective on how a fine-dining kitchen works. It is an interactive table where the guests talk to the chef and cooks directly.

Complimentary valet parking is available. It is wheelchair accessible. Reservations are accepted. Park Avenue Grill is open seven days a week for breakfast, lunch, and dinner.

PASEO GRILL $–$$$$
2909 Paseo
(405) 601-1079
www.paseogrill.com
Located in the heart of Oklahoma City's historic Paseo Arts District, this restaurant features classic American cuisine with international flair. Guests are seated at either tables or booths, both equally pleasing. Red walls, dark curtains, and tile floors make this a casual, yet sophisticated dining experience. Dress is casual, elegant, business attire. Patio seating is also available where guests can view the Spanish villa–style art galleries and decide which one they want to visit after their meal.

For lunch, appetizers include fried green beans, hummus bi tahina, and tuna tartar. Salads and soups are served as well as sandwiches and entrees, such as a black bean burger, classic club, chicken pot pie, and paseo grilled chicken.

Some of the dinner items to choose from are New York strip steak, rib eye, pork chops, duck breast, Chilean sea bass, and Southwest meatloaf. There is an extensive wine list and specialty drinks are made-to-order.

Ample parking is available. Reservations are accepted and recommended and required for parties of five or more. The Paseo Grill is open Mon through Thurs from 11 a.m. to 9:30 p.m., Fri from 11 a.m. to 10 p.m., and Sat from 5:30 to 10 p.m.

PRAIRIE THUNDER BAKING COMPANY $
1114 Classen Dr.
(405) 602-2922
www.prairiethunderbaking.com

Come for the bread, but stay for breakfast or lunch. This artisan bakery and cafe starts early in the morning to make sure their clientele has the freshest of items. The breads range from the traditional baguette to the five-grain levain and beyond. All breads are made from the simplest ingredients possible, contain no preservatives, and are 100 percent natural. Currently, four breads are baked daily with a large selection of others rotating in and out each day.

Pastries are a staple here and like the breads are made on-site with the highest-quality and freshest ingredients available. Some of the pastry items are traditional and chocolate-filled croissants, fresh fruit tarts, scones, eclairs, and brownies. Due to the pastries popularity, management asks that you order a day in advance for a dozen or more of any single item.

The cafe, decorated to remind patrons of the traditional cafes of Europe, welcomes guests to relax and enjoy fresh, delicious food in a warm congenial setting. Breakfast is served Mon through Sat from 7 to 10:30 a.m. and includes croissant sandwiches, breakfast quiche, and pastries. The lunch menu runs Mon through Sat from 11 a.m. to 2 p.m. Guests can order a stuffed baguette, chicken panini, lunch quiche, or four different salads. Prairie Thunder Baking Company is closed on Sun.

ℹ Let these three Web sites help you to find even more restaurants in Oklahoma City: www.eataroundokc.com, www.okclive.com/restaurants, and www.ok gazette.com.

ROCOCO RESTAURANT AND
WINE BAR $–$$$$
2824 N. Pennsylvania Ave.
(405) 528-2824
www.rococo-restaurant.com
Bruce Reinhart and Jason Bespumonte opened their restaurant in June 2004. They wanted to bring an East Coast–style restaurant to the Midwest. According to their customers, they have succeeded. The ambience is elegant but casual

and guests will feel comfortable in jeans or a tux.

Some of the menu items include crab cakes, pastas, steaks, chops, and fresh seafood. There is a large bar and an elaborate martini list. The *Oklahoma Gazette* named the Rococo the Best New Restaurant when it opened and the *General Record* named it the Inventor of the Year for its Mayor's Menu.

There is plenty of well-lit free parking. Rococo is open seven days a week for lunch and dinner and serves a Sun brunch.

RUNWAY CAFÉ (BETHANY) $–$$
5915 Phillip J Rhoads Ave.
(405) 787-7732

For a casual mom-and-pop dining experience, head to Wiley Post Airport where this cafe is located. The current owner, Ron, has owned the restaurant since 2005, but people have been coming to eat at this location since the 1960s. It is in the same building as the tower and diners can watch planes land through the atrium-style all-around windows. Ron serves southwestern style cuisine, like chicken fried steak, meatloaf, and hamburger. Breakfast here consists of cinnamon rolls or his special oven-baked omelets. For dessert, diners might want to try the nutty fruit quesadillas or a bowl of peach, cherry, or apple cobbler.

The cafe is open Tues through Sat from 8 a.m. to 2 p.m. Don't worry about parking. There is plenty of it.

SAUCED $–$$
2912 Paseo Dr.
(405) 521-9801
www.yoursauced.com

Located in the Paseo District, this restaurant is a unique place. On a daily basis, it serves local senators, military personnel, local bohemians, and the art-culture crowd from some of Oklahoma's finest oil and watercolor painters to premiere musicians. The restaurant can seat a minimum of 80 people on their patio and just under 30 inside.

Sauced serves typical cafe food, such as salads and pizza. Appetizers include humus and chips and fresh salsa (made daily). Freshly baked

sweet treats are also available. The house salad is considered by many to be the best in town and the pizza choices are so unique and special tht they get rave reviews from people who live in Chicago, New York, and San Francisco all the time. Wine, beer, and cider is also available.

Sauced is open from 10 a.m. to midnight Sun through Thurs and 10 a.m. to at 2 a.m. on Fri and Sat. Reservations are accepted but not required unless you have a large party or want a specific seat for a special occasion.

SONIC, AMERICA'S DRIVE-IN $
300 Johnny Bench Dr.
(405) 280-5000
www.sonicdrivein.com

SONIC, America's Drive-In may be a chain but this chapter wouldn't be complete without it. Why? Because it opened in 1953 in Shawnee, Oklahoma, as a hamburger and root beer stand called Top Hat Drive-In. The name was changed to SONIC Drive-In in 1959. Today, the company headquarters can be found in downtown Oklahoma City. As a matter of fact, drive downtown and the corporate office is easy to spot. SONIC is spelled in bright red letters across the side of their building.

SONIC has now grown to more than 3,500 drive-ins from coast to coast. In Oklahoma City, it seems there's one on every other block. That's fine with patrons. A testament to its popularity, more than a million customers eat at SONIC every day.

And why not? There's a lot going for this fun and unique establishment. Pull in to a spot, push the red button, order from the menu, and your order will be delivered to you by a personal, friendly, and at some locations, skating carhop. You never have to leave your car. Just sit back and eat in the comfort and privacy of your own vehicle.

Items on the menu include TOASTER sandwiches (sandwiches served on thick Texas toast), delicious onion rings, extra-long chili-cheese coneys (hot dogs with chili and cheese), fresh hamburgers, Tater Tots, a plethora of dessert choices, and more than 168,000 drink combinations. Whether you're thirsty for a cherry limeade or a vanilla cherry diet Dr Pepper, any combination is acceptable here. And if it's early and you want a burger instead of a breakfast sandwich, no problem. SONIC is open seven days a week from 6 a.m. to midnight or later. Most have extended summer hours. If guests need assistance with ordering, carhops are available to help.

Asian

BUDDHA TAO ASIAN BISTRO $-$$$
2737 W. Memorial Rd.
(405) 751-9700
www.buddhatao.com
Oklahoma City's only Pan-Asian restaurant, this establishment serves sushi and Asian style cuisine. As in the Zen-Master style, décor is deep reds, taupe, and rich fabrics with Asian and Japanese accents throughout.

Depending on what guests are hungry for they can order traditional or unique sushi, noodle bowls, rice bowls, soups, salads, skewer and kabob grills, and other hot entrees or specialty desserts. Buddha Tao has Oklahoma's largest selection of sake. They serve import and domestic beer, fine wine and make a variety of martinis.

Because the restaurant also has a bar and lounge, guests have a wide range of seating options. They can sit in the main dining room or choose a private dining room, at the sushi bar, at the outdoor courtyard, or in the Opium Lounge. On Thurs, Fri, and Sat nights guests can enjoy music played by local, regional, and national deejays.

The restaurant and bar are open Tues through Sat at 11:00 a.m. and close at 2:00 a.m. They are closed Sun and Mon. On Mon however, they will hold private parties upon reservation.

CANTON $-$$
2908 N. MacArthur Blvd.
(405) 946-8512
While this restaurant may not look like much at the end of the small strip mall along MacArthur, appearances can be deceiving. Since 1972, this family restaurant has cooked up some of the best Cantonese cuisine in town. Locals can be found eating here five or six times a month. Canton serves egg drop soup, crispy egg rolls, shrimp balls, General Tsa's chicken, and garlic fritter chicken. You'll leave checking your schedule to see when you can come back and eat more. If you don't have time to eat in, you can order carryout.

The Canton is open Tues through Sun from 11:15 a.m. to 9:00 p.m. The restaurant is closed Mon.

MUSASHI'S $-$$$$
4315 N. Western Ave.
(405) 602-5623
www.musashis.com
Opened in July 2001, Musashi's is a contemporary, open-space restaurant that is dim to moderately lit. On one wall are iron symbols of the elements (water, earth, void, fire, wind) found in Japan's greatest Samurai, Miyamoto Musashi's book, *The Book of Five Rings*. Each has a track light focused on it. This provides a warm, almost mysterious feel. While the restaurant feels quiet and tranquil, the burst of fire when the teppanyaki Chefs cook on the grill bring the establishment to life.

Completed in Feb 2007, the Fire Room is a sushi bar and lounge located inside Musashi's. It is peaceful on most nights and has large windows. It offers a more intimate and relaxed setting for those not necessarily interested in the grill show. Behind the sushi bar is a fun light that changes colors, providing a magical feel. And because of the the windows, customers can enjoy their sushi while gazing outside at the traffic that passes by. It's like sitting outside without actually sitting outside. During the summer months, a deejay plays music on the patio every other Wed.

The restaurant's most ordered special from the lunch menu (served until 4 p.m.) is the chicken yakisoba (yack-i-soba) which consists of stir-fried noodles and grilled chicken breast cooked to perfection. On the dinner menu, the family-style dinner combination consists of shrimp, chicken, and New York steak. Dinner entrees come with grilled vegetables, steamed rice, and a soup or salad. On the sushi menu, the popular crazy cajun roll has crawfish on the inside and is topped with fresh salmon, masago, spicy sauce, eel sauce, and green onion. For more reserved customers who aren't ready for fresh fish just yet, the tootsie roll is also a favorite. It has deep fried cream cheese, salmon and a spicy sauce. Reservations are strongly recommended for the restaurant's teppanyaki grill (where the chef cooks in front of you). Walk-ins are accepted based on availability.

SUSHI NEKO   **$–$$$$**
4318 N. Western
(405) 528-8862
www.sushineko.com

This Japanese sushi bar and restaurant has an Asian contemporary interior. It offers a full bar, where guests can order all their alcoholic favorites Some favorite sushi items include sassy shrimp, crazy cajun, and hot lips. For those who aren't sure about sushi, the restaurant has a Sushi Virgin Sampler and those who have a big appetite should try the Tastes of Japan, a sampler of sushi. For those not in the mood for sushi there are other dishes available, like New York sirloin steak and crispy chicken. Seating can be limited in the evenings and especially on the weekends. There are about 75 seats inside and 20 outside. Reservations are accepted and they can be made online.

Barbecue

THE COUNTY LINE   **$–$$**
1226 NE 63rd St.
(405) 478-4955
www.countyline.com

Located minutes from the capitol, zoo, and Remington Park, this barbeque restaurant has built a reputation for fine barbeque with sides that will be remembered.

Opened in 1935 as the Silver Club, it has a notable history. The Silver Club soon became the Oakcliff Nite Club and in 1939, it changed owners again and opened as the Ramada Club.

The Ramada Club was known as the most modern and beautiful nightclub in the state. It was also known for its unsavory reputation. Law enforcement officials raided the club on several occasions and confiscated everything from slot machines to gambling dice. Guests brought their own alcohol in brown bags and the club provided tonic water, soda, and so forth.

Inside, guests could sit in one of the many private dining rooms that were built like horse stables around the east and west walls of the main dining area. Each year, the name of the winning horse of the Kentucky Derby would be painted above a room.

In 1981, after another name change, the County Line opened. With its 1940s atmosphere preserved, guests can still sit in one of the horse stable rooms and enjoy lickin' good barbecue. From ribs and brisket, to homemade potato salad and bread, this restaurant is notorious once again, but now for the food it serves. Portions are large and ample. Some will say messy, but that shouldn't stop anyone from coming. After the meal, warm, wet washrags are brought to the table so guests can clean up before leaving.

The Country Line is open Sun through Thurs from 11:00 a.m. to 9:00 p.m. and Fri and Sat from 11:00 a.m. to 10:00 p.m.

EARL'S RIB PALACE   **$–$$**
6816 N. Western
(405) 843-9922
www.earlsribpalace.com

When four partners, all from Oklahoma City, opened the first Earl's on Western in 1996, they hoped the community would take to an upscale barbecue place. It did and Earl's expanded into four other locations. All five of the Earl's smoke their own meats on the premises. They make their own barbecue sauce and serve fresh roasted corn on the cob. Side order items are made fresh daily. Ribs and brisket seem to be the most popular items, but fried okra, green beans, and char-grilled burgers come in a close second. Desserts include peach, apple, and blackberry cobbler and brownies. No store-bought stuff here.

Dress is casual. The clientele is varied. Look for the businessmen though. You'll recognize them from the ties thrown over their shoulders.

Ample parking is available at all locations. The restaurants are wheelchair accessible, accept reservations for large parties, offer take-out, and have children's menus. This restaurant is open Mon through Sat from 11:00 a.m. to 9:30 p.m. Closed on Sun.

4414 W. Reno, (405) 949-1220
2121 S. Broadway (Edmond), (405) 715-1166
216 Johnny Bench Dr., (405) 272-9898
920 SW 25th (Moore), (405) 793-RIBS

IRON STARR URBAN BBQ $-$$$
3700 N. Shartel Ave.
(405) 524-5925
www.ironstarrbbq.com

Named after Belle Starr, the notorious female Oklahoma outlaw, this barbecue restaurant might be considered an outlaw when compared to other barbecue establishments. While dress is casual, this restaurant combines fine dining with true smokehouse flavor in the upscale area of Nichols Hills/Crown Heights. Besides the usual fare of ribs, chopped brisket, and pulled pork, this restaurant serves quail, salmon, shrimp, and a green chili cornbread sure to keep guests coming back for more. Desserts include buttermilk pie, homemade banana pudding, and peach crisp.

The Iron Starr is wheelchair accessible. Parking is ample in the restaurant's private lot. The restaurant is a nonsmoking establishment. Call the number above or go to the Web site to make a reservation. Open Mon through Thurs from 11:00 a.m. to 9:30 p.m. and Fri and Sat from 11:00 a.m. to 10:30 p.m.

JACK'S BAR-B-QUE $-$$
4418 NW 39th St.
(405) 605-7790

Located at Northwest 39th and Meridian on historic SR 66, this restaurant is an institution in the community. Opened in 1963, it has a long history here and has been named to the list of top 100 restaurants on SR 66. When guests settle in to one of the 54 seats, they can also take a walk down memory lane by looking at the SR 66 and soda memorabilia on the wall. Clientele here is varied.

A businessman is as likely to walk in as a grandma.

Jack's serves the usual barbecue fare, but sliced brisket and smoked pork ribs are the most popular. Meats are smoked on the premises so guests know they are getting their food fresh. Deviled eggs are also made daily here.

No alcohol is served, making Jack's especially family friendly. There is a large parking lot and the restaurant is wheelchair accessible and has a children's menu.

Hours are Mon through Sat from 11 a.m. to 8:30 p.m.

Cajun

i The Oklahoma Restaurant Association (ORA) started in 1933 with 75 members. Today over 4,500 restaurants receive guidance from the ORA. If you want to know if your favorite restaurant is a member, visit www.okrestaurants.com or call (405) 942-8181 or (800) 375-8181.

BOURBON STREET CAFÉ $-$$$$
100 E. California
(405) 232-6666
www.bourbonstreetcafe.com

This restaurant serves authentic cajun and creole dishes, and your mouth waters just reading the menu. Appetizers include coconut shrimp, fried alligator bites, and their most popular, Calamari Royale and hot crab dip. Also on the menu is gumbo, sandwiches, salads, steaks, chicken, pork, and seafood. The BB shrimp and crab cakes are wonderful, but so is the chicken breast topped with a crab and shrimp alfredo sauce served over dirty rice and the blackened catfish topped with crawfish étouffée over dirty rice. Drinks include soft drinks, tea, wine, and domestic and imported beers.

The cafe has live music on the weekends featuring such artists as Brent Blount, Garret Jacobson, and Hal Corn.

The restaurant is open Mon through Sun from 11:00 a.m. to 9:30 p.m.

French

LA BAGUETTE BISTRO & BAKERY $-$$$
7408 N. May
(405) 840-3047
www.labaguettebistro.com

La Baguette Bistro & Bakery is located in the corner of a small strip mall, but don't be fooled. Inside, the food is big on taste. Brothers Alain and Michel Buthion opened the bistro in 1988 and ever since patrons have been flocking here to not only have breakfast, lunch, and dinner, but also to buy bakery goods meats. Items which must be tried are the chicken walnut salad, the focaccia sandwich, the tortilla club wrap, Dave's meatloaf, meatballs, carrot cake, and chocolate divine cake. Fortunately, the bakery items come in several sizes, so whether you are serving a few or many, it has the perfect size for you.

Parking is limited, so plan ahead and avoid the noon rush. You can view the full menu on the Web site. Bakery items can be ordered ahead of time, especially if you want a specific size. Hours are Mon through Thurs from 8 a.m. to 10 p.m., Fri through Sat from 8 a.m. to 11 p.m., and Sun from 9:30 a.m. to 2:30 p.m.

Italian

BELLINI'S RISTORANTE & GRILL $-$$$
6305 Waterford Blvd., Ste. 100
(405) 848-1065
www.bellinis.net

Located on the southwest side of the Waterford Office complex overlooking the duck pond, Bellini's offers diners a casual but elegant experience inside or a relaxing, scenic experience outside. Open since 1990, the restaurant serves both Italian and American cuisine with equal pride. Lunch and dinner menus are available. Appetizers include fresh bruschetta and hot artichoke dip. One of the best salads around can be found here. It is the Honey Roasted Pecan Salad. Don't miss it. Bellini's serves steaks, seafoods, pastas, and a specialty called Greco Gamberetti. It is made with sautéed shrimp, black olives, red peppers, roma tomatoes, and penne pasta in a Mediterranean

garlic wine sauce garnished with feta cheese. Top of your meal with one of Bellini's decadent desserts like crème brûlée, white chocolate raspberry cake, turtle brownie, or tiramisu.

Bellini's is open Mon through Thurs from 11:00 a.m. to 10:00 p.m., Fri and Sat from 11:00 a.m. to 11:00 p.m., and Sun from 10:30 a.m. to 9:00 p.m.

CAFFE PRANZO $-$$
9622 N. May Ave.
(405) 755-3577
www.caffepranzo.com

This restaurants claims its secret to success is "excellent food and service at a very reasonable price." Patrons agree. A friendly neighborhood Italian restaurant, it is worth the short drive to the north side of the city. For lunch you can get sandwiches, like the meatball sandwich or Italian melt. There is also lasagna, spaghetti with homemade meatballs, fettuccini, brick oven pizza, and salads, like their pesce insalate made with shrimp, scallops, red onions, capers, black olives, roma tomatoes, and Italian vinaigrette dressing served over linguini and fresh salad greens. Appetizers include French onion soup, bruchetta, or grilled marinara pizza. For dinner, try the grilled portobello pasta or the grilled vegetable lasagna. Brick oven pizza is available for dinner, too, as well as veal, chicken, and seafood specialties. Wholewheat linguini is available upon request.

Top off your meal with a decadent dessert, such as tiramisu, Kahlua torte, or New York cheesecake shipped in from the Carnegie Deli. You can also get desserts to go. On the way out check out the refrigerated display case. There you'll find soups, salads, and lasagna to go, too.

Hours are Mon through Thurs, 11:00 a.m. to 2:30 a.m., Fri and Sat 5:00 to 10:00 p.m. Closed on Sun.

FALCONE'S PIZZERIA AND DELI $-$$$
6705 N. May Ave.
(405) 242-2222
www.falconesokc.com

Want a little taste of Italy? Danny, the owner and

a second-generation Italian American, invites you to his restaurant. Born and raised in Little Italy in New York City, he brought some of the recipes that have been in his family for hundreds of years to Oklahoma City. He makes his own meatballs for his pasta and sandwiches and serves only the finest quality Boar's Head and Italian cold cuts. Of course, he serves pizza, whole or by the slice and for a little added kick on anything, ask for the famous Bada-Bing. Danny is sure the hot onions will set off anything you order. He also has a location in Bricktown at 208 Johnny Bench Dr. (405-702-1500).

Falcone's is open Sun through Wed from 11:00 a.m. to 9:00 p.m. and Thurs through Sat from 11:00 a.m. to 11:00 p.m.

HIDEAWAY PIZZA $-$$
6616 N. Western Ave
(405) 840-4777
www.hideawaypizza.com
The first Hideaway Pizza was founded in Stillwater, Oklahoma, in 1957. It was very popular with college students so in 1993, the company expanded into Oklahoma City and Tulsa. Today, you will find four locations in the Oklahoma City region and four in the Tulsa area. The restaurant has won numerous awards, such as the Best Pizza Around from the *Daily Oklahoman* (Reader's Choice Award 1999 to 2006) and Best Pizza from the *Oklahoma Gazette* (1998 to 2006), *Oklahoma Magazine* (2000 to 2006), and *Edmond Life and Leisure* (2005).

Items on the menu include starters, like chicken wings and fried ravioli; salads; and of course, pizza. There are numerous specialty pizzas, like Pizza of the Gods, Big Country, Maui Magic, and Sooner Schooner. Most people may balk at pizza with pineapple and mandarin oranges, but it is one of the favorites. If you're not into specialty pizza, you can build your own or try pasta or a sandwich. Eat in or get it to go. It's all good either way.

Hideaway Pizza is open Sun through Thurs from 11:00 a.m. to 9:30 p.m. and Fri and Sat from 11:00 a.m. to 10:30 p.m.

MEIKI'S ITALIAN AMERICA $-$$
6916 NW Expressway
(405) 721-5522
Opened in 1990 Meiki's serves selected Italian and American favorites. For 16 years, Meiki's was located on SR 66 and lent itself to Route 66 decor. Two years ago when it relocated to Northwest Expressway, the decor changed to relaxing, casual, and romantic.

Customers say Meiki's pizza and calazone are the best this side of Canada. Their sauces, alfredo lasagna, manicotti, and rigatoni are made from scratch. The home-cut fries that are served with the burgers and sandwiches are popular. One of the specialties is the chicken pocket sandwich which is made from a baked pillow of homemade pizza dough.

This restaurant gives great service. It has many repeat customers and considers those customers extended family. There is no bar. Meiki's is wheelchair accessible, has a large parking area, and accepts Visa and MasterCard.

Hours are Mon through Thurs from 11 a.m. to 9 p.m. and Fri and Sat from 11 a.m. to 10 p.m. for lunch and dinner.

SOPHABELLA'S $-$$
1628 N. May
(405) 879-0100
www.sophabellasrestaurant.com
This restaurant sits just south of Wilshire on May. It is named after the owner's two daughters. Opened in 2000, it has quickly become an Oklahoma City favorite. Everything is made from scratch here. Sophabella's serves prime-aged beef, seafood, which is brought in fresh everyday, and true Chicago–style pizza. This restaurant was Oklahoma City's first to serve deep-dish Chicago style–pizzeria. On Sun, a large brunch is offered with French crepes, crab hollandaise, and $1 mimosas.

There is plenty of parking for this upscale, casual eatery. Reservations are preferred since the restaurant only holds 115 people. Hours are Mon through Thurs 11 a.m. to 10 p.m., Fri and Sat 11 a.m. to 11 p.m., and Sun from 10 a.m. to 9 p.m.

Mediterranean

JAMIL'S STEAKHOUSE $–$$$
4910 N. Lincoln Blvd.
(405) 525-8352
www.jamilssteakhouseokc.com

Just north of the capitol, on the East side of Lincoln under several big trees, you will find this one-of-a-kind, Lebanese restaurant. Established in 1964, it has built a reputation that keeps locals coming back.

Jamil's serves both lunch and dinner. At lunch, soups, salads, and sandwiches are the fare. The sandwiches include smoked turkey, Senator's Smoked Bologna, and smoked pit ham. Some of the dinner favorites are Rose's Cabbage Roll Dinner, the Smoked Bologna Dinner, or angus steaks. Jamil's famous appetizers include tabouli, hummus dip, relish tray, crackers, cabbage roll, and smoked bologna.

Dress is casual. Parking is ample on the east side of the building, so pull in at the narrow gravel entrance on the north side. Guests enter the restaurant at the back. The restaurant is wheelchair accessible and child friendly. It has a full bar with a great wine list. So come for the food, come for the atmosphere, but most of all just come. You'll be glad you did.

Hours are Mon through Sat from 11:00 a.m. to 2:00 p.m. and 5:00 to 10:00 p.m. Closed on Sun.

MEDITERRANEAN IMPORTS
AND DELI $–$$
5620 N. May
(405) 810-9494
www.medimportsokc.com

Mediterranean Imports and Deli is a specialty foods store and a deli. Whether you're looking for grape leaves or cheeses, this store has it all. Crammed full with items stacked on shelves and in coolers, Mediterranean Imports features foods from all around the Mediterranean and the world. Here you will find items from Italy, Greece, Turkey, France, Spain, England, North Africa, and Central and South America. You will find the owner, Atif Asal, working here, running back and forth from the back bringing out items that he doesn't have the space to display out front.

Lunchtime is crowded here. Besides the traditional ham and cheese sandwich, guests should try the falafel sandwich or a gyro. By ordering the Middle Eastern Platter, guests will get to sample a little bit of everything—kibbe, grape leaves, falafel, hummus, and tabouli. For dessert, try the baklava. It is a sweet treat made with pecans, honey, butter, and paper-thin phyllo pastry sheets.

Before leaving, check the gourmet grocery section, the deli case, and the buckets filled with olives, and the cheeses sitting by the cash register. Whatever your taste in cheese, from Gruyère to manchego, you can get 8 ounces or 3 pounds here. Spices from around the world, imported dried fruits and nuts, exotic jams and preserves, and assorted breads and pitas, including the famous Arabic flat breads can be found here as well.

Parking can be a little tight especially during lunch hour, but if the lot is full, guests can park just south of the deli. Operating hours are 9:30 a.m. to 6:30 p.m. Mon through Sat.

NUNU'S MEDITERRANEAN CAFÉ
AND MARKET $–$$
3131-B W. Memorial Rd.
(405) 751-7000

Janet, the owner of Nunu's, learned to cook Lebanese food from her mom. Since opening her restaurant on Mar 6, 2008, she has had an ever-growing clientele. Guests love the casual atmosphere. The decor is cheerful, reminding diners of a cross between Tuscany and the mountains of Lebanon. One wall has a mural, while stone arches grace the entry.

Everything here is fresh and homemade right down to the clarified butter. Menu items include grape leaves, kibbe, cabbage rolls, chicken kabob, and Greek salad with chicken breast. There is a vegetarian menu with a variety of choices.

Visit the market before you leave. There you'll find 30 different kinds of cheese and deli items available for purchase.

Parking may become a little cramped during the noon hour and at dinnertime as the lot is shared by other businesses. The cafe is open Mon through Thurs from 11 a.m. to 7 p.m. and Fri and Sat from 11 a.m. to 8 p.m.

OLIVE BRANCH CAFÉ $-$$
1 N. Hudson Ave.
(405) 272-5144

New to the area, this Mediterranean cafe has already made an impression on the locals. The staff's happy personalities add to the charm. The owner's dad is the cook and he's been cooking Mediterranean for 18 years. The menu inlcudes beef, chicken, lamb kabobs, and hummus. There is also make one Italian dish—pizza. Guests can get a 16-inch, five-topping pizza for $12.

Dress is casual. The restaurant does not serve alcohol and there is no children's menu. Parking is available on the street at meters and across the street in a large parking lot. Reservations are requested for parties over six. Olive Branch Café are open Mon to Sat from 11 a.m. to 9 p.m.

ZORBA'S MEDITERRANEAN $-$$
6014 N. May
(405) 947-7788
www.zorbasokc.com

For a truly unique Mediterranean dining experience, go to Zorba's. This restaurant was established in 1991 and up until 2006 was in a location just south of its present one. The decor has a casual Mediterranean feel and live entertainment adds to the unique atmosphere.

Everything on the menu is excellent here. Hummus (whipped chickpeas, sesame-seed paste, olive oil and seasonings), dolma (grape leaves filled with rice and seasonings), falafel (ground bean crispy patties with herbs and spices), spanakopita (spinach and feta cheese wrapped in fillo dough), and tiropita (cheese pie) are just few of the items offered. The gyros are, hands down, the most popular item on the menu. Gyro meat piled high in a warm flour pita, garnished with onions and tomatoes and topped with yogurt sauce will satisfy any hearty appetite. Burgers and wraps, stews, salads, and a wide range of dinner choices are available as well.

Don't be worried about limited parking. If spaces fill up out front or along the sides of the restaurant, there is a big parking lot behind the building. Zorba's is wheelchair accessible. If you don't have time to eat in, order take-out. Customers can call, and then go to the north side of the building where there is a special entrance and waiting area just for guests picking up take-out.

Zorba's is open Mon through Sat from 11:00 a.m. to 10:00 p.m. and Sun from 11:00 a.m. to 9:00 p.m.

Mexican

ADOBE GRILL $$-$$$
5120 N. Shartel Ave.
(405) 848-7250
www.adobegrill.com

ServingOklahoma City since 1966, the Hernandez family has been familiarizing patrons with authentic Mexican cuisine for years. From 11 a.m. to 2 p.m., the Adobe serves Mexican favorites, like pork tamales and cheese and chicken enchiladas, but it also offers specialties like Frida y Diego, grilled sirloin steak served with skewered shrimp; chile relleno, made with poblanos and stuffed with cheese and chicken, pork, or beef; and the Adobe Original Chimichanga, beef, chicken, pork, or spinach fried to a golden brown and served with your choice of toppings. The Adobe has the standard cream cheese sauce, salsa ranchero, salsa de chipotle, and hot sauce, but it also has specialty sauces like the Adobe's Special Relish made with broccoli, cauliflower, carrots, and soy sauce. It has 12 different sauces in all and once you try one you'll want to try them all.

> **i** The Oklahoma Cattlemen's Association (405-235-4391; www.okcattlemen.org) is the "Voice of Oklahoma Cattle Producers." To find the latest news on beef, check them out at 2500 Exchange Ave.

Sandwiches

BROWN'S BAKERY $
1100 N. Walker Ave.
(405) 232-0363

Since 1946, Brown's has been baking up sweet treats for the Oklahoma City area. This third-

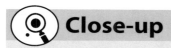 **Close-up**

Ted's Café Escondido

The original Ted's Café Escondido restaurant (2836 NW 68th St., 405-848-8337, www.tedscafe
.com, $–$$$) in Oklahoma City opened in Oct 1991. The location is not highly visible from
the street so that is why it was named Café Escondido. *Escondido* in Spanish means "hidden."
Ted's Café Escondido was opened with a vision of creating an intimate restaurant atmosphere
that guaranteed the best Mexican food and service in the state of Oklahoma. The owners
and staff are committed to consistently providing the greatest tasting food, made from the
freshest and highest-quality ingredients and served by well-trained, knowledgeable, and
enthusiastic staff.

Guests are greeted by a host who can't wait to take them to a comfortable Mexican cafe table.
Once seated, guests are served complimentary salsa, chips, cheese sauce, and tortillas. This is
only the beginning of the dining experience.

Ted's is a casual setting where you are treated like family. The clientele are people from all
walks of life who enjoy a fun and friendly atmosphere. Ted's is often the first stop for visi-
tors who have heard of its reputation for great food and great service. The restaurant has
won Best Mexican Restaurant and/or Best Mexican Food awards given by numerous Oklahoma
publications for over 10 years

One of Ted's specialties is Ted's World Famous Fajitas. The meat is marinated with a blend of
secret spices, grilled to perfection, and served with fresh sautéed green peppers and onions in
a red-hot skillet. Fajitas are served with rice and beans, shredded cheese, pico de gallo, real
sour cream, guacamole that is made fresh daily, and fresh, homemade flour tortillas.

Another favorite is the chicken fajita enchiladas, two flour tortillas filled with chicken fajita
breasts sautéed in butter, cheese, and pico de gallo. They are served covered with sour cream
sauce and cheese and your choice of side items, such as rice, refried beans, steamed beans,
steamed corn, corn con crema, or pappas Mexicanos.

Ted's Café Escondido is open seven days a week for lunch and dinner from 11:00 a.m. to 10:00
p.m.. Seating is on a first-come, first-served basis. Business is always brisk, but on Fri and
Sat nights, the restaurant is very busy. So come early or be prepared to wait. Forty minutes
to an hour is not uncommon. On nights when you're in a hurry or the wait is long, take-out
is an option.

You can enjoy a great dining experience at the original location at 2836 NW 68th St. in
Oklahoma City or in Edmond at 801 E. Danforth, South Oklahoma City at 8324 S. Western,
Norman at 700 N. Interstate Dr., or Broken Arrow at 3202 W. Kenosha.

generation, family-owned and -operated bakery
is the largest independently owned full-line retail
and wholesale bakery in Oklahoma. The donuts,
some say, are the best in the world, Danish,
cookies, cakes, pies, and breads are all here to
tempt a person's taste buds. Between 200 and
300 people stop here each weekday and over
500 stop in on Sat. The bakery is also a favorite of

the Oklahoma Bicycle Society. Every Sat a group
rides in for a donut stop and then heads out after
having their fill.

The bakery opens at 6 a.m. and closes at 3
p.m. It serves lunch from 11 a.m. to 2 p.m. The
deli serves up sandwiches made with their own
bread and some of the finest ingredients found
anywhere.

CLARK'S PASTRY SHOP AND DELI $
6744 NW 39th Expressway (Bethany)
(405) 789-5792

This old-fashioned bakery first opened back in 1945. David and Gail, the owners since 1997, say not much has changed here. The interior still has its 1950s feel with black and white tiles on the floor and red tablecloths on the tables. A lot of locals eat here and out-of-towners keep coming back for the cinnamon bread, six-grain bread, and thumbprint cookies. Donuts, cookies, brownies, custom cakes, breads, and sandwiches, including turkey, ham, and two kinds of chicken salad are also available.

Parking is limited in the front. It is difficult to pull out onto 39th St. after you park, so you might want to check out the parking behind the building. The shop is wheelchair accessible. It is open Tues through Fri from 6 a.m. to 5 p.m. and Sat from 6 a.m. to 4 p.m. It is closed Sun and Mon.

Tearooms

A SPOT FOR TEA $-$$
3812 N. MacArthur Blvd.
(405) 720-2765
www.aspotfortea.com

Want to get away from the hustle and bustle of regular restaurants? Try out this one. In 1996 A Spot for Tea started out as a store, selling tea, teapots, and inspirational books. In Jan 2003, Tammy Seibert, one of the owners, attended a seminar in Florida where she learned how to own and operate a tearoom. On Apr 1, 2003, she served her first customer. Today, A Spot for Tea serves sandwiches, salads, soups, cakes, and, of course, tea. English Lunch is served from 11 a.m. to 3 p.m. Queen's Tea is served at 11 a.m. and 1 p.m. Reservations are preferred for Queen Tea time. There are five specialty rooms for parties for all ages and occasions in addition to the main dining room. The tearoom was featured in the fall 2004 issue of *Tea Time* magazine and the winter 2007 issue of *Tea A Magazine*. It is open Tues through Sat.

TEA ROOM $-$$
4413 N. Meridian Ave.
(405) 495-2252

Three-fourths of a mile north of SR 66 on Meridian Avenue, sitting next door to an antiques store, this Victorian-style cottage has a charm all its own. Here visitors are served by ladies who really enjoy what they do. House specialties are chicken salad, broccoli salad, and, some say, the best quiche in the state. After your main course, don't leave without trying dessert—baked fudge, buttermilk pie, or bread pudding with rum sauce. Open Mon through Fri 11 a.m. to 2 p.m. The Tea Room fills up fast, so call to make your reservations.

EDMOND

American

BOULEVARD STEAKHOUSE $$-$$$$
505 S. Boulevard St., Edmond
(405) 715-2333
www.boulevardsteakhouse.com

This restaurant opened in Dec 1998. It sits next door to its sister restaurant, Café 501. More upscale in appearance, Boulevard Steakhouse offers diners a fine-dining experience. It was the first restaurant in Oklahoma to offer steaks made only from prime beef.

The most popular items on the menu are the 7- and 10-ounce filets, lobster, and fresh seafood. There is a full bar here and the restaurant has won the *Wine Spectator* Award of Excellence for the past 10 years.

Free, self-parking is available on the south side of the building. Boulevard Steakhouse is open seven days a week for dinner only starting at 5:00 p.m.

CAFÉ 501 $-$$$
501 S. Blvd., Edmond
(405) 359-1501
www.my501cafe.com

Café 501 owner Sheree Holloway traveled to France and learned how to bake bread in the French tradition. When she came back to

Edmond, she decided to open a restaurant. Café 501 opened in Aug 1995. The inside has been recently remodeled and has been referred to as rustic European. There's a lot of wood throughout, a mural painted on one wall, and a full bar with a big screen television hanging over it. Guests can choose to sit at a booth or one of the many tables in this casual atmosphere.

The menu is an eclectic mix of French meets Californian meets Moroccan. Chef Noureddine Bennai adds the Moroccan influence. While more women come in for lunch, at dinner there is a nice family mix. The ladies like the 501 salad and the cobb salad. The grilled portobello mushroom sandwich and Thai shrimp wrap are popular as well. For dinner, guests order the slow-cooked sirloin or fish. When ordering the fish, guests choose from three types: ahi tuna, tilapia, and salmon. They can then choose how it's cooked and the sauce they would like on top.

Bakery items are available and include artisan breads and desserts, like New Orleans bread pudding and chocolate lava cake.

Guests may park in front of the cafe, although space there is limited. A better option is to park directly east, across the street or south of the complex in the large parking lot.

Hours are Mon through Thurs 10:30 a.m. to 9 p.m., Fri 10 a.m. to 10 p.m., and Sat from 8 a.m. to 10 p.m. Sun brunch is served from 9 a.m. to 2 p.m.

JOHNNIE'S CHARCOAL BROILER (OKC CORPORATE) $–$$
6641 NW Expressway, Edmond
(405) 721-7974
www.johnniesok.com
Johnnie Haynes opened the first Johnnie's Charcoal Broiler in Sept 1971 at Military Avenue and Britton Road. He started in the restaurant business in 1946 on the West Coast and had 18 years experience before starting his own restaurant. His first drive-in had 12 stalls for cars where car hops delivered food. Inside, were 12 booths which could seat 48. . Expansion started in 1977 and today there are eleven Johnnie's located in Oklahoma City, Edmond, Tulsa, Norman, Stillwater,

and Broken Arrow. Johnnie's employs more than 500 people in these communities.

The food at Johnnie's is cooked over real charcoal. His hamburgers are made with meat that is ground fresh daily. With more than 30,000 hamburgers being served each week, one knows there has to be favorites. People order the #9 Cheese Theta more often than any other burger. It is topped with Johnnie's special sauce, a house made hickory sauce. Also popular is the #4 Caesar Burger served with Caesar dressing. The dressing is made with a secret family recipe and to make sure that recipe stays a secret, co-owner David Haynes makes a batch of the dressing himself every day.

By slicing real onions and battering them, homemade onion rings are made fresh here every day as well. Five hundred pounds of onions are used for each location. French fries are made from real potatoes which have been cut and then made ready to fry. Tea is freshly brewed each day and guests can buy it by the cup or gallon.

Johnnie's continues to be voted "Best Burger" by the locals who have come to appreciate the quality taste and freshness of their burgers. Oklahoma City residents knows Johnnie's prepares quality food at affordable prices with great friendly service and that what keeps bringing them back. All Johnnie's are open seven days a week. The restaurants have dine-in seating, walk up carryout, and drive through.

The following are open from 11 a.m. to 10 p.m. daily for lunch and dinner:
2652 W. Britton Rd., (405) 751-2565
33 E. 33rd St., (Edmond) (405) 348-3214
6629 NW Expressway, (405) 721-9018
421 SW 74th, (405) 634-4681

Locations below are open from 7 a.m. to 10 p.m. and serves breakfast, lunch, and dinner:
13900 N. May Ave., (405) 748-5440
620 W. Danforth, (405) 216-8020
1230 W. Main, (Norman) (405) 573-7744

TWELVE OAKS RESTAURANT $$–$$$$
6100 N. Midwest Blvd., Edmond
(405) 340-1002

Bill Horn opened his dream restaurant in June 1994 in a house originally built in Guthrie in 1896 and moved to its present location. Twelve Oaks offers diners a fine dining experience with an understated *Gone with the Wind* theme. Sitting atop one of Oklahoma County's tallest hills, the restaurant allows guests to gaze down upon cattle and oil wells.

Items on the menu include steaks, lamb chops, quail, salmon, shrimp, and lobster. There is a full bar. Don't pass up the house dessert called I'll Think About It Tomorrow. It is a lightly toasted slice of pound cake topped with vanilla ice cream, warm praline sauce, roasted pecans, whipped cream, and a cherry.

Reservations are required here. Valet parking is available on Fri and Sat nights. The restaurant is wheelchair accessible. Hours are Mon through Sat from 5:30 to 10 p.m. Because this restaurant is out in the country, you may want to call for directions and, of course, reserve a table.

VIRGINIA'S COZY KITCHEN $-$$
2828 E. 2nd St., Edmond
(405) 340-4473

Virginia's Cozy Kitchen is located in a small strip mall on the corner of Second Street and Coltrane. The current owners took possession of this restaurant in Apr 2009. The restaurant has been here since 1985, so locals are familiar with the location and continue to return. This is a casual, place to eat with owners who are down-to-earth, hard-working people trying to please the public and earn a living.

Virginia's serves chicken fried steak, fresh hamburgers, real mashed potatoes and gravy, homemade pies, fresh hot rolls, and cinnamon rolls.

The parking lot is shared by all the business in the strip mall. During lunchtime, you probably won't find parking in front of the restaurant, but you can find it down a ways. Thr restaurant's hours are 6 a.m. to 3 p.m. seven days a week. On Fri nights from 6 to 9 p.m. is all-you-can-eat catfish.

Asian

DOT WO $-$$
64 E. 33rd St., Edmond
(405) 341-2878
www.dotwoedmond.com

From the lucky cat waving at you to the friendly manager's greeting, you know you have come to a special restaurant when you step inside. Open since 1995, this Chinese seafood restaurant has something for everyone's taste buds. From jeans to business suits, everyone can feel at home here. The dining hall is decorated in light blues, gold, and burgundy. The staff is friendly and manager Andy Sheung greets everyone personally to make sure your dining experience is a pleasant one. He picks up fresh seafood from the airport three times a week and fresh ingredients arrive by truck every morning.

While there are many items to choose from, the sweet and sour chicken, orange chicken, and Mongolian beef are bestsellers. Dot Wo has received recognition from the *Daily Oklahoman, Oklahoma Gazette,* and *Edmond Evening Sun* in their "Best" awards.

Hours are Mon through Fri from 11 a.m. to 2:30 p.m. and from 5 to 9:30 p.m. Sat and Sun hours are 11 a.m. to 9:30 p.m. Dot Wo is closed on July 4th, Thanksgiving, and Christmas Day.

Barbecue

BILLY SIMS BBQ $-$$
924 W. Edmond Rd., Edmond
(405) 562-1331
www.billysimsbbq.com

Diners who like to eat barbecue while watching their Oklahoma Sooners play think this place is heaven. Named after a University of Oklahoma (OU) legend, Billy Sims, guests here are surrounded by the Heisman Trophy winner's pictures adorning the walls. Five televisions are available so sports fans won't miss any of the action. Sometimes they get to shoot the breeze with Billy or Steve Owens, another OU great, who come in to the restaurant every now and then.

Don't wait to be seated here. This restaurant serves assembly-line style. Guests approach the cutting-board station, request the type of meat they want, and watch while it's cut. Then they move on down to where they can choose side dishes, like cole slaw, baked beans, green beans, baked potatoes, side salad, or corn on the cob. There are no fried foods here. Favorite meats of choice are the ribs and pulled pork.

At lunch, from 11 a.m. to 4 p.m., guests can get a single-meat sandwich, one side, and a drink for $7. On Tues nights, it's all-you-can-eat ribs.

There is plenty of parking here. The restaurant is wheelchair accessible. Hours are Sun through Thurs 11 a.m. to 9 p.m. and Fri and Sat 11 a.m. to 10 p.m.

i Not that you'll ever need the Oklahoma City County Health Department (405-427-8651; www.cchdoc.com), but just in case, the main office is located at 921 NE 23rd St.

Italian
OTHELLO'S $–$$
1 S. Broadway, Edmond
(405) 330-9045
www.othellosofedmond.com
Located on the southwest corner of Main and Broadway in downtown Edmond, this Italian restaurant has a past. Before it became a restaurant it was Edmond's first hospital upstairs and Edmond's first movie theater downstairs. The current restaurant opened here in 1999 and seats about 125 people.

The owner says they serve "anything with red sauce," which means mainly Italian. Menu items include pastas, like ravioli and spaghetti; pizza; and seafood. On Sun, guests will want to try the half-price pizza special. Now that's a deal. Othello's opens daily at 4:00 p.m. and closes at 10:00 p.m.

Tearooms
INSPIRATIONS TEA ROOM $–$$
2118 W. Edmond Rd., Edmond
(405) 715-2525
www.inspirationstearoom.com

Seeing the opportunity and need for a tearoom, Larry and Tamara Rhoads opened this restaurant in 2005. They have five dining areas, ranging from casual to fine dining. They can seat 160 inside and 32 on the main deck outside. The clientele is mostly female but men and families are always welcome. Their mission statement is "Encouraging Faith, Family, and Friends."

Some of the more popular items on the menu are the Tea Room Trio, quiche, chicken salad, and scones with lemon curd. This tearoom has the largest selection and best quality of tea in Oklahoma.

The tearoom has been featured on the weekly travel television program, Discover Oklahoma and the magazine MetroFamily has given the restaurant its highest review. Parking is good, but limited during peak hours. Reservations are recommended as the tearoom fills up fast. It consistently serves from 800 to 1,000 customers a week.

Hours are Tues through Sat from 11:00 a.m. to 5:00 p.m. Closed Sun and Mon.

NORMAN

American
BRAUM'S $
Corporate Office
3000 NE 63rd St., Norman
(405) 478-1656
www.braums.com
The first Braum's opened in Oklahoma City in Mar 1968. Today Braum's has 275 locations in Texas, Kansas, Arkansas, Missouri, and Oklahoma. There are 19 locations in Oklahoma City proper, 5 in Edmond, and 4 in Norman, with more opening on a regular basis. All locations are owned and operated by the Braum family.

At each Braum's location, guests will find Braum's Grill, Braum's Fountain, and Braum's Fresh Market. The grill serves breakfast, lunch, and dinner. Breakfast is served from 6 a.m. to 10:30 a.m. Mon through Sat and 6 a.m. to 11 a.m. on Sun. Lunch and dinner is served thereafter. The fountain sells ice cream, sundaes, banana splits,

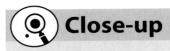

Close-up

Legend's Restaurant

Legend's Restaurant (1313 West Lindsay St., Norman, 405-329-8888, www.legendsrestaurant .com, $-$$$) goes back quite some time in Norman history. It started in 1967 as a pizza delivery service called LEMUAL B. LEGEND'S, LTD. The business was located behind the laundromat on Norman's South Navy Base. The original owner, Lemual Legend opened the business to pay for his University of Oklahoma college tuition and expenses. He drove all over Norman in his old Rolls Royce delivering pizzas.

After its first year, the business was so successful the eleven owners moved the restaurant to Lindsey Street, its present location. Décor here was something akin to the Gay Nineties. Each table had its own telephone, which was unique at the time. Customers used these phones to not only order their food, but "ring up" patrons at other tables.

Joe Sparks and two other partners bought out the remaining eight in 1971.They had a new vision and direction for the restaurant. The phones were taken out in 1972, and instead of serving pizza they started offering a more cultured menu. They also changed the name of the restaurant to Legend's Restaurant.

It was at this time, too, that they purchased a private club license and built wooden bottle storage lockers for alcohol. These lockers are still used today, and they hold Legend's extensive wine inventory. The restaurant sells 20 wines by the glass, 75 different wines by the bottles, and 15 different kinds of beer plus specialty liquor drinks.

In 1981, Sparks bought out the remaining two partners, and he and his wife Rebecca still own it today.

Legends has always supported the community of Norman by hiring University of Oklahoma students to work in the restaurant. Over the 40 years of its existence, the restaurant has employed more than 3,000 Oklahomans here.

The atmosphere at the restaurant is casual and relaxing. Wood floors, brass railings, plants and fresh flowers welcome each guest. Legend's goal is to give people an excellent dining experience, quality service, and quality food at reasonable prices. They serve everything from steaks to seafood, sandwiches to soups. They have a large fresh salad bar and make their own soups and desserts.

Their customers come from all walks of life. On any given day, you will find families, dates, out-of-towners, and locals dining here. Guests come wearing whatever they feel most comfortable in be it jeans or a business suit.

Legends Restaurant has won too many awards to list here. However, some of the more notable recognitions include the "Silver Knife Award" given by the Oklahoma Beef Commission, and *Bon Appetit* magazine recognized them for their excellent homemade desserts.

Legend's is open seven days a week for lunch and dinner. Sun Brunch starts at 10 a.m. They are closed on holidays like Labor Day, Christmas, New Year's Day, July 4th, and Memorial Day.

shakes, and malts, and the market sells fresh meats, bakery items, vegetables, fruits, and dairy products from milk to ice cream.

Quality is important to the Braum family. At the Braum's processing plant and distribution center in Tuttle, Oklahoma, 40 minutes southwest of Oklahoma City, 800 Holstein dairy cows are milked every 32 minutes, which add up to over 10,000 dairy cows a day. Because Braum's has their own processing plant, milk and milk products get to consumers faster and fresher. Braum's has their own fleet of refrigerated trucks and their products are delivered every other day in that fleet. All Braum's locations are within a 300-mile radius of this distribution center.

A Braum's store is the first stop locals make after being away on vacation or a business trip. Whether it's one of their hamburgers or a pecan caramel sundae, everyone finds something they like here.

CITY BITES $
3770 W. Robison St., #100
Norman
(405) 579-8500
www.citybitesinc.com
In 1986 brothers Eric, Brad, Gary, and Mark Blevins opened City Bites in Bethany. Today there are 18 locations. City Bites is a casual restaurant with whimsical decor that includes a full-size rhino head breaking out of the wall and a wrecking ball swinging back and forth from the ceiling. Each of the 18 locations has its own decor making a visit to each a unique experience.

City Bites is business-lunch friendly as well as kid friendly. Clientele includes families, coworkers, business associates, students, and travelers passing through.

On the menu, the California club is a long-time favorite and is still winning over new customers each day. It is made with turkey, bacon, alfalfa sprouts, and avocado. The Philadelphia cheese steak and Fleetwood are popular as well. You must try a freshly baked pumpkin cookie with cream cheese icing to complete your visit. City Bites has such a variety every customer is sure to find a favorite.

City Bites does not serve alcohol. It has large parking lots available to all types of vehicles, including buses and the restaurant is wheelchair accessible. City Bites is open seven days a week for lunch and dinner at 14 locations.

This location is open Mon through Sat from 11:00 a.m. to 8:00 p.m. and Sun from 11:00 a.m. to 3:00 p.m.

Four locations serve breakfast and lunch only so check the Web site or call the other locations for hours of operation.

O'CONNELL'S IRISH PUB AND GRILLE $
120 E. Lindsey St., Norman
(405) 364-8454
www.oconnellsnorman.com
Open in 1968, this pub serves American and Tex-Mex food. The decor leans toward sports and the dress is casual. Favorite foods here are the ranch-hand burger, Monte Cristo, and buffalo wings. O'Connell's serves beer and wine, is wheelchair accessible, and has a children's menu. It is open seven days a week for lunch and dinner. Parking is somewhat limited so be prepared to walk from parking areas nearby.

O'Connell's is open seven days a week from 11:00 a.m. to 2:00 p.m. Happy Hour is from 2:00 to 7:00 p.m.

RAISING CANE'S $
1130 Alameda, Norman
(405) 307-9618
www.raisingcanes.com
This restaurant is located on the east side of Norman at the intersection of 12th and Alameda. It opened on Nov 2005 and is owned and operated by Chad and Amanda Achord, current Norman residents. They have a wide variety of clientele from students to retirees. The dress is casual and the atmosphere is modern and upbeat. Raising Cane's specializes in cooked-to-order, fresh-never-frozen chicken fingers; grade-A, extra-long crinkle-cut fries; Texas toast; fresh coleslaw; and Cane's signature sauce, made daily. This restaurant is known for its quality chicken fingers, great crew, customer service, and involvement with the community.

Raising Cane's does not serve alcohol. The restaurant is wheelchair accessible and has a children's menu. The hours are Sun through Thurs 10:30 a.m. to 11 p.m. and Fri and Sat from 10:30 a.m. to midnight.

Indian

MISAL'S OF INDIA BISTRO $-$$
580 Ed Noble Pkwy., Norman
(405) 579-5600
www.misalofindia.com

The owner of Misal's, Neelam Misal, came here from India in 1972. He immediately fell in love with Oklahoma, but missed his native Indian food. Like so many people with an entrepreneurial spirit, he opened his own restaurant. Today, Misal's cousin, Nasir Ghouri, is his partner.

Everything served here is prepared fresh; even the yogurt for dressings and marinades is homemade and is either low fat or no fat. There are no additives, MSG, or artificial colors added to Misal's food. Most menu items qualify as heart healthy. For those of you looking for authentic Indian cuisine, the menu items include naan, samosa, chicken korma, tandoori chicken, dal, and much more.

Misal's has been voted "Best Lunch Buffet and Best Place to Take a Date" by the *Norman Transcript* and the *Oklahoma Gazette*. Hours are 11 a.m. to 3 p.m. for the lunch buffet and from 5 to 10 p.m. for dinner, seven days a week.

NIGHTLIFE

Whether you like to go to movies, attend concerts, sip martinis, or watch real cowboys riding bulls, Oklahoma City has a nightspot for you. This chapter is filled with places you can go alone, with a partner, or with a group to kick back and have some fun. Not every nightspot in the area is listed here, but from clubs to concert venues, it's a good place to start.

North Western Avenue between 36th and 50th has many popular clubs. Bricktown is another area where people go to hear music, dance, and have a drink. Club Rodeo sits on South Meridian and along Pennsylvania and 39th, there are several alternative-lifestyle clubs. There are a number of movie theaters listed here as well as a comedy club and several concert venues.

Before you venture out though, there are a few things you should know. Most clubs that feature live music charge a cover charge. Meals and drinks are not included in cover charges so be prepared to pay extra. Cover charges range from $5 to $15. If a big-name musical band is performing, the cover charge may be higher. You can always find out the cover in advance by calling ahead or checking the club's Web site.

All Oklahoma City bars and clubs covered here close at 2 a.m. on the weekends and in some cases earlier on the weekdays. I have included information about times in almost all the listings. Some establishments open at 11 a.m.; others don't open until 4 p.m. All hours, of course, are subject to change. So if you are planning a night out, be sure to call ahead.

Oklahoma's legal drinking age is 21. Minors are not allowed in bars or clubs that serve alcohol. If you have just turned 21 or could pass for a 16-year-old, make sure you carry identification because you will be carded.

Drinking and driving is never a good idea in Oklahoma City. If you do plan to drink, appoint a designated driver who will be sober or call a cab. Police are on the lookout for erratic behavior and will pull you over. The fines and consequences for drinking and driving in Oklahoma are significant.

As stated earlier, there are many fine establishments not listed here. When you're looking for current nighttime things to do, pick up the *Oklahoma Gazette* (www.oklahomagazette .com), Oklahoma City's cultural newspaper. It reviews and lists happenings across the city. It is published weekly, is free, and can be found just inside the front doors of convenience stores, restaurants, and clubs.

BARS AND LOUNGES

BAKER STREET
2701 W. Memorial
(405) 751-1547
Open here for three and a half years, this all-smoking establishment has a friendly Cheers-type atmosphere. The only Baker Street in Oklahoma, this pub has a wraparound deck, a dance floor, two pool tables, three dartboards, and video games. It is decorated in red and black and the English style is enhanced by deep wood and items like Sherlock Holmes memorabilia.

Traditional English food is served, like fish-and-chips and shepherd's pie. You can also order burgers, steak, and pasta.

There is live music six nights a week. Music ranges from the 1970s to the 1990s. There is no cover charge to listen to the music. All age groups are usually represented in the crowd. Average drink price here is $3.75.

Hours are 11 a.m. to 2 a.m., seven days a week.

BIN 73
7312 N. Western Ave.
(405) 843-0073
www.bin73.com

Located in the Kamber's Shopping Center in Nichols Hills for four and a half years, this is a relatively small venue but one that offers a great intimate feel. The clientele ranges in age from upper twenties to fifties. There is no designated dance floor, but that doesn't mean the crowd won't dance. Live music is offered Thurs and Sat nights at 10 p.m. The music is acoustic and all of the musicians bring speakers. The staff adjusts the volume according to how many people are in the bar and the level of conversation. During the day at lunch they play acoustic covers from satellite radio, 1980s and 1990s during happy hour, and pop late at night.

Over 50 wines are available by the glass and there is an extensive beer list as well as a full-service bar. A nitrogen preservation system helps Bin 73 offer unique wines without running the risk of them going bad. Wine tastings are held once or twice a month offering four or five wines with a tasting plate that complements the wines featured, as well as complimentary green chile queso at the start of the tasting. The tastings are held on Wed at 7 p.m. and cost $17.50 per person (not including tax or gratuity).

BIN 73 serves lunch as well as dinner. The full menu is served until 11 p.m. daily. Hours are Mon through Wed, 11 a.m. to midnight, Thurs and Fri 11 a.m. to 2 a.m., and Sat from 4 p.m. to 2 a.m. There is no cover charge.

BLUE NOTE LOUNGE
2408 N. Robinson Ave.
(405) 524-5678
www.myspace.com/okcbluenote

This club is known for having the best drink prices in Oklahoma City. Here visitors will find two pool tables, two dartboards, a dance floor, and a jukebox. Old country, bluegrass, rockabilly and rock are the music of choice. Live bands perform here on Fri, Sat, and Sun. Past bands include Deke Dickerson and Riverboat Gamblers. On some nights the music can get loud so come prepared.

There is no cooked food here, but patrons can buy locally made beef jerky and chips. The lounge has been nominated for the *Oklahoma Gazette*'s Best of award for the last four years and was in the top three every year.

The average drink price here ranges from $4 to $6. Hours are 2 p.m. to 2 a.m., seven days a week. There is a cover of $5 to $10 on Fri and Sat nights when the bands play.

BRICKTOWN BREWERY
1 N. Oklahoma Ave.
(405) 232-2739
www.bricktownbrewery.com

Located in a 115-year-old brick warehouse, this club was the second restaurant-bar in the area. It was the first brewpub to open in Oklahoma, making it the oldest brewery in Oklahoma. It has been in this location for 17 years.

There are pool tables, darts, shuffleboard, and video games. There is no dance floor but a lively jukebox. As a matter of fact, the second floor can become quite loud. Patrons will find live music here on New Year's Eve and St. Patrick's Day.

Brewpub food, like burgers, salads, and ribs, is available. The brewery has a full bar with alcohol and wine and, of course, handcrafted beer which is the specialty. Average drink price is $5.

Bricktown Brewery opens at 11 a.m. and closes at midnight Mon through Thurs and at 1 a.m. on Fri, Sat, and Sun.

BUDDHA TAO ASIAN BISTRO
2737 W. Memorial Rd.
(405) 751-9700
www.buddhatao.com

On the north side of Oklahoma City sits Buddha Tao. It is a Pan-Asian restaurant, bar and lounge that features contemporary Asian cuisine and traditional and one of a kind sushi. As in the Zen-Master style, décor is deep reds and browns with lush fabrics and Asian and Japanese accents throughout. The upstairs bar, called Opium

Lounge, offers comfortable seating, low tables, candlelight and deejay driven music that makes Buddha Taoa unique experience in Oklahoma City's dining and nightlife options. Food is served on most nights until close.

Buddha Tao has Oklahoma's largest selection of sake. They serve import and domestic beer, fine wine and make a variety of martinis. Prices range from $3 for domestic beers to $12 glasses of wine.

The establishment has a dance floor that is nearly 800 square feet. Dancing is always encouraged. A variety of music is played like Top 40, old school 80's, current R&B, classic rock. During happy hour while the music is contemporary and tends on the rock side, it does allow patrons to carry on conversation without any trouble. On Thurs, Fri, and Sat nights starting at 11 p.m., guests can enjoy music played by local, regional, and national deejays.

The restaurant and bar are open Tues through Sun for lunch beginning at 11 a.m. and closes at 2 a.m. Closed Mon, but will open for private parties. Please call to confirm hours.

CITYWALK IN BRICKTOWN
70 N. Oklahoma
(405) 232-9255
www.citybrickwalk.com
For one cover charge, you can visit seven different clubs under one roof. This 30,000-square-foot warehouse is home to a karaoke club, a rock club, 1980s and disco club, a piano bar, and more. Visit Tequila Park, which has the largest tequila selection in the southwest, or City Rocks, where Fri and Sat nights you can hear live local or out-of-state bands. Find one you like and stay all night or hop from one club to another. It's all up to you.

CLUB RODEO
2301 S. Meridian Ave.
(405) 686-1191
For a wild and definitely crazy time, this is a club you must visit. There is a huge dance floor. Dance the night away to country-and-western music with a mix of R&B and the latest hits. But undoubtedly the most unique thing about this club is the rodeo ring at the south end of the building. Only in Oklahoma can you find a club with bull riding. On Fri and Sat nights, people stand around the bullring or in the balcony and watch real cowboys ride real bulls. There's bucking and snorting enough for even the wildest person's taste. Above the dance floor is the timekeeper clock, so you can keep track of how long a rider rides. This is so real, there's even a clown to save the riders when they are thrown.

Drinks like beer, wine, and mixed drinks are served here, but no food so eat before you come.

While there are a fair number of cowboys who come here, the crowds are always mixed. Be ready to pay a cover charge and expect to have lots of fun.

DEEP DEUCE GRILL
307 NE Second St.
(405) 235-9100
www.deepdeucegrillokc.com
The Deep Deuce is located in an area settled in the Land Run of 1889 by the first African Americans to come to Oklahoma City. The Deep Deuce area, called Deep Second for some time, was home to jazz legends Jimmy Rushing and Charlie Christian and author Ralph Ellison.

The restaurant's building was built in the early 1900s by Jimmy Rushing's father, Andrew. In the late 1930s and early 1940s it was a medical clinic.

Today, guests can see bits and pieces of Oklahoma City's history everywhere here. A pew from the Calvary Baptist Church where Martin Luther King Jr. applied to be a minister was made into a bar top and granite blocks from the destroyed Alfred P. Murrah Federal Building were used for the patio.

Those who enjoy the nightlife won't be disappointed. Specialty drinks include the Deep Deuce Hurricane, the Deuce LIT, and the Blues Traveler. In celebration of the drinks, there is a cocktail of the month every month. Special events are held here. Check the Web site to see what's happening at Deep Deuce.

EDNA'S
5137 N. Classen
(405) 840-3339
www.ednasokc.com

This nightspot is considered one of the best neighborhood bars in Oklahoma City. Edna has been in business for herself since 1980 and has been responsible for outstanding service and entertainment ever since. Rumor has it Edna will dance on the bar if you play Jerry Lee Lewis's "Great Balls of Fire" on the jukebox. The building was renovated in 2008 and a patio was added out front. The interior walls are covered with dollar bills from patrons leaving their mark on Edna's for the last 20 years. Crowds here are quite eclectic.

There is one pool table, a dart machine, and a jukebox. The music is not excessively loud but has a tendency to increase in volume as the night progresses. All types of music are played. There is never a cover charge at Edna's and the average drink price is $4.

The hours are 11 a.m. to 2 a.m. Edna's is also a restaurant. See the "Restaurant" chapter for what Edna's offers in the way of food.

 Had a little too much to drink? Don't drink and drive. Call 800-TAX-ICAB.

51ST STREET SPEAKEASY
1114 NW 51st St.
(405) 463-0470
www.myspace.com/51stspeakeasy

Step back in time to the 1930s. This neighborhood-style pub has a tin-punch ceiling, dark reddish-brown walls, period light fixtures, and black and white Prohibition-era pictures on the walls. Music includes red dirt, bluegrass, and country. Volume depends on the music being played. There is live music on Thurs, Fri, and Sat and every other Mon, patrons can enjoy stand-up comedy. Don't worry about a cover charge. There's not one here. One of this pub's goals is to become a notable live-music venue.

Smoking is allowed here. Food, such as sandwiches, burgers, nachos, and brisket tacos, are served Mon through Sat from 5 to 10 p.m.

All alcohol served here is 6.0 or higher. Moose Drool, Golden Ales, Big Sky, St Peter's English, and Coop Ale Works are served. Alcoholic drink prices range from $3 to $6 and higher. This pub is open Mon through Sat from 3 p.m. to 2 a.m.

MICKEY MANTLE'S STEAKHOUSE
7 Mickey Mantle Dr.
(405) 272-0777
www.mickeymantlesteakhouse.com

Mickey Mantle's opened in the fall of 2000 and offers a full-service bar and lounge. Their cellar stays full of new and old world wines with over 500 different selections. Cigars are sold in the bar and the lounge is smoke friendly. The lounge offers live entertainment on Thurs with acoustic ensembles and Fri and Sat night you can always catch the hottest jazz and blues bands.

Happy hour is offered in the lounge Mon through Fri from 4:30 to 7 p.m. Happy hour specials consist of a complimentary buffet, a half-priced appetizer list, and domestic beer specials.

Valet parking is offered to all guests. Mickey Mantle's is wheelchair accessible. The lounge opens at 4:30 p.m. every day.

O'CONNELL'S IRISH PUB AND GRILLE
120 E. Lindsey St., Norman
(405) 364-8454
www.oconnellsnorman.com

As a restaurant by day and a pub by night, this establishment serves a mix of patrons according to the time of day. Open in 1968, it is the oldest bar/restaurant in Norman. There is no dance floor here, but guests can play pool, darts, and shuffleboard. On special occasions bands play here. Pop is the music of choice and the volume is never overwhelming. This is a place where everybody feels comfortable.

Food is available here and beverages include wine and a selection of beers and mixed drinks. Average drink price is $4.75. There is no coverage charge. Special events are commonplace here on St. Patrick's Day, Cinco de Mayo, Mardi Gras, and University of Oklahoma game days.

Hours are 11 a.m. to 2 a.m.

PROHIBITION ROOM AT THE GOLD DOME
1112 NW 23rd St. #102
(405) 601-0363
www.prohibitionroom.com

Located in the historic Gold Dome Building off Classen Boulevard, this nightspot celebrates its one-year anniversary in 2009. Already a local favorite, it has live bands, which play Mon, Fri, and Sat nights. Musical guests who have played in the past include Edgar Cruz, Cami Stinson, Ricki Derek, and the Vegas Six. The music includes jazz, Big Band swing, and acoustic.

Prohibition serves contemporary American food with a 1930s touch, including soups and sandwiches, steaks, and pastas. Desserts include bread pudding with whiskey caramel sauce, bananas foster, and pineapple upside down cake.

This nightspot has the largest liquor selection in Oklahoma and The most popular drink is the Jack Rose Cocktail made with applejack, fresh lime juice, and pomegranate. The average drink price is $5.50 and up for spirits and $1.75 and up for beer. Prohibition is open from 11 a.m. to 2 a.m. every day.

ROCOCO RESTAURANT AND WINE BAR
2824 N. Pennsylvania Ave.
(405) 528-2824
www.rococo-restaurant.com

This restaurant and wine bar has a contemporary black exterior with red lighting accents, soft leather seating, a fireplace, an exquisite bar, and comfortable "gangster" booths. There is a small dance floor and if it gets full, people have been known to dance in the aisles.

During the day, the restaurant serves excellent food. Some say it has the best crab cakes anywhere. At night, the restaurant turns into a nighttime hot spot. Blues, jazz, and classical music is played here. Local musicians vary. Live bands, such as Jazzaholics, and singers, like Denise Smith, perform on Fri and Sat nights.

All types of alcohol are served here and there is an extensive martini menu. Average drink price is $8.25.

Hours are Mon through Thurs from 11 a.m. to 10 p.m., Fri and Sat from 11 a.m. to 11 p.m., Sun from 11 a.m. to 10 p.m. (brunch is served until 3 p.m.).

ROK BAR BRICKTOWN
119 E. California
(405) 235-7625
www.okcrokbar.com

If you like to party hearty, this place is for you. Located in Bricktown, the ROK has a pool table, darts, and four huge flatscreen televisions so guests can watch games or fights. You'll find live entertainment here, too. Performers are chosen for their talent and the way they can move a crowd so you know concerts are always lively. Performers in the past have included Dirty Penny, Hinder, and Yellow Card. If you want to dance the night away or rub shoulders with celebs and rock stars, stop by.

The Rok Bar is open daily from 4 p.m. to 2 p.m. A full-service menu is served from 4 p.m. to midnight daily.

SKKYBAR ULTRA LOUNGE
7 S. Mickey Mantle Dr., 4th floor
(405) 272-9222
www.skkybar.com

Located in the heart of Bricktown, on the 4th floor of JDM Place, above Mickey Mantle's Steakhouse is the SKKYBAR Ultra Lounge. Like any lounge and nightclub, the interior is warm and friendly. Deep, rich colors and fabrics, candlelight, low tables, comfortable seating welcome guests to come in and stay for a while.

Several of the walls in the lounge are adorned with large canvas paintings by artist Kip Frace and the hot spot boast a 3000-square-foot balcony. There is a VIP room that has a private bar, balcony and restroom facilities that can be reserved.

Local, regional and national deejays play modern and trendy music like adult top 40, retro-dance hits, and classic rock late into the night.

The main lounge is open from 9 p.m. Tues through Sat. Closing time is 2 a.m. on all evenings. The club is available for private parties on Sun, before opening hours Tues through Sat, and at all times in the VIP room.

VZD'S RESTAURANT AND CLUB
4200 N. Western
(405) 524-4200
www.vzds.com

This neighborhood bar and grill used to be store #21 of the Bill Veazey Drug Store chain back in 1978.Today, it is simply a place that serves good food and fun. It sits on the east side of Western on the south end of a small strip mall.

Voted the Best Place in Oklahoma City to See Live Music by the *Oklahoma Gazette* Reader's poll in 1999–2000, this club showcases local, regional, and national bands every Fri and Sat night. Previous bands to play here include Bo Diddley, the Dixie Chicks, and Junior Brown. Shows start at 10 p.m. on the weekends for ages 21 and up. There is a cover charge for the weekend concerts. For out of town bands, the cover charge is $10 to $15 and for local bands, it's $5.

There is a full bar available here. In the daytime, guests can order burgers, salads, sandwiches, and homemade stew chili and cornbread. At 5:30 p.m. a night menu with more elegant cuisine is offered. For dessert, check out the pecan pie or turtle cheesecake.

Hours are Mon through Thurs, 10:30 a.m. to midnight, Fri and Sat from 10:30 a.m. to 2 a.m.

WORMY DOG SALOON
311 E. Sheridan
(405) 601-6276
www.wormydog.com

For some good old boy music and a cold brew, make your way to the Wormy Dog. Friends, couples, and singles come here for a good time in a relaxed atmosphere. Live shows are a staple here. Past performers include Shooter Jennings, Jackson Taylor, and Blue Static. Ticket prices range from $5 to $15. There's always something going on here, so check out the Web site or better yet in person.

ALTERNATIVE-LIFESTYLE CLUBS

HABANA INN
2200 NW 39th Expressway
(405) 528-2221
www.habanainn.com

The Habana Inn complex is a hotel with two dance clubs, a restaurant, a piano bar, and a unique gift shop. You can have fun at the clubs here and the hotel offers reasonable rates. The friendly service will make you feel comfortable and welcome.

Located in the heart of Oklahoma City's gay district and a popular spot for the gay community it is conveniently located near local attractions, like the Oklahoma City Zoo, Remington Park, and the Oklahoma City National Memorial & Museum downtown. There are also movie theaters, restaurants, golf courses, and malls within minutes of the inn.

The Copa, located here since the 1980s, is a club with a small game room and a medium-size, stainless-steel dance floor. Dance music is played by a deejay and is loud. All ages are welcome here, but the average is from 21 to 40. Wine, beer, and mixed drinks are all served. Average drink price is $4. Pageants, shows, and other events are held here on a regular basis. Sometimes a cover charge is collected for the special events. Hours are from 9 p.m. to 2 a.m.

At the inn's other dance club, Finish Line, guests can dance to country music on a large wooden dance floor. There are pool tables and during special events and on weekends, guests can sit by the pool in the outdoor seating area. A deejay spins the music and it stays at a moderate level so you can enjoy a your conversation. All ages are welcome, but from 25 to 50 years of age is the average.

Hours are from noon to 2 a.m. daily.

The on-site piano bar, Ledo, entertains crowds of typically 30 years of age and older. Guests can order food here from Gushers, the adjoining restaurant. Wine, beer, and mixed drinks are all served and the Ledo is known for having the best martini in town. Average drink price is $4.

Hours are from 4 p.m. to 2 a.m., seven days a week.

HI-LO CLUB
1221 NW 30th St.
(405) 843-1722
www.myspace.com/hiloclub

This club has been in the same location since it opened in the 1950s. It has a classic, vintage look with unique 1950s lighted signs. There is a small dance floor. Very diverse music is played via the jukebox and is dictated by patrons who pay the quickest. On Tues nights, live bands perform. Bands are local or touring national acts. Some nights the volume of music is loud, depending on the crowd.

No food is served here, just beer, wine, and a wide variety of spirits. Hi-Lo is renowned for its Bloody Marys, martinis, and signature drink, the Pearl Driver. Drinks start at $1.75.

This club welcomes everyone over 21 years of age. Hours of operation are noon to 1:45 a.m., 365 days a year.

PARTNERS 4
2805 NW 36th St.
(405) 942-2199
www.partners4club.com

While this may be an all women's club, boys are welcome too. But be forewarned guys, all activities here are for the girls. On Tues and Wed patrons can shoot pool free and buy cheap beer. On Thurs and Sun, you can sing karaoke, watch or participate in the dart tournament, or just enjoy music with deejay Storm. The club has one of the largest dance floors in Oklahoma City where Sat nights you can dance the night away. On the second Fri of every month is Professional Oklahoma Women's (POW) Night. This is a night where women over 40 can come, relax, enjoy 80s music and light snacks. Hours vary so call or check the Web site.

CONCERTS

CIVIC CENTER MUSIC HALL
201 N. Walker Ave.
(405) 297-2584
www.okcciviccenter.org

The Civic Center Music Hall is not only a beautiful structure with its art-deco design, but a building that has through renovation become nationally known for its "near perfect accoutsics." Originally called the Municipal Building, the building was part of President Franklin D. Roosevelt's New Deal Program and was completed in 1937. At the time, it could seat 6,000 people and was used for numerous events like conventions, sporting events (boxing and basketball) and performing arts.

In 1966, the hall went through a renovation and its name was changed to the Civic Center Music Hall. Beginning in 1998, the hall went through a second major renovation. Since the building is owned by Oklahoma City, it was to benefit from the 1993 tax-based initiative known as MAPS (Metropolitan Area Projects). Then in Sept 2001, three years later, the $52.4 million-newly renovated 2,500-seat Civic Center Music Hall reopened its doors. The new hall is striking and stylish In 2006, a study was done and the Music Hall was rated "one of the top 3 acoustic halls in the United States. The Canterbury Choral Society, Lyric Theatre, Oklahoma City Ballet Company and Oklahoma City Philharmonic make their home here. Nationally known singers, musicians and artists like Mikhail Baryshnikov, Michael Buble, Placido Domingo, The Gaithers, and Itzhak Perlman have performed here,

Three different performance theatres as well as two banquet spaces are located in the Civic Center Music Hall. The main hall is the Thelma Gaylord Performing Arts Theater. It seats 2,418 and features ballet companies, Broadway musicals, choral performances, orchestras and more,

The 286-seat Freede Little Theatre is a smaller space than the Thelma Gaylord theater and is typically used for seminars and recitals. This theatre hasn't changed much through the years and still has much of its original décor like its seats, sconces, and more. The black-box-style CitySpace theater is located in the basement of the Civic Center Music Hall. It seats 90. Being smaller in size it is perfect for the smaller theater companies who want to produce an intimate experience for guests. Next is the 5,300-square-foot Meinders Hall of Mirrors. This historic ballroom still has its parquet wood floors, original sconces, chandeliers, and its 20 foot windows and mirrors. Banquets, fundraisers, and weddings are often held here. Joel Levine Hall, a smaller and modern version of the Meinders can seat up to 100. There is street-level parking around the building, both on the street and in municipal lots around the complex. Metered parking spaces are free after 6 p.m. on weekdays and on weekends. Fees vary for the lots but generally range from $6 to $8 per space. Admission prices vary for each performance. Individual tickets for season performances and special limited engagements can be purchased at the box office in person, by phone (405-297-2264 or 800-364-7111) or on the Web (www.okcciviccenter.com or www.myticketoffice.com). The box office is located at 201 North Walker Ave. and the hours are Mon through Fri from 9 a.m. to 5 p.m. and two hours before each show time. Season tickets for any of the center's resident performing groups can be purchased by contacting the individual group.

COX CONVENTION CENTER
1 Myriad Gardens
(405) 602-8500
www.coxconventioncenter.com
Formerly known as the Myriad Convention Center, the Cox Convention Center is an approximately 1-million-square-foot, 15,000-seat arena, located in the heart of Oklahoma City. This is a historic area for Oklahoma City for when the City was born, this is where all the action took place. About one mile east of where the Cox Center is located now, near the Santa Fe railroad tracks, a tent city sprang up literally overnight. Entrepreneurs like "Kid Bannister," a Texas gambler, set up his business in a tent across from the Santa Fe Train Depot and declared the first territorial bank open for business. The 'bank' was located on the northeast corner of where the Cox Center is located today. Bannister's neighbors, located on the same block was a saloon, the Two Johns, and the first Oklahoma City Post Office.

In the fall of 1972 the $22-million Myriad Convention Center (now the Cox Convention Center) opened its doors. Through the years, the Center has hosted a number of events like basketball games, banquets, concerts, and conventions. It has also been home to several sports franchises like the Oklahoma City Blazers hockey

team, the Oklahoma City Calvary basketball team, and Oklahoma Wranglers football team. Major sporting events like All-College basketball tournament, the National Finals Rodeo, and the 2007 Big 12 Women's Basketball Championships to name a few have been held here. Sesame Street Live, Stars on Ice, and the Harlem Globetrotters have performed here as well as entertainers like Elvis, Brad Paisley, Janet Jackson, and the Rolling Stones to name a few. Republic Parking Systems manages parking for the Center. There are over 900 parking spaces located in the underground parking garages beneath the Cox Center. For guests driving properly licensed or tagged vehicles, handicapped parking spaces are available near the four-level elevator entrances for easy entrance and exit. There are parking entrances to the building on the east side off E.K. Gaylord and the west side off North Robinson. Currently, parking prices are $6 per vehicle per event. Prices are subject to change.

Street parking is also available throughout the downtown area. There are over 18,000 spaces and around 1,300 parking meters accessible to those who are attending events. For further information on the center's parking garage and other city parking facilities, you may call (405) 235-PARK or visit www.parkingokc.com.

Guests can keep track of all the events being held at the Cox Convention Center by visiting the center's Web site. Tickets can be purchased by phone (800-745-3000), online at www.coxconventioncenter.com, or by visiting the U.S. Army Box Office at Ford Center. Ford Center is just south of the Cox Convention Center at 100 West Reno Ave.

> **i** Look here to find out what's happening tonight: **www.oklahomanightlife.com** and **www.communityokc.com**.

FORD CENTER
100 W. Reno
(405) 602-8700
www.okfordcenter.com
Construction began on the $89-million Ford Center in the spring of 1999 and it opened on June 8,

2002. It is owned by Oklahoma City and was paid for through Metropolitan Area Projects (MAPS), a capital improvement program.

Since its opening, the Ford Center has undergone many improvements, such as new restaurants, video boards, and speakers. In Mar 2008, voters approved another temporary sales tax, which will allow more upgrades to the Ford Center. These upgrades will include new concession areas, loge boxes, rooftop gardens, and a family fun zone.

The Ford Center has a total of 586,000 square feet with a seating capacity range of about 5,000 to 20,000, depending on the event. There are 49 private suites and 48 total restrooms, including 12 family restrooms.

Currently three restaurants and 23 concession stands are available for hungry guests. The Ford Center has six passenger elevators, six escalators, and two primary sets of stairs so getting around isn't a problem. Three ATMs are available. Smoking is prohibited in the arena and concourse areas. Certain items, like laser pens, oversize bags, and outside food and drinks are not allowed. A full list of prohibited items is available on the Web site.

Visitors don't have to worry about missing any of the action during sports games or concerts. Newly renovated in 2009, the Ford Center has a new Daktronics four panel center hung scoreboard, which will allow the action as well as scores, timeouts, messages and more to be seen and clearly seen from anywhere in the arena.

More than 200 television monitors are located in restrooms, bar areas, and restaurants.

The Ford Center is home to the Oklahoma City Blazers, Oklahoma City Yard Dawgz, and Oklahoma City Thunder. It also hosts concert events at various times throughout the year.

For events, tickets can be purchased on-site at the U.S. Army Box Office, by phone (800-745-3000), or online at www.ticketmaster.com. The box office is open 10 a.m. to 6 p.m., Mon through Fri and on weekends and holidays depending on the event.

ZOO AMPHITHEATRE
2101 NE 50th St.
(405) 364-3700
www.zooamp.com

If you like to listen to music in the open air and under the wide-open sky, then you will love this venue. While there is a huge stage with a state-of-the-art sound system, seating is on the lawn. Be sure to bring a lawn chair or a blanket. Constructed in 1935 and 1936 by the Civilian Conservation Corps and made from native sandstone, this amphitheater saw hard times in the 1960s, but was restored in the late 1970s. Past performers include Sheryl Crow, Journey, Charlie Daniels, Stevie Nicks, and Chris Isaak.

While all guests are invited to have fun, there are some things that you can't bring with you. Security does not allow pets, ice chests, outside food or beverages, cameras, tape recorders, video equipment, or weapons of any kind. General admission and VIP seats are available. Depending on the concert, ticket prices can range from $28 to $125. Guests should know that once tickets sold exceeds 6,000, no more lawn chairs will be allowed and all sales are final. There are no refunds or exchanges.

COMEDY CLUB

LOONY BIN COMEDY CLUB
8503 N. Rockwell Ave.
(405) 239-4242
www.loonybincomedy.com/ok

Opened in 2002, this comedy club is one of four Loony Bin locations. The other three are located in Little Rock, Arkansas; Wichita, Kansas; and Tulsa, Oklahoma. The owners, Jeff Jones, Larry Marks, and Terri Libby, have over 50 years of comedy experience combined. This is adult entertainment for the over-21 crowd.

There are two table levels here-upper and lower. The club features national headline acts. Past performers include Tommy Chong, Michael Winslow, Rodney Carrington, and Dave Attell.

The club seats 230 people. Food is available, including appetizers and sandwiches. Shows are held on Wed and Thurs at 8 p.m., Fri and Sat at 8 p.m. and 10 p.m., and Sun at 9 p.m. Prices are $6 to $20 per ticket with a one-item purchase minimum.

MOVIE THEATERS

AMC CROSSROADS 16
1211 E. I-240
(405) 775-OAMC
www.amctheatres.com

A little sister to AMC Quail Springs 24 (see below), Crossroads 16 opened in Feb 1999. It has 16 stadium-seating auditoriums with a total of 3,367 seats. The largest auditorium here is #9 with 417 seats. The stadium seats feature rocking backs and cupholder armrests that lift up. All auditoriums have six-channel digital surround sound.

Traditional concession items are offered from nine stations, including special AMC items such as Clip Gummi Stars and AMC MovieNachos.

Ticket prices are $8.50 for adults, $7.50 for seniors, and $5.50 for children. The matinee price is $6.50. On Sat, Sun, and all holidays, the 10 a.m. show is just $4. Matinee movies are shown until 6 p.m. Mon through Thurs and from noon until 4 p.m. Sat and Sun. You can buy tickets at the theater or ahead of time online at www.movietickets.com.

You'll want to visit the early part of the week, as typically the weekends are the busiest. All auditoriums have wheelchair-accessible seating.

AMC QUAIL SPRINGS 24
2501 W. Memorial Rd.
(405) 775-OAMC
www.amctheatres.com

Opened in Dec 1998, this theater has 24 stadium-seating auditoriums with a total of 5,134 seats. The largest auditorium is #2 with 527 seats. The stadium seats are an AMC exclusive and ultra-comfortable They are loveseat-style seats, featuring rocking backs and cupholder armrests that lift up. All auditoriums have six-channel digital surround sound.

Traditional concession items are sold from 18 stations, including special AMC items such as Clip Gummi Stars and AMC Movie Nachos.

Tickets prices are $9 for adults, $8.00 for seniors, and $7 for children. The matinee price is $7. On Fri, Sat, Sun, and all holidays, the 10 a.m. show is just $5. Matinee movies are shown until 6 p.m. Mon through Thurs. and from noon until 4 p.m. Sat and Sun. You can buy tickets at the theater or ahead of time online at www.movietickets.com.

Typically the weekends are the busiest times so early in the week is the best times to come. All auditoriums have wheelchair-accessible seating.

HARKINS BRICKTOWN CINEMAS 16
150 E. Reno Ave.
(405) 231-4747
www.harkinstheatres.com

Located along the Bricktown Canal downtown, this 16-auditorium theater opened in Oct 2004. Auditorium sizes range from approximately 120 to 400 seats in 15 of the theaters with the Cine Capri theater holding nearly 600. All auditoriums have stadium seating and feature the Ultimate Rocker, high-back, rocking love seats—an innovation that Harkins Theatres introduced to the industry in 1997. Auditoriums are wheelchair accessible and include state-of-the-art digital sound technology.

One concession stand is located in the main lobby. The theater boasts an unprecedented gourmet snack bar with an extensive menu, including pizzas, popcorn chicken, and cheese sticks. It features Coca-Cola products, as well as Dr Pepper and diet Dr Pepper.

In the busy summer months, the theater typically opens between 9 and 9:30 a.m. Generally, the first shows are around 10 a.m. throughout the year. The last show is usually around 10 or 10:30 p.m. unless there is a midnight screening. Ticket prices are $9 for adults, $6 for seniors,and $5 for children. The matinee price is $7. Moviegoers can purchase tickets via phone, Internet, or at the abundant on-site kiosks.

NOBLE THEATER AT THE OKLAHOMA CITY MUSEUM OF ART
415 Couch Dr.
(405) 236-3100
www.okcmoa.com/film

On Apr 12, 2002, this state-of-the-art theater opened inside the new Oklahoma City Museum of Art. It is appropriate that a theater should open here as the grounds formerly held Oklahoma City's last downtown movie palace, the Centre Theatre, built in 1947. Since opening, the Noble Theater has offered more than 1,000 screenings of the finest independent, foreign-language, and classic films for Oklahoma City audiences. The theater seats 250 and shows films Thurs through Sun. It has a surround-sound system and a green room, where actors or special guests can wait on the north side of the stage. Parents should be aware that many of the films shown here are not rated and may be inappropriate for younger viewers.

The Noble Theater participates in the Sundance Art House Project. Twelve art houses throughout the country are chosen to receive and show films in an effort to build audiences for independent films at the local level.

Tickets can be purchased at the Noble Theatre box office two hours before show time. Advance tickets may be purchased the same day of the showing (with the exception of Sun) at the museum's admission desk from 10 a.m. to 5 p.m. or with a credit card by calling (405) 278-8237. Film tickets do not include entrance to the galleries. Prices are $8 for adults and $6 for seniors and students. If you are a museum member, the ticket price is $5. Dinner and a movie packages are available for $28 per person.

OKLAHOMA CITY OMNIDOME THEATRE
2100 NE 52nd St. (in the Science Museum
(405) 602-3663
www.sciencemuseumok.org
Located inside the Oklahoma Science Museum, this is Oklahoma's first large-format, dome-screen theater. A 70-foot diameter dome screen virtually surrounds the audience, while worlds of adventure envelop the senses due to Iwerks Entertainment's 15/70 projection system, the largest, most technologically advanced in the world. A state-of-the-art, 36,000-watt digital sound system provides heart-pounding sound and effects to complete the experience.

Movies shown here are science related. Each movie runs for a full year with new ones being rotated into the schedule every six months. Showtimes start at 10 a.m. and run until 5 p.m. Mon through Sat and on Sun from noon to 5 p.m. Tickets are $8.25 for adults 13 to 64 and $6.75 for seniors 65 and over and children 3 to 12. Tickets do not include admission to the museum.

SHOPPING

Oklahoma City has been a shopping destination since people settled here after the Land Run of 1889. While shopping is spread across the city, there are a few general areas you will want to know about before you head out.

Located along Reno Avenue from I-44 west to Meridian, you will find a number of furniture stores, like Mathis Brothers, Bob Mills, and Lorec Ranch. At May Avenue and Northwest 10th and along Western Avenue from Northwest 36th to about Northwest 50th, antiques enthusiasts will discover clusters of antiques stores. If you are interested in going to one area to mall shop, get groceries, or find something for a baby shower, head to Northwest Expressway and Pennsylvania. There are two malls, numerous restaurants, and a Super Wal-Mart nestled close to each other. Along Classen Avenue and Northwest 23rd, you will find a number of good Asian food markets and on 23rd between Meridian and MacArthur, there are several Mexican food stores.

In this chapter I have included sections on antiques, bakeries, bookstores, specialty shops, and the most prominent malls in Oklahoma City. Of course not every shopping experience is covered here, but it's a good place to start. As you venture out and about, you will find your favorite places to shop. Keep a list and when you get the chance, drop me a line so I can share them with others.

ANTIQUES

ALL ABOUT ANTIQUES
2625 W. Britton Rd.
(405) 752-2882
Richard Cravens and Peter Cypert have been in business since 1984. They buy from individuals and conduct estate liquidations. They have a large selection of vintage and antique furniture from the 1800 and 1900s and a large selection of contemporary and vintage prints. There is a small selection of jewelry, books, memorabilia, and some linens and dishes. They sell their items from a space inside the French Quarter Antiques store. If you need an appraisal, call for an appointment. They'll be happy to look at your item.

> **i** Get your Antique Guide, a map to antiques stores in Oklahoma City, by calling (405) 751-3885. You can also find the guide in your favorite antiques store.

ANCIENT OF DAYS ANTIQUE MALL
2714 NW 10th
(405) 942-2115
www.ancientofdaysantiquemall.com
In its original location for 12 years, this store prides itself on a vast collection of quality oak furniture, primitives, and great country store showcases and collectibles. Established in 1997, this 5,000-square-foot mall features more than 20 dealers. Take a walk back in time with their massive collection of tin types and Civil War collectibles. This store is known to have the best collection of Civil War items in the Southwest.

All of the merchandise has been purchased from all over North America from estate sales, private sales, and auctions. There is a large selection of furniture, dishes, and paintings, a medium selection of jewelry, a small selection of tools and memorabilia, and some books and linens.

Shoppers receive a 10 percent discount on merchandise on the first Sat of every month during the mall's eight-hour sale. Layaway plans are available. The mall is open Mon through Sat from 10 a.m. to 6 p.m. and Sun from 1 to 5 p.m.

ANOTHER TIME ANOTHER PLACE ANTIQUE MALL
2830 NW 10th
(405) 948-8200

This 5,000-square-foot store has around 19 vendors. Sue Barnard, the owner, is a member of the Antique Dealers Association and has been in this location for over three years. She has lots of late Victorian-era furniture, dishes, some silver, handkerchiefs, a small amount of vintage clothing, and a large selection of vintage jewelry. Framed vintage pictures line the wall and if you are looking for something unique, you will find it here. Prices are more reasonable than most stores. Come prepared to take your time and look in all the nooks and crannies.

THE ANTIQUE AVENUE MARKET
5219 N. Western
(405) 842-1010
www.antiqueavenuemarket.com

Whether you are a collector or just want to furnish your house, this market is a must visit. In business for five years, the market has 24 dealers renting space here. Items are gathered from auctions, estate sales, antiques sales, and flea markets. Shoppers will find late-18th-century to mid-19th-century furniture, collectibles, lighting, art, and decor items available for purchase. The market has consistently been voted Favorite Antique Store by the Daily Oklahoman's Reader's Choice. Hours are Mon through Sat from 10:30 a.m. to 5:30 p.m. and Sun from 1 to 5 p.m.

ANTIQUE HOUSE
4409 N. Meridian
(405) 495-2221
www.antiquehouseokc.com

This three-generation family-run business sells merchandise they have collected on their own. They have gone and bought some of their merchandise from New York for 25 years. They will accept consignment items if the items are of high quality. There is a large selection of Victorian

and oak furniture. They carry a small selection of jewelry and books, a large selection of antique glass, and the largest selection of antique linens in Oklahoma City. Hours are Mon through Sat from 10 a.m. to 5 p.m. or by appointment.

APPLE ORCHARD ANTIQUE MALL
2921 NW 10th St.
(405) 946-3015

This mall has 50 antiques dealers. Some dealers rent more than one space. The owner has several spaces herself. The mall carries a large selection of jewelry, books, linens, dishes, and memorabilia. There are paintings, tools, and furniture, but these selections are small. There's also a large selection of price-guide books, with 98 percent of those books being current or new. The mall is open Mon through Sat from 10 a.m. to 5:45 p.m.

APPLE TREE ANTIQUE GALLERY
6740 NW 39th
(405) 495-0602
http://appletreeantique.com

Located on historic SR 66 in downtown Bethany, this 12,000-square-foot gallery has a large selection of competitively priced antiques. The gallery has been in business for 10 years and has over 53 dealers. Items come from estate sales, auctions, and overseas. There is a large selection of dishes and memorabilia and a medium selection of furniture, jewelry, books, linens, and paintings. Visitors will enjoy the large selection of restored carousel horses, dollhouses, and dollhouse miniatures that are for sale here.

The gallery is open Mon, Tues, Wed, Fri, and Sat from 10 a.m. to 6 p.m.; Thurs from 10 a.m. to 7 p.m.; and Sun from 1 to 5 p.m.

COLLECTIBLES, ETC.
1511 N. Meridian
(405) 524-1700

Opened in May 1983, this store moved to its present location in 2000. It carries a large selection of jewelry; vintage and new designer apparel; Marilyn Monroe, Elvis Presley, and Betty Paige memorabilia, and Steiff toys. Hours are Tues through Sat from noon to 5 p.m.

COVINGTON ANTIQUE MARKET

7100 N. Western

(405) 842-3030

This market has been open for 14 years. It sells only its own merchandise. There are no dealers. The owners shop in France for their antiques and specialize in French chandeliers, scones, and decorative pieces. They have a large selection of French mirrors, 19th-century furniture, and 19th- and 20th-century dishes and memorabilia. They also offer a full design service, providing designer fabrics and wall coverings. Hours are Tues through Sat from 10 a.m. to 5 p.m.

FARMERS PUBLIC MARKET

311 S. Klein

(405) 232-6506

www.okcfarmersmarket.com

In 1928, when the Farmers Public Market opened, it just sold fresh produce. A lot has changed since then. It still sells produce, but now it also houses 17 dealers in its one-story horseshoe-shaped building. Antiques shoppers will find hundred of different items here. There is Depression glass, Hall tea pots, Big E Levi's, furniture, jewelry, record albums, rock 'n' roll memorabilia, ladies vintage clothing, knives, fishing lures, coins, baseball cards, books, toys, advertising, primitives, pottery, one-of-a-kind jewelry, handmade Indian items, old clocks, swords, toy guns, cars, trucks, and tractors.

Visitors can enter the building on the north, east, or west. A lot of people enter from the west however, as there is a parking lot there. All dealers are closed on Mon and most are closed on Sun. Hours vary with each dealer so be sure to check the Web site to find when the store you are interested in is open.

FRENCH QUARTER ANTIQUES

2625 W. Britton Rd.

(405) 749-8855

www.frenchquarterantiquesokc.com

Opened in 2004, this 25,000-square-foot mall has 15 dealers. Each dealer brings something unique to their area. There are bronzes, old crystal chandeliers, Strauss chandeliers, artwork, jewelry, and French and English furniture, like beds, desks, chairs, and buffets. Don't be in any hurry and wear comfortable clothes because once you get inside, you'll want to allow plenty of time for browsing. Hours are Mon through Sat from 10 a.m. to 6 p.m.

JODY KERR ANTIQUES & FINE ART

7908 N. Western

(405) 842-5951

Jody Kerr has been in business since 1989 and in her current location since 1991. She is an estate sales expert and all merchandise in her store is personally selected by her. She travels extensively always looking for and purchasing "special" items. She carries a large selection of 19th-century furniture, paintings, and porcelain, including Meissen and KPM. Hours are Wed through Sat from 11:30 a.m. to 4 p.m. and by appointment.

LANGHORNE PLACE ANTIQUES

9115 N. Western

(405) 848-3192

Originally opened in 1978, this store moved to its current location in 1980, a charming bungalow with the original wooden floors and old tin ceiling. There are about 30 dealers here and the owner travels around the country and occasionally out of the country to purchase items for the store.

Shoppers will find a large selection of American and European furniture, costume jewelry from the 40s and 50s, Native American jewelry, children's books, and all kinds of dishes. There is a medium selection of children's toys and a small selection of linens and paintings. The store specializes in lamps, table lamps, and hanging features like pictures and wall art.

Hours are Mon through Sat from 10 a.m. to 5 p.m.

MARY'S SWAP MEET

7905 NE 23rd

(405) 427-0051

www.marysswapmeet.com

The oldest flea market in Oklahoma, this business has been in operation for 42 years and in the same location. Every Sat and Sun from daylight until dark, vendors bring their items to sell. There are spaces for 500 vendors. Items include furniture, jewelry, books, linens, dishes, paintings, tools, and memorabilia. Visitors here will be impressed with the large variety of items available. Plan to take some time looking at everything. Wear comfortable shoes.

MICHAEL'S ANTIQUE CLOCKS
5920 W. Hefner
(405) 722-3300
www.michaelsclocks.com

Since the 1980s this family-operated business has been buying, selling, and repairing clocks in the Oklahoma City area. It is one of the larger antique clock shops in this part of the country with four showrooms and 800 to 1,000 clocks on hand. People from as far away as Scotland, England, France, and the Netherlands purchase clocks from Michael's. There is a large selection of antique wall, mantle, statue, and grandfather clocks, as well as a large selection of new clocks by Howard Miller and Bulova.

Hours are Tues through Fri from 8 a.m. to 5 p.m. and Sat from 9 a.m. to 3 p.m. The shop is closed on Sun and Mon.

NOTTING HILL ANTIQUES
7204 N. Western
(405) 842-1500
www.nottinghillokc.com

This antique store has been in business for 16 years. There are no dealers. All items are for sale by owner, Lee, and come from England, where she and her husband take yearly trips to find the items they sell in their store. They carry a line of handmade necklaces and earrings custom-made in Notting Hill, England, created especially for the store. They also carry English china, furniture, prints, and silver. Their goal is to offer the best-quality items for the best price and only carry items that they would want to have in their home.

Hours are Tues through Sat from 10 a.m. to 5 p.m.

RINK GALLERY
3200 N. Rockwell Ave.
(405) 787-7465
www.rinkgallery.com

The largest antiques mall in the Oklahoma City area opened in July 2006 off Rockwell. It offers about 150 booths operated by about 75 dealers. There is a huge variety and selection of merchandise, including antique, vintage, retro, primitive, shabby chic, prairie chic, western, midcentury, and modern furniture; jewelry; books; linens; dishes; art; and collectibles. According to shoppers, Rink Gallery has the best prices in town and new items are brought in daily. The gallery hosts a special event called Sun at the Rink with free food and live music from 3 to 5 p.m. every Sun.

Hours are Mon through Wed from 10 a.m. to 6 p.m., Thurs through Sat from 10 a.m. to 8 p.m., and Sun from 1 to 6 p.m. It is open every day except Thanksgiving and Christmas.

SCRANTON'S UNIQUES: THRIFT & GIFTS
7512 N. Western
(405) 848-9300

This store has been in business since 1971 in three different locations all along North Western. The owner and three other sellers collect merchandise from local estate and garage sales. They also acquire items from people who come in wanting to sell their belongings. There is a large selection of books which dates from the early 1900s to present. Shoppers will also find some vintage clothing and military surplus items here. This store is currently evolving into a thrift store. The shop is open Tues through Sat from 10 a.m. to 4:30 p.m.

23RD STREET ANTIQUE MALL
3023 NW 23rd
(405) 947-3800
www.antiques23.com

In July 2009, this mall celebrated its 20th anniversary. For eight years, it was located in an old movie theater and known as the May Antique Mall. Then it moved to its present location and became known as the 23rd Street Antique Mall. The mall has about 70 dealers, and sells items on consignment. Many of the dealers have been in the mall for the entire 20 years and have built up a large clientele themselves.

From 1995 to 2008 the mall won the *Daily Oklahoman*'s Reader's Choice Award for the Best Antiques Store in Oklahoma City.In 2008, they won the *Daily Oklahoman*'s Reader's Choice Award for Best Furniture Resale and then in 2009 won *Oklahoma Magazine*'s Best of the Best Antique Shop in the State award.

The mall has a large selection of items, including American Indian pottery, jewelry, baskets, and arrowheads. Furniture includes Victorian walnut pieces from the 1800s and American oak pieces from 1895 to 1915. There are a number of 1830s to 1890s firearms, art glass by Tiffany, Edison phonographs with exposed horns, Sterling flatware, Depression glass, and more. There are so many items shoppers will not have a problem finding something of interest.

Hours are Mon through Sat from 10 a.m. to 5:30 p.m.

WESTERN TRAIL TRADING POST
9100 N. Western
(405) 842-8306
Located here for over 30 years, this antiques store is an antiques hunter's paradise. The owner describes his place of business as a "Classic Route 66 Trading Post." From floor to ceiling, shoppers will be surprised with what they find. Merchandise is acquired from estate sales, auctions, and walk-ins. There is a large selection of furniture, books, linens, dishes, and memorabilia, especially from the 19th and 20th centuries. Seekers of postcards and photos need to stop here as there is quite a selection.

When you go in, plan to spend several hours. Don't hurry through this gold mine. Hours are Mon through Sat 10 a.m. to 5 p.m.

Bethany
BETHANY ANTIQUE MALL
3909 N. College
(405) 495-7091
In business since 1993, this mall has 35 dealers. Located in a quaint area of downtown Bethany,

people come from across the state to see what's new and to shop. Here visitors will find a large selection of furniture dating from the late 1900s to the 1960s and a large selection of paintings. There is a moderate amount of jewelry, books, linens, and dishes.

The mall is open Mon through Sat from 10 a.m. to 6 p.m. and Sun from noon to 4 p.m.

Edmond
ANTIQUE BOUTIQUE
111 S. Broadway, Edmond
(405) 359-9408
www.antiqueboutiqueedmond.com
For 16 years, this store has been located in historic downtown Edmond in a 1915 building with its original tin ceiling. There are 20 dealers here. The owner, Judy Thorwart, also sells items here. She has a large selection of books, dishes, toys, and memorabilia; a medium selection of furniture, linens and paintings; and a small selection of jewelry and tools. Hours are Mon through Sat from 10 a.m. to 5:30 p.m.

BROADWAY ANTIQUES
114 S. Broadway, Edmond
(405) 340-8215
There are over 30 dealers selling their items in this half-market, half-antiques store in the first block on the east side of downtown Edmond. Everything from furniture to books, stamps, and postcards can be found here. And if you are looking for the perfect decorative item for your house, look here. There are lamps, doilies, folk art, and more. The store's motto is "inspiration from every day." Broadway Antiques won the *Daily Oklahoman*'s Readers Choice Award for Best Antique Store in 2008.

COURTYARD ANTIQUES
3314 S. Broadway, Edmond
(405) 359-2719
Courtyard Antiques has been in business for 13 years. It has three dealers but the majority of the store is filled with items being sold by the owners who import items from Europe quarterly. The store carries a large selection of 1800s furni-

ture, new paintings, and 18th- and 19th-century leather books. It specializes in timeless accessories, chandeliers, Fortunata, and elegant lamps.

Hours are Mon through Sat from 10 a.m. to 5 p.m.

ELKS ALLEY MERCANTILE
1201 S. Broadway, Edmond
(405) 340-2400
Originally opened in 2003 in Guthrie, this family-owned and -operated mercantile moved to Edmond in Nov 2005. It imports European antiques and deals in unique home accessories. The owners shop markets and dealers all over Europe and hand pick each piece and then ship them by containers into the United States 600 to 700 pieces at a time. The 14,000-square-feet store offers a large selection of furniture. As visitors weave their way through the narrow aisles, they step back in time to when furniture was made to last a lifetime. As each piece is tagged with a label, visitors can spend a lot of time just reading the labels and learning about when the furniture was made and where it came from. A visit to the store is an education in itself whether visitors buy anything or not.

Hours are Tues through Sat from 10 a.m. to 5:30 p.m.

BAKERIES

BIG SKY BREAD COMPANY
6606 N. Western Ave.
(405) 879-0330
www.bigskybreadokc.com
Big Sky Bread Company opened for business in Mar 1996. It is an old-fashioned bakery, offering baked goods made from scratch. No preservatives and very few oils are added to most breads, making them virtually fat free.

Big Sky makes 8 to 10 varieties of breads—including whole grain items—Tues through Sat, plus cookies, muffins, brownies, scones, cinnamon rolls, granola, crumb cake, and biscotti. Most products are out of the oven by noon.

Honey wholewheat, three seed, and cinnamon walnut raisin are the three most popular breads. Chocolate chip cookies are the most popular cookies while blueberry is the favorite among muffin and scone customers. The bakery ships granola all over the country via FedEx and UPS.

The bakery is open Tues through Fri from 7 a.m. to 6:30 p.m. and Sat from 7 a.m. to 5 p.m. It is wheelchair accessible.

BROWN'S BAKERY
1100 N. Walker Ave.
(405) 232-0363
www.brownsbakery.net
Since 1946, Brown's has been baking up sweet treats for the Oklahoma City area. This third-generation family-owned and -operated bakery is the largest independently owned full-line retail and wholesale bakery in Oklahoma. Donuts that some say are the best in the world, danish, cookies, cakes, pies, and breads are all here to tempt a person's taste buds. Brown's offers a large selection of delicious traditional and specialty baked goods as well. Between 200 and 300 people a day stop here throughout the week and over 500 on Sat. The bakery is home to the Oklahoma Bicycle Society. Every Sat a group rides in for a donut stop and then heads out after having their fill.

The bakery opens at 6 a.m. and closes at 3 p.m. It serves lunch from 11 a.m. to 2 p.m. in their deli. The deli serves up sandwiches made with the bakery's bread and some of the finest ingredients found anywhere.

INGRID'S KITCHEN
3701 N. Youngs Blvd.
(405) 946-8444
www.ingridskitchen.com
Whether it's an item you custom order or select right from the case, you will find something sure to please here. Ingrid's Kitchen makes homemade authentic German products and more. For 30 years, it has built its reputation on high-quality foods and service. The bakery has bagels, cookies, cakes, specialty breads, and large cream horns. The breads include roggeli, black forest, soya, sour dough, and challah. You can order a salad, a made-to-order sandwich, and dessert all at one place.

Ingrid's Kitchen is open Mon through Fri from 7 a.m. to 6:30 p.m. and Sat from 7 a.m. to 5 p.m.

RED VELVET BAKERY
2824 E. Second St., Edmond
(405) 330-8127
www.redvelvetbakery.net

Tammy Morgan, the owner of Red Velvet Bakery, has been baking cakes for Edmond residents since 1983. She used to own Desert Rose, but moved to this location in 1996. Morgan makes everything she sells. On any given day, shoppers can purchase fresh bakery items, like sugar cookies, red velvet cupcakes, sweet breads, pies, and bonbons. Come early though, the case empties quickly and when items are gone, they're gone for the day. Busiest days are Sat and Sun.

Morgan also makes and decorates custom cakes, like wedding and birthday cakes. For those who are looking to special order, Morgan suggests ordering at least a week ahead.

Hours are Mon through Fri 9 a.m. to 5:30 p.m. and Sat from 9 a.m. to 4 p.m.

i Get your "Shopper's Guide to Pesticides" at www.foodnews.org. It is available in a PDF download and as an iPhone app.

BOOKS

ALADDIN BOOK SHOPPE
5040 N. May Ave.
(405) 942-2665
www.aladdinbookshoppe.com

This bookshop was established in 1930. In 2006, however, it was in danger of closing until three partners, two of whom are librarians, stepped in to save it. There is 2,400 square feet of retail space filled with 25,000 titles. Another 25,000 titles are available online. The biggest genres the shop carries are nonfiction, science fiction, and fantasy and it specialize in out-of-print, collectible, and rare books. Each month a selection of books is offered at half price.

Two of the owners work in the bookstore, so you will always get personal service. The shop is wheelchair accessible and open Mon through Sat from 10 a.m. to 5:30 p.m.

BARNES AND NOBLE BOOKSELLERS
13800 N. May Ave. (Quail Springs)
(405) 755-1155
www.barnesandnoble.com

On the northeast corner of Memorial Road and May Avenue sits this bookstore. Parking is located to the south and east side of the building. As you walk in the front door, you are greeted by the latest book arrivals, to the left are magazines, and on the right are books that have been discounted. Music CDs can be found at the very back of the store.

Halfway through the store on the west side of the building is the children's section. Tucked away in this area, are books for infants as well as grown children. A large tree with a stage at its base invites children to sit and read under its limbs. This is also where story time is held during the week. Check the local Oklahoma events calendar on the Web site for the story time schedule.

If you need a pick-me-up, a place to meet friends, or just a place to sit down and look through your purchases, stop in at the coffee shop. There are tables and chairs and Wi-Fi available.

BARNES AND NOBLE BOOKSELLERS
6100 N. May Ave.
(405) 843-9300
www.barnesandnoble.com

This bookstore is laid out much the same way as the Quail Springs location (see above). Entering and exiting is a little tricky as May Avenue running north and south in front of the store is always a busy street. There are book readings for children, author events, and other activities happening here.

BEST OF BOOKS
1313 E. Danforth Rd.
(405) 340-9202
www.bestofbooksedmond.com

This bookstore opened in the fall of 1984. In 1992 two employees purchased the business from its original owner after working here for a number of years. In 1993, they expanded to store to its present 3,150-square-feet. Both owners are book lovers and they employ a knowledgable staff. They can recommend a variety of books on many subjects.

Best of Books carries over 25,000 titles. The largest sections are fiction, mystery, children's books, and young adult books. You'll also find educational toys, puzzles, crafts for children, and a variety of unique sidelines like games and small craft projects for adults.

Every Sat at 11 a.m. children can enjoy story time. Other events and activities include art classes for children, a reading group for children, a book club for adults, and autographing events for children and adults.

Hours are Mon through Sat from 9 a.m. to 8 p.m. and Sun from 1 to 5 p.m.

BORDERS BOOKSTORE

3209 NW Expressway
(405) 848-2667
www.borders.com

Located next door to the Marriott Hotel, this bookstore sits off the Northwest Expressway on the north side. It has 25,000 square feet of space and carries over half a million titles. It also has a large magazine section and a larger local interest section than any other bookstore in the area. For coffee lovers, there is a Seattle's Best Coffee located in the store. Be sure to check out the Borders Reward card.

FULL CIRCLE BOOKSTORE

1900 NW Expressway (in 50 Penn Place)
(405) 842-2900
www.fullcirclebooks.com

Full Circle was founded more than 40 years ago as a small counterculture bookstore in Norman. Since its acquisition by Jim Tolbert in 1978, it has morphed into the largest independent bookstore in Oklahoma and one of the largest in the Southwest. Now covering 7,500 hundred square feet with more than 60,000 titles, the bookstore

also features a cafe and terrace garden, three fireplaces, rolling ladders, and oak bookshelves. It is a book lover's paradise.

Full Circle offers a very broad selection with great strength in fiction, literature, poetry, history, biography, science, Native American studies, politics, current events, art, architecture, audio books, travel, and books for children and young adults. Perhaps the greatest appeal of Full Circle beyond the strong inventory is the exceptional personal service provided by its knowledgeable staff. Book signings, book group meetings, poetry readings, children's story times, and regularly scheduled live music in the cafe help make Full Circle a center of cultural life in the Oklahoma City community.

There is ample parking including reserved spaces at the north entrance. The store is wheelchair accessible. Hours are Mon through Thurs from 10 a.m. to 9 p.m., Fri and Sat from 10 a.m. to 10 p.m., and Sun from noon to 5 p.m.

WALDENBOOKS

2501 W. Memorial Rd. (inside Quail Springs Mall, East End)
(405) 755-4773
www.borders.com

This bookstore is located on the second floor of Quail Springs Mall between Dilliard's and Sears. It has a children's section in the back and stocks new releases of science fiction, mysteries, romances, and magazines.

WALDENBOOKS

1901 NW Expressway, #2048 (inside Penn Square Mall)
(405) 843-9510
www.borders.com

Owned by Borders, this small bookstore can be found on the Cheesecake Factory side of Penn Square Mall, on the second floor, west end, near Macy's. It sells bestseller-list books and graphic novels and has a large selection of science-fiction books. Check out the bargain shelf. A new selection comes in weekly.

WALDENBOOKS

7000 Crossroads Blvd., #2148 (inside Crossroads Mall)

(405) 634-5811

www.borders.com

Located on the west side of Crossroads Mall, on the second floor. If you need a quick gift or want to pick up the latest book by a well-known author, stop in here. There is a medium-size magazine rack.

CANDY

42ND STREET CANDY STORE

4200 N. Western Ave.

(405) 521-8337

The 42nd Street Candy Store opened on Valentine's Day in 1979. Teresa Wall, the present owner, purchased it in Mar 2000. She began in a space of about 600 square feet, but in July 2007 moved to a larger space in the same building. The store now has just under 1,500 square feet.

Inventory expanded tremendously after the move to the new space. The store now offers chocolate bars from Belgium, Spain, Germany, the United Kingdom, Switzerland, Italy, Holland and Australia. The bulk candy ranges from jelly bellies to gummi bears to chocolate covered fruits and nuts. The best-selling items are the fine chocolates in the chocolate case and the chocolate covered sunflower seeds.

The store has walk-in customers as well as a nice base of corporate customers who call for client gifts and seasonal treats for their offices and it offers events and sales on a regular basis. On Wed, there is a gift with purchase in support of the Wed on Western Program, where local businesses offer special incentives like gifts, discounts, or sales for customers who shop the businesses on Western on Wed. Each summer there is the annual sidewalk sale and the store also host events in the store to raise money for nonprofit organizations that focus on services for women and children. In 2005 the store won a People's Choice Award and in 2007 a Best Presentation Award.

The store's hours are 10 a.m. to 6 p.m. Mon through Fri and 10 a.m. to 5 p.m. Sat.

WOODY CANDY COMPANY

922 NW 70th St.

(405) 842-8903

www.woodycandy.com

This company began manufacturing candy in 1927. It has been family-owned for 82 years. Second generation Claude Woody Jr. owns and manages the business. The company makes 90 percent of what it sells and what it sells are treats that can't be beat. On any given day, you might find turtles, English toffee, Aunt Bill's brown candy, chocolate pecan fudge, or chewy pralines with pecans and walnuts. This company can make any kind of candy, but the season determines what they mix. This company strives for the highest quality and freshest ingredients in their confections.

Consumers can find Woody Candy pralines in 675 Cracker Barrel Old Country Stores or they can buy a large range of products from this manufacturer at reasonable prices.

Hours are Mon through Fri from 10 a.m. to 5 p.m. It is also open Sat through the Christmas season.

FOOD

AVALON SEAFOODS

7712 N. May

(405) 843-3474

www.avalonseafoodsokc.com

Avalon Seafoods was established in 1997 with one idea in mind—to bring the freshest seafood available to the Oklahoma City area. Avalon is centrally located at 7712 N. May Ave. It carries a huge variety of fish and shellfish. On any particular day you may find, salmon, halibut, sole, trout, catfish, mahimahi, tuna, sword, roughy, wahoo, snapper, flounder, shark, barramundi, eel, and much, much more. For shellfish you will find gulf shrimp, Prince Edward Island mussels, little neck clams, manilla clams, sea scallops, bay scallops, blue crabs, Dungeness crabs, king crab legs, snow crab legs, gulf oysters, West Coast oysters, East Coast oysters, and much more.

Avalon's employees excel at service, giving customers expert advice on preparing the perfect meal for family or friends. Want to do a crawfish boil for 4 or 400? They can guide you. Want to make dinner for two? How about pan-seared yellow fin tuna? Want to have a tailgate party? How about grilled salmon, halibut, or golden trout flown in fresh from Idaho? Anything you need to know, just ask and they can help you.

Cooking classes are offered Tues nights where you can learn how to prepare a different dish each week. There are also hundreds of recipes available.

Hours of operation are Mon through Sat from 9 a.m. to 6 p.m.

FARMER'S PUBLIC MARKET
311 S. Klein
(405) 232-6506
www.okcfarmersmarket.com
During the summer, local farmers come here to sell their produce, but there are five businesses that are here year-round.

Sterling's Produce (405-235-2815) is a family-owned and -operated produce market that has been here for 30 years. On any given day, you will see sisters, Linda and Suzanne, stocking produce or helping customers. They sell local produce in season, baskets, honey, relish, Amish jellies and jams, and nuts in season, like peanuts from Oct to June. Sterling's is open Mon through Sat from 8 a.m. to 5 p.m.

Angels Produce (405-236-2948) is another produce market located here. It offers fresh fruit and vegetables, Mrs. Renfro's specialty sauces, Oklahoma honey and spices, aloe vera leaves, cornhusks, tamale mix, and a variety of Mexican chilies. Angels is open Sun from 9:30 a.m. to 5 p.m. and Mon through Sat from 8:30 a.m. to 6 p.m.

Pinata Produce (405-232-1314) sells fruits and vegetables, Mexican candy, Mexican ice cream and sodas, and fresh roasted peanuts. It is open Mon through Sat from 8:30 a.m. to 5:30 p.m. and Sun from 9:30 a.m. to 5 p.m.

For those who like to garden, Pam's and J&M Bedding Plants are the places to go for all your plant needs. For 25 years, Pam's (405-270-0507) has been growing bedding and vegetable plants from seed and selling them to the public. It carries a full line of produce plants, a full assortment of fall flowers, pumpkins, gourds, hay, cornstalks, Christmas trees, landscaping trees, shrubs, and firewood. The nursery-owned J&M Bedding Plants (405-278-8555), offers annuals, perennials, house plants, shrubs, shade trees, fruit trees, berry vines, flowering baskets, pots, and bowls.

FURNITURE

GALLERIA FURNITURE
3700 W. I-40 Service Rd.
(405) 942-9222
www.galleriaokc.com
The Owens family opened Galleria Furniture in June 2005. It is their goal to provide a furniture shopping experience in a relaxed environment. The 170,0000-square-foot store carries a wide range of affordable, stylish items. Some of the manufacturers include Sealy, Kathy Ireland, and England, a La-Z-Boy Company. In addition to the furniture selection, the store has one of Oklahoma's largest accessory showrooms. An in-house decorator is available to help shoppers with their decorating needs.

Shoppers can place special orders with several lines. Massoud, Mayo, England, and Best Chair offer a wide variety of frames and fabrics.

Galleria Furniture delivers locally, out-of-town, and out-of-state. With the exception of occasional back orders, the furniture is in stock and ready for carryout or delivery. There is a large parking area and open parking for those pulling a trailer.

Wells Fargo is Galleria's financing company and they offer 3, 6, and 12 months no-interest financing. Layaway is also available. Hours are Mon through Sat from 10 a.m. to 10 p.m. and Sun from 11 a.m. to 7 p.m.

JUDE 'N' JODY & SONS FACTORY DIRECT
509 SW 29th
(405) 631-1505
This family-owned and -operated furniture store opened in 1964 in its present location. It has a 38,000-square-foot showroom and a

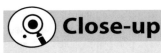 **Close-up**

Super Cao Nguyen Market

Super Cao Nguyen Market (2668 N. Military, 405-525-7650, www.caonguyen.com) is a specialty international grocery store. They carry products from Japan, Hong Kong, Thailand, Vietnam, Taiwan, UAE, Italy, Mexico, Canada, Australia, France, and Belgium, just to name a few countries. It is a family-run business and celebrated its 30th anniversary in 2009.

The original Cao Nguyen Market was started by the Luong family as a 1,000-square-foot store in 1979. The store was named after a region in Vietnam by the same name, which means "the highlands." As the Asian population in Oklahoma grew, so did the store. As the store grew, it gained a loyal following from food lovers and gourmet enthusiasts looking for something other than the meat and potatoes typically available in the Midwest. In 2003, the market moved into a new 50,000-square-foot building a block away to meet the needs of a growing Oklahoma City.

The new Super Cao Nguyen, as it was known, drew inspiration from gourmet and international markets from all over the United States. The idea is to transport visitors to another part of the world without ever leaving the city limits. It is not uncommon to hear five or six different languages being spoken inside the store.

At last count, Super Cao Nguyen stocks grocery items from over 50 different countries and 6 different continents. Hot French baguettes are baked on-site daily; sushi is handmade daily; bánh mì sandwiches are made-to-order; fresh exotic produce arrives daily; and the meat counter sells freshly butchered pork. Super Cao Nguyen stocks the largest selection of Japanese food in the Southwest region. Those who love seafood will enjoy the fresh and live seafood, such as sushi-grade tuna, Dungeness crabs, lobsters, crawfish, blue crabs, and clams from New Zealand. A few times a year, Super Cao Nguyen will bring in live Alaskan king crabs and spiny lobsters from Australia.

Super Cao Nguyen draws a diverse clientele from throughout the Midwest region. It is not uncommon to see regular customers from Texas, Kansas, Missouri, Arkansas, and even Aspen, Colorado. Super Cao Nguyen also attracts tourists and out-of-town visitors from all of the country. Local restaurant chefs will also peruse the aisles for their daily and weekend specials.

This specialty store keeps its prices low as it strives for great customer service. It knows the highest quality products at the most reasonable prices are what customers look for so they keep those prices competitive with other stores in the area. Super Cao Nguyen is open seven days a week from 9 a.m. to 8:30 p.m.

28,000-square-foot warehouse and sells affordable furniture like Ashley, Harden, and Lady Americana Mattress.

The owners, Jude Northcutt and Jody Taylor, are country-and-western singers and had a television show for 28 years. They appeal to middle-class, blue-collar farmers and ranchers because they still write and sing country music.

They appear at different venues around the state promoting their furniture store.

The store offers payment plans and same-day free delivery. Hours are Mon through Sat from 10 a.m. to 7 p.m. and Sun from 1 to 6 p.m.

This is not a high-pressure sales store. As an added bonus, Jude and Jody give their customers free CDs and DVDs of their television shows.

LIFESTYLES
1801 W. 33rd St., Edmond
(405) 348-7422
www.lifestylesstores.com

For years, residents of the Oklahoma City area knew this store as The Lighting Center. It was founded in 1971 and sold lighting fixtures and ceiling fans to homebuilders and their clients for their new homes. In 1999, the owners decided to build a 30,000 square foot show room to replace the original Oklahoma City location. Today, the store, renamed Lifestyles sits on the north side of 33rd between Kelly and Santa Fe. The new expanded store allows for a new merchandise mix to include furniture, rugs, home decor, and hardware. In the spring of 2001, LifeStyles moved into the Tulsa market and in 2005 it began doing business in the Plano, Texas, market. Still family-owned and -operated, LifeStyles has grown to be the region's largest lighting and home furnishings retailer.

LifeStyles shoppers include new homeowners, builders, decorators, and retail customers. Besides lighting, shoppers will find furniture, lamps, rugs, florals, bedroom groups, dining sets, accessories, and hardware. Lifestyles also offers financing.

Hours are Mon through Fri 9 a.m. to 6 p.m., Thurs from 9 a.m. to 8 p.m., Sat 10 a.m. to 6 p.m., and Sun from noon to 5 p.m.

i **Look for more places to shop at www .oklahoma.city.retailguide.com, www .shopping.newsok.com, and www.keyokc .com/shopping.html.**

JEWELRY

B.C. CLARK
101 Park Ave., Ste. 100
(405) 232-8806
www.bcclark.com

"Jewelry is the gift to give, 'cause it's the gift that will live and live." From just after Thanksgiving through Dec when residents of Oklahoma City hear that jingle, they know Christmas is not far away. For B.C. Clark and Oklahoma City that jingle is a tradition and it kicks off B.C. Clark's anniversary sale.

B.C. Clark was founded in 1892, three years after Oklahoma City was settled and 15 years before statehood when the area was still considered Indian Territory. It is a fourth-generation family business and the oldest retail store in Oklahoma with the same family ownership and name. The business is currently led by the executive team of Jim Clark and his sons, Coleman and Mitchell Clark.

B.C. Clark sells fine jewelry, watches, and gifts, including many of the most prestigious brands and designers. It specializes in loose diamonds, engagement rings, and fine watches and has one of the largest selections of David Yurman and Roberto Coin jewelry in the Southwest.

Besides the anniversary sale, B.C. Clark offers a Pray for Rain promotion to customers who purchase diamond engagement rings. If it rains 1 inch or more in Oklahoma City on the day of the customer's wedding, the customer may be eligible for a refund of up to $5,000. The store also runs a Church Coupon program. At the time of purchase, a customer may fill out a church coupon requesting that B.C. Clark give 3 percent of the customer's purchase price to the church of the customer's choice.

B.C. Clark has three stores in the Oklahoma City area, one in Northpark Mall, one in Penn Square Mall, and one in downtown. The two mall stores have mall parking and the downtown store has metered parking on the street. The downtown store gladly refunds parking expenses for those who choose to visit them.

B.C. Clark has won the *Daily Oklahoman* Reader's Choice Award and the *Oklahoma Gazette*'s "Best of" award. It offers in-store credit. The downtown and Northpark store hours are Mon through Sat from 9:30 a.m. to 5:30 p.m. The Penn Square location hours are Mon through Sat from 10 a.m. to 6 p.m.

INDIAN ART OKLAHOMA
4716 N. MacArthur Blvd.
(405) 495-1800
www.indianartoklahoma.com

For a unique and fun experience, come and check out the largest Indian trading post in Oklahoma

City. Sister store to Jeweler's Bench (see below), Indian Art Oklahoma has been open since 1995. It has increased steadily in size to its present 2,000 square feet. The store offers turquoise jewelry, pottery, artwork, artifacts, movies, music, pow-wow regalia, beadwork, Leanin' Tree cards, flutes, sculptures, moccasins, and dream catchers. The best-selling item is silver turquoise jewelry.

The store is wheelchair accessible and parking is available in front and back. Hours are Wed through Fri from 10 a.m. to 5 p.m. and Sat from 10 a.m. to 2 p.m.

JEWELER'S BENCH
4716 N. MacArthur Blvd.
(405) 495-1800
www.jewelersbenchokc.com
Mike and Valerie Mon, owners of Jeweler's Bench, had their original store in Breckenridge, Colorado, in 1973. They were inspired by nature's beautiful stones and thought what better way to share them than in jewelry. In 1975, they returned home to Oklahoma and opened a store across from Shepherd Mall. There they stayed until 1995 when they relocated to their present location in Warr Acres.

Mike and Valerie make and sell custom-design gold and silver jewelry, which are their best-selling items. Also available are natural stones and gemstones and Native American jewelry and gifts. From mid-Nov through Dec the store has an annual sale event to celebrate the holiday season. If you are interested in learning how to make jewelry yourself, silversmithing and other jewelry-related classes are available.

Parking is available in front and back of the store and the store is wheelchair accessible. Hours are Wed through Fri from 10 a.m. to 5 p.m. and Sat from 10 a.m. to 2 p.m.

KAMBER'S ON NORTH WESTERN
7308 N. Western
(405) 840-2122
Kamber's opened in 1922 and was owned and operated by the Kamber family. Now it is owned by Kevin Mashburn, who worked for Kamber's since 1974. He purchased the store in 2007 and continues the Kamber family's tradition of old-fashioned customer service.

In the 3,000-square-foot retail space, guests will find luggage, travel items, hard-to-find gifts, chess sets, and canes. Kamber's is a high-end store and most of the clientele are women. Kamber's offers free embossing, engraving, and gift wrapping. Periodically throughout the year, there are special sales.

The store is open Mon through Sat, from 10 a.m. to 5:30 p.m. and is wheelchair accessible.

MALLS

CROSSROADS MALL
7000 Crossroads Blvd.
(405) 631-4421
www.shopcrossroadsmall.com
This mall is located on the northeast side of I-35 and I-240 in south Oklahoma City. It was built in 1974 and sits on 112 acres, with 1.3 million square feet of stores. Two floors feature 100 stores, including American Eagle Outfitters, Bath & Body Works, and Victoria's Secret. There are no food courts here, but there are restaurants, like Texas Roadhouse, Chinese Express, and Gyros City. Special events include car shows, music performances, trade shows, Santa Claus, and the Easter Bunny. The mall has security around the clock.

50 PENN PLACE
1900 NW Expressway
(405) 848-7488
www.50pennplace.info/retail.htm
For an upscale shopping experience, stop in and visit 50 Penn Place's boutiques, salons, and galleries. It's easy to find as it is right across the street from Penn Square Mall on the south side of the expressway. Originally built in 1973, it has had many renovations since then. It is a multistory building totaling over 320,000 square feet and three levels of that, or 132,580 square feet, is retail space. There are five restaurants: Belle Isle Brewery, Urban Market, Saffron Grill, I Love Sushi, and the Café Garden, which is located inside Full Circle Bookstore. Other businesses here include Balliet's, a high-end retail and cosmetic store;

Route 66;, Mystique Fragrances;, 50 Penn Place Hair Designers; and Pendleton Woolen Mills, which sells women and men's clothing. The retail outlet employs 24-hour security so shoppers needn't worry about their safety.

NORTHPARK MALL
12100 N. May Ave.
(405) 751-1453 or 755-3565
www.northparkmallokc.com
If you prefer a smaller mall, visit this one located in the northwest part of Oklahoma City at Northwest 122nd and May Avenue. The first phase opened in 1972 and the mall has been going strong since. It sits on 22 acres and has 200,000 square feet of leasable retail space. It is one story so you don't have to worry about stairs, escalators, or elevators. The mall has 40 upscale specialty stores, like B.C. Clark, Shoe Gallery, Geno's Furs; a cleaners; three salons; and two restaurants, Shogun's and City Bites. Northpark Cinema 7 is located here and offers great deals on movies before and after 6 p.m. The box office opens at 12:15 p.m. In Apr, the mall holds a "girl's night out." Women of all ages can enjoy games, food, and live entertainment.

PENN SQUARE MALL
1901 NW Expressway
(405) 842-4424
www.pennsquaremall.com
Located on the northeast corner of the Northwest Expressway and Pennsylvania Avenue, this mall has something for everyone. There is a food court and movie theater located on the upper level. Three department stores, Macy's JCPenneys, and Dilliard's, anchor the mall on the north, east, and west side. Four sit-down restaurants, 10 fast-food establishments, 8 specialty food shops and over 100 other stores are here to entice shoppers.

Parking is ample and security patrols 24 hours a day.

QUAIL SPRINGS MALL
2501 W. Memorial Rd.
(405) 755-6530
www.quailspringsmall.com
Sitting on eight acres, this mall has over 125 stores, including Macy's, Dilliard's, JCPenney, Sears, the Disney Store, and Abercrombie & Fitch. It originally opened in 1980 and underwent renovation and expansion in 1998 and 1999. It now totals 1,117,485 square feet. Over 13 million customers visit this three-level, enclosed mall annually.

If you tire of shopping, stop by the 24-screen AMC theater and catch a movie. This theater is rated the number-one movie theater in the state of Oklahoma. Two concession stands are located inside the theater, one at the front and one at the back, so you can order snacks quickly and get to your movie.

For food, look no further than the Drive-In, a 1950s-themed food court. Available here are tacos, chicken sandwiches, pizza, hamburgers, and Chinese food. Restaurants, like BJ's Restaurant and Brewhouse, Longhorn Steakhouse, and El Chico Mexican Restaurant, are available, too.

There are children's soft play areas and family restrooms throughout the mall. Visitors will have no problem finding a parking space in the 5,500 parking space lot and while security is always present, it is still wise to hide valuables and lock your car before heading in to shop.

Hours are Mon through Sat from 10 a.m. to 9 p.m. and Sun from 11 a.m. to 6 p.m.

SPECIALTY

BACKWOODS
12325 N. May Ave., Ste. 103
(405) 751-7376
www.backwoods.com
Repeat customers keep this store open. In Oklahoma City since 1974, this 7,000-square-foot store sells items for backpacking trips, rock climbing, flyfishing, and more. International travel enthusiasts will find water filters and freeze-dried food. Footwear includes everything from flip-flops to boots and the clothing ranges from thermal underwear to outerwear. This store is always on the lookout for cutting-edge products and the newest is Five Fingers footwear from Vibron. They are toe socks with boot bottoms.

The store is open Mon through Fri from 10 a.m. to 7 p.m., Sat from 10 a.m. to 6 p.m., and Sun from 1 to 5 p.m.

NORTH POLE CITY
4201 S. I-44 Service Rd.
(405) 685-6635
www.northpolecity.com

Nothing will put you in the Christmas spirit quicker than stopping by this store. Open and decorated year-round, this shop offers trees, tree ornaments, Christmas decorations, and many collectibles, including. Precious Moments, Boyd's Plush, and Ty products. If you are looking to expand your holiday decorations, Dickens Village, Snow Village, and Snowbabies may be the place to start. Purchase them all at once, buy one piece a month, or one piece a year. Whatever you decide, all the Christmas items will be here when you're ready. Be sure to check out the porcelain dolls, crystal, and handcarved wood figures. There is something here for everyone's taste and budget.

Hours vary so be sure to call in advance.

OKLAHOMA'S RED DIRT EMPORIUM
Bricktown Canal Level
115 E. California
(405) 415-6779
www.reddirtemporium.com

Founded in 2007, this store specializes in products made in Oklahoma. Products include art, films, books, music, food, and clothes. If you are looking for something unique, you will find it here.

The emporium is open seven days a week from 10 a.m. to 9 p.m.

PAINTED DOOR
124 E. Sheridan
(405) 235-4410
www.painteddoor.com

Located on the first floor of a 100-year-old brick warehouse, this unique store has a variety of products in all price ranges and tastes. Items include home decor, baby items, greeting cards, lip gloss, bath products, gourmet prepackaged foods, wedding gifts, clothing, and accessories. The owner, Avis Scaramucci, says that she wants to offer items that everyone can afford, so visitors will find items ranging from $5 to $500.

There is a bridal registry and complimentary gift wrap while you wait. The store is wheelchair accessible

Scaramucci also owns Nonna's, the restaurant just next door. Stop in and shop at Painted Door, then grab something delicious to eat at Nonna's before heading out. If you become familiar with the store and need a gift quickly, you can call ahead and the staff will have the gift wrapped and ready to go by the time you arrive.

SHOPPING IN STOCKYARDS CITY

NATIONAL SADDLERY
1307 S. Agnew
(405) 601-4438
www.nationalsaddlery.com

Some of the most sought-after saddles in the country come out of this unassuming storefront next door to a restaurant. The building that houses National Saddlery has been a saddle shop since 1926. The original brass ceiling tiles are still in place and there is what looks like a cowboy stuck in the ceiling. When replacement tiles couldn't be found to fix a hole in the ceiling, owners John David and Dona Kay Rule filled the spot with a pair of stuffed jeans attached to cowboy boots. John David makes custom saddles and belts for the likes of Garth Brooks. Prices start at $1,400. Rule also makes all the trophy saddles for the Professional Rodeo Cowboy Association's National Finals Rodeo. The saddle shop is open Mon through Sat from 9 a.m. to 6 p.m. Rule's workshop is in the back; visitors are welcome to watch him work.

OKLAHOMA NATIVE ART AND JEWELRY
1316 S. Agnew
(405) 604-9800

This store's original location was one block north of the Alfred P. Murrah Federal Building. After the bombing in 1995 and the building was damaged,

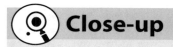 **Close-up**

Sealed with a Kiss

Sealed with a Kiss (SWAK) (3124 N. Classen, 405-600-YARN, www.swakknit.com) started as a design studio in 1993, offering original sewing patterns and kit designs through mail order. The mail-order business expanded and the studio started wholesaling its patterns to yarn shops across the United States and Canada. In 1997 SWAK opened a small shop and design studio on the west side of Guthrie. In 2001 it expanded, moving into one of the historic buildings in downtown Guthrie (109 East Oklahoma). SWAK grew to become one of the largest and best-known yarn shops in the United States.

In 2007 SWAK expanded again, opening a second location in Oklahoma City at 3124 North Classen in the quirky arts/Asian district. SWAK is owned by Keely Northup and her mom, Sherry Stuever. Both have been involved in various aspects of the needlework business for most of their lives and thoroughly enjoy what they do. Keely and Sherry are recognized as the leading authorities on the intarsia knitting technique and their knowledge extends well beyond this one technique.

The Oklahoma City location is housed in a large, historic home that is painted lime green. The shop occupies the entire lower level, approximately 2,000 square feet. It sells yarns and supplies of all sorts for those who love to knit and crochet. Supplies include needles, accessories, tote bags, patterns, books, and just about anything one would need to knit or crochet. SWAK is also a Prairie Gypsies retailer, selling their Oklahoma-made jams, mustards, and treats.

While most of the customers are women, men are also coming in and buying products at the stores. The largest growing number of their clientele is under 35 urban women who are modern but very traditional as well. Many of their customers are stay-at-home moms who are interested in homemaking and crafts. These customers are internet savvy and have online social groups that circle around crotchet and knitting. Keely, the owner of SWAK, feels that's the reason their website continues to receive so many orders. Both stores are wheelchair accessible. The wheelchair ramp at the Oklahoma City store is located on the southeast corner of the deck. The Oklahoma City store also offers a wheelchair-accessible bathroom. Parking here is available on 31st Street, in the lot shared with the Red Cup and Denton's Framing.

The Oklahoma City store hours are Mon and Tues from 10 a.m. to 3 p.m., Wed from 10 a.m. to 10 p.m., Thurs through Sat from 10 a.m. to 6 p.m., and Sun from noon to 4 p.m. The Guthrie store hours are Fri to Wed 10 a.m. to 5 p.m. and Thurs from 10 a.m. to 8 p.m.

the owner, Yolanda White Antelope had to relocate and chose Bricktown along the canal. The store remained in that location for the next eight years. In 2007, several merchants in the Stockyards are asked her to relocate to Stockyards City because they thought her business would be a nice fit for the area and it did.

In its current location the store has over 2,000 square feet and sells only authentic American Indian items, including jewelry, pottery, Kachinas, framed and unframed prints and original artwork, sculptures, long bows, lances, arrows, flutes, and bags. There are seven silversmiths who make jewelry for the store and there is always a silversmith on-site for custom work and sizing.

Free street parking is available. The store is wheelchair accessible. It does not except American Express. Hours are Tues through Sat from 9 a.m. to 9 p.m. and Sun and Mon from 10 a.m. to 8 p.m. It is closed Christmas Day.

SHEPLER'S
812 S. Meridian Ave.
(405) 947-6831
www.sheplers.com

The original branch of this western store opened in Wichita, Kansas, in 1909. The Meridian Avenue location is the place local shoppers go to find western wear. Wrangler, Levi, Justin, Stetson, and Carhartt are only a few of the brands available. The store carries over 2,000 pairs of boots and can fit almost any foot. For men, there are jeans, boots, shirts, hats, coats, belts, and buckles. Women's items include jewelry, handbags, hats, jeans, and wedding dresses. Kids will have fun shopping for stick ponies, board games, toy spurs, toy barns, and more.

i For coupons, free shopping lists, recipes, and more, go to www.allfree printables.com.

SHORTY'S CABOY HATTERY
1206 S. Agnew
(800) 853-4287
www.shortshattery.com

The owner of Shorty's is Lavonna Koger, who advertises her shop as the only female-owned hattery in North America. Koger makes hats from 100 percent beaver "blanks" that she imports from France, shaping them with her collection of vintage wooden hat blocks and machinery. Koger, who's called on by Hollywood from time to time, specializes in jobs requiring vanishing expertise, like putting a tight "pencil curl" around the brims of hats.

Koger is happy to have visitors watch her work and she likes to show off her equipment, most of which is nearly impossible to come by anymore. Prices for Koger's hats range from about $300 to $450. The hattery is open Mon through Sat from 8:30 a.m. to 3 p.m.

TENER'S WESTERN OUTFITTERS
4320 W. Reno Ave.
(405) 946-5500
www.teners.com

In 1930 Ray F. Tener opened his first western store in Oklahoma.It was to be one of many. He loved people and through tenacity and strength of character he built the business into what it is today. His first store has grown to four and now there are locations in Shawnee, Oklahoma, Sherman and Wichita Falls, Texas. After all these years, Tener's still sells quality products for cowboys and cowgirls of all ages and is still owned and operated by Oklahoma born and raised families.

This 28,000-square-foot store has a full range of western wear, including boots, hats, belts, buckles, jewelry, tack and clothes for all ages. Most popular are the boots, jeans, shirts, and hats. Tener's always has something on sale and it guarantees the lowest prices in town. If you find a better price, they'll beat it.

Hours are Mon through Sat from 9 a.m. to 8 p.m. and Sun from 12 to 6 p.m.

ATTRACTIONS

Are you interested in learning about the history of the state? Want to dip your toes in a cool stream? Interested in seeing botanical gardens? Then look no further than downtown Oklahoma City.

In the heart of downtown is the Myriad Botanical Gardens and Crystal Bridge Tropical Conservatory. To the west of downtown on Reno Avenue is White Water Bay and just north of downtown, are the Oklahoma History Center and the National Cowboy Hall of Fame and Western Heritage Center.

Some of the attractions can be seen in a couple hours. Others take all day. I have noted those attractions where visitors should plan to spend all day. In all cases, guests should take their time. Each attraction has something different and unique to offer.

There are a number of attractions that are across the street, down the street, or next door to one another. The Oklahoma History Center is across the street from the Governor's Mansion and the Oklahoma City Zoo is a short walk away from the Science Museum and across the street from Remington Park. Once you go to one, you may be tempted to pop into another. The zoo and Science Museum, however, will each take an entire day.

You will find that most of these attractions are the busiest in the summer months so plan a visit for the spring or fall if you want to avoid crowds. Spring and fall are also the best times to visit because it is not so hot. Summer months—June, July, and Aug—can be brutal because of the heat. If you decide to go to an outdoor attraction during these months, go early in the morning, saving indoor attractions until the afternoon when you will want to escape the heat.

All months in Oklahoma have the potential for severe weather, but spring is when the most severe weather occurs. It can be clear at 1 p.m. and by 3 p.m. torrential rain and hail may be falling. Be prepared. Take raincoats and umbrellas and always keep an eye to the sky.

Hours and admission prices in the listings below were current at the time of this writing. They are always subject to change, however, so it is good to call ahead or check the attraction's Web site before you go.

This chapter does not provide a comprehensive list of everything there is to do in Oklahoma City. You can also check the Kidstuff, Nightlife, the Arts, and Annual Events chapters in this book for more ideas on things to do.

As you read or flip through this book, you will find that there is a lot to do in and around Oklahoma City, so you better get started.

BRICKTOWN
One block west of the Cox Convention Center
(405) 236-8666
www.bricktownokc.com
Located just east of downtown, Bricktown is a renovated hotspot of activity. Historically significant, this 15-block area has sprung to life more than once. Two years before the Land Run of 1889, the Santa Fe Railroad built its tracks here. Rock Island, Frisco, and the Katy soon followed. Large freight operations shipped out raw products and accepted manufactured ones. After oil was discovered in Oklahoma City's oil fields, it too was shipped from here by rail. Coming and going on the trains were residents and salesmen.

To accommodate commerce and passenger traffic, redbrick buildings were built here. From 1898 to 1930 there was a building boom and then when the Great Depression hit, building stopped. After World War II, suburban sprawl began and new industrial parks grew away from this commercial center because of cheap land and the development of the trucking industry.

By 1980 the area had become a virtual graveyard of brick buildings. Enter Oklahoma City and its MAPS program. With vision, leadership, and a plan to revitalize the area, Bricktown came back to life.

Today, visitors will find a movie theater, restaurants, clubs, shopping, and river rides. The Bricktown Ballpark is here and home to the Redhawks, Oklahoma City's minor league baseball team. With so much history and so many things to see and do here, this is one place, you don't want to miss.

COLES GARDEN
1415 NE 63rd St.
(800) 334-5576
www.colesgarden.net
When visitors walk through the large iron entrance gates which belonged to Napoléon, they are transported to another world. There are not many large gardens like this in Oklahoma. Coles Garden is 13.5 acres of flowers, trees, and a 70-foot wide waterfall nestled in the heart of Oklahoma City. The flowers change with the season. Beds contain flowers and foliage that are native to Oklahoma as well as some that are not.

In the summer, hibiscus abound. In the spring, the Fleur de Lis Garden shows off its tulips. The wildflower garden exhibits its colors and allows visitors to appreciate natural beauty. The waterfall spills from one Koi pond to another. Visitors are allowed to feed the Koi with special food. The serene sounds of nature surrounds visitors as they rest on stone benches and explore the gardens within the garden.

Visitors are allowed to take pictures. The garden is wheelchair accessible. Parking is free, abundant, and secure. Hours are Tues through Fri, 9 a.m. to 6 p.m. and Sat by appointment. A lot of weddings are held here so weekends are pretty packed, especially in the summer. There is no gift shop or snack bar. Admission is $5 per person. Children 11 and under are free with a paying adult. Unless you have a big group, the garden typically does not take credit cards for admission.

DEVON OIL AND GAS PARK
Oklahoma History Center
2401 N. Laird Ave.
(405) 522-5248
www.oklahomahistorycenter.org
Outside the Oklahoma History Center, located on the northeast corner of Northeast 23rd and Lincoln Boulevard, across the street from the Oklahoma capitol, you will find this park. As you pull into the history center's parking lot, the park is on the northeast part of the property. A concrete path will lead you around to the oil equipment. Each piece explores the drilling, production, and transportation phases of the Oklahoma oil and gas industry. There are four oil derricks, including a 1950 portable rotary platform rig, which represent the types of derricks used throughout Oklahoma's gas and exploration history. Placards are located on each piece of equipment so visitors can read and learn about each. Feel free to park in the history center's lot. Admission is free to the Devon Oil and Gas Park.

i If you are planning to do a lot of activities in the Oklahoma City area, check out the "Entertainment Book." For $15, you will get coupons to many of the local attractions, restaurants, and businesses. For more information or to order, call (888) 231-SAVE.

EXPRESS RANCHES CLYDESDALES CENTER
12701 W. Wilshire
(405) 350-6404
www.expressclysdale.com
Guests are invited to visit the 1,800-to-2,300-pound Clydesdales in their specially constructed barn, originally built in 1936. Today, the barn is a welcome center for visitors from around the

world. The barn features pine wood and walnut trim and brass fixtures throughout. There are 10 stalls. The upstairs loft is available for rent for birthday parties and other gatherings. Outside there are smaller four-legged animals to see, like a zebra and a couple of miniature horses.

Once a year, the center holds a barn party to help raise funds for the Children's Miracle Network. There are wagon rides and hot dogs and drinks are sold. The cost to attend is minimal.

After visiting the Clydesdales, guests can purchase memorabilia in the gift shop. It has a wide variety of items to choose from, such as hats, jackets, candles, T-shirts, beanie Clydesdales, coffee mugs, and much more. The center accepts Visa and Mastercard.

Picture taking is always allowed, there is ample parking, and the center is wheelchair accessible. Comfortable walking shoes and jeans or shorts are encouraged. Admission is free.

45TH INFANTRY MUSEUM
2145 NE 36th St.
(405) 424-5313
www.45thdivisionmuseum.com
Military history buffs will want to stop at this museum, named after the division that General George Patton called "one of the best, if not the best, divisions in the history of American armies." The museum covers the history of Oklahoma soldiers from 1841 to the present but some of the most popular exhibits are connected with the 45th. Division member and cartoonist Bill Mauldin first drew "Willie & Joe" for the 45th Infantry newsletter and a collection of his drawings is on display. The 45th was the first division to reach Munich and to enter Adolf Hitler's apartment there; consequently, the museum displays the world's largest collection of items that once belonged to Hitler.

Outside, military vehicles, weapons, and aircraft are on display. The museum is open Tues through Fri from 9 a.m. to 4:15 p.m., Sat from 10 a.m. to 4:15 p.m., and Sun from 1 to 4:15 p.m. Admission is free.

FRED JONES JR. MUSEUM OF ART
University of Oklahoma (OU)
555 Elm Ave.
(405) 325-3272
www.ou.edu/fjjma
Fred Jones Jr. Museum of Art , located at the University of Oklahoma is an exceptional university art museum. It has 12,300 objects of art in its permanent collection like Asian Art, ceramics, French Impressionism, Native American Art, photography, 20th Century American painting and sculpture and more. A new building designed by architect Hugh Newell Jacobsen, exhibits works by such artists as Ansel Adams, Claude Monet, Georgia O'Keefe, Vincent Van Gogh and other recognizable artists.

In addition to permanent collections and temporary exhibitions, the museum hosts multiple programs and educational events each month, including guest lectures, art activities for children, live concerts, and family activities.

Photography is allowed of the permanent collection and some exhibitions. Be sure to ask. Flash photography is not allowed as it can damage certain pieces. Visitors should dress comfortably. There is free parking across Boyd Street to the north of the museum, immediately west of the Baptist Student Union. Visitors may also use metered parking on campus or in the Elm Avenue parking garage to the west of the museum. Metered parking is typically $1 per hour.

The museum gift store is a fun place to visit because many of the items on sale here mirror what the museum has in its collection. Guests will find art books, Native American Indian jewelry, puzzles and more. You can get 10 percent off your purchases by becoming a museum association member. Admission is $5 for adults, $4 for seniors 65 and older, $3 for children 6 to 17, and free for children under six, museum association members, and University of Oklahoma students with a valid ID. Admission is free for everyone on Tues. Hours are Tues through Sat from 10 a.m. to 5 p.m., Fri from 10 a.m. to 9 p.m., and Sun from 1 to 5 p.m. The museum is closed Mon.

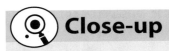

Close-up

Frontier City

If you and your family want fun, Frontier City (I-35 between NE 122nd and Hefner Road, 405-478-2140, www.frontiercity.com), Oklahoma's only theme park, is the place you need to visit. It will transport you and your family back to the Wild West. It opened in 1958. Jimmy Burge started the park because he wanted to create a place "where good guys always won." Located in the middle of Oklahoma, on the northeast side of Oklahoma City, just off I-35, the park has dozens of rides, shows, and attractions, including Oklahoma's only suspended-track roller coaster, the Steel Lasso. It opened in the summer of 2008. In addition, Frontier City features three other roller coasters, two water rides, and Kiddie Land, home to Tiny Timber Town. Frontier City also presents a summer concert series each season withartists appearing in the Starlight Amphitheater. Concerts are free with paid admission.

Frontier City officially opens at the end of Mar and stays open until the end of Oct. If you don't like crowds, the best time to come is Mon through Thurs during the summer months and when the park is open during the early and late season months of Apr, May, Sept, and Oct. Call or visit the park's Web site before you go for operating hours. Certain rides may need to close when severe weather blows in, but after storms blow over, the park re-opens the rides.

Pictures are allowed within the park. You will want to capture the memories and fun you had at Frontier City. Don't hesitate to ask a staff member to assist so the entire family will be in the photo. Dress for comfort, however, clothing with offensive wording or graphics is not allowed. A shirt and shoes must be worn at all times. Skates or skate shoes are not allowed. The weather is always changing in Oklahoma so you might want to bring a sweater or light jacket for cool evenings and a rain jacket in case of rain showers. Guests can rent a locker inside the park for storage of valuables.

A lot of parking is available in the main parking lot located just north of the park. Park entrance is easily accessible from this area. Parking is $7 per vehicle. Season parking passes are available for $29.99 for the 2009 season. Sometimes special parking promotions are offered on the park's Web site. Frontier City is wheelchair accessible and offers wheelchair rental, as well as wagon rentals for children.

In 2009 the price of a one-day general admission ticket is $34.99 plus tax for adults and $19.99 plus tax for seniors and for children 48" and under. Children under three are always free. Season passes, Double Park Season Passes, which entitles you to unlimited visits to Frontier City and White Water Bay, and group tickets for 10 or more are also available. Tickets may be purchased at the front gate, by phone, or on the park's Web site. If you wish to leave the park and return the same day, get your hand stamped at the main entrance and you will be readmitted at no extra charge. Due to special events, however, readmission may not always be allowed. Notices will be posted at the main entrance.

Several gift shops offering a wide variety of souvenirs and apparel are located in the park. The Frontier Trading Company is the largest gift shop, selling Frontier City apparel, stuffed animals, and other souvenirs. There is also an old-time portrait studio, offering guests the opportunity to have their photos taken wearing period costumes.

Frontier City offers a variety of food at numerous restaurants and snack bars located all around the park. Alcoholic beverages are served at some of the locations but are not permitted outside the park.

GAYLORD-PICKENS OKLAHOMA HERITAGE MUSEUM
Northwest 13th Street and Shartel Avenue
(405) 235-4458
www.oklahomaheritage.com

The Gaylord-Pickens museum provides visitors hands-on opportunities to learn about the famous and not-so-famous people who have made Oklahoma what it is today. Housed inside the refurbished Hefner Mansion, a historic landmark built in 1927, the museum houses electronic interactive exhibits that allow people to learn about Oklahoma's history.

Popular permanent exhibits include the Oklahoma Through Its People gallery, which focuses on the five characteristics that every Oklahoman shares—perseverance, individualism, optimism, pioneer spirit, and generosity. The 30 Oklahomans featured here are diverse in age, profession, ethnicity, and socioeconomic status, so that every guest can find someone with whom they can identify.

Also popular is the Oklahoma Hall of Fame gallery, which honors the more than 600 individuals who have been inducted since 1927. Computer touch screens allow guests to look up biographies, photos, and fun facts about inductees and even take a quiz to test their Oklahoma history knowledge.

The Gaylord-Pickens museum was named Best New Attraction in Oklahoma in 2008 by the Oklahoma Tourism Industry Association and the 2008–2009 Nickelodeon Parents' Pick for Teens in Oklahoma City.

The museum is open Tues through Fri from 9 a.m. to 5 p.m. and Sat from 10 a.m. to 5 p.m. It is closed Thanksgiving, Christmas, and New Year's Day. Admission is $7 for adults, $5 for seniors 62 and over, students ages 6 through 17, and free for children five and under. Free admission is offered every year on the museum's anniversary, May 10, and on or around Statehood Day.

HARN HOMESTEAD MUSEUM
1721 N. Lincoln Blvd.
(405) 235-4058
www.harnhomestead.com

The focus of the Harn Homestead Museum is Oklahoma's territorial period, from 1889 until statehood in 1907. On the grounds of this museum are houses, barns, a school, and outbuildings. They sit on what was originally the homestead of William Fremont Harn. Harn was a lawyer who came to the territory in 1891 to sort out hundreds of land disputes after the 1889 Land Run . When his job was abolished two years later, Harn stayed.

In 1986, he settled on a 160-acre homestead and built the museum's centerpiece, the Queen Anne–style farmhouse. The stone-and-wood exhibit barn, enclosing part of a windmill, is based on the original Harn barn. In addition to a carriage and farm equipment, the barn holds historical photos from prestatehood days. Two more farmhouses and another barn, along with vegetable and herb gardens, are located here. They are used to illustrate the daily life of pioneer families.

The museum is open Mon through Fri from 10 a.m. to 4 p.m., and from 10 a.m. to 2 p.m. the first Sat of each month. Admission is $5. Children ages three and under get in free.

HEARTLAND FLYER
Santa Fe Train Station
100 S. E.K. Gaylord
(800) 872-7245 (USA-RAIL)
www.heartlandflyer.com

Anyone who has not experienced a train ride should hop on the Heartland Flyer. It operates out of the same train station that brought settlers to Oklahoma City during the historic Land Run of 1889. The silver and blue beauty leaves the station every morning at 8:25 a.m. and makes a 418-mile roundtrip to Fort Worth, arriving back in Oklahoma City at 9:39 p.m. Along the way it stops at Norman, Purcell, Pauls Valley, Ardmore, and Gainesville, Texas.

The train is a push-pull operation, which means the superliner coaches are pushed down to Texas and pulled back up or vice versa. It runs on the Burlington Northern Santa Fe Railway tracks and is funded by a partnership between Texas, Oklahoma, and Amtrak.

Two refurbished superliner coaches run all the time with two more being added when needed. These coaches have reclining seats, large windows, and individual reading lights. One of the coaches on the lower level has 12 wheelchair-accessible seats on one end and restrooms on the other. A full-service cafe car is available with sofa-style seating. The cafe serves snacks, sandwiches, soft, drinks, and cocktails.

With all four coaches running, the flyer can carry 280 passengers. In June 2009, the Heartland Flyer celebrated its 10-year anniversary. In those 10 years, 640,000 people have ridden on the train. Rates range in price from $26 to $36 one-way.

INTERNATIONAL GYMNASTICS HALL OF FAME
2100 NE 52nd St. (inside the Science Museum)
(405) 364-5344
www.ighof.com
If you are interested in gymnastics, then head down to the exhibit located on the second floor of the Science Museum. Inside you will find portraits of the 68 inductees from 20 nations who have been instrumental in promoting the sport of gymnastics. The board of directors chooses their inductees from all over the world. Many are athletes, but not all. They include Mary Lou Retton, Stoyan Deltchev, Bela Karolyi, Karin Janz, Valery Liukin, Shannon Miller, Bart Conner, and Nadia Comaneci. Beside the portraits, visitors will find placards that provide information about the inductees. Included in the exhibit are videos and gymnastics equipment. This is an exhibit unlike any other. As a matter of fact, it can't be seen anywhere else in the world.

ISTVAN GALLERY
1218 N. Western Gallery
(405) 831-2874
http://istvangallery.com
At this art gallery visitors can expect to see a variety of artwork by local artists, including sculptures, glass, oil, acrylic, watercolor, and other mediums. There are quarterly exhibits throughout the year which feature a different artist and his or her artwork.

Istvan Gallery believes art comes in every form, so it hosts monthly story slams, film and video viewings, poetry readings, and other community events. Story slams are events where people get together to tell stories that revolve around a set topic. These events are free.

Visitors are allowed to take pictures. The gallery welcomes casual wear and is wheelchair accessible. There is no gift shop, but the artwork on display is for sale. Admission to the gallery is free. On-site parking is free. The gallery is open Tues and Thurs from 1:30 to 5 p.m., Sat and Sun from 1 to 5 p.m., and by appointment.

JOHN E. KIRKPATRICK HORTICULTURE CENTER
400 N. Portland
(405) 945-3358
www.osuokc.edu
Visitors who come here can see the center's 40 acres of horticulture teaching and demonstration gardens, as well as the All America Trial gardens. Oklahoma State University–Oklahoma City (OSU–OKC) is the only two-year college chosen to participate in the All American Selection trial gardens for flowers and vegetables. The winners of the trials are displayed in the gardens.

The John E. Kirkpatrick Horticulture Center was built in 1981. In the mid-1990s, the OSU–OKC Farmers' Market opened on the grounds and is now housed in and around the Horticulture Pavilion. In 2008, a new, state-of-the-art facility, the OSU–OKC Agriculture Resource Center, opened on the grounds and houses both the OSU–OKC Horticulture Department and Vet Tech Department.

Here visitors can see grounds which are carefully planned and planted with demonstration and display gardens for flowers, fruits, and vegetables, as well as tree and shrub collections and a five-hole golf course that is also used as a living teaching laboratory. The horticulture center is also home to the year-round OSU–OKC Farmers' Market on Sat. This market features products made in Oklahoma. A number of annual celebrations are held at the farmers' market throughout the year. For details of what's coming up at the farmers' market, check the Web site at www.osuokc.edu/agriculture. Admission is free.

MARTIN PARK NATURE CENTER
5000 W. Memorial Rd.
(405) 755-0676
www.okc.gov/parks/martin_park/index.html
This nature park gives visitors a break from the concrete jungle and lets them enjoy nature while still close to modern conveniences. The park is 140 acres in size and it a wildlife sanctuary and an environmental education area. There is a small nature museum here and 3.5 miles of hiking trails. The main trail is about a mile long. There are native plants and animals in the park. Guests will enjoy watching the squirrels gathering their food and the birds flying among the blackjack trees. There is not one time of year that is better than another for visiting. It's all good.

Admission to the park is free. There is plenty of parking and the entire park is wheelchair accessible.

The park is located in the far northwest corner of Oklahoma City, between North MacArthur Avenue and North Meridian off the Kilpatrick Turnpike on the south side of West Memorial Road. It is just west of Mercy Hospital. The gate is open Wed through Sun from 9 a.m. to 6 p.m. For information about education programming or special events, call the number above.

MELTON ART REFERENCE LIBRARY
4300 N. Sewell
(405) 525-3603
www.marl-okc.org
Are you interested in art and the artists who create great pieces? Whether you are a collector, student, dealer, or someone merely interested in learning more about artists, this library is for you. It is designed for the access of information on over 100,000 different artists. The library has over 5,000 research materials, including biographies, monographs, resource tomes, and sales catalogs. In addition, it houses sales records, reproductions, and individual articles on many lesser-known artists.

The library is open to the public Mon through Fri from 10 a.m. to 5 p.m. and admission is free.

Plan to spend an hour or all day reading and learning about different artists.

MYRIAD BOTANICAL GARDENS AND CRYSTAL BRIDGE TROPICAL CONSERVATORY
301 W. Reno
(405) 297-3995
www.myriadgardens.com
If you like plants, particularly tropical plants, the Myriad Botanical Gardens is a place you must visit. Located in downtown Oklahoma City, the grounds offer 17 acres of manicured lawns and gardens like the Meinders Garden featuring perennials and flowering shrubs and a two-acre lake filled with fish and water-loving plants. Situated in the middle of the acreage is the Crystal Bridge Conservatory. It has over 1,000 species of tropical and subtropical plants like begonias, bromeliads, gingers, orchids, palms and more.

Guest follow a gray, concrete path through the Conservatory and can take their time as they read about and admire the many plants presented here. Overhead is a cylindrical glass dome that gives guests the impression they are in a huge greenhouse. There are two different habitat regions represented here—the Tropical Rain Forest Zone and the Arid Tropical Zone.

The Garden Water Stage is located outside on the northwest side of the grounds. It is a lakeside amphitheatre. Through the year events like concerts, festivals, and Oklahoma Shakespeare in the Park are held here.

Special exhibits are common at the Myriad Botanical Gardens and usually begin each June and run through Nov or Dec.

Visitors are allowed to take pictures here. This is one of Oklahoma City's most photographed locales. Monopods are welcome inside the Crystal Bridge, but tripod use is restricted as it impedes traffic flow on the path. Please refer to the Web site or call for professional photography fees ad policies.

Visitors wishing to explore the tropic climates of the conservatory need to dress for the tropics, especially during Oklahoma's hot summer. The average temperature inside the Crystal Bridge remains a toasty 78 degrees, although that temperature can rise depending on the temperature outside. The humidity can also get quite high, especially along the wet mountain area, which mimics the bioclimate of a tropical rain forest.

The Crystal Bridge Gift Shop, located outside the main entrance to the Crystal Bridge, has a wide array of gift items for anyone on your list. Visitors will find everything from gardening statuary and accessories to children's toys and educational gifts, ornaments, jewelry, candles, and more.

There is not a restaurant or snack bar on the premises, however soft drinks, bottled water, and candy are available for purchase in the gift shop during regular business hours.

Most areas in the Crystal Bridge are wheelchair accessible. There is an elevator which can transport visitors from the first to third levels.

Parking is available in the visitors' lot on the northwest corner of Reno and Robinson (across from the Cox Convention Center). Parking is $6 per car and includes one free adult admission to the Crystal Bridge Tropical Conservatory.

The outdoor grounds are open from 7 a.m. to 11 p.m. unless otherwise noted. The Crystal Bridge Tropical Conservatory is open Mon through Sat from 9 a.m. to 6 p.m. and Sun from noon to 6 p.m.

Admission is $6 for adults, $5 for seniors 62 and over and students 13 to 18 or with valid college ID, $3 for children 4 to 12, and free for children under 12. Coupons for $1 off admission can be found in *Key Magazine* and other local publications in Oklahoma City. Limit one coupon per person.

NATIONAL COWBOY HALL OF FAME AND WESTERN HERITAGE CENTER
1700 NE 63rd St.
(405) 478-2250
www.nationalcowboymuseum.org
Founded in 1955, this museum sits on a hill off I-44 to the north and is a giant as far as museums go. The museum's 12 galleries, encompassing thousands of square feet, present different aspects of the West, showing the broad spectrum of western heritage and art. Each year, this

museum welcomes close to 10 million visitors.

Prosperity Junction, Art of the American West, Native American Gallery, Western Performers Gallery, and the Children's Cowboy Corral are only a few of the different areas of the museum. Prosperity Junction is real-size replica of a Western town. Visitors can step inside a frontier school, church, blacksmith shop, and railroad depot. Don't neglect the barbed wire room. Drawers pull out to show visitors the many different types of barbed wire used in the American west. The 15,000-square-foot Art of the American West exhibits paintings and sculptures. At its entrance is the 18-foot-tall marble Canyon Princess made by sculpture Gerald Balciar. Inside the Native American Gallery, visitors will see how the Native American's lived through exhibits showing their culture. The Western Performers Gallery features such western notables as John Wayne, Barbara Stanwyck, and Tom Selleck. The Children's Cowboy Corral is an interactive discovery area for children. Here, children can dress up in spurs and chaps and even hop a ride on an imaginary horse. After exploring the west end of the museum, be sure to check out the five Windows to the West paintings at the east end in the Sam Noble Special Events Center.

If you get hungry, across the hall from the events center is the museum's restaurant, Persimmon Hill. Decorated with blue cornflowers and yellow sunflowers, it is a full-service restaurant overlooking another one of the museum's attractions, the Western States Plaza pool and fountains. There is a buffet in addition to a full menu. Try one of the restaurants decadent desserts, such as chocolate Italian cream cake, strawberry torte, or bread pudding. The restaurant is open daily from 11 a.m. to 3:30 p.m.

On your way out, stop by and pick up a souvenir from the Museum Store. Located at the entrance on the west side, visitors will find jewelry, pottery, books, food items, and more.

The museum's hours are 9 a.m. to 5 p.m. daily. It is closed Thanksgiving, Christmas, and New Year's Day. As the museum is extensive, comfortable clothing and shoes are strongly encouraged. It is wheelchair accessible. In some galleries, visitors are allowed to take pictures. The museum map indicates where photographing is allowed.

i **Got some time to read? Check out these three unique and different books on Oklahoma:** *Roadside History of Oklahoma* **by Francis L. Fugate,** *Oklahoma Place Names* **by George H. Shirk, and** *Ghost Towns of Oklahoma* **by John W. Morris.**

NATIONAL SOFTBALL HALL OF FAME
2801 NE 50th St.
(405) 424-5266
www.asasoftball.com/hall_of_fame
If you are interested in softball, then this is the museum for you. Visitors here will see memorabilia of the greatest softball players in the United States. Colorful exhibits trace the history of the sport from its invention in 1887 to the present. If time permits and a game is scheduled, visitors can watch an actual softball competition in the renowned Hall of Fame Stadium, which annually hosts some of the most prestigious events in the sport including the NCAA College World Series. Guests won't want to miss the Olympic Room which has pictures and memorabilia from the three gold-medal winning U.S. teams. There is a timeline tracing the Amateur Softball Association from its beginning in 1933 to the present.

Besides being a hall of fame and museum, this location is also the headquarters of softball's national governing body, the Amateur Softball Association, which celebrated its 75th anniversary in 2008.

Two premier events in softball, the NCAA College World Series and the World Cup of Softball, are held at the ASA Hall of Fame Stadium just northwest of the museum building.

There is a gift shop located on the first floor. It sells items like books, videotapes, T-shirts, hats, and jackets. The museum is wheelchair accessible. Admission is $6 for adults, and $3 for children 12 and under. Admission to games depends on the event. The museum is closed on the weekends from Oct through Apr, but open weekdays. Weekday hours are Mon through Fri,

9 a.m. to 4 p.m. May through Sept and weekend hours are Sat 10 a.m. to 4 p.m. and Sun from 1 to 4 p.m.

99'S MUSEUM OF WOMEN PILOTS
4300 Amelia Earhart Rd.
(405) 685-9990
www.museumofwomenpilots.com
This museum features the history of women pilots, from the early 20th century to today. It is one of the few museums in the world solely dedicated to the history of women pilots. There are permanent exhibits on Amelia Earhart, the Women's Air Force Service Pilots (WASP), and airline, military, and international women pilots. In 2009, the museum is adding a flight simulator and some audio-visual displays.

An open house, called the Aviation Celebration, is held annually. It is held on a Sat in early June. There are a number of activities for children and families to introduce them to the museum and the history of women pilots. The open house is free to the public.

The museum is located on the second story and there is an elevator available. All exhibits are wheelchair accessible. Casual and comfortable clothing is recommended. Visitors are allowed to take pictures. The gift shop has books by and about women pilots for adults and children, T-shirts, mugs, posters, jewelry, and aviation toys.

The museum is open Mon through Fri from 9 a.m. to 4 p.m. and on Sat from 10 a.m. to 4 p.m and closed most major holidays. Admission is $5 for adults, $4 for seniors 65 and over, and $3 for students.

OKLAHOMA CITY'S ADVENTURE DISTRICT
822 N. Broadway Ave.
(405) 290-7529
www.okcadventure.com
In 1999, northeast Oklahoma City was home to seven of the state's most outstanding attractions—all within a 2-mile radius. However, tourists often visited one attraction, not aware that others were just around the corner. In 2000, these attractions—the National Cowboy & Western Heritage Museum, the Oklahoma City

Zoo and Botanical Garden, Cinemark Tinseltown USA Theatre, Remington Park Racing Casino, the Oklahoma State Firefighters Museum, the Science Museum, and the ASA National Softball Hall of Fame—began combining their resources in cooperation with Frontier Country Marketing Association to promote the area as an entertainment destination for tourists and local residents.

By 2003, the Adventure District was recognized by the City Council of Oklahoma City as an official entertainment district. Oklahoma City's Adventure District is funded by its members, the seven charter attractions, and by its marketing partners.

Today, more than 3 million people visit the district each year, not only to watch a great horse race or softball game but also to visit 2,200 exotic animals, learn about space, try on firefighting gear, watch Hollywood's greatest movies, and see John Wayne paraphernalia. The district is a complete vacation getaway for all members of the family. Special discounts can be found in the district's brochure, which may be requested by phone, and on the Web site. Coupons are available to download. The district's exclusive hotel partner, the Sheraton Oklahoma City Hotel, located in downtown Oklahoma City, offers special packages on hotel stays and attraction tickets on its Web site at www.sheraton.com/okadventures.

OKLAHOMA CITY MUSEUM OF ART
415 Couch Dr.
(405) 236-3100
www.okcmoa.com

The Oklahoma City Museum of Art offers visitors more than three floors exhibiting fine works of art. The museum's Special Exhibitions Gallery, located on the ground floor, presents national and international traveling exhibits. The second and third floor galleries display works from the museum's permanent collection. The museum is home to the world's most comprehensive Dave Chihuly collection of glassworks and also has the tallest glass tower in the world at 55 feet. The museum also offers films and arts education.

The Museum Store is located on the ground floor. It offers a wide variety of merchandise, including books on key artists, music, decorative objects, and jewelry. It also has a children's section and and a section dedicated to Dave Chihuly.

The Museum Café serves lunch, dinner, and Sun brunch. It is located on the ground floor of the museum as well. The cafe's metropolitan ambience, superb cuisine, and exceptional service bring a taste of Chicago, San Francisco, and London to Oklahoma City. The full-service restaurant offers fine dining with a French flair. Patio tables are available for seasonal dining along with an array of coffees, teas, espressos, cappuccino, and a full bar. Dinner and Sun brunch reservations are suggested. Call (405) 235-6262.

The museum is located downtown. On weekdays parking is $1 for two hours at a meter or $8 in a parking lot north of the museum. On weekends, meters are free. The museum is wheelchair accessible and it provides wheelchairs as well as strollers free of charge.

Admission is $12 for adults, $10 for seniors and students, and free for children under five and museum members.

OKLAHOMA CITY NATIONAL MEMORIAL & MUSEUM
620 N. Harvey Ave.
(405) 235-3313
www.oklahomacitynationalmemorial.org

The 1995 bombing of the Alfred P. Murrah Federal Building in Oklahoma City changed our nation and our world. It remains the costliest act of domestic terrorism on American soil. The Oklahoma City National Memorial & Museum offers a breathtaking glimpse of the hope and resilience this community and this nation showed in the face of unspeakable tragedy. The Outdoor Symbolic Memorial and the Memorial Museum form the site. The site incorporates many symbolic elements, including monumental Gates of Time, the Field of Empty Chairs, the Survivor Tree, the Reflecting Pool, and a special children's area.

The Outdoor Symbolic Memorial incorporates the space where the Murrah building once stood, the adjacent street, and the nearby area where the Survivor Tree stands. The symbolic memorial is open 24 hours a day, 365 days a year. A cell phone tour featuring the designers of the site is available for visitors.

The Memorial Museum is in the historic Journal Record Building on the Northwest end of the Outdoor Symbolic Memorial. The Memorial Museum tells the story of the Murrah building bombing, the response that followed, and how the experience changed the lives of those involved forever. Each person who steps off the elevator into the Oklahoma City National Memorial Museum is taken back in time to that beautiful spring morning of Apr 19, 1995. Traveling through the day, weeks, months, and years since the bombing, visitors hear the story and experience firsthand the impact of the violence. Visitors leave the museum knowing the courage of a community whose spirit would not be destroyed. They will clearly understand the hope of a nation that refuses to be defeated by terrorism.

The Memorial Store features hundreds of items from apparel and books to children's toys and home accessories.

Personal (noncommercial) photos are allowed to be taken on the Outdoor Symbolic Memorial and in the Memorial Museum lobby. Photographs are not permitted in the Memorial Museum exhibit areas.

Paid public parking is available in several areas surrounding the Oklahoma City National Memorial & Museum, including public lots and metered spaces around the site. The memorial does not offer any parking.

In 2009, admission is $10 for adults, $8 for seniors 62 and over, $6 for students six to college age with valid college ID, and free for children five and under. The Outdoor Symbolic Memorial is open 24 hours a day, seven days a week. The Memorial Museum is open Mon to Sat from 9 a.m. to 6 p.m. and Sun 1 to 6 p.m. The last ticket is sold at 5 p.m. daily. The Memorial Museum is closed New Year's Day, Thanksgiving, Christmas Eve day, and Christmas Day.

The Oklahoma City National Memorial & Museum is an affiliate of the National Park Service and does not receive any funds from federal, state, or local government. Museum admissions, store sales, the Oklahoma City Memorial Marathon, earnings from an endowment, and private fund-raising allow the memorial and museum to be self-sustaining.

OKLAHOMA GOVERNOR'S MANSION
820 NE 23rd
(405) 522-8871
www.governor.state.ok.us
The Dutch colonial Oklahoma Governor's Mansion, once leaky and dowdy, received a one-million-dollar facelift and coverage in *Architectural Digest* several years ago. Highlights of the renovations to the 1928 mansion, made through a collaboration of seven interior designers, are rugs woven with the names of Oklahoma's governors and an image of the state seal, a Montgolfier chandelier, and art on loan from Oklahoma museums. Free tours are conducted on Wed from 12 to 2 p.m., except in Dec and Jan.

OKLAHOMA HISTORY CENTER
2401 N. Laird Ave.
(405) 522-5248
www.okhistorycenter.org
Across the street from the capitol, sitting on the northeast side of Lincoln and 23rd is the Oklahoma History Center. This 18-acre, three-story, 215,000-square-foot center is home to five state-of-the-art galleries, a huge library, and archives. Visitors will learn not only about the Native American culture of Oklahoma, but also about its sports heroes, arts and crafts, and dust bowl days. The center also exhibits some Oklahoma landmark inventions, like the shopping cart, parking meter, and trencher, a machine that digs trenches. The Gemini 6 space capsule, a Civil War cannon, and a wagon from the Land Run of 1889 also have a home here. After visitors absorb Oklahoma history through the exhibits, they might want to check out their ancestry. The center's library and archives are a must for genealogists and those looking to see if they might be on the Indian rolls.

While exploring this complex, visitors may find they are hungry. By taking the stairs or eleva-

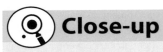

Close-up

Oklahoma City Zoo

One of the premiere attractions in Oklahoma City is the Oklahoma City Zoo (2101 NE 50th St., 405-424-3344, www.okczoo.com). It is the state's number-one attraction. The zoo is also an accredited botanical garden. The incredible community support it receives allows for the development of state-of-the-art animal environments and makes the zoo one of the top accredited zoos in North America. The zoo currently utilizes 110 landscape acres with 203 total acres available, including a lake.

The zoo's animal collection features over 2,200 creatures from around the globe. Many of the animals are endangered or a part of important conservation efforts. Bears, sea lions, snakes, gorillas, and African lions thrill visitors of all ages. The zoo also offers family-friendly rides, playgrounds, and diverse educational programs. Favorite exhibits and rides include Great Escape, Cat Forest/Lion Overlook, swan paddleboats, the safari tram, the endangered species carousel, Aquaticus, and Oklahoma Trails. Oklahoma Trails, the zoo's newest addition, is 8 acres. The $10.3-million naturalistic habitat is a wonder to behold. A suspended, wooden boardwalk takes visitors past cougars, bobcats, turkey vultures, black bears, river otters, and Mexican gray wolves. A new children's zoo is scheduled to open in the spring of 2010 and Expedition Asia, showcasing elephants and other Asian species in the most elaborate undertaking in zoo's history, is scheduled to open 2012.

The zoo has numerous gift shops which carry plush animal toys, books, gift cards, ecofriendly items, apparel, sculptures, animal created paintings, and much more. There are also snack bars and restaurants on the premises that sell hamburgers, hot dogs, pizza, smoothies, salads, and other kid-friendly choices.

Seven or eight events are held at the zoo every year. For more information on these events, look in the "Events" chapter of this book or check the zoo's Web site. One of their premier events is Haunt the Zoo for Halloween, a six-night, family-friendly trick or treat. The Ostrich Egg Breakfast is another popular event. The price varies each year. Entertainment and unique collectible T-shirt keepsakes are part of the festivities.

The zoo is open daily from 9 a.m. to 5 p.m. It is closed Thanksgiving, Christmas, and New Year's Day. Spring, early summer, and fall are especially beautiful as the botanical aspects of the zoo are in full regalia. Since the zoo is fairly large and there is a fair amount of walking, comfortable shoes are recommended. State law prohibits smoking inside the zoo.

Admission is $7 for adults, $4 for seniors 65 and over and children 3 to 11, and free for children two and under. The best deal at the zoo is a ZooFriend Membership. For a nominal price, individuals who join will receive unlimited admission to the zoo for one year, quarterly members-only newsletters, invitations to Family Fun Night and special events, and more. There are several levels of membership so almost anyone can join.

tor upstairs to the Winnie Mae café, located on the third floor, they'll discover drinks and sandwiches. The Oklahoma History Center is open Mon through Sat 9 a.m. to 5 p.m. and Sun from noon to 5 p.m. Admission is $5 for adults, $4 for seniors 65 and over, $3 for students, and free for children five and under.

OKLAHOMA NATIONAL STOCKYARDS
107 Livestock Exchange Building
(405) 235-8675
www.onsy.com

The Oklahoma National Stockyards is the world's largest stocker and feeder cattle market. It originally opened in 1910, three years after statehood and is two miles southwest of downtown Oklahoma City. In 1915, Morris, Wilson, and Armour established and operated packing facilities here. Faced with complete overhaul, the plants decided to close in 1961. This did not hurt the area as sales went from private agreement between seller and buyer to public auction.

Today, auctions are held every Mon and Tues morning. Each week, approximately 10,000 head of cattle are bought and sold. Tourists are welcome and encouraged to sit in on the auction and walk over the catwalk. The catwalk is a long, overhead bridge that allows you to look over the cattle pens and walks you to the auction barn. Going into the stockyards is like going back in time.

While visitors will see lots of cowboys wearing jeans, boots, and cowboy hats, visitors should wear clothing they feel comfortable in. Parking is ample and free.

OKLAHOMA RAILWAY MUSEUM
3400 NE Grand Blvd.
(405) 424-8222
www.oklahomarailwaymuseum.org
How would you like to take a ride on a real passenger train and visit a red caboose, an authentic dining car, or a Pullman car that once ferried generations across the country? At the Oklahoma Railway Museum, you can do that and more.

The museum is an educational experience for both young and old. It provides the experience of railroad travel either in a 1940s or 1950s streamliner passenger train once operated across the state.

The museum operates a variety of different diesel locomotives and passenger equipment from the 1920s to the 1950s. In addition, there are many pieces of freight equipment and display locomotives. The museum also houses artifacts from the Oklahoma Railway Company that operated the trolley system across Oklahoma City until it was shut down in 1946. The depot is the restored 1905 depot from Oakwood, Oklahoma, that served the Kansas City, Mexico, and Orient Railroad, which was later purchased by the Santa Fe Railroad. The trains operate over the former

Missouri, Kansas, and Texas railroad line (the Katy) in Northeast Oklahoma City.

Train rides are available on the first and third Sat of each month, Apr to Aug, the first Sat in Sept, and the third Sat in Oct. The train leaves Oakwood Depot at the museum at 10 a.m., 11 a.m., noon, 1:30 p.m., and 2:30 p.m. Tickets are $8 for guests 15 and over, $5 for children 3 to 14, and free for children under 3.

OKLAHOMA STATE CAPITOL
2300 N. Lincoln Blvd.
(405) 522-0836
www.ok.gov
www.oklahomadome.com
Turn onto Lincoln Boulevard from I-44 heading south and it's impossible to miss the capitol. It is the centerpiece of Lincoln. In 1910, a homesteader, William Fremont Harn donated 40 acres to Oklahoma City for the Capitol. The Capitol building would sit in what was once Harn's pasture land. The state capitol had been located in Guthrie, north of Oklahoma City about 40 miles, but was moved to the City after much haranguing and a U.S. Supreme Court decision.

The original design sported a dome on top of the Capitol, but with World War I and a steep shortage, plans for a dome right away were scratched. The Capitol was completed in 1917. For years, politicians and citizens spoke of adding the dome, but there was always some cause for postponing. Finally, in 2002, the dome was completed at an estimated cost or $20 to $21 million. On top of the dome is a 22-foot bronze statue of an Indian called *The Guardian*.

The inside ceiling is literally a work of art. Murals illustrate the history of Oklahoma from Francisco Vasquez de Coronado's visit to the area in 1541 to the forced march of southeastern tribes to Indian Territory in the 1830s to the 1889 Land Run. Artist Charles Banks Wilson also painted full-length portraits of state heroes, including Sequoyah and Will Rogers. Full-length portraits of Sequoyah and Will Rogers, painted by artist Charles Banks Wilson, can also be seen at the Capitol.

Oil wells dot the lawn of the Capitol complex. Petunia Number One, named after the flower bed it was drilled in sits outside the north door. Even though it is not operational now, it is a reminder of Oklahoma's glory days, when oil was king. East of the oil rig, guests will find a 37 flag plaza. These flags represent the federally recognized Native American tribes headquartered in Oklahoma.

The state capitol is at 23rd Street and North Lincoln Boulevard. Tours are conducted hourly Mon through Fri from 9 a.m. to 3 p.m. Tours are not conducted from 12 to 1 p.m.. A self-guided tour brochure is available for weekends. The capitol is open every day except Thanksgiving and Christmas. Use the west entrance lower level. For tour information call (405) 521-3356.

OKLAHOMA STATE FAIR SPEEDWAY
500 Land Rush St.
(405) 948-6796
www.statefairspeedway.com
The State Fair Speedway is a $3/8$-mile clay oval dirt track located on the historic state fairgrounds. Auto racing at the speedway has been a summer staple since 1954. The State Fair Speedway is one of the premier racetracks in the Southwest. The grandstands are featured in the 1962 movie, *State Fair*, starring Pat Boone and Ann-Margaret. Some of the top drivers in auto racing have competed on this speedway on their way to national fame. They offer fans and sponsors great value for their dollar. Every Fri night from Mar through Aug they offer exciting races with special shows in Oct. They feature open wheel sprint cars and full-bodied cars as well.

Fans are encouraged to visit the pit area after the races where they can meet their favorite driver, collect autographs, take photos, and even sit in race cars. Comfortable clothing, jeans, T-shirts, sweatshirts, and tennis shoes are encouraged. Fans are also encouraged to bring hats, gloves, blankets, and jackets at the start of the season as the temperature often drops once the sun goes down. Auto racing is a loud event so for small children or first-time guest, earplugs or protective ear wear is advised.

The speedway has plenty of free parking right outside the grandstand gates. There is plenty of handicap parking and ramps, and a spe-

cial section for wheelchairs on the ground level.

There is a souvenir booth that sells T-shirts, hats, die-cast cars, checkered flags, and earplugs.

Concession stands are open during the races. Food includes corn dogs, curly fries, hamburgers, pretzels, hot dogs, chicken baskets, nachos, and popcorn.

Please check out the Web site for ticket information as the touring shows vary in cost. A typical Fri night show is $10 for adults, $7 for seniors 65 and over and students 12 to 17, $2 for children 6 to 11, and free for children 5 and under.

The speedway offers a variety of free admission nights starting Apr 17 with Oklahoma City Night. There are also Fan Appreciation Night and a School's Out Bash, where kids 15 and under are admitted free with a paid adult admission.

i **If you are looking for more information on Oklahoma and its history, visit www.blogoklahoma.us. In 2006, this blog was the Okie Blog Award winner for Best Culture Blog.**

OKLAHOMA STATE FIREFIGHTERS MUSEUM
2716 NE 50th St.
(405) 424-3440
www.osfa.info
On a visit to this museum, visitors can see antique firefighting equipment, like fire trucks from 1910, 1920, and 1928. There is a replica of an old firehouse, modern firefighting equipment, a patch collection, and a mural painted by artist Lynn Campbell. The mural depicts different pieces of firefighting equipment from the period of the horse-drawn steamer to the mid-1950s. In the main hall of the museum, guests will see the Murrah Memorial. It acknowledges the Apr 19, 1995, bombing of the Alfred P. Murrah Federal Building. This museum has the distinction of being the only fire museum owned and operated by firefighters.

Children will enjoy the Junior Firefighter Activity Center playground. It has fire safety messages and teaches children about life and fire

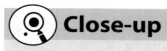 **Close-up**

Science Museum Oklahoma

Formally the Omniplex (2100 Northeast 52nd St., 405-602-6664, www.sciencemuseumok.org), the institution's name change to Science Museum Oklahoma was the first step in an exciting plan that will launch the museum to national prominence. Since the name change in Nov 2007, the museum has opened five new exhibits and is in the process of developing and building more. The constant state of evolution keeps visitors excited about returning to the museum time and time again to see what's new. The exhibits open now at the museum are Kidspace, Gadget Trees, the Tinkering Garage, the Train Exhibit, Aviation, Destination Space, and the Planetarium.

All kinds of activities await guests at Kidspace. The are brain-teasers for kids of all ages, blocks, puppets, and facepainting to choose from at this exhibit. Babies and toddlers have a play area and older kids can play in the currents building dams or having water fights.

Next is Gadget Trees. It has one of the largest trees in North America, a two story tree house, and the tallest spiral slide in Oklahoma. Welcomed by the sound of a soothing brook and birds singing, visitors learn about how science interacts with nature when they enter this exhibit. There is much to see, learn, and do here.

In the Tinkering Garage, children of all ages are encouraged to build, dream up, investigate and design with hands-on projects. Some of the tools, visitors will see and can use are Bumpity Blocks, Legos, and a peg wall.

Be sure to visit the Train Exhibit here. It is located in the south west part of the building. Here guests can marvel at the 1000 square foot miniature town and the Pullman car.

For guests who are interested in air flight, they'll want to visit the Aviation and Space exhibit. Here guests will find World War II parachutes, the Mercury Capsule Simulator, a 1946 Stinson Voyager, airplanes, astronaut uniforms and more. Be sure to visit the Oklahoma Aviation and Space Hall of Fame before you leave.

The newest exhibit is Destination Space. It lets visitors investigate and explore what it's really like to be an astronaut. The actual Apollo Command Module Mission Simulator is always a big hit.

Since 1985, the Planetarium has shown guests what's in our galaxy and what is beyond it in other parts of the universe. Oklahoma's first public-access planetarium, there are daily shows and occasionally astronomy events are held here. On Jan 11, 2006, NASA's mural-sized Hubble Space Telescope image was uncovered. Guests can enjoy the image displayed by the Planetarium.

Besides these exhibits, the Dome Theater, Red Earth Gallery, and International Gymnastics Hall of Fame are located inside the museum complex. Museum hours are Mon through Fri from 9 a.m. to 5 p.m., Sat from 9 a.m. to 6 p.m., and Sun from 11 a.m. to 6 p.m. It is closed Thanksgiving, Christmas eve, and Christmas Day.

Museum admission is $9.95 for visitors 13 to 64 and $8.75 for seniors 65 and over and children 3 to 12. Admission includes a complimentary planetarium show based on seating availability. Prices here fluctuate depending on if there is a traveling exhibit. Please call ahead or check the Web site for admission to other areas inside the museum. Membership options are available as well. Hours and prices here are subject to change without notice. Picture taking is encouraged.

safety. Adults will enjoy the audio tour, which brings the museum to life.

Parking is free in front of the building and the museum is wheelchair accessible. Hours are Mon through Sat from 9 a.m. to 4:30 p.m. and Sun from 1 to 4:30 p.m. It is closed major holidays. Admission is $5 for adults, $4 for seniors 56 and over, $2 for children between 6 and 12, and free for children under six.

ORR FAMILY FARM
14400 S. Western
(405) 799-3276
www.orrfamilyfarm.com
There's a lot to do for adults and children alike at this farm. The owners expect you to "come and have a good time." And who couldn't with all there is to do. Visitors can ride the train. It holds about 100 people and looks, puffs, and sounds like a steam engine, but for safety reasons is a diesel. When that activity is over, guests can go fishing, ride a carousel, pet animals, take a pony ride, ride the pedal cars, jump on the Jumping Pillows, or watch Jethro P. Hogg, an animatron who sits on a stool, and sings and plays guitar. If that doesn't hold your attention, what about making your way through a maze or mining for gemstones at the Neal Simpson Mine?

Besides the guest activities, this is a working horse farm. With 240 stalls, the Orr Family Farm is considered the largest horse-training center in Oklahoma.

The farm has two gift shops, which sell private-label fudge, jellies, and jams. At the snack bar, guests can settle down to barbeque brisket, hot dogs, chili dogs, and snow cones.

There is an asphalt parking lot. Dress is always casual here. A great many children come here on field trips during the week. The farm is open to the general public on Fri evening from 6 to 8 p.m. and on Sat from 10 a.m. to 6 p.m. Prices vary according to the activity.

OVERHOLSER MANSION
405 NW 15th St.
(405) 528-8485
www.nscda.org/museums/oklahoma.htm

This 1904 three-story, French chateau–style house, was built by Henry Overholser, who came to Oklahoma Territory in the Land Run of 1889. Inside, the home still contains the original furnishings of the family, including Brussels lace curtains and English carpets. Some of the walls of the 15-room house are hung with handpainted canvas and the rooms are filled with heavy mahogany, oak, and teak furniture and brocade covered sofas. The house is now owned by the Oklahoma Historical Society. With the assistance of the National Society of Colonial Dames of America, Historical Preservation, the Women's Architectural League, and Friends of the Overholser, this museum was restored and is open to the public. Museum hours are Tues through Sat from 10 a.m. to 3 p.m. It is closed Mon, state holidays, and the month of Jan. Admission is $3 for adults, $2.50 for seniors, $1 for children 6 to 18, and free for children under six.

PELICAN BAY AQUATIC CENTER (EDMOND)
1034 S. Bryant
(405) 216-7649
http://edmondok.com/parks/pelicanbay
Pelican Bay is a family-oriented water park without throngs of people. It operates with a maximum number of 600 guests in the park at one time. The park is an exciting place for every member of the family. It features a spray deck with interactive features for curious infants and toddlers and an aquatic playground with more interactive features and a double slide. Guests can float through Salamander Springs or take a spin in the vortex pool. For the more adventurous Pelican Bay offers two body slides and a rock-climbing wall.

In 2009, two sand volleyball courts were added where guests can strike up a game or join a volleyball league. Overlooking the courts is a pool deck, allowing families to lounge in the sun or enjoy a delicious snack from the Pelican Bay Café. No glass containers, ice chests, or coolers are allowed on the premises. This is for everyone's safety. The cafe offers treats, drinks, appetizers, and meals.

Street clothes are not allowed in the water. Swimsuits must be worn by anyone entering the water and infants and toddlers must wear swim diapers.

Admission is $4 for children five and under and $7 for children six and up. Admission price is also $7 for adults. Infants who cannot walk are free. Parking is free and if the west lot is full, there is overflow parking in Hafer Park, on the east side of the center, with convenient access via the wheelchair-accessible bridge.

Pelican Bay prides itself on having highly trained and experienced staff. Lifeguards are always on duty. The center is open from 1 to 8 p.m. Mon through Wed and 1 to 7 p.m. Thurs through Fri. From Memorial Day to Labor Day it is also open 11 a.m. to 6 p.m. Sat and 1 to 6 p.m. Sun. Fri through Sun are the busiest days.

RED EARTH MUSEUM
2100 NE 52nd St. (inside the Science Museum)
(405) 427-5228
www.redearth.org
Casual attire and comfortable shoes are recommended for visits to this museum. Always interesting Native American artwork can be found here. This museum houses over 1400 items of detailed beadwork, textiles, incredible basketry, pottery and fine art in its collection. Visitors will want to take their time and appreciate the treasures displayed. The Red Earth Museum has the only collection of Native American totem poles in the region. It is also home to the renowned Deupree Cradleboard Collection. This exclusive collection is one of the best in North America.

Since the museum is located inside Science Museum Oklahoma, admission to the Red Earth Museum is free with paid admission into the Science Museum. There is a gift shop inside the museum complex. Hours are Mon through Fri from 9 a.m. to 5 p.m., Sat from 9 a.m. to 6 p.m., and Sun from 11 a.m. to 6 p.m.

REMINGTON PARK
1 Remington Place
(405) 424-1000
www.remingtonpark.com

Remington Park is a state-of-the-art entertainment center that includes horse racing and casino gaming. It is one of the leading tourism sites in Oklahoma and has received numerous awards for its customer service and guest amenities. It was built in 1988 at a cost of more than $100 million. In 2000, a $31-million casino was added. The center is 333,000 square feet and sits on 375 acres. It includes a row of private suites overlooking the racetrack and several upscale restaurants, such as Silks Fine Dining and Remis Buffet.

Besides the casino gaming area, which offers games for penny players and high rollers, Remington Park offers thoroughbred and quarter-horse racing and is regarded as one of the leading racetracks in the country. There are hundreds of monitors throughout the facilities to show live racing and simulcasts from tracks throughout the country.

Remington Park hosts numerous special events throughout the year, including several major racing events with purses in excess of $100,000. In addition, ethnic food festivals, family fun nights, free merchandise nights, regular rewards for the Lucky Circle 20 Club, bands, and other entertainment go on throughout the year.

All parking is free, including valet parking at the casino as well as the racetrack clubhouse.

Hours are Sun through Wed from 10 a.m. to midnight, Thurs from 10 a.m. to 2 a.m., and Fri and Sat from 10 a.m. to 3 a.m. Simulcasts are shown seven days a week starting at 10 a.m.

THE RODEO OPRY
2221 Exchange Ave.
(405) 297-9773
www.rodeoopry.com
Governor Brad Henry declared this attraction "Oklahoma's Official Country Music Show." It is located in historic Stockyards City. The Opry Heritage Foundation of Oklahoma operates the Rodeo Opry. The foundation's goal is to educate committed entertainers and help advance their skills as they pursue their interest in country and western music. The organization is non-profit.

The opry was started over 30 years ago by Oklahoma legend and founder Grant Leftwich.

Artist development workshops and showcase concerts are scheduled throughout the year as well as the popular Writers from the Row Workshop and Concert Series, where country music's top writers come to Oklahoma and facilitate songwriting critiques, workshops, and performances. Popular songwriters such as Steve Seskin, Barbara Cloyd, Jason Matthew, Bryan White, Jeff Wood, and Julie Vassar-Wood have all led successful workshops and concerts.

Parking is free in the stockyards area. The facility is wheelchair accessible. The snack bar sells Coca-Cola products, candy bars, nachos, root beer floats, water, and coffee.

The regular Rodeo Opry show is every Sat at 7:30 p.m., excluding holiday weekends such as July 4th, Memorial Weekend, Thanksgiving, and Christmas. Special events are scheduled at a variety of times throughout the week and year. Tickets are $10 plus tax for adults and $6 plus tax for children.

ROUTE 66 PARK
9901 NW 23rd St.
(405) 297-3903

Route 66 Park is the first themed park in the Oklahoma City Parks and Recreation Department, and it is dedicated to the "Mother Road." Route 66 Park is not on SR 66, but adjacent to it. It is located about a mile south of SR 66 on the west side of Oklahoma City's Lake Overholser.

A plaza area with inlaid tile provides visitors a bird's-eye view of the historic road's route from the skyscrapers of downtown Chicago to the Santa Monica Pier. This greater-than-life-size map includes 34 landmarks along the route, which crosses through eight states.

In addition, the Cyrus Avery Observation Tower gives visitors a sweeping, panoramic view of the 148-acre park's three ponds, as well as Lake Overholser. An outdoor plaza and amphitheater is the perfect place for small concerts and outdoor events, and picnic shelters abut a themed Route 66 playground. The tower is open only to persons who rent the plaza area for special events.

Anglers will love the fishing opportunities in the park's wetland ponds. A series of plank walkways and bridges take visitors through the wetlands where they can observe native wildlife, as well as fish for largemouth bass, channel catfish, blue catfish, crappie, and flathead catfish.

Several projects from the park master plan are underway. A new Skate Plaza for boarders and bikers opened in the Summer 2009. The park is open daily from 8 a.m. to 11 p.m.

SAM NOBLE OKLAHOMA MUSEUM OF NATURAL HISTORY
University of Oklahoma Campus
2401 Chautauqua Ave.
(405) 325-4712
www.snomnh.ou.edu

This museum with its 50,000 square feet of exhibit space is the nation's largest university-based museum. It has five galleries and exhibits that give visitors an in-depth tour of more than 300 million years of Oklahoma's natural history.

The Hall of Ancient Life exhibit takes visitors on an adventure through more than 4 billion years of Earth's history. In the Hall of People of Oklahoma, visitors learn how the state's first people lived and worked thousands of years ago. Experience the bison hunt and see the Cooper Skull, the oldest painted object from the New World. Also here, visitors will get to see a collection of artifacts representing many of the tribes living in Oklahoma today. The Hall of Natural Wonders shows visitors the sights and sounds of Oklahoma's native landscape, while the Gallery of World Cultures features cultural rarities from all over the world.

This museum has unique exhibits, like the two Guinness-World-Record-holding dinosaurs *Pentaceratops* (world's largest dinosaur skull) and the head and neck of *Sauroposeidon* (world's tallest dinosaur).

Visitors are allowed to take pictures of all permanent exhibits. Sometimes there are restrictions against photos in special exhibitions. Those galleries are clearly marked when that is the case. If you are in doubt, ask.

The museum temperature is usually cool, so a light sweater might be a good idea. Also remember you will be walking and the museum is large. Comfortable shoes will make your visit more enjoyable. The museum gift shop, Excavations, is a natural history store. It offers souvenirs, books, educational toys, jewelry, decorative items, Native American art, and more.

If hunger strikes while you are visiting, the Redbud Café serves ready-made sandwiches, soups, coffee, snacks, and desserts. It is open Tues through Sat from 10 a.m. to 3 p.m. It is closed on Sun.

There is ample free parking. The museum is wheelchair accessible and there are wheelchairs available for free loan at the information desk.

Admission is $5 for adults, $4 seniors 65 and over, $3 for children 6 to 17, and free for children 5 and under. The museum is open Mon through Sat from 10 a.m. to 5 p.m. and Sun from 1 to 5 p.m. It is typically quieter in the afternoons, particularly during the busy spring field-trip season.

STATE FAIR PARK
333 Gordon Cooper St.
(405) 948-6704
www.okstatefairpark.com

Located on the northeast corner of I-40 and the I-44 junction, this Oklahoma City landmark covers 435 acres. State Fair Park has been in its present location for over 50 years. In 2005, the park began renovations to transform the grounds into a modern destination for tourism, livestock shows, and exhibit facilities. There have been many improvements and more are planned to come. The park is a multiuse complex with its many buildings and barns. Events like car, horse, RV, boat, gun, and craft shows are held on the grounds throughout the year. Probably the biggest event however, and the one most people are familiar with is the annual Oklahoma State Fair, which is held here in Sept. The City Arts Center, a place where artists of all ages can take classes and learn about specific art disciplines, is located on the east side of the park. If you get lost, look for the red, white, and blue space tower.

STOCKYARDS CITY
1305 S. Agnew Ave.
(405) 235-7267
www.stockyardscity.org

Historic Stockyards City started up at the same time the stockyards opened and was originally known as Packingtown. It served as a mercantile district for the stockyard. The old city is centered around Agnew and Exchange Boulevard and is two miles west of downtown Oklahoma City. In its early days it had a hay market, cotton gin, cotton compress, wagon factory, and harness factory. Today, it is a historic district with food, entertainment, and shopping.

Since 1992 Stockyards City has been affiliated with the national Main Street Association. The association is dedicated to revitalizing commercial districts through its four-point approach of organization, promotion, design, and economic restructuring.

Christmas time and the summer months are the busiest times of the year. A majority of the tours are in the summer, which brings more people than usual. Parking is free and primarily on the sides of the road. There is, however, a large parking lot behind Cattlemen's Steakhouse where parking is generally easy to find.

If you are worried about security here, don't be. Police are on duty during the day and Homeland Security recently put up cameras throughout the stockyards since it is a major food distribution area for the country.

WHITE WATER BAY
3908 W. Reno
(405) 943-9687
www.whitewaterbay.com

White Water Bay is the largest water adventure park in Oklahoma. Located in the heart of Oklahoma City, it is easily accessible from I-40. It offers over 30 rides, slides, pools, and activities. The rides range from mild to wild. Try the Mega-Wedgie, a 277-foot-long speed slide that features a 64-foot free fall that is sure to take your breath away. Ride the waves in the 500,000-gallon wave pool or just lay back and relax in Castaway Creek, White Water Bay's version of a lazy river. People are encouraged to take pictures to ensure they remember forever all the fun they had at White Water Bay.

There are two gift shops. Tabago Trading sells swimwear, towels, and souvenirs. Papaya

Pete's Sweets is smaller and offers a variety of candy and novelty items. The park provides inner tubes and inflatable tubes to rent for the wave pool and other activities. Lockers are available so patrons can lock up their valuables. Several food stands around the park sell everything from pizza to ice cream.

White Water Bay enforces a dress code. No denim cutoffs, shorts, thong bikinis, or swimsuits with buttons, zippers, rivets, or snaps on back are allowed. Shoes, aqua socks, and shirts are not allowed on some attractions.

White Water Bay offers many promotions throughout the season, such as Dive-In Movies. Every Fri night in July guests can watch movies in the wave pool from the comfort of their inner tube.

There is ample parking for guests in a parking lot just north of the park. This allows for easy access to the park's entrance. Parking in the north parking lot is currently $5 at the gate. White Water Bay is wheelchair accessible. Admission is $25.99 plus tax for adults and $21.99 for seniors, handicapped individuals in wheelchairs, guests 48 inches and under, and free for children three and under. Season passes are available as are group rates.

The water park opens in late May and during the summer months (June, July, and part of Aug) is open seven days a week. Mon through Thurs the park is open from 10:30 a.m. to 7 p.m. and is the park's least busiest time. On Fri, Sat, and Sun, the park is open from 10:30 a.m. to 8 p.m. In Sept park hours are limited and it closes for the season after Labor Day. Operating days and hours change so check the Web site to get the latest updated information.

WILL ROGERS HORTICULTURE GARDEN
3400 NW 36
(405) 943-0827
www.okc.gov/parks/will_rogers
Will Rogers Horticultural Garden is part of Will Rogers Park, a 30-acre park in Northwest Oklahoma City. The park is located on the southwest corner of 36th Street and Portland Avenue. It is one of the city's historic parks and is open year-round.

The garden features a seven-acre arboretum with a broad spectrum of Oklahoma native trees, two ponds, intensely landscaped winding paths and walkways, and the beautiful Charles E. Sparks Rose Garden, which houses over 90 varieties of roses and serves as a test garden for growers across the United States. In addition, the Will Rogers Horticultural Garden is home to the Ed Lycan Tropical Conservatory, which houses Oklahoma's largest collection of succulents and cacti. The historic greenhouse is an original Lord and Burnham Greenhouse and dates back to the 1930s.

The garden is also home to the Will Rogers Garden Exhibition Center, which hosts multiple garden-related workshops and exhibitions throughout the year, many of which are free to the public.

There is no admission to visit the garden or attend park-hosted events or workshops. Events hosted by outside organizations may charge a small fee for admission.

Hours of operation are 7 a.m. to 7 p.m. from Apr through Oct and 7 a.m. to 4 p.m. from Nov to Mar. Exhibition center hours are Mon through Fri from 7 a.m. to 4 p.m.

WORLD ORGANIZATION OF CHINA PAINTERS MUSEUM
2641 NW 10th
(405) 521-1234
www.theshop.net/wocporg
This museum displays handpainted china from its members around the world. It is one of the few museums in the United States dedicated to the preservation of handpainted china. On display visitors will find vases, plates, bowls, cups, and portraits painted on porcelain. Most of the pieces are award winners. Every piece of china is unique.

There is a gift shop where visitors can purchase painted china and painter's supplies. Classes and seminars are offered here as well. This museum is located on the north side of 10th Street.

Admission to the museum is free. Donations are appreciated. Hours are Mon through Fri from 10 a.m. to 4 p.m. The museum is closed on holidays.

KIDSTUFF

Adults shouldn't have all the fun. Kids should have fun too. That's what this chapter is all about. Some of the entries in this chapter are also listed in the "Attractions" chapter, but here's the twist: This chapter gives information on what children can specifically do at these places.

Throughout the Oklahoma City area, parents will find all sorts of activities to involve their children in. Some require only child participation, while others require parents be on hand to supervise. In all instances, parents are responsible for the safety of their child. If you do not feel comfortable with leaving your child, then don't. A good rule of thumb is to check with other parents to get their take on activities where you will not be present.

When parental supervision or participation is required, use the opportunity to bond with your child. Don't hesitate to jump into these activities with your children. Many classes are offered for parents and children from science to art. Classes and camps are offered by different organizations at different times throughout the year. Some have after-school programs or weekend programs, while others have weeklong activities.

The Oklahoma area offers a number of entertainment options, including fun parks, a zoo, activity centers, playgrounds, and movie theaters. There are several museums, such as the Science Museum, that offer hands-on activities that keep children entertained.

Keep in mind that the weather plays a large part in which activity you will want to involve your child. Early mornings work better for outdoor activities in the months of June, July, and Aug. It gets hot quickly in these months. If you do decide to go outdoors during the heat, take plenty of water and wear a hat, and light-colored clothing. In the afternoon, indoor activities would be wise.

During the year, there are many events with special activities for children. Check out the "Annual Events" chapter to learn more about those. You can also look in the "Sports and Recreation" chaper where I have listed bowling alleys, tennis courts, parks, and playgrounds where children can run off that pent-up energy.

Another good source for activities for your children can be found in *MetroFamily* magazine (405-340-1404; www.metrofamilymagazine.com). Each month, this publication lists a calendar of events. Sarah Taylor, the publisher, also has a family-friendly Web site that offers activities and events for children. At www.exploringok.com, parents can connect with other parents, find coupons for some of the area's attractions, and learn about new or upcoming events.

CACTUS JACK'S FAMILY FUN CENTER
1211 N. Council Rd.
(405) 789-9846
www.cactusjacksokc.com
Adults have their casinos, kids have Cactus Jack's. Opened in 1976, this fun center is a family-friendly environment where kids and families come to play and have fun. The owners, brothers Jim and Sam Kamas, used to own Kamas Vending Company. They placed electronic arcade like games in stores and when those games weren't in use, they needed someplace to store them.

They found their present location, but it needed lots of work. With help from friends, the brothers began gutting the building. As they added new stuff, they took out the old and hauled it to the dump. The guy at the dump was so grumpy, everybody dreaded going there. They started calling him Cactus Jack. After three months of fear from going to the dump, they decided to name the game room after the old man.

Nobody dreads coming to Cactus Jack's today. There are so many games, everyone is happy. There is Skee-Ball; air hockey; redemption games; video games; classic games, like Tetris and Ms. Pacman; pinballs; pool tables; kiddie rides; foosball tables; and photo booths.

No smoking or drinking is allowed here. Vending machines are available for snacks and sodas. The games use tokens. The majority of games cost one token. Pool is three tokens and the deluxe games are two or three tokens. Tokens are 25 cents.

Hours are Mon through Thurs from 10 a.m. to 10:30 p.m., Fri and Sat from 10 a.m. to 12:30 a.m., and Sun from 1 to 11 p.m.

CELEBRATION STATION
509 Westline Dr.
(405) 942-7888
www.celebrationstation.com

Covering six acres, just off south Meridian and I-40, this fun spot will keep kids of all ages busy for hours. There are go-karts, bumper boats, three 18-hole miniature golf courses, batting cages, pool tables, and a 25-foot slide. Two stories of arcade fun can be found here. Driving games, air hockey, prize crane, and over 100 video and redemption games are here. A restaurant on the premises offers hot dogs, pizza, nachos, buffalo wings, and more.

Prices vary per activity but range from $2 to $70. Special price packages are available.

CITY ARTS CENTER
3000 General Pershing Blvd.
(405) 951-0000
www.cityartscenter.org

Besides being a great place to go check out artwork of all mediums, the City Arts Center holds summer camps for kids of all age ranges from May to Aug. Each camp runs for a week, from 9 a.m. to 4 p.m. daily. Children get hands-on experience working with clay, acting, puppetry, painting, and more. Prices range depending on which medium child decides to study.

The center also offers a spring break camp in Mar. Children, ages 5 to 12 and up, can choose from drawing, painting, and working with clay. This camp lasts a week and costs approximately $140. Hours are 9 a.m. to 4 p.m. each day. Before and after-hours care is offered at $5 per child.

Call or check the Web site for more detailed information on classes and camps.The City Arts Center is located on the east side of the Oklahoma State Fairgrounds.

EDMOND ALL-SPORTS
301 S. Bryant, Ste. A-500
(405) 340-4766
www.edmondallsports.com

Edmond All-Sports (EASI) is an organization that provides league sports like baseball, softball, golf, flag and tackle football to the young people of Edmond and the surrounding area. The athletes experience league play as well as play in seasonal tournaments held for each sport. It also offers a golf program with Kickingbird Golf Club in the summers, along with a just recently started adult kick-ball league. The organization is nonprofit.

Ages for baseball and softball are 3 to 13. Flag football is available for children in kindergarten through the sixth grade and tackle football is offered for children in second grade through seventh grade. The golf program is offered to 8 through 17-year-olds. Softball and most of the football games are played at Mitch Park in Edmond. The baseball games and some flag football are played at Hafer Park. The adult kick-ball league is also played at Mitch Park. Spring sign up for baseball and softball is the first three weeks in Feb and the season runs from the end of Mar through the middle of June. Golf sign up is in June for the July to Aug program. Fall sign up for baseball, softball, and football is the first three weeks in Aug. The baseball and softball season runs from the beginning of Sept through the middle of Oct and the football season runs from Sept through the middle of Nov. Cost varies between $45 and $95 depending on age of the child and the sport. EASI currently has over 4,000 kids participating in its programs each year. Each season EASI also hosts baseball and softball tournaments, which bring in teams from all over Oklahoma and the surrounding states. It hosts the USSSA (United States Specialty Sports Association) state tournament in June and the six, seven, and eight-year-old USSSA World Series in July. EASI also host camps. See the Web site for more information.

i Wondering if the pool toys you purchased for your children are safe? Contact the United States Consumer Product Safety Commission, 4330 East West Highway, Bethesda, MD 20814; (800) 638-2772; www.cpsc.gov.

FRONTIER CITY
11501 NE Expressway
(405) 478-2414
www.frontiercity.com
Frontier City is located on the west side of I-35 on the service road, just north of Hefner Road. It transports guests back in time to the Old West, with western-themed facades and rides. Smaller members of the family will have fun on their rides in Kiddie Land, home to Tiny Timber Town. Older children will enjoy the roller coasters, water rides, shows, and other attractions. Some rides require a height limit, so be on the look for those.

Frontier City opens at the end of Mar and stays open until the end of Oct. Weekday operation begins the end of May and continues through the end of Aug. Mon, Tues, Wed, and Thurs during the summer, and Sat and Sun during the months of Apr, May, Sept, and Oct are the best days to visit the park as that is when attendance is lightest.

Since children are young only once, visitors are encouraged to take pictures of the family fun. Admission for adults is $28.99, children 48 inches and under is $19.99 plus tax. Children under three are free. As always prices are subject to change, so check the Web site for current pricing.

GAYLORD-PICKENS OKLAHOMA HERITAGE MUSEUM
Northwest 13th Street and Shartel Avenue
(405) 235-4458
www.oklahomaheritage.com
The Gaylord-Pickens Museum provides visitors hands-on opportunities to learn about the famous and not-so-famous people who have made Oklahoma what it is today. This attraction was named Best New Attraction in Oklahoma in 2008 by the Oklahoma Tourism Industry Association and the 2008–2009 Nickelodeon Parents' Pick for Teens in Oklahoma City.

The museum has many activities for children. The free field trip program allows schoolchildren to tour the museum each year. Summer camp is offered every year in June for ages 5 through 15. Campers learn about notable Oklahomans and the history of Oklahoma and take behind-the-scenes tours of the museum. Through the Scholarship program, the Heritage Museum makes more than $400,000 in cash scholarships and tuition grants available each year to Oklahoma high school students. During Heritage Week, 4th through 12th graders compete in poster and essay competitions for cash prizes.

Visitors may take pictures and should stop by the Bust Garden, where they can take a picture of their own head atop a pedestal. Children really enjoy doing this.

Hours are Tues through Fri from 9 a.m. to 5 p.m. and Sat from 10 a.m. to 5 p.m. The museum is closed Thanksgiving, Christmas, and New Year's Day. Admission is $7 for adults, $5 for seniors 62 and over and students ages 6 through 17, and free for children five and under. Free admission is offered every year on the museum's anniversary, May 10 and on or around Statehood Day.

HARN HOMESTEAD TERRITORIAL FUN DAY CAMP
1721 N. Lincoln Blvd.
(405) 235-4058
www.harnhomestead.com
This weeklong summer camp is for elementary-age schoolchildren. The camp is held during daytime hours. Students learn about territorial and

homestead living in Oklahoma prior to Oklahoma becoming a state. Arts and crafts along with core curriculum materials are provided. The camp also offers before and after care as well. Children must bring their own lunch.

In 2009, the fun camp celebrated its third year. In 2008, it was voted the Best Summer Camp by Nickelodeon's Parent Pick Award program. The Harn Homestead decided to offer the camp because of numerous requests they received from parents. They like to have groups of 25 children attend.

Children can attend one day or all week. Registration is $25 per day or $100 for the entire week.

MITCH PARK (EDMOND)
Located at Covell between Kelly and Santa Fe
(405) 359-4630
www.edmondok.com/parks/cityparks/mitch
This park is located on the northwest side of Edmond. Children can visit this park and play on swing sets, slides, merry-go-rounds, and other playground equipment. In July and Aug, children ages 5 to 12 can participate in Summer Blast, a program organized by the Edmond Parks and Recreation Department. Here they can play dodgeball and other games, experience relay races, and learn about everything from science to arts and crafts. The park has a recreation center where classes are held.

OKLAHOMA CHILDREN'S THEATRE
2501 N. Blackwelder
(405) 606-7003
www.oklahomachildrenstheatre.org
Nationally recognized for its educational live theater experiences for young children, this organization holds school year productions; summer, winter, fall, and spring-break camps; and after-school creative-drama programs for school-age children. Nearly 900 children participated in the camps in 2009. The theater serves children in the public school system and offers a homeschool program as well as a preschool program. Some of the skills students learn in the classes are basic

theater skills, stage direction, theater terminology, and voice projection.

Tuition for classes is $80 per class and camps run from between $100 and $400.

OKLAHOMA CITY MUSEUM OF ART
415 Couch Dr.
(405) 236-3100
www.okcmoa.com
At this museum children learn how to appreciate art by creating it. The museum offers classes for toddlers to teens throughout year and holds summer and spring-break camps. Hours vary depending on class schedule. Classes for ages 15 months to 36 months focus on texture, color, and shape, while classes for children 3 to 5 years old explore collage and jewelry making. Children ages 6 through 9 learn about pottery and story quilts and ages 10 through 13 explore kite making, collage, and pottery. A parent or guardian must be present while their child attends class. Prices range from $9 for the younger children to $15 for the older children. Camp prices vary from year to year so call or check the Web site for current prices. Everyone is encouraged to wear comfortable clothing to class.

OKLAHOMA CITY ZOO
2101 NE 50th St.
(405) 424-3344
www.okczoo.com
While children always enjoy going to the zoo and seeing the bears, lions, and giraffes, there's more for them to do than just looking at the animals at the Oklahoma City Zoo. On the west side of the zoo, there is Jungle Gym, a playground area made just for kids. They can also catch a ride on the Centennial Choo Choo. On the east side of the zoo, at the Adventure Zone, there's another playground, a rock wall to climb, and rides, like the Endangered Species Carousel and Kiddie Train.

In 2010, the Children's Zoo is scheduled to open. Set on 2.5 acres, this $8-million endeavor is funded by a one-eighth of a cent sales tax approved by Oklahoma City voters in 1990 and by private donations. Children will have many options for educational play in their new zoo. The Secret Forest will allow them to climb through mysterious structures. They'll get to splash in Waterway while admiring a waterfall and dig in the ground in the Underground Zone and discover what lives under the surface of dirt. There are other activities not listed here, but parents will appreciate all that's included that will keep their children busy and entertained.

The zoo has many events for children, including HOPabaloo and the Easter Egg Hunt. The Zoo Explorers educational program is available for all ages. For more information on Zoo Explorers call (405) 425-0218.

The zoo is open from 9 a.m. to 5 p.m. daily. It is closed on Thanksgiving, Christmas, and New Year's Day. Admission is $7 for adults 12 to 64, $4 for seniors 65 and over and children 3 to 11, and free for children 2 and under. Same day reentry is allowed. Strollers are available for rent on the west side of the plaza area just beyond the main entrance. Parking is ample and free.

ORR FAMILY FARM
14400 S. Western
(405) 799-3276
www.orrfamilyfarm.com
There's a lot to do for adults and children alike at this farm. The owners expect everyone to "come and have a good time." And who couldn't with all there is to do. While there is a lot to see here, the farm does focus on children. A quick ride on the train can put any child in a good mood. The train holds about 100 people and looks, puffs, and sounds like a steam engine, but for safety reasons is a diesel. When that activity is over, children can go fishing, ride a carousel, pet animals, take pony rides, ride the pedal cars, jump on the Jumping Pillows, or watch Jethro P. Hogg, an animatron who sits on a stool, sings, and plays his guitar. There are mazes to explore and volleyball and horseshoes to play. If all that doesn't hold your child's attention, then he or she can mine for gemstones in the Neal Simpson Mine.

In Sept and Oct hayrides and picking out pumpkins are also part of the fun.

Dress is always casual here. A great many children come here on field trips throughout the week. The farm is open to the general public on

Fri evening from 6 to 8 p.m. and on Sat from 10 a.m. to 6 p.m. Prices vary according to the activity.

PELICAN BAY AQUATIC CENTER
1034 S. Bryant Ave.
(405) 216-7649
www.edmondok.com/parks/pelicanbay
Pelican Bay is child friendly. It features a spray deck with interactive features perfect for curious infants and toddlers. In the zero-depth beach entry, older children will enjoy the aquatic playground with more interactive features and a double slide.

Children should wear swimwear. Street clothing is not allowed. For infants or toddlers to enter the water, Oklahoma State Bathing Code requires them to wear a swimsuit or appropriate swim diaper.

Lifeguards are on duty, but please be responsible for your children and keep an eye on them.

Special events are held from May through Sept. Please check the Web site for the dates and times of these events.

THE PLAY ZONE
7212 W. Hefner Rd.
(405) 728-0500
www.dynamogym.com
Need to find a place where your child can run off some energy? Come to the Play Zone. The interior of the Play Zone is decorated in fun colors, like red, yellow, green, and blue. The walls are painted with different cartoon characters and clouds in different shapes. The bathrooms are also brightly painted.

The Play Zone is a three-story indoor playground. It can entertain over 100 children and has an air bounce, a zipline, four different slides, a balance beam, nets to climb, and plenty of different obstacles to climb through.

Parents must supervise their children. They may play in the Play Zone too if they wish. No food is served, but there are juice and soda vending machines. Children from 15 months to approximately 13 years of age are welcome here.

Hours are Mon through Thurs from 9 a.m. to 8 p.m., Fri from 3 to 8 p.m., and Sat from 9 a.m. to 12 p.m. Reservations for birthday parties or group play are required.

Cost is $5 for two hours per child and free for parents. Everyone in the play zone must wear socks.

RONALD J. NORICK DOWNTOWN LIBRARY
300 Park Ave.
(405) 231-8650
www.mls.lib.ok.us

This library offers some great programs for kids, such as Storytime, Toddlertime, Parachute Play, music and dance presentations, and 1, 2, 3 Play with Me. From June 1 to the end of July the main library and its branches also host the Summer Reading Program. The program always has a theme and reading goals for the attendees. Age-appropriate prizes are given when child finishes the program. Participants may sign up at any branch.

Check the library's Web site for more information about the children's programs, and for branch locations. Branch locations are also listed in the "Relocation" chapter of this book.

SAM NOBLE OKLAHOMA MUSEUM OF NATURAL HISTORY (NORMAN)
2401 Chatauqua Ave.
(405) 325-4712
www.snomnh.ou.edu

The museum of natural history offers a number of children's program for age levels. Children in grades one and two can attend a program where they become time travelers and learn about the changing Oklahoma prairie. For high school students the museum offers a two-week residential paleontology program.

The museum also offers ExplorOlogy, a series of programs for all ages to "do science" by getting out and experiencing the world of science. Children can join Spike's Club, Scouts, or sign up for one of the many workshops offered. Space is limited in all these programs and preregistration is required. The cost varies per program.

Family programs are offered throughout the year as well. Field trips are offered where you can travel to a dig site in Oklahoma in search of fossils. Family Night Out can include anything from building habitats for the birds to using trees to tell time..

Programs change yearly, so check the Web site or call the Education Department at (405) 325-4712 for more information.

SCIENCE MUSEUM
2100 NE 52nd St.
(405) 602-3760
www.sciencemuseumok.org

During the summer, the Science Museum holds six one-week camps. These camps run from the middle of June to the end of July and are open to students in grades one through three and four through six. The cost is $200 per student for Science Museum members and $235 per student for nonmembers. Register for two or more camps and receive a 10 percent discount. Registration includes admission to the museum, hands-on activities; lunch each day, and a commemorative T-shirt. Camp hours are 9 a.m. to 4 p.m. each day.

Besides the summer camps, the museum also has a Camp in Science program where children can spend the night at the museum exploring the exhibits and participating in other activities. Birthday party packages and science demonstrations are also available. Call the number above for availability and pricing.

i To learn about car safety, lake safety, and fire prevention, contact Safe Kids Oklahoma, 940 Northeast 13th St., Oklahoma City, OK 73104-5008; (405) 271-5695; www.oksafekids.org.

WHITE WATER BAY WATER PARK
3908 W. Reno Ave.
(405) 943-9687
www.whitewaterbay.com

This is the largest water adventure park in Oklahoma. It offers 30 rides, slides, pools, and activities. There are wild rides for teenagers and adults and younger children can cool off in the Kid's Kove. In Kid's Kove children will find outrageous creatures to play on and fun fountains to splash around in. The best time to visit is Mon through Thurs. Denim cutoffs, shorts, and swimsuits with buttons, zippers, rivets, or snaps on the back are not allowed.

ICE SKATING AND ROLLER SKATING RINKS

ARTIC EDGE ICE ARENA

14613 N. Kelly Ave.

(405) 748-5454

www.blazers-icecentre.com

If you or your family is interested in ice skating, check out this ice rink. Skating enthusiasts have two ice rinks to choose from, both 200 feet by 80 feet. Top-40 music is played here. You will also find a pro shop and game room. If you don't like to skate, there are bleachers and tables where you can sit and watch. For those who need a warmer seating area, tables and booths are available in the heated lobby.

Hockey tournaments, ice shows, and University of Central Oklahoma hockey games are held here. Individuals can also take skating lessons. A five-week course costs $125.

Hungry? The arena has a concession stand. It serves chicken fingers, French fries, hot dogs, nachos, and drinks.

The ice arena is open seven days a week, from 9 a.m. to 10 p.m. The busiest times are on the weekends from noon to 10 p.m. Admission is $7. Skate rental is $3. Family nights are Tues from 7:15 to 8:45 p.m. The cost is $6, including skates. Skates are also available for purchase. Figure skates start at $68 and hockey skates start at $39.

BLAZERS ICE CENTRE

8000 S. I-35 Service Rd.

(405) 631-3300

www.blazers-icecentre.com

This 50,000-square-foot facility has one 200 foot by 80 foot concrete base ice surface rink. There are six locker rooms available so storing equipment, purses, and coats won't be a problem while you skate.

Owned by the same company as the Artic Edge Ice Arena (see above), this center offers many of the amenities. There is a pro shop, game room, and concession stand. This rink is home to the University of Oklahoma men's hockey team and is the practice facility for the Oklahoma City Blazers.

Birthday party packages are available and start at $125. Packages include personalized cake,
ice skating admission and rental, and decorated private party room. Skate admission is $7.00 and skate rental is $3.00. Skating classes are available and run about $125 for a five-week course.

Hours are typically from 9 a.m. to 10 p.m. seven days a week. Times are subject to change.

SOUTHWESTERN ROLLER RINK

6401 S. Western

(405) 632-5484

www.swskate.com

This skating rink has an electric atmosphere. It is known as the skating rink with the bumps. You walk in, look around, and immediately start moving to the beat of the music. Young and old enjoy the top-40 pop and teenie bop music played over the sound system. The 176 foot by 76 foot hard rock maple floor gets single skaters as well as couples moving. The inside walls are decorated in bright glow neon with black lights. If you get hungry, there is a snack bar area. Garlic butter crust pizza, nachos, and hot dogs are served. For those who don't wish to skate, there is an area where you can sit and watch the skaters.

The weekends are the busiest times to skate here. You can rent skates or buy a pair from the pro shop. Skating classes are available year-round and cost $6.

Individual skating can run as low as $3.50 to as high as $7.50. There is not rental fee for regular skates. However, inline skates rental is $4.00. Family nights are Tues, Wed, and Thurs. These nights are for families with elementary age children. Families come to skate and have fun. On Tues and Thurs admission is $4.50. Wed, also known as "Cheap Skate," admission is $3.50 per person.

Hours at this rink vary according to what night of the week it is. Call or check the Web site for hours and prices.

Every parent's nightmare is losing their child. To keep track of how near or far away your child is, check out a personal alarm system. You can read about Child Guard at www.yourpersonalsecurity .com or call (866) 282-7162.

SPORTS AND RECREATION

This chapter is devoted to fun—fun in the sun, fun in the water, and fun with games, be they played or watched. In this chapter you will find four different categories of fun activities to enjoy—casinos, participation sports, spectator sports, and parks and recreation.

In the "Casinos" section below, you will learn that there is one casino, Remington Park, within the Oklahoma City limits. Most Oklahoma City residents travel to casinos at the edges of the county to play games. These casinos are within 30 to 45 minutes driving time, so I have listed those for you.

In the "Participation Sports" section, you will find sports activities that you can take part in. Participation sports are hot around Oklahoma City. Leagues in tennis and bowling play throughout the year. Many tournaments are held and whether you are a novice or seasoned player, there is a league for you.

If you like to play golf, Oklahoma City has a number of public courses. People drive in from all across the state for a round. Rates vary according to the time of the year. Because Oklahoma observes daylight savings time, many courses in Oklahoma City extend twilight time during the summer, something you may want to consider when temperatures soar above 95 degrees.

Oklahoma City is fast becoming popular for its professional teams and the "Spectator Sports" section covers professional and college teams that play at home in Oklahoma City or nearby. The Thunder, Blazers, Redhawks, and Yard Dawgz make their homes downtown. While the Redhawks have quite a history here, the Thunder is a new franchise steadily gaining its legs. In addition to the pro teams, Oklahoma City has several college teams that keep Oklahoma City suburbs in the spotlight. The Oklahoma Sooners and Oklahoma State Cowboys are located in Norman and Stillwater, respectively, but Oklahoma City residents support these teams and follow them on television or radio whenever they play.

With Oklahoma City's hot summers, many will be looking for places to cool off. While Oklahoma City lakes may fit the bill, the city has a number of parks with swimming pools and spraygrounds located in neighborhoods. Under the "Parks and Recreation" section, you will find those lakes and city parks listed. I have included five lakes that sit in or near Oklahoma City. Fishermen or water enthusiasts can run out to these lakes for an afternoon and be home before dark. As for parks, Oklahoma City maintains over 200, Norman over 55, and Edmond over 25 There was no way to include them all, so only a sampling is given space here. Contact information for park and recreation departments is included so you can visit the Web sites or call for more information.

Whether you intend to go to a lake, a park, or an outdoor game, keep Oklahoma City's environment in mind. June, July, and Aug are body melters. Temperatures in July and Aug have been known to go over 100 degrees. Apply sunscreen often and drink plenty of nonalcoholic beverages, like water or Gatorade. Remember too that many lake attractions near the city fill up quickly on weekends and holidays, so make your plans early.

This chapter is intended to get you started. Try these places and then explore to find your favorite thing to do and place to go. Enjoy and remember to have fun.

CASINOS

FIRELAKE CASINO
41207 Hardesty Rd.
(405) 878-4862

Open since May 2003, this casino is owned and operated by the Citizen Potawatomi Nation. It is located 25 minutes east of Oklahoma City. There are over 800 games here including slots, poker, blackjack, craps, and bingo. Average payout depends on play. Players win jackpots here regularly. On Aug 16, 2009, the casino had a jackpot winner of over $23,000.

Guests can find food at the Bistro Buffet and buy their favorite drinks from the Lucky 7's Bar. The casino offers gaming specials throughout the week, the New Players Club, and the Player Reward Program. Smoking and nonsmoking areas are available. The casino is open seven days a week, 24 hours a day.

FIRELAKE GRAND CASINO
777 Grand Casino Blvd.
(405) 964-7263
www.firelakegrand.com

This casino has over 1,800 games, including slots, poker, blackjack, craps, spinette/roulette, keno, and Ultimate Texas Hold 'em. Jackpots are won on a regular basis here. In Aug 2009, this casino had a jackpot winner of over $34,000. Players will find four restaurants—the Grandstand Sports Grille, the Grand Buffet, Embers Steakhouse, the Roasted Bean Café, and one bar, the Fire & Ice Lounge.

This casino opened in Oct 2006 and is owned and operated by the Citizen Potawatomi Nation. It is located 15 minutes east of Oklahoma City on I-40. It offers gaming specials throughout the week and special events on a regular basis. In the past, country and western singer Blake Sheldon and comedian Rodney Carrington have performed. Cage fighting is also popular here. In 2008, the casino won two Addy Awards. In 2009, they were voted Best Place to Place Your Bet in *Oklahoma Magazine*'s Best of the Best poll.

The casino is open seven days a week, 24 hours a day.

REMINGTON PARK
1 Remington Place
(405) 424-1000
www.remingtonpark.com

Remington Park is a state-of-the-art entertainment center that includes horse racing and casino gaming. It is one of the leading tourism sites in Oklahoma and has received numerous awards for its customer service and guest amenities. It was built in 1988 at a cost of more than $100 million. In 2000, a $31 million casino was added. The center is 333,000 square feet and sits on 375 acres. It includes a row of private suites overlooking the racetrack and several upscale restaurants, such as Silks Fine Dining and Remis Buffet.

Besides the casino gaming area, which offers games for penny players and high rollers, Remington Park offers thoroughbred and quarter-horse racing and is regarded as one of the leading racetracks in the country. There are hundreds of monitors throughout the facilities to show live racing and simulcasts from tracks throughout the country.

Remington Park hosts numerous special events throughout the year, including several major racing events with purses in excess of $100,000. In addition, ethnic food festivals, family fun nights, free merchandise nights, regular rewards for the Lucky Circle 20 Club, bands, and other entertainment go on throughout the year.

All parking is free, including valet parking at the casino as well as the race track clubhouse.

Hours are Sun through Wed from 10 a.m. to 12 a.m., Thurs from 10 a.m. to 2 a.m., Fri and Sat from 10 a.m. to 3 a.m. Simulcasts are shown seven days a week starting at 10 a.m.

RIVERWIND CASINO
1544 W. State Highway 9
(405) 322-6000
www.riverwind.com

This premiere casino opened in 2006. It is located just south of Norman, off I-35, 30 minutes from downtown Oklahoma City. Owned by the Chickasaw Nation, it is 200,000 square feet of fun and excitement. There are 2,300 games, 55 poker and blackjack card tables, an off-track betting lounge, the state's largest buffet, fast-food restaurants, fine-dining restaurants, and an 1,500 seat theater.

Past performers have been Merle Haggard, the Four Tops, Lee Ann Womack, Michael Bolton, and Glen Campbell. In Oct 2008, the casino won the Best Casino Award in the *Oklahoman Reader*'s Choice Awards and was voted Friendliest Casino by *Oklahoma Gazette* readers.

The casino is open 24 hours a day, seven days a week. Visitors must be 18 years old or older to play here.

ORGANIZATIONS

EDMOND ALL-SPORTS

301 S. Bryant, Ste. A-500
(405) 340-4766
www.edmondallsports.com
Edmond All-Sports (EASI) is an organization that provides league sports like baseball, softball, golf, flag and tackle football to the young people of Edmond and the surrounding area. The athletes experience league play as well as play in seasonal tournaments held for each sport. It also offers a golf program with Kickingbird Golf Club in the summers, along with a just recently started adult kick-ball league. The organization is nonprofit.

It also offers a golf program with Kickingbird Golf Club in the summers. While in the past EASI has focused on youth play, spring 2009 they introduced a new adult kick-ball league.

The season for the kick ball league starts in Mar. Registration opens in Jan and runs through Feb. The cost is $475 per league with no gate fees. The season consists of 14 games played as doubleheaders on Mon, Tues, or Thurs nights. Games are played at Mitch Park in Edmond.

OKLAHOMA CITY ALL SPORTS ASSOCIATION

211 N. Robinson, Ste. 250
(405) 236-5000
www.okcallsports.org
This organization was started in 1957 to promote and sustain the All-College Basketball Tournament. In 1983, it enlarged to host more than 265 events in Oklahoma City. This includes 30 NCAA Championships. Each year, because of these events, $30 million is brought to Oklahoma City. Some of these events include the NCAA Women's College World Series, the All Sports Golf Invitational, and the All College Basketball Classic.

The Oklahoma City All Sports Association is managed by seven staff members and supervised by 41 non-paid board members. It is a non-profit organization and exists to bring and promote amateur sporting events to Oklahoma.

Sports lovers and corporations from across the state belong to the Oklahoma City All Sports Association. Anyone is welcome to join. Membership is $375 a year for elite membership and $225 a year for VIP.

The association puts out a quarterly newsletter and publishes an annual membership guide along with *Sooner State Games* handbooks.

PARTICIPATION SPORTS

Bowling

AMF BOWLING CENTER (YUKON)

500 E. Main
(405) 354-2516
www.amf.com
This facility is Yukon's favorite entertainment center. It has a nice family atmosphere and is kept clean by the staff. You will find bowlers who came here as children and are now bringing their own children in to bowl.

If you like bowling and want to join a league, this might be the place for you. This 24-lane bowling center is known as a "league house." At least 24 bowling leagues play at the facility and sometimes even more. During the fall, Mon through Fri, leagues begin playing at 6 p.m. and go for two or three hours depending on the number of players in each league. If you are interested in joining a league, visit the center or hop on the Web site where you can sign up.

Sun through Thurs after league play (about 8 p.m.), guests can play for $1.29 a game. If you're an early riser who likes to bowl on Sun, you can play for two hours between 10 a.m. and 2 p.m. for $5.

You can bring your own shoes and ball or rent from the center. Shoe rental runs about $3.75 for adults. If you want to buy your own equipment, there is a pro shop. It sells shoes, balls, bags, towels, and anything else related to the sport.

There is instruction available for young bowlers. Music is played through a jukebox hooked up to the Internet. Listen to the latest or choose your own. A snack bar serves burgers, pizza, popcorn, fries, or any other snack food you might be hungry for.

The center is open from 11 a.m. to 11 p.m. Mon and Thurs, noon to 11 p.m. Tues and Wed, 10 a.m. to 11 p.m. Fri and Sat, and 10 a.m. to 10 p.m. Sun. Hours are subject to change so call ahead. You may also want to call and reserve a lane or check league play status.

Other AMF centers in the surrounding area are: **Boulevard Lanes,** 3501 S. Blvd., Edmond, (405) 348-3210; **Moore Lanes,** 420 SW 6th St., Moore, (405) 799-3344; **Sunny Lanes Bowling,** 4330 SE 15th St., Del City, (405) 677-6616.

HERITAGE LANES
11917 N. Pennsylvania
(405) 755-7575
www.heritagelanesokc.com
On the north side of the city, just off Pennsylvania, is this 40-lane facility. In addition to a bowling alley, guests will find a game room, billiard room, and a double meeting room. This facility is a smoke-free, friendly-family place. A member of the Oklahoma City Chamber of Commerce, it is involved in the community, holding fund-raisers and welcoming school fieldtrips.

The pro shop sells balls, bags, shoes, and other sport-related items. Bowling instruction is available. There is a full-service lounge and a snack bar. For those who like to watch music videos, there are five drop-down video screens that play the latest videos over the bowling lanes. Forty-two inch big screens project sporting events or news in the common area. Leagues play here Mon through Thurs and hold their tournaments on the weekends.

You may bring your own balls and shoes or rent shoes from the facility. Shoe rental is $3.29 plus tax for adults and $2.99 plus tax for children. Bowling prices are $2.89 plus tax before 5:00 p.m. and $3.89 plus tax after 5:00 p.m. Heritage Lanes offers a family pass and a summer program where kids bowl free. Check out the summer special by visiting www.kidsbowlfree.com/heritage.

Hours are Mon and Tues from 9 a.m. to 11 p.m., Wed and Thurs 9 a.m. to midnight, Fri and Sat 9 a.m. to 2 a.m., and Sun 11 a.m. to 11 p.m.

WINDSOR LANES BOWLING
4600 NW 23rd St.
(405) 942-5545
www.amf.com/windsorlanes
Windsor Lanes Bowling offers 40 lanes and you can bring your own shoes and balls or rent from the center. Leagues play here so you might want to call ahead and ask about the best times to visit. This facility does not offer bowling classes. There is a snack bar that serves pizza, cheeseburgers, quesadillas, and more. Beer, wine, and mixed drinks are also served here. Hours are Sun through Thurs from noon to 10 p.m. and Fri and Sat from noon to 1 a.m.

> **i** With over 200 golf courses scattered across the state, you might want to check out the Oklahoma Golf Association. Since the early 1900s, this nonprofit organization has been promoting the game of golf within the state of Oklahoma. Call (405) 848-0042 or visit www.okgolf.org to learn more.

Golf
BROADMOORE COURSE
500 Willow Pine Dr.
(405) 794-1529
Located in Moore, this golf course has been damaged by tornados over the years, but is back in tip-top shape for golfers to enjoy. It is an 18-hole course, designed in 1967 by Duffy Martin. Par is 71 and course yardage from the regular men's

white tees is 6,196. Fourteen holes have water hazards, with number 17 being the most scenic, 18 the most popular, and 8 the most difficult. There are trees, wide fairways, and the course is in excellent shape.

Open all year, shirts and soft spike shoes are required. The course has a pro shop, which sells items like balls, gloves, and hats, and offers golf lessons. There is also a driving range and putting green for those inclined to improve their skills. A snack bar sells sandwiches, soft drinks, beer, and other items for those who get hungry and thirsty.

At this course, golfers can walk or ride. Golfers can bring their own cart and pay a trail fee. Reservations are accepted for Sat, Sun, and the holidays. Reservations must be made one week in advance to play on Sat morning. Weekdays are open play. Green fees for 18 holes are $18 on weekdays and $20 on weekends. The green fee for seniors is $11. If you come late in the day and want to play, the green fee is $16.50 and at dusk, $13.00. These fees do not include cart rental.

BROOKSIDE
9016 S. Shields Blvd.
(405) 632-9666

This nine-hole course is a good one for seniors and beginners. It has water hazards on six holes and sloping greens. Course yardage from the men's white regular tees is 2,543 and par is 34/35. The most scenic hole at this course is number 3. The most popular is 7 and the most difficult is 8.

Shirts and soft spike shoes are required. There is a driving range and putting green. No tee times are used here. It is an open, walk-on course. Golfers may ride, but it is an easy walk. Green fees are daily fees. They are $12 until noon and $11 after noon on weekdays. On weekends and holidays, fees are $13 until noon and $12 after noon.

COBBLESTONE CREEK (NORMAN)
1350 Cobblestone Creek Dr.
(405) 872-2582
www.cobblestonecreekgolfclub.com

This nine-hole course was designed by Tripp Davis in 2000. His philosophy for the course was "you've hit a drive down the middle on a regula-

tion course and you now have an approach shot." The course has been open since 2002 and has had three rounds under par from the back tees: one by an Oklahoma University All-American, one by the 2006 Norman City Champion, and one by the owner. It is a real challenge with 20 traps, water on 7 holes, and lots of trees on holes 5 through 8. It's a beautiful course on the south side of Norman with an upscale neighborhood surrounding it.

Par is 27. Total yardage is 1,532 from the back tees, 1,334 from the middle tees, and 1,050 from the front tees. The most scenic hole is number 7 and the most difficult is number 4. The course does not have a driving range, but does have a practice green.

The course has a 6,000-foot clubhouse with a bar. It serves hot dogs and sandwiches. Beverages include soft drinks, beer, and mixed drinks.

Cobblestone Creek is open year-round and golfers can book to play as far ahead as they want. To play on Sat, it only requires a reservation made the day before. There is no public play during tournaments. Green fees for 9 holes are $14 for adults, $10 for seniors and children below 18 and in high school and $12 for students. Carts are available and you may bring your own. Cart fees are $6.00 for 9 holes and $10 for $18.00. Carts must remain on the cart path at all times. Collared shirts and soft spikes are required.

COFFEE CREEK
4000 N. Kelley Ave.
(405) 340-4653
www.coffeecreekgolfclub.com

Built in 1990, this course ranks in the top five for courses you can play. It consists of 18 holes with Bermuda grass fairways and bent-grass greens. The front nine consists of rolling natural fairways, while the back nine carves through some dense forest with tight, tree-lined fairways. Par on this course is 70, while the yardage is 6,700 from the regular men's white tees. The most popular hole is number 13 and seven holes have water hazards.

There is a full-service pro shop, a driving range, and a putting and chipping green. The Out of Bounds Grill, located inside the clubhouse, serves burgers and sandwiches.

Golfers need to make their tee time reservations one week in advance. Parking is on the west side of the club house. Go in the south door to check in. No personal carts are allowed. Also prohibited are sleeveless shirts, cut-off shorts, jeans with holes, and metal spike shoes. Collared shirts are preferred.

Green fees for 9 holes is $13.50 Mon to Friand $22.50 San and Sun. Green fees for 18 holes is $34.50 Mon to Friand $39.50 San and Sun. Twilight time and prices vary throughout the year. Coffee Creek is located on the northwest side of Edmond.

EARLYWINE GOLF
11600 S. Portland Ave.
(405) 691-1727
www.okcgolf.com
There are two courses here. The north course was designed in 1993 by Randy Heckenkemper. Par is 72 and course yardage from black tees is 6,721 yards. The hilly, tree-lined course has creeks and bent grass greens with Bermuda fairways tees and roughs. Golf Digest gives it a four-star rating. The north course is recognized as one of the best public layouts in the Oklahoma City Metro.

The lakes on the south course were originally designed in 1976 by Floyd Farley. Mark Hayes renovated three holes in 1999. Par on this course is 70 and total yardage from black tees is 6,505. The course has lakes on seven holes, creeks, green side bunkers, and fairway bunkers. Golf Digest gives this course 3.5 stars.

Earlywine is open year-round. Casual golf wear and soft spikes are required. There are three putting greens, a short game practice area, and three practice bunkers available. A restaurant is on the premises and is open daily. Tee times can be made one week in advance. The green fee is $21 for walking. Twilight costs $18.50 and the dusk fee is $13.75. Various promotions are held throughout the year.

JAMES E. STEWART GOLF COURSE
824 Frederick Douglass Ave.
(405) 424-4353
www.okcgolf.com

This is a nine-hole golf course. It was redesigned by Randy Heckenkemper and reopened in 1999. Par is 35 and the course yardage from the regular tees is 3,105. Hole number 8 is the most scenic with a par 5 and water hazard down the right side and fronting the green. Four holes have water hazards and nine holes have bunkers. There is a driving range, chipping green, restaurant, and pro shop here. Lessons are available.

Guests may bring their own cart. Shoes, soft spikes only, and shirts must be worn. Open year-round, the course is open to the public unless a tournament is scheduled. Tee times are available one week in advance. Green fee for nine holes is $8 for adults, $6 for seniors, and $2 for juniors, under 18 and in high school.

JIMMIE AUSTEN GOLF CLUB (NORMAN)
1 Par Dr.
(405) 325-6716
http://ougolfclub.com/golf/proto/jimmieaustingolf
This 18-hole course was designed by Perry Maxwell in 1951 and redesigned by Bob Culp and completely renovated in 1996. In 2007 all greens were resurfaced and all bunkers were rebuilt and received new white sand. Several new tees were installed and over 200 trees were added. Now with lots of trees, native areas, 86 great white-sand bunkers, the course is challenging with lots of movement. There is a live creek running through the course providing nice aesthetics. An Oklahoma State champion burr oak tree is also on the course at hole number 7. Course yardage from the regular men's white tees is 6,615 and par is 72. Hole number 18 is the most popular and 14 holes have water hazards as the creek runs through the course.

There is a golf shop which offers almost all services, but shoe repair. The Clubhouse Grill serves typical golf course food.

Members need to make their tee time reservations 14 days in advance while the general public need only make their reservations 7 days in advance. Guests may not bring their own cart. Visitors must walk or rent one of the club's carts.

Green fees, including golf cart and practice facilities, are $60 Mon to Fri and $75 Sat and Sun. The course is open year-round and requires collared shirts for men and collared and sleeved shirts for ladies. Soft-spiked shoes are required.

JOHN CONRAD (MIDWEST CITY)
711 S. Douglas Blvd.
(405) 732-2209
www.midwestcityok.org/golf-john-conrad
This 18-hole golf course has rolling hills with tree-lined fairways and beautiful green side bunkers. It was designed by Floyd Farley in 1971. Ten holes have water hazards. Number 17 is the most difficult and popular. Par is 72 and total yardage is 6,390. There is a pro shop, which offers full service; a driving range; and a putting green. Golfers can bring their own cart. The restaurant, Conrad Grill, serves hamburgers, hot dogs, chicken strips, and salads.

Tee time reservations should be made on Fri for the following week. To play on Sat or Sun, reservations need to be made the previous Sat. Green fees are $15 for 9 holes and $21 for 18 holes. Cart fees are $11.86 plus tax for 9 holes and $23.72 for 18 holes.

KICKINGBIRD GOLF COURSE
1600 E. Danforth
(405) 341-5350
www.kickingbirdgolf.com
Floyd Farley originally designed this 18-hole course in 1971. It was redesigned in 1997 by Mark Hays. Today this Edmond course has new greens, continuous cart trails, and redesigned holes with new tees and new sand traps. This course offers tree-lined fairways and a gently contoured green. There is a driving range, which is lighted, and a 10,000-square-foot putting green. Par on this course is 70. Course yardage from the regular men's blue tees is 6,282. Four holes have water hazards and the most difficult hole is number eight. A restaurant is on the premises. Golf lessons and limited club repair are also available.

There are limitations to play. On Thurs morning from Mar through Oct, no one is allowed to play. Tee times can be made one week in advance. On weekends, no parties of five before 11 a.m. allowed.

Green fees for 18 holes are $19.50 Mon to Thurs and $24.50 Fri to Sun. Green fees for 9 holes are $12 Mon to Thurs and $15 Fri to Sun. A special twilight fee of $14.00 is offered Mar through Oct after 4 p.m. and Nov to Feb after 2 p.m. A super twilight fee of $11.50 is offered Apr through Oct after 6 p.m. A cart for 9 holes is $12 and for 18 holes is $23. A pull cart runs $2.32 plus tax. Guests can bring their own cart, but a trail fee of $11.50 plus tax is required. Golfers must wear soft spikes only and no tank tops or cut offs are allowed.

Kickingbird is open year-round except for Thanksgiving and Christmas Day.

LAKE HEFNER GOLF CLUB
4491 S. Lake Hefner Dr.
(405) 843-1565
www.okcgolf.com
Located on the south end of Lake Hefner, Lake Hefner Golf Club offers two courses that are popular with city golfers. Both courses have 18 holes, are dotted by water hazards, and have bunkered fairways and greens.

The North Course opened in 1951. It was designed by Perry Maxwell and in 1994 was redesigned by Randy Heckenkemper. The slope on this course is 127 and course rating is 73.8. Par is 72 and yardage is 6,459 from the blue tees and 6,970 from the black.

The South Course was designed by Floyd Farley and opened in 1964. It is the shorter of the two courses. Par is 70. Yardage is 6,305 from the blues. Slope is 123 and course rating is 71.4.

Guests will find a pro shop, restaurant, and cart rental here. A driving range, putting green, and chipping green are only some of the practice facilities.

The green fee for 18 holes is $18. Twilight costs $15. These fees do not include sales tax. Golf cart fees for 18 holes start at $20.

LAKESIDE
9500 S. Eastern Ave. (Oklahoma City)
3400 N. Eastern Ave. (Moore)
(405) 794-0252

Despite being blown away by several tornadoes, this golf course continues to come back. It is a 9-hole course, designed by David Reed in 1993 and redesigned by him in 2000. Par is 35 and the total yardage from the men's regular blue tees is 2,653 on the nine. The most difficult hole here is number 7, while the most popular is number 1. While all the holes have water nearby, six holes have water hazards. The fairways are fast and the greens are good. You will find no dress code, although you will need to wear soft-spike shoes. You can bring your own cart and reservations are not required. Currently there is no driving range. It blew away in the last big tornado. The green fees for 9 holes is $7.50 if you walk and $5.50 for seniors. On weekends, the price for everyone is $8.50.

LINCOLN PARK GOLF COURSE
4001 NE Grand Blvd.
(405) 424-1421
www.okcgolf.com

This golf course has a long history in Oklahoma City. It was the city's first municipal golf course. It has two courses, the East Course and the West Course. The first 18 holes were built in 1922 and the second 18 in 1933. Both courses were designed by Arthur J. Jackson. Randy Heckenkemper designed the renovation in 1999 and 2008. In 1999, the West Course received new tees, bunkers, greens, cart trails, irrigation and beautification of the grounds. In 2008, the East Course got new tees, bunkers, cart trails, irrigation, and water feature enhancements. Both courses are tree lined with changing elevations.

Par on the West Course is 71 and the yardage is 6,137. The number 16 hole on this course is challenging with number 5 having the most water hazards.

On the East Course, par is 70 and the yardage from the regular men's white tees is 6,023. The number 15 hole is the most difficult and number 6 has the most water hazards.

Proper golf attire is required as well as soft-spiked shoes. Private golf carts are allowed.

A full-service golf shop, a driving range, and a putting green are available. Visitors need to make

tee time reservations one week in advance and if they want to play Sat morning, they must reserve that time the Sat before.

Fergie's Place serves a full range of burgers, sandwiches, breakfast, beer, and soft drinks.

This course is open year-round. The green fee for 18 holes or less is $18 plus tax. The twilight fee is $15 plus tax and the dusk fee is $11 plus tax. There is a discounted fee for seniors and students.

THE LINKS
700 NE 122nd St.
(405) 936-9214

Located between Hefner Road and Northeast 122nd, off North Kelley Avenue, is this nine-hole course. It was designed by Lyndy Lindsey in 1996 and is one of 38 courses in nine states that Lindsay Management owns. Course yardage is 1,880 yards. Number 7 is the signature hole, 172 yards over water with a fountain. The course has water and slope so your skills will be tested. A putting green is available to help you sharpen your skills as well.

No private carts are allowed. Soft spikes are required. A pro shop is available to golfers, but no restaurant or snack bar. No alcoholic beverages are allowed on premises.

The Links is open year-round to the public. There are no tee times. Management claims it will get you out within 15 minutes of check in. If you want to play nine holes, the green fee is $10.85. Eighteen holes is $16.25.

MIDWEST CITY MUNICIPAL COURSE (MIDWEST CITY)
3210 Belaire Dr.
(405) 732-9999
www.midwestcityok.org/golf-nine-hole

This nine-hole course was designed in 1957 by Floyd Farley. Par is 30 and total yardage from the men's regular white tees is 3,894. There are big trees on this course as well as a creek. Six of the holes have water hazards, number 6 is the most scenic, 5 is the most popular, and number 4 is the most difficult.

Open year-round, golfers can bring their own cart. There is a putting green. Nine holes of golf cost $8.75.

SILVERHORN GOLF CLUB
11411 N. Kelley Ave.
(405) 752-1181
http://silverhorn.americangolf.com
Silverhorn Golf Club is an 18-hole championship golf facility. It offers picturesque landscape with 170 acres of lush turf, native grasses, oaks, elms, hackberries, and four winding creeks built to challenge avid golfers without frustrating the novices. It was designed in 1991 by Randy Heckenkemper. Par is 71 and the total yardage from the regular men's white tees is 6,071. The most scenic, popular, and difficult hole is number 13. Twelve of the holes have water hazards.

Private carts are not allowed. Club rentals are available along with a selection of clothing, accessories and equipment in the pro shop. Soft-spike shoes are required and no tank tops or cut offs are allowed on the course. The snack bar which serves hot dogs and burgers for lunch is also open for breakfast.

The club is open year-round. Golfers can make tee time reservations seven days in advance. Green fees, including cart, are $29 Mon to Fri and $37 Sat and Sun. After 2 p.m. on weekdays, the rate drops to $22. After 2 p.m. weekends, it drops to $25.

TROSPER PARK
2301 SE 29th St
(405) 677-8874
www.okcgolf.com
Trosper was designed by Tom Harris. It is an 18-hole course. The first nine holes were completed in 1957 and the second nine holes were completed in the spring of 1958. This beautiful course features rolling hills, tree-lined fairways, 20 well-maintained bunkers, and many creeks. A chipping green, practice putting greens, and driving range are also available.

Par on this course is 70. Yardage is 6,601 from the championship (blue tees) and 5,963 from the white (men's) tees. The senior tee yardage is 5,235 and the ladies (red) tees are 4,676. The most scenic, popular, and difficult hole is number 18. It is a 573-yard, par 5 that plays into the south wind most of the time. It has an elevated green with a large creek in front. It is always the most difficult 18th hole in Oklahoma City on all the local surveys.

You may bring your own cart. Golfers must wear shoes, soft spikes only, and a shirt. The course is always open to the public unless a tournament is scheduled. There is a full-service pro shop where lessons are available.

The green fee for 18 holes or less is $21 plus tax. There are discounts for twilight and dusk. There are also junior and senior rates. Tee times may be reserved one week in advance.

Tennis

EARLYWINE TENNIS CENTER
Southwest 119th and May Avenue
(Earlywine Park)
(405) 691-5430
www.okc.gov/parks/tennis/earlywine_tennis.html
Located on the southwest side of Oklahoma City, this facility reopened in Apr 2007 after being renovated. It offers 12 lighted, outdoor courts; a full-service pro shop; an air-conditioned snack and pro area; stringing and gripping services; and locker rooms with showers. For more amenities, please check the Web site.

Clinics and tennis lessons are available to the public. Lesson fees run from $18 for semiprivate to $35 per hour for private lessons.

Court fees are $5 per court per hour whether single or double. Walk-ins are welcome, but courts are available by reservation, so when guests arrive they will need to reserve a court. Guests may also purchase an annual court pass. The cost is $185 plus tax for a family of four, $120 plus tax for a single adult, and $75 plus tax for children ages 5 to 17.

Summer hours are Mon through Sat from 9 a.m. to 10 p.m. and Sun from noon to 8 p.m. Winter hours are Sun through Fri from noon to 8 p.m. and Sat from 10 a.m. to 8 p.m. The tennis center closes when the temperature falls below 38 degrees Fahrenheit. It is closed Thanksgiving, Christmas, and New Year's Day.

KICKINGBIRD TENNIS CENTER
1500 E. Danforth Rd., Edmond
(405) 348-3120
www.kickingbirdtennis.com

Located on the southeast corner of Danforth and Bryant in Edmond, this tennis center has 11 lighted outdoor courts, including a stadium court with seating and three indoor courts. There is a patio seating area with a view of the courts if you'd rather watch than play.

A pro shop is available here. It sells clothes, shoes, sunglasses, sports watches, and rackets. Free stringing is offered with every racket sold or you can pay $15 plus string to get your own restrung.

Beginning and advanced classes are available for children and adults. These are taught by on-site tennis pros. Private lessonsrun $45 for one hour and $30 for a half-hour lesson.

Many different leagues are also available. The adult leagues form year-round. They are offered in the day and evening according to your skill level. There are single, double, and ladder leagues. All you have to do is choose the one for you. In the fall, the World Team Tennis leagues form and in Jan the U.S. Tennis Association (USTA) leagues form. From Apr through Oct the USTA Pro Circuit tournaments are held here. Visit the center's Web site to view the schedule.

Court fees are $8 per hour for the outdoor courts and $12 per hour for indoor. If you don't have a racket, don't worry. You can rent one for $5 a day. If you are playing indoors, you can also rent a ball machine for $25 an hour. Nonmarking shoes are required for play.

The tennis center is open seven days a week from 8 a.m. to 10 p.m. It is closed on Easter, Thanksgiving, and Christmas.

OKLAHOMA CITY TENNIS CENTER
3400 N. Portland (in Will Rogers Park)
(405) 946-2739
www.okc.gov/parks/tennis

Renovated in 2006 at a cost of $1.8 million, this center offers 24 lighted courts, a full-service pro shop, misting stations, and covered seating.

Lessons are available throughout the year. They run from $32 per hour per person to $9 per hour per person if four people are taking the class. Summer camps are held for ages 6 through 18 for $70 a week. Five sessions run from June into July, Mon through Fri from 8 to 11 a.m. League play is available through the week throughout the year. U.S. Tennis Association tournaments are held on the weekends.

Court fees are $6 an hour for singles and $8 an hour for doubles. Lighted courts are $2 an hour plus the court fee, and ball machines rent for $10 an hour plus the court fee. Summer hours are Mon through Thurs from 9 a.m. to 10 p.m., Fri from noon to 6 p.m., Sat from 9 a.m. to 9 p.m., and Sun from 1 to 6 p.m. Winter hours vary so check the Web site or call before going.

OKLAHOMA CITY TENNIS COURTS
(405) 297-2211
www.okc.gov/parks/tennis

The Oklahoma City Parks and Recreation Department maintains 50 tennis courts around the Oklahoma City area. Listed below are the courts with three playing courts or more available to visitors. To see all the courts available visit the Web site.

Goodholm Park, 2701 N. Robinson (located on Northwest 26th between Robinson and Harvey), 5 outdoor courts available; **Hosea Vinyard Park,** Southwest 41st and Walker, 5 outdoor lighted courts available; **Memorial Park,** 3600 N. Classen Blvd., 5 outdoor courts available; **Sellers Park,** 8301 S. Villa Ave., 3 outdoor courts available; **South Rotary Park,** 1800 Westwood Blvd., 3 outdoor courts available.

WESTWOOD TENNIS CENTER
2420 Westport Dr., Norman
(405) 366-8859
www.westwoodtennis.com

This tennis center was named the Outstanding Facility of the Year by the U.S. Tennis Association in 2007. It is a 12-court outdoor facility and a full-service pro shop that offers stringing services for tennis, racquetball, and badminton rackets. Guests also can enjoy a lounge area with two flatscreen televisions.

Many programs are available for children and adults. Adults can sign up for private lessons, clinics, drill groups, and leagues. Lessons range from $16 for a half hour to $40 for a full hour per person. Junior clinics run in the spring, summer, and fall for ages 3 to 18. Prices and times vary so call for more information.

Leagues and tournaments are played here and the men's and women's tennis teams of the University of Oklahoma practice here.

Court fees are $2.25 per person per hour on off-peak times, which are typically weekday mornings from 9:00 a.m. to noon and $3 per person per hour 5:30 to 8:30 p.m. Annual passes are $175 for families, $95 for adults, and $65 for seniors, 65 and older, and children 3 to 18.

Hours are 9 a.m. to 9 p.m. Mon through Sat and 9 a.m. to 6 p.m. Sun.

PARKS AND RECREATION

Lakes

ARCADIA LAKE
East of I-35, off 15th Street
(405) 216-7477
www.edmondok.com/parks/arcadialake

Just east of Edmond, between 15th Street and Second Street is Arcadia Lake. It was built in 1987 by the City of Edmond and the U.S. Army Corps of Engineers. It was constructed to supply water to Edmond, to provide flood control for the Deep Fork River Basin, to be a habitat for fish and wildlife, and to be a recreational and educational area for the community. Residents who have visited this lake will tell you it has fulfilled its purpose.

This lake has a lot of wooded areas surrounding it, making it perfect for wildlife viewing. It has scenic trails, where visitors can enjoy hiking, biking, equestrian rides, or mountain biking. There is a heated fishing dock where fishermen can catch bluegill, catfish, and bass. Boating and other water activities, like Jet Skiing wakeboarding, and waterskiing can all be enjoyed here. Anyone under the age of 13 must wear a life jacket at all times while on the water.

There's plenty of room for those who like to camp here as well. Arcadia Lake has 145 total campsites. Ten full hookups include electricity, water, and sewage. There are 72 regular campsites with water and electricity and 63 primitive sites. Showers are available in all camping areas.

Visitors will also find playgrounds, picnic tables, outdoor grills, a swimming beach, volleyball, and disc golf. Pets are allowed at Arcadia.

Arcadia Lake has four premiere events that take place during the year. In Jan, visitors can come and see the eagles during Eagle Watch. A Kids Fishing Derby is held in June. Aug finds those who love the lake and want to keep it clean working to pick up trash during Lake Sweep. And finally in Oct is Storybook Forest. Read about the Eagle Watch and Storybook Forest in the "Annual Events" chapter of this book.

The lake has 26 miles of shoreline and over 1,800 surface acres. A fee is charged for entrance, but it varies, so check the Web site or call ahead.

LAKE HEFNER
Located on the west side of Lake Hefner Parkway
(405) 299-0005
www.lakehefner.org
www.okc.gov/lakes/hefner.html

This lake sits on the northwest side of Oklahoma City and is no doubt the easiest of all the lakes to get to. Driving north or south on Hefner Parkway, you can exit off Hefner or Britton; go west to one of the parking lots. You can also reach the lake from the Northwest Expressway; turn north on Portland or Meridian.

Lake Hefner was built in 1947 and has 18 miles of shoreline. It has 2,500 surface acres, is 94 feet at its deepest, and has an average depth of 29 feet. It is owned by Oklahoma City. On its southwest corner is a canal that connects it to Lake Overholser, another Oklahoma City–owned lake. Water flows in to Hefner from the North Canadian River and the Canton Reservoir.

There's a lot to do here—fishing, power-boating, sailing, windsurfing, kite flying, flying remote-controlled airplanes, biking, running, walking, bird-watching, and picnicking. For those interested in fishing, channel cat, walleye, bass, crappie, and sunfish make their home here. Lake Hefner also has a 9.1-mile asphalt multipurpose trail that runs around the lake. The trail is 12-feet wide on three sides and then drops down to a 6-foot-wide pedestrian-only trail on the east side. Lake Hefner hosts a number of special events throughout the year that raise money for organizations like the Red Cross, Make-A-Wish Foundation, and Cystic Fibrosis Foundation.

Stars and Stripes Park is located on the south side of the lake. There is a playground and softball field here. Hefner Golf Course is on the southwest side of the lake. If guests get hungry, they'll find a number of restaurants on the west and east sides.

LAKE OVERHOLSER
Located off SR 66, between Council and Morgan Road
(405) 299-0005
www.okc.gov/lakes/overholser.html
www.outdoorsok.com/Oklahoma/Overholser
This is Oklahoma City's oldest water reservoir. It was built in 1919 and named for Ed Overholser, Oklahoma City's sixth mayor. The lake provides water to a treatment plant still operating at Northwest 6th and Pennsylvania. In 2007, Overholser Dam was added to the National Register of Historic Places.

There are 7 miles of shoreline with 1,500 surface acres. The lake is 13 feet at its deepest, with an average depth of 6 feet. A covered picnic pavilion can be reserved for family or company gatherings. Some of the activities enjoyed here are picnicking, sailing, boating, and fishing. Fishing enthusiasts will find catfish, crappie, white bass, largemouth bass, and hybrid striped bass available here. There is a covered fishing pier, boat ramps, outdoor grills, picnic tables, and handicap facilities. However, no swimming is allowed.

LAKE STANLEY DRAPER
Located Minutes from I-240 and Sooner Road
Marina: 8301 SE 104th St.
(405) 799-0870
www.okc.gov/lakes/draper.html
Located on the southeast side of Oklahoma City, this lake is 98 feet deep with an average depth of 34 feet. It has 34 miles of shoreline and 29,000 surface acres. Built in 1963, it takes in water from Lake Atoka and McGee Creek Reservoir.

Those who like the water will find plenty to do here, including fishing, boating, camping, dirt-bike riding, and picnicking. Skiing is allowed in open water, but swimming is prohibited. There are four covered fishing piers, covered wet slips, and dry storage areas that can be rented from the marina. The marina is open seven days a week. Operating hours vary according to the season.

Motorboats, sailboats, and Jet Skis are allowed on the water. As the lake is owned by Oklahoma City, a city boating permit is required for all watercraft. Fees are $5 a day or $25 for a yearly pass. Boating permits and fishing licenses can be purchased from the marina.

LAKE THUNDERBIRD
13101 Alameda Dr.
(405) 360-3572
www.touroklahoma.com
One of the Oklahoma City area's largest lakes, Lake Thunderbird is located in 1,874-acre Lake Thunderbird State Park, just east of Norman. The lake is the water reservoir for Norman, Midwest City, and Del City. It has over 6,000 surface acres and 86 miles of shoreline. For those who want a lot to do without being far from the city, this is the lake for you.

There is a swim beach, two marinas, an archery range, a nature center, horse rental, equestrian trails, hiking trails, as well as bicycle trails. Water sports include paddleboating, canoeing, sailing, wakeboarding, Jet Skiing, and waterskiing. Interested in fishing? Here fishermen will find channel cat, crappie, white bass, largemouth bass, and saugeye.

The park has 447 campsites, including 200 full RV hookup sites. For those wanting to get back to nature, primitive camping is available as well as tent sites. Showers are located throughout the campgrounds. Restrooms, outdoor grills, picnic tables, and drinking water can be used by daytime or overnight visitors.

Fees are charged but they vary according to location and season, so call ahead to find out current prices.

Parks

EARLYWINE AQUATIC CENTER
3033 SW 119th St.
(405) 692-6050
www.okc.gov/parks/pools/earlywine.html
Want to have some fun in the water? Head to the Earlywine Aquatic Center. There are swimming lanes, bubbling geysers, slides, large mushroom water curtains, and buckets that drop water on swimmers from 15 feet in the air. The center employs 15 lifeguards, eight of which are on duty at all times. If you tire of water activities, visit the huge sandbox or gather a team and play a game of volleyball. When guests get hungry, there is a full-service concession stand that sells pretzels, pizza, ice cream, and more.

Summer hours are from May 30 to Aug 16 noon to 9 p.m. daily. From Aug 21 to Sept 7, hours are Fri from 3 to 9 p.m. and Sat and Sun from noon to 6 p.m. Admission is $5; $3 after 6 p.m. Season passes are available and cost $50 for individuals and $150 for a family of four.

Swim lessons for all age levels are offered here. Dates, times, and cost vary, so call for more information.

MAT HOFFMAN ACTION SPORTS PARK
1700 S. Robinson
(405) 297-2211
www.okc.gov/parks/skatepark
Named after 10-time BMX World champion Mat Hoffman, this skate park is the only park of its kind in Oklahoma City. Hoffman helped design the park, which is for skateboards, inline skating, and BMX freestyle biking only.

National Geographic ranked the park as one of the top 10 skate parks in the United States in its 2009 book, *The 10 Best of Everything Families: An Ultimate Guide for Travelers.*

The park is divided unto two areas. The first area is the flow course. It consists of bowl combinations of varying shapes, depths, and heights. Bowl depths range from 5 feet to 11 feet. Second is the street course with ledges and handrails.

The park has a picnic bench, lighting, and free admission. Protective gear and helmets are required. No food or drink is allowed in the fenced area. Weapons of any kind are prohibited on the grounds. Graffiti, tagging, and stickers are prohibited. The Oklahoma City Police Department and Oklahoma River security monitor the park regularly.

This park is a use-at-your-own-risk, nonsupervised facility. It is open from dawn to 11 p.m. every day.

> **i** To receive your Parks Guide contact the Oklahoma City Parks and Recreation Department at (405) 297-2211 or download a guide in pdf form from www.okc.gov/parks.

OKLAHOMA CITY PARKS AND RECREATION DEPARTMENT
(405) 297-2211
www.okc.gov/parks
Oklahoma City owns and/or maintains over 200 parks across the metro area. A list of them is available on the city Web site at www.okc.gov/parks/parks_maps/list.html. There you can find out what each park offers and if it is near where you live. If you have questions about a specific park, you can call the Parks and Recreation Department at the phone number above. Not all the parks have the same amenities. There are some with baseball fields, basketball courts, gymnasiums, tennis courts, picnic shelters, spray grounds, tennis courts, and some that only have a swimming pool and playground. Check the Web site for a park that has the amenties that you are most interested in.

PAW PARK
Northwest 73rd and Grand Boulevard
(405) 297-2211
www.pawok.com
This two-acre off-leash dog park was rated one of the top 10 dog parks in America by the magazine Dog Fancy in Oct 2008. This park was built by the Partners for Animal Welfare of Oklahoma in cooperation with Oklahoma City. The cost of construction was $85,000. It has water stations, trees, two fenced-in areas (one for smaller dogs and senior dogs and one for larger dogs), a swimming pool, and a bright-red fire hydrant.

Dog owners know that 20 minutes of off-leash activity equates to two hours of walking on a leash, so owners bring their canine friends here to run and romp with them and their other dog friends. There are several benches and shaded areas for noncanines who may need to rest. You should know the area is restricted to dogs and their owners. No one under age 10 is allowed. There are other regulations that you should know before you go. They are listed on the Web site.

ROUTE 66 PARK
9901 NW 23rd
(405) 297-2756
www.okc.gov/parks/route_66
Route 66 Park is the first themed park in the Oklahoma City Parks and Recreation Department, and it is dedicated to the "Mother Road." Route 66 Park is not on SR 66, but adjacent to it. It is located about a mile south of SR 66 on the west side of Oklahoma City's Lake Overholser.

A plaza area with inlaid tile provides visitors a bird's-eye view of the historic road's route from the skyscrapers of downtown Chicago to the Santa Monica Pier. This greater-than-life-size map includes 34 landmarks along the route, which crosses through eight states.

In addition, the Cyrus Avery Observation Tower gives visitors a sweeping, panoramic view of the 148-acre park's three ponds, as well as Lake Overholser. An outdoor plaza and amphitheater is the perfect place for small concerts and outdoor events, and picnic shelters abut a themed Route 66 playground. The tower is open only to persons who rent the plaza area for special events.

Anglers will love the fishing opportunities in the park's wetland ponds. A series of plank walkways and bridges take visitors through the wetlands where they can observe native and wildlife, as well as fish for largemouth bass, channel catfish, blue catfish, crappie, and flathead catfish.

Several projects from the park master plan are underway. One of the projects, the new Skate Plaza for boarders and bikers, opened in Summer 2009.

The park is open daily from 8 a.m. to 11 p.m.

FIVE OKLAHOMA CITY PARKS

Oklahoma City has over 200 parks. Here are five parks that have varying activity centers and fields.

Douglass Park, 900 Cloverdale Dr., (405) 427-8712
Baseball field, basketball goals, gymnasium, golf course, playground, recreation center, sprayground, and swimming pool.

Macklanburg Park, 2234 NW 117th, (405) 751-2473
Baseball field, gymnasium, playground, recreation center, tennis court, and sprayground.

Memorial Park, 1150 NW 36th St., (405) 297-2211
Basketball goals, playground, recreation center, soccer field, sprayground, tennis courts, and trail.

Sellers Park, 8303 S. Villa Ave., (405) 685-4027
Baseball field, gymnasium, playground, soccer field, sprayground, swimming pool, and tennis court.

Woodson Park, 3028 SW 36th St., (405) 681-9776
Baseball field, gymnasium, playground, picnic shelter, softball field, senior center, and trail.

Edmond Parks
EDMOND PARKS AND RECREATION DEPARTMENT
2733 Marilyn Williams Dr., Edmond
(405) 359-4630
www.edmondok.com/parks

Edmond has 26 parks and you can find a list of them on the city's Web site, www.edmond ok.com/parks/cityparks. This Web site provides information about what each park has to offer. While all the parks are nice and clean, the two listed below are Edmond's premier parks.

HAFER PARK
1034 S. Bryant, Edmond
Hafer Park is located between 2nd and 15th Streets off the east side of Bryant. Built in 1979, it has a 6.5-miles trail. It runs along the far eastern side of the park and hooks up with Fink Park downtown. The park itself covers 121 acres and is quite heavily wooded. There are playgrounds, a volleyball court, an exercise station, a stage, restrooms, picnic tables, drinking fountains, and a kids fishing pond where several families of ducks hang out. To the north is an athletic complex for baseball and softball games. This park is used heavily, so be prepared to wait for facilities on weekends and holidays. There is plenty of parking.

MITCH PARK
1501 W. Covell, Edmond
Located on the northeast corner of West Covell Road and North Santa Fe, this 280-acre park has something for everyone. There are 5 miles of trails, playgrounds, a disc golf course, basketball courts, an exercise station, a volleyball court, a skate park, picnic tables, restrooms, an amphitheater, and an athletic complex for baseball and softball. There aren't many trees at the front of the park, but is fairly wooded toward the back along the trail. Use caution when on the trail as some areas are quite secluded. Plenty of parking is available.

Norman
CITY OF NORMAN PARKS AND RECREATION
201 W. Gray St., #C, Norman
(405) 366-5472
www.ci.norman.ok.us
The Norman Parks and Recreation Department maintains 55 neighborhood and community

---

MORE PARKS IN OKLAHOMA CITY AREA

To learn about parks in other Oklahoma City suburbs, please call or visit the Web sites of the departments listed below.

City of Bethany Parks and Recreation Department, (405) 789-2146, www.cityofbethany.org

Del City Parks and Recreation Department, (405) 677-2443, www.cityofdelcity.com/parks.htm

Midwest City Parks and Recreation Department, (405) 739-1296, www.midwestcityok.org

City of Moore Parks and Recreation Department, (405) 793-5090, www.cityofmoore.com

City of Yukon Parks and Recreation Department, (405) 350-8937, www.cityofyukonok.gov

---

parks. Pavilions and shelters are available for rent in several of them. For information on the city's parks, contact the Parks and Recreation Department at the number above or visit the city's Web site.

LIONS PARK
Flood Avenue and Symmes Street
Norman
Located 5 blocks northwest of the University of Oklahoma, Lions Park is a nice neighborhood park with lots of trees. There are picnic tables, backstops for softball and baseball practice, a gazebo, a picnic shelter, a trail for walking or jogging, lighted tennis courts, a lighted baseball field available for rent, and restrooms that are open from Apr through Oct.

REAVES PARK

2501 S. Jenkins Ave., Norman

More than 3,000 volunteers helped build a 13,000-square-foot playground for this park in five days. Designers took suggestions from children and incorporated them into the design, making this a true children's park. The children's area has a dinosaur slide; games, like tic-tac-toe; swings; a tree house; and a rock wall. Of course, there are the usual park facilities like picnic tables, back stops for baseball and softball practice, a shelter, a jogging and walking course, and restrooms available Apr through Oct.

Reaves Park is home to the Medieval Festival in Apr and it hosts numerous softball games. To learn about the Medieval Festival, visit the "Annual Events" chapter of this book. To learn more about the softball games, visit www.reavespark.org.

SPECTATOR SPORTS

ASA HALL OF FAME TOURNAMENTS

Amateur Softball Association of America (ASA)
2801 NE 50th St.
(405) 424-5266
www.asasoftball.com

The NCAA College World Series, which annually draws more than 63,000 spectators from around the nation, and the World Cup of Softball are two premier softball events held at the Amateur Softball Association (ASA) Hall of Fame Stadium. These two events bring together the best in college softball and the best women's fast-pitch teams from various foreign countries. The ASA Hall of Fame Stadium is the mecca of softball in the United States and the dedicated ASA staff and volunteers ensure the best in hospitality to everyone who visits there.

Games are played from Mar through Oct and are the premier events in softball. The cost of admission depends on the event and tickets are available online or in person at the hall of fame gift shop. Dates are booked well in advance. You can find out more information about who's playing by visiting the ASA's Web site. Parking is available for more than 1,000 cars and buses. Visi-

tors have to pay for parking for selected events, including the NCAA College World Series.

The Hall of Fame Stadium has a complete concession area with everything from hot dogs to chicken and brisket sandwiches. Hours vary depending on event.

OKLAHOMA CITY BLAZERS

105 N. Hudson Ave., #101
(405) 235-7825
www.okcblazer.com

Hockey has a rich history in Oklahoma City. It dates back to the mid-1930s. From 1965 to 1982, hockey existed in Oklahoma City as a primary farm team for three different National Hockey League clubs. The current Blazers franchise began play in 1992 in the Central Hockey League (CHL). The Blazers have been the gold standard in the CHL during the last 17 seasons. They won the CHL championship in 1996 and 2001 and own the CHL record for wins. That record is 652 games in 17 seasons.

In each of the last five hockey seasons from 2004 to 2009, it has hosted a School Day Game. For each event the team brought nearly 4,000 kids from Oklahoma City public schools to attend a hockey game.

The Blazers coach, Doug Sauter, has the most wins in the Central Hockey League. Sauter has been with the team since 1994. Under his guidance, the Blazers teams have qualified for the playoffs 11 times, won 7 CHL division regular season titles, won 4 regular season championships, made 3 CHL Finals appearances, and won 2 CHL championships.

The regular season for the Blazers begins in mid-Oct and runs through mid-Mar. The playoffs begin immediately following the regular season and can last until mid-May. The Blazers play at the Ford Center. Ticket prices range from $10 to $30.

OKLAHOMA CITY REDHAWKS

2 S. Mickey Mantle Dr.
(405) 218-1000
www.oklahomaredhawks.com

The Oklahoma City Redhawks baseball club started out as the Oklahoma City Indians back in 1918. In 1962, the team was the 89ers and from 1962 to 1997 it played games at the All Sports Stadium on the state fairgrounds. In 1998, the 89ers officially became the Oklahoma Redhawks when the team moved to the AT&T Bricktown Ballpark, located to the east of downtown. At the end of the 2008 season, the Redhawks announced another name change to Oklahoma City Redhawks to acknowledge the commitment Oklahoma City residents made 10 years earlier by approving MAPS, a one-cent sales tax to build a professional baseball stadium.

The Redhawks play all home games at the AT&T Bricktown Ballpark. The $23.6-million ballpark seats more than 13,000 fans. To date the Redhawks have had five playoff appearances and continue to attract some 752,000 fans to the ballpark annually.

The team is a Triple-A affiliate of the Texas Rangers. It hosts several nonprofit events throughout the year, including the Susan G. Komen Race for the Cure, Alzheimer's Memory Walk, Down Syndrome Buddy Walk, United Way Pancake Breakfast, Autism Speaks, and the American Heart Walk to name a few. The Redhawks season begins in late Mar or Apr and runs through Sept. Tickets range from $7 to $22

OKLAHOMA CITY THUNDER

Two Leadership Square
211 N. Robinson Ave., Ste. 300
(405) 208-4800
www.nba.com/thunder

The Oklahoma City Thunder played its first season in Oklahoma City in 2008, following relocation from Seattle. On July 2, 2008, a settlement with Seattle was announced which permitted the team to move. On Sept 3, 2008, Chairman Clay Bennett announced the team would be renamed the Thunder. The Thunder played its first regular season home game in the Ford Center on Oct 29, 2009, against the Milwaukee Bucks.

As the Seattle Supersonics, this franchise won a National Basketball Association (NBA) Championship in 1979. It's all-time winning percentage is 52 percent. The Thunder plays in the Northwest Division of the Western Conference of the National Basketball Association.

Scott Brooks was named head coach of the Thunder on Apr 15, 2009, after serving as interim head coach since Nov 2008 and assistant coach prior to that. Brooks graduated from UC–Irvine where he played for the Anteaters. He had an 11 year NBA career playing with seven teams during that time. and then spent six years as an NBA assistant coach with the Sacramento Kings (2006–2007), Denver Nuggets (2003–2006) and finally for the Thunder (2007–2008). The Thunder is active in the community and takes significant initiatives in the areas of education, physical fitness, arts, and youth basketball They visit schools and community venues to discuss and encourage young people to get involved in physical fitness. The NBA schedule is released in early Aug. The 82-game regular season begins on or about Nov 1 and ends in mid-Apr. The regular season consists of 41 home games and 41 road games. There is a preseason schedule of approximately seven games in Oct. The Thunder plays its 41 regular season home games in the Ford Center. Nonpremium seating ranges from $10 per seat to $250. NBA requires teams to provide at least 500 seats for $10 a seat. The Thunder offers 3,500 seats.

i If you are a Sooners fan and want to find out what's happening in Sooners sports, look no further than the *Sooner Spectator* (www.soonerspectator.com). This magazine covers it all from football to baseball. Subscriptions are $39.95 for one year. To subscribe call (405) 488-0242.

OKLAHOMA SOONERS

University of Oklahoma
660 Parrington Oval
(405) 325-0311
www.soonersports.com

Twenty minutes south of Oklahoma City is the University of Oklahoma, home to the Oklahoma Sooners. The Sooners have a rich tradition of sports in the state and fans will tell you the "Sooner Nation" takes precedent over any other sports program in Oklahoma. While the Sooners have sports, like baseball, tennis, golf, track

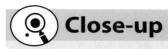 **Close-up**

Oklahoma City Yard Dawgz

This franchise was founded in 2004 by Jeff Lund, Horn Chen, and Barry Switzer and is currently owned by Phil Miller, who also owns several Oklahoma City–based businesses. In its six-year history, the Yard Dawgz (100 W. Main, Ste. 175, 405-228-3294, www.okcyarddawgz .com) has made the playoffs every year with the exception of the 2008 season. The team belongs to the Arena Football League's minor league, arenafootball2 (af2), and has a regular season win percentage of 60 percent.

The team has had two af2 Kicker of the Year recipients, Peter Martinez (2004) and A. J. Haglund (2006), and also one af2 Lineman of the Year recipient, James Landers (2004). In 2005, Al Hunt was named to the All-af2 Second Team and in 2007; Al Hunt, Barry Giles, and Gene Frederic were named to the National Conference All-af2 team. In 2008, Al Hunt was named to the af2 All-Ironman Team. Hunt is the only player to be with the team since 2004 and could finish his career as the best wide receiver in af2 history.

Currently the Yard Dawgz is coached by Sparky McEwen. The Yard Dawgz players, coaches, dancers, and mascots make numerous appearances throughout the year all over Oklahoma City. In 2008, the organization won second and third place awards for best Community Relations Department in af2. The Yard Dawgz also donated over $10,000 in tickets and merchandise to several organizations, including the American Lung Association, the Paralyzed Veterans of America, the Muscular Dystrophy Association, and Meals on Wheels.

The team hosts two Junior Dance Clinics every year in which schoolage girls learn dances with the Yard Dawgz Dance Team and have the opportunity to perform in front of thousands during half-time. The Yard Dawgz Football Academy offers middle school and high school boys the opportunity to receive individualized instruction from professional players and coaches in their indoor training facility. There are four camps throughout the season, beginning in Mar.

Since 2006, The Yard Dawgz mascot, Deizel Dawg, has won af2 Mascot of the Year three times.

Regular season for the Yard Dawgz begins at the end of Mar and runs through July. Playoffs are scheduled for Aug. All home games are played in the Cox Convention Center. Single game tickets start at $10 and the average ticket price is $30.

and field, volleyball, gymnastics, rowing, soccer, and cross country, they are best known for their women's and men's basketball programs and the football program.

Beginning in Aug, a change sweeps over the state. All eyes turn to Norman and all talk turns to the Sooners football team and its chances for the season. Since 1915, when the Sooners won its first conference title, the team has had the attention of not only the state, but also the nation. Head coach Bob Stoops has been with the Sooners since 1999. Stoops has led the Sooners to six Big 12 Conference crowns and one national championship title. Overall the Sooners have won seven national championships and 42 conference titles. The football program has had five Heisman Trophy winners and 148 All Americans. Some of the more notable figures to come out of the program have been Billy Sims, Brian Bosworth, and Roy Williams. The Sooners football team plays its home games at Gaylord Family–Oklahoma Memorial Stadium in Norman. The stadium has a capacity of over 82,000 and those who attend will tell you every seat is always taken.

Following a close second in popularity is the Sooners basketball team. Coach Jeff Capel has led the team since 2005and the team plays home games in the Lloyd Noble Center. The team's overall record includes 20 conference titles and it has made it to the NCAA tournament 26 times. Basketball season runs from Nov through Mar.

The Sooners women's basketball team is another program to be reckoned with. Head coach Sherri Coale has been with the program since 1996. Under her guidance, the women's basketball team made it to the Final Four in the Women's NCAA Tournament in 2002 and in 2009 the team won the Big 12 Title, making it a Big 12 Champion.

To catch all the action, tune in to KOKC, 1520 AM, the Sooner Sports Radio Network, or visit the Sooner's Web site. You'll find statistics, schedules, information on players, and where to get tickets for all Sooner sports programs.

OKLAHOMA STATE COWBOYS (STILLWATER)
Oklahoma State University
(405) 744-5000
www.okstate.com
The Oklahoma State Cowboys have a rich sports heritage. Oklahoma State has football, basketball

cross-country, soccer, golf, tennis, wrestling, baseball, softball, and equestrian. The sports program has produced Olympic gold medalists, NCAA champions, a Heisman Trophy winner, the NCAA Baseball Player of the Century, college and pro hall of fame inductees, and some of the greatest wrestlers in history. The men's golf program has qualified for the NCAA championship in each of its 61 seasons and won 50 conference championships. Both the men's and women's cross-country teams have impressive records. They finished in the top 10 in 2005, won four NCAA championships, have had more than 50 All-Americans, have one world record holder, and an Olympian.

To learn more about the Oklahoma State Cowboys sports programs, find schedules, get statistics on players and teams, learn about their coaches and players, and how and where to get tickets, visit the Oklahoma State Web site.

ℹ **To hear what's happening in sports around Oklahoma, tune in to 640 AM or 98.1 FM, WWLS, the Sports Animal (www .thesportsanimal.com). You will find 24 hours of sports commentary and interviews on this station.**

ANNUAL EVENTS

Oklahoma City and its surrounding cities and towns have a lot going on during the year. Jan, Feb, and Mar see a lot of events preparing people for summer. From Apr through Aug, festivals and marathons are highlighted, along with our nation's independence celebrations. In Sept, the Oklahoma State Fair takes center stage along with a few fall festivals. Oct is full of events for those interested in celebrating on the scary side. Nov and Dec are about all things Christmas.

Listed in this chapter are some events just for children and some just for adults. Most however, incorporate children's events into the celebration so children will have as much fun as their parents.

About half the events charge admission; those that do are noted. Parking at most events in the suburbs and along the fringes of Oklahoma City is free, however, if the event is taking place downtown, be prepared to pay to park.

Weather is always a consideration in this area. In the winter months, ice and snow may cause an event to be postponed or canceled. If the highway patrol is urging everyone to stay off the roads, it might be wise to stay home. In the spring, visitors need to be prepared for sudden downpours and the possibility of severe weather. Take an umbrella and a raincoat and keep an eye on the sky. If you are attending an event in the middle of summer and it is outdoors, keep yourself hydrated by drinking plenty of water.

Be sure to wear weather-appropriate clothing when you attend these events. In the winter, dress in layers. In the spring and fall it is a good idea to carry a sweater or a light jacket. Dressing in layers is also a good idea because so you can shed clothing if you become too hot. In summer, wear light clothing and a hat to shield you from the sun.

Although most of the events listed here have been held in the same location for years, event locations do change from time to time. Always call and confirm the event's location before you go.

Good sources of information for events not listed here are the Oklahoma City Convention and Tourism Bureau (405-297-8912; www.okccvb.org), Downtown OKC (405-235-3500; www.downtownokc.com), Oklahoma State Tourism and Recreation (800-654-8240; www.tourokla homa.com), and the City of Oklahoma City (www.okc.gov, click on "Things To Do").

JANUARY

ANNUAL EAGLE WATCH
Arcadia Lake
Edmond
(405) 216-7471 or (405) 216-7470
www.edmondok.com/parks/arcadialake/
events
For the past 12 years, the City of Edmond, has invited visitors to Arcadia Lake to experience one of nature's most beautiful wonders—the bald eagle. About 800 people per year have attended the event in the past and attendance increases each year, testifying to the popularity of the event.

Visitors start at the Lake Park Office, where they can watch a film about eagles and view posted information about the bald eagles as well as other birds that inhabit the park. There is also a mounted eagle on display.

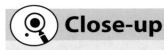 **Close-up**

Oklahoma Bluegrass Club Oklahoma Bluegrass Concerts (Del City)

Monthly indoor Bluegrass Concerts (405-677-1509, patpogue@cox.net, www.okbgc.org) are held the first Sat of each month from Oct through Apr. The Oklahoma Bluegrass Club with the assistance of the Oklahoma Arts Council puts on these events. In 2009, the organization celebrated its 40th year anniversary concert.

These concerts are held at Kerr Middle School, 2300 South Linda Lane, in Del City. The concerts start at 7 p.m. and three scheduled bands play at each event. There are jam sessions throughout the building where professional and nonprofession musicians of all ages come together to share their music in a family oriented atmosphere where alcohol or drugs are not allowed. Some of the past performing bands are, The Faris Family, Village Singers, The Arbuckles, Boggy River Bluegrass, Cedar Ridge, and South Bound Mule just to name a few.

Visitors paying admission to the concert are allowed to take pictures. There is a concession serving, hot dogs, nachos, Frito pies, soft drinks, coffee, and homemade desserts. The bands playing the concert sell their T-shirts, CD's, pictures, and other items that pertain to their band or Bluegrass Music.

There is plenty of close, free parking and the facility is handicapped accessible. The Oklahoma Bluegrass Club expects between fifteen hundred and two thousand people to attend the concerts each year. There is a nominal fee charged. General admission is $6 for adults, Oklahoma Bluegrass Club members, $5, ages 14-16 years old, $1.50, under fourteen years is free. Children are encouraged to attend the concerts in an effort to learn about Bluegrass Music so it will continue to be passed down from generation to generation.

In addition to the Oklahoma City concerts, the Oklahoma Bluegrass Club, which was started in 1969 and was the first Bluegrass Club formed in Oklahoma, sponsors the annual Skyline Bluegrass Festival, with the assistance of the Oklahoma Arts Council, the first weekend in May at Wewoka Lake Park, Wewoka, Oklahoma, I-40, Wewoka/Cromwell exit 212, Hwy. 56, south 15 miles then west three miles. Admission to the festival is $10 on Thurs and Fri $12 on Sat. Children 12 years of age and under are free. A three-day pass is available for $30. R.V. hook-ups are available for $10 per day. Numerous Bands are scheduled to perform from various states as well as Oklahoma. Those attending the festival may participate in the Bluegrass instrument workshops. Bluegrass Music is noted for its acoustical sound made with nonelectric instruments such as fiddles, guitars, banjos, mandolins, dobros, and upright bass. Bluegrass Music has become very popular in recent years as it is heard and enjoyed by all ages.

When visitors are ready to look at the eagles, they proceed outside where they will be directed to where the eagles are. There are designated viewing areas, so visitors can walk or ride to those areas. No matter what guests will need binoculars or a spotting scope to see the eagles up close, so visitors need to bring those items when they come as they are not provided by the park.

If visitors get hungry, food vendors are present. In the past, the park has served free coffee and hot cocoa. The park also has items like chips, 20-ounce sodas, and candy bars for sale at all times and Arcadia Lake merchandise, such as caps, T-shirts, and sweatshirts.

This is a come-and-go event meaning visitors don't have to stay at one place for any given period of time. People are at one location for a short time before they move on to the next.and then if they want to go back to a location, they can. Where parking is necessary like at the Lake Park Office, there are paved parking spots complete with wheelchair-accessible spots.

The fee for the event is $3 per vehicle with up to five people. Tickets are sold at the Park Office. Visitors are given maps and explanation of the event at that time.

INTERNATIONAL FINALS RODEO
2304 Exchange
(405) 235-6540
www.iprarodeo.com

The International Finals Rodeo (IFR) is held the third weekend in Jan each year at the State Fair Arena in Oklahoma City. Hosted by the International Professional Rodeo Association, it's the culmination of the entire rodeo season, where the top 15 cowboys and cowgirls have the opportunity to compete for more than a quarter of a million dollars in prize money as well a world championship. The International Finals Rodeo attracts more than 25,000 people annually.

The IFR consists of four live performances with 120 contestants competing in each. The first performance is held Fri night. The second is Sat afternoon, the third Sat night, and the final round, where the world champions are crowned, is Sun afternoon.

Also part of this event is a trade show that offers merchandise for sale, such as saddles, ropes, clothes, house goods, food, boots, belts, hats, western furniture, and jewelry. There is also a booth that sells IFR merchandise, including hats, sweatshirts, beanies, T-shirts, jackets, and an array of souvenirs.

Tickets cost $15, $18, and $25 depending on where you sit. You can purchase them ahead of time online at www.tickets.com or by going to the box office at the State Fair Arena. There is no charge for parking. Still photos are allowed.

OKLAHOMA CITY BOAT SHOW
Oklahoma State Fair Park
Northwest 10th and May
(405) 948-6704
www.okcboats.com

In 2008 the Oklahoma City Boat Show celebrated its 54th annual show. Attracting more than 10,000 people a year, the show is held in three buildings at State Fair Park.

Besides boats, guests can check out the latest in personal watercraft, like Jet Skis and wakeboards. Boating manufacturers are available to answer questions about boat construction and the Coast Guard and Oklahoma City Police Department are also on hand to answer water-safety questions and provide other educational information. Vendors are also here to sell you boat-related merchandise. If you are interested in buying the latest and greatest boat, financing is available at this show.

Tickets are $5 for adults. Admission is free for children 12 and under. Discount tickets are available from boat dealers and at 7-Eleven convenience stores around the metro area.

OKLAHOMA CITY HOME AND GARDEN SHOW
Oklahoma State Fair Park
Northwest 10th and May
(405) 948-6704
www.oklahomacityhomeshow.com

Held since 1982, this is Oklahoma City's largest home and garden show. The event provides an opportunity to shop for hundreds of products and services for your home.

More than 400 local and national exhibitors offer ideas and advice. National celebrity home and garden experts give entertaining and educational presentations throughout the event. Large, full-size landscape features allow guests to experience products.. Food vendors are also at the show, offering specialty items, like dips, mixes, nuts, and wine. If you get hungry, you'll find concessions serving corn dogs, burritos, nachos, hamburgers, funnel cakes, and cinnamon rolls.

The show is held in five buildings at the State Fair Park. In 2009, over 35,000 people attended. There is plenty of free parking. Admission prices vary. Check the Web site for current prices.

NORMAN EAGLE WATCH (NORMAN)
Lake Thunderbird State Park
Discovery Cove Nature Center
1201 Clear Bay Ave.
(405) 321-4633
www.touroklahoma.com

This event is held at the Discovery Cove Nature Center at Lake Thunderbird State Park. Included in the approximately three-hour program is a presentation about bald eagles given by a naturalist and a drive around the lake, with stops at preset locations to look for eagles. Very little walking is required. Attendance is usually 20 to 40 people. Well-behaved children are welcome

The event is free but please call to make a reservation as space is limited. The eagle watch will be canceled in the event of freezing precipitation or hazardous road conditions. Ample parking is available.

FEBRUARY

AN AFFAIR OF THE HEART
8409 Gateway Terrace
(405) 632-2652
www.aaoth.com
First held in Feb 1985, An Affair of the Heart will celebrate its 25th anniversary in 2010. It is an Oklahoma tradition and people travel from across the United States to attend. Annual attendance is between 40,000 to 50,000 people. Exhibitors come from 25 states and occupy seven large buildings at the State Fair Park in Feb and Oct.

Vendors at the event offer a wide selection of items for sale, including arts, crafts, antiques, collectibles, furniture, decorative items, jewelry, and clothing. If shopping makes you hungry, there are food vendors available selling everything from strudel to strawberries Newport.

Parking is free and trolleys are available to transport guests to and from the parking areas.

There is a one-time admission fee of $6, good for all three days of the show. Tickets can be purchased in advance at the An Affair of the Heart office in Oklahoma City. Children 12 and under are admitted free.

CHOCOLATE FESTIVAL IN THE FORUM AT THE UNIVERSITY OF OKLAHOMA
1704 Asp Avenue, Norman
(405) 329-4523
www.normanfirehouse.com
First held in 1982, this festival is a fund-raising event for the Firehouse Art Center. Years pre-vious, this event was held at the Art Center; however in 2009, the event outgrew the facility. The 2010 event will be held in the Forum on the University of Oklahoma campus. It was ranked third among Best Food Festivals in the United States by the Food Network. It has been featured in *Southern Living* magazine and it won Frontier Country Grand Award for Best Food in Central Oklahoma in 2008. In 2009, approximately 4000 people attended this event.

The festival features approximately 40 chocolate vendors and chocolate-tasting sessions are offered at 11:30 a.m., noon, 12:30 p.m., 1 p.m., and 1:30 p.m. A premiere, one-hour tasting session is held from 10:30 a.m. to 11:30 a.m. and includes 15 chocolate samples, a container to take home leftovers, and a complimentary drink. Throughout the festival, guests can watch hundreds of children create with paint, clay, and mixed media. Firehouse Art Center faculty and fine arts students from the Oklahoma University are on hand to assist the children.

Tickets go on sale Dec 1 at the Firehouse Art Center Tickets are $15 for members of the Firehouse Art Center and $18 for nonmembers and include 10 chocolate samples. Tickets for the premier tasting are $25 for members and $30 for nonmembers.

FONDUE FANDANGO
Harn Homestead
1721 N. Lincoln Blvd.
(405) 235-4058
www.harnhomestead.com
This is a fondue competition and tasting party. The first Fondue Fandango was held in 2007. It is one of the most unique cooking competitions in Oklahoma City. Chefs from area restaurants compete for the best sweet and savory fondues. Guest can enjoy sampling those fondue creations from various restaurants, dance to live music, and bid on fabulous chance drawings and live auction prizes. This event is for adults 21 and over.

Each year, between 350 and 400 guests attend. It is held in the barn at the Harn Homestead. Tickets are $75 in advance and $85 at the door. Valet parking is complimentary.

GROUNDHOG DAY

Oklahoma City Zoo
2101 NE 50th St.
(405) 424-3344
www.okczoo.com

Held at the Oklahoma City Zoo, this event started about 1994. Groundhog Day is a traditional, yet unconventional celebration here. The zoo does not have any groundhogs, so other zoo animals are chosen to be official Groundhog Day delegates. Popular prognosticators have included bison, pot-bellied pigs, a prairie dog, and grizzly bear brothers, Will and Wiley. These two bears are the most popular delegates with zoogoers.

On the morning of Feb 2, a zoo employee reads the Groundhog Day proclamation. Then children, adults, and zoo employees watch as the animal ambassador comes out into his exhibit. If the weather mammal sees his shadow, six more weeks of winter is forthcoming. But if no shadow is detected, spring is on the way. Zoo guests are treated to complimentary hot chocolate and donuts while they watch as this wild event takes place.

The event is free with paid zoo admission. The excitement begins at 10:30 a.m. This event is typically held outdoors. If the zoo is closed due to inclement weather, the event is canceled. Parking at the zoo is ample as they have a large parking area. Attendance varies depending on the weather.

LEAKE CAR AUCTION

Oklahoma State Fair Park
Northwest 10th and May
(800) 722-9942
www.leakecar.com

If you are interested in cars, this is the event for you. The Leake Auction Company has been coming to Oklahoma City and holding this auction since 1984. Leake Auction was established in 1964 as one of the first car auctions in the country. More than 40 years later, the auction company has sold over 30,000 cars.

People who come to this event are impressed with the size of this auction. In two days, approximately 400 cars are sold. The event features two auction rings and a large variety of cars from 1930 Lincolns to a 2009 Shelby. The 2008 show resulted in total sales of $4.2 million and total bids of $7.1 million. The top-selling car was the 1959 Cadillac Series 62 and it sold for $216,000.

Each year about 2,000 people attend this two-day event held at the Cox Pavilion at the Oklahoma City Fairgrounds. Tickets are $10 for adults and $5 for children and may be purchased at the gate

MARDI GRAS PARADE

Downtown Norman
(405) 329-5108

In the true spirit of Mardi Gras, this parade is a family-friendly tradition that celebrates the arts and community spirit with a nighttime moving carnival. Jeanne Flanigan, a local costume shop owner, started the parade in 1994. Over the years, it has grown and today it is overseen by the Norman Mardi Gras Parade Committee, which includes a number of local artists.

Parade participants include performers, floats, bands, dancers, and animals. Among the nearly 50 entries in 2009 were the Jedi Oklahoma City Star Wars Fan Club, the Society of Creative Anachronism, the Oklahoma Victory Dolls Derby Team, Rowdy the Redhawk, the Oklahoma National Guard, fire dancers, and animals from the Little River Zoo. Longtime participant, Krewe of Buckeus tosses hundreds of stuffed animals into the crowd along the parade route, while the Krewe of Bogus throws mini–Moon Pies.

Parade watchers should dress warmly and in layers. There is ample, free public parking within a half block of the parade route. The parade usually draws 5,000 to 6,000 people and is free.

i **If you want to get in the Mardi Gras spirit, you can order a King Cake from an authentic Mardi Gras bakery in New Orleans. Haydel's Bakery (800-442-1342; www.haydelsbakery.com), ships King Cakes from Jan through Mar only. Randazzo's Camellia City Bakery (800-684-2253; www.kingcakes.com) bakes and ships King Cakes all year long.**

OKLAHOMA CITY STORYTELLING FESTIVAL
400 W. California
(405) 270-4848
www.artscouncilokc.com

The Oklahoma City Storytelling Festival celebrates the ancient art of storytelling. It is held at Center Stage in downtown Oklahoma City and consists of a series of live storytelling performances. Past storytellers have included Donald Davis, Sid Lieberman, Nancy Donoval, Dovie Thomason, and Steve Poltz.

Storytellers are alone on stage and tell their stories with no visual props. The stories vary and they are all very entertaining.

Because of length, subject matter, and the lack of visual elements, the festival is recommended for children 13 and up. Parking is available on the street and in the Arts Council of Oklahoma City's parking lot next to Center Stage. Ticket prices vary based on performances and can be purchased online from the Arts Council about two months before the event.

MARCH

RV SUPER SHOW
Oklahoma State Fair Park
Northwest 10th and May
(405) 948-6704
www.rvshowokc.com

The RV Super Show is held at the Oklahoma State Fair Park.It is open to the public and gives those who are interested in owning and RV, or upgrading their existing RV the opportunity to view what's on the market, and what's new in RVing in one location.

There are hundreds of different RV makes and models to see here. Guests can "compare" shop and see which RV would fit into the family budget, be it a Fifth Wheel, Motorhome, or Pop-Up camper. Visitors will find RV displays throughout the grounds and in the Centennial Building, Cox Pavilion, and the Travel and Transportation Building. Besides the RV dealers, RV industry experts will be on hand to answer any questions about RVs and what's right for you.

A normal booth exhibit area at the RV show includes a variety of RV-product and service-related companies, such as repair services, parts, accessories, storage, rentals, loans, destination resorts, campgrounds, parks, hitches, portable generators, tow-behind vehicles, four-wheelers, scooters, motorcycles, pickup trucks, truck parts and accessories, stock brokers, satellite TVs and phones, satellite Internet, and travel-friendly food items. These types of product and service companies recognize the tremendous advantage of meeting Oklahoma's RV audience up close and face-to-face.

There is abundant free parking available. The event averages about 6,000 visitors per show with some recent shows reaching an estimated 12,000 people. An admission fee is charged.

SAINT PATRICK'S DAY PARADE
Bricktown
(405) 753-9887
www.saintpatricksdayparade.com/
oklahoma_saint_patricks_day_parade.htm

Oklahoma City's St. Patrick's Day Parade began in 1983 when a small group of individuals decided that the city needed a celebration of Irish heritage. The parade begins at the corner of Walker and Sheridan and proceeds east on Sheridan into Bricktown, ending at Joe Carter Avenue. The review stand is located in Bricktown. Parade participants have included Oklahoma University, color guard groups, shriners, Choctaw Indians, trained dog groups, clowns, and dancers. The parade goes on regardless of the weather. Attendance is between 10,000 and 15,000 people.

TASTE OF YUKON (YUKON)
Robertson Activity Center
SR 66 and Mustang Road
(405) 350-7677
www.canadianoklahoma.com/city/yukon/
events

This event gives attendees the opportunity to sample food from 20 different local restaurants. Taste of Yukon is held indoors at the Robertson Activity Center and around 1,000 guests are expected each year. The event enjoyed its 10th year in 2009. Tickets are $8 in advance and $10 the day of the event for adults and $5 for children 10 and under.

APRIL

OKLAHOMA CITY MEMORIAL MARATHON
Oklahoma City National Memorial & Museum
620 N. Harvey Ave.
(405) 235-3313 or (888) 452-HOPE
www.okcmarathon.com

The Oklahoma City Memorial Marathon was started as a way to honor the victims and survivors of the 1995 bombing of the Alfred P. Murrah Federal Building. The marathon is a Boston-qualifying, USA Track and Field sanctioned event on a certified 26.2-mile, single-loop course. Participants have the opportunity to register for the full marathon, a half marathon, a relay marathon, or a memorial walk. Participants must be 16 years of age or older on race day.

There is a Kid's Marathon (25 miles plus 1.2 miles) for all young athletes, including physically and mentally challenged athletes, age 11 and under who have run 25 miles prior to race day. All children will run the final 1.2 miles on race day and receive a special finisher's medal.

Fees range from $5 for the Kid's Marathon to $175 for the 5-person relay.

FESTIVAL OF THE ARTS
Downtown Oklahoma City
(405) 270-4848
www.artscouncilokc.com/festival-of-the-arts

This festival is produced by the Arts Council of Oklahoma City and is known as Oklahoma City's rite of spring. Typically held the third week of Apr, this event has garnered national attention as a premier event. Locally, it's known as a great place to stop, get a bite to eat for lunch or dinner, and enjoy the sounds of free music and the sites of downtown. For more detailed information, see "The Arts" chapter.

HOPABALOO
Oklahoma City Zoo
2101 NE 50th St.
(405) 424-3344
www.okczoo.com

In 2003, the Oklahoma City Zoo starting holding this event on Easter Sun and it has gained in popularity over the years. The fun begins with a brunch served from 11 a.m. to 2 p.m. in the Canopy Restaurant with the Easter Bunny. At 1:30 p.m. an egg hunt for children three and under begins. The egg hunt for four-year-olds begins at 2 p.m. and the five-year-olds get their chance starting at 2:30 p.m. Each egg hunt is limited to 100 participants.

The egg hunts are free with paid zoo admission. Zoo admission and brunch costs $14 for adults and $12 for seniors 65 and up and children 3 to 11. Children two and under eat free. Advance reservations are required. Zoo Friends receive a 10 percent discount.

JUNGLE GYM ART PARTY
Oklahoma City Zoo
2101 NE 50th St.
(405) 424-3344
www.okczoo.com

Held at the Jungle Gym Playground at the Oklahoma City Zoo, children 11 and under discover art through a variety of activities, such as cookie decorating, storytelling, and more.

The 30,000-square-foot playground was made possible by thousands of volunteers, individual donors, artists, civic organizations, and businesses. The Jungle Gym is a gift to the community from the Junior League of Oklahoma City, the Oklahoma City Zoo, and the Oklahoma Zoological Society.

Attendance varies depending on the weather. The event is held outside and is held rain or shine. Both children and adults are welcome. The event is free with paid admission to the zoo.

MEDIEVAL FAIR (NORMAN)
2501 Jenkins Avenue
(405) 288-2536
www.medievalfair.org

The Medieval Fair began in 1976 as a one-day fair and it has grown into a three-day event. Today it is the third-largest event in Oklahoma. The fair is a living history fair with art, crafts, food, games, and a vast array of entertainment for all ages. It is held in Reaves Park, 2501 Jenkins Ave., in Norman.

There are six stages with continuous performances. There are jousting tournaments with knights on horseback, human chess games, jugglers, minstrels, magicians, a falconer, a balancing act, dancing, and Shakespearean comedy. Visitors are allowed to take pictures and will want to as the king and queen and their court make their rounds through their kingdom.

Over 35 food vendors offer such fare as Indian tacos, funnel cakes, smoked turkey legs, gyros, roasted corn, crepes, Italian gelato, homemade root beer, sarsaparilla, and cream soda. More than 200 artists and craftspeople display and sell their items here. Visitors can buy wooden crafts, jewelry, journals, chain mail, Renaissance and medieval costumes, baskets, musical instruments, dolls, incense and oil, fine art, glass art, and more.

Parking is free at a lot adjacent to the fair. Visitors only need to follow the crowds to find their way to the entrance. Admission is free. With thousands of people attending, be prepared for a crunch, especially on Sat if the weather is nice. The best time to go is Fri afternoon while most people are at work and kids are in school.

OKLAHOMA CENTENNIAL HORSE SHOW
Oklahoma State Fair Park
Northwest 10th and May
(405) 948-6704
www.okcentennial.com/history.htm
Want to see a real horse show? Then head for the Oklahoma Centennial Horse Show. Held at the State Fair Arena in Oklahoma City, the show holds live performances that are actually the horse show division competitions themselves. A very colorful horn blower calls each division into the arena. Occasionally, live musicians play on Fri night while the horses compete.

This event has been held since 1988 and is run by volunteers. All proceeds benefit the Coffee Creek Riding Center for the Handicapped in Edmond.

Approximately 2,500 people attend per year. Admission and parking is free.

PARTY FOR THE PLANET
Oklahoma City Zoo
2101 NE 50th St.
(405) 424-3344
www.okczoo.com
Feeling up to a party? Head for the Oklahoma City Zoo and celebration of Earth Day. Leap into action and discover the importance of conserving wildlife and wild places. Held in honor of Earth Day, zoos and aquariums across the United States and Canada host this event, making it one of the largest Earth Day celebrations in North America. Families will enjoy fun activities, crafts, live entertainment, giveaways, and more.

The event is held outside on the Global Plaza and takes place rain or shine. Free with zoo admission.

PSCYCLE FOR FAMILIES BIKE RIDE
Edmond Family Counseling
1251 N. Broadway
(405) 341-3554
www.edmondfamilycounseling.org
Ready, set, ride. If you and your family are interested in riding bikes, this event is for you. Starting at the Edmond Family Counseling office, there are 14-, 30-, and 62-mile rides to choose from. All rides end at Flat Tire Burgers, where all bike riders and volunteers are served a free burger.

Registration is open to anyone 14 years and older. However, if children under 14 do want to participate, they will not need to register, but must be accompanied by a registered adult. Helmets are suggested for all distances. The registration fee is $25 and each preregistered biker will receive an event T-shirt for free.

The Edmond Fire Department B.E.R.T. team conducts a Bicycle Rodeo for children under 12 from 9 a.m. to 11 a.m.

This event is an annual fund-raiser for Edmond Family Counseling. All proceeds go toward funding counseling programs and services. There are no refunds for inclement weather and no rain dates are scheduled.

REDBUD CLASSIC
6421 Avondale Dr., #207A
(405) 842-8295
www.redbud.org
This annual two-day community event promotes fun, fitness, and philanthropy. It is put together by the nonprofit Redbud Foundation and in 2009 celebrated its 27th year. Held in Nichols Hills, the Redbud Classic was the first organized 10K in the Southwest. There are cycling tours, 10k and 5k running events, and a 2-mile fun run. When the first classic was held in 1983, it drew approximately 1,100 participants. Today, it draws approximately 6,500 participants with another 4,000 to 5,000 observers. Bands play live music along the course and sponsors offer donuts, pancakes, bagels, fruit, and yogurt to the runners. There is a free 1-mile fun run for children and afterward they can enjoy a carnival. Sat night, participants and visitors can enjoy live music and Pasta on the Pond, a pasta dinner.

There is ample parking throughout the neighborhood. Shuttle service is available in certain areas. All post and prerace events are free. A registration fee of $25 for runners and cyclists of events is required.

SOUTHWEST STREET RODS NATIONAL
State Fair Park
Northwest 10th and May
(405) 948-6704
www.nsra-usa.com
This is Oklahoma's largest automobile event. More than 1,900 pre-1949 street rods and antique vehicles from all over the Southwest and other areas of the United States and Canada descend upon State Fair Park. The total value of the cars in attendance total $65 million dollars minimum.

On Fri, there is a street rod parade through downtown Oklahoma City. At 1 p.m. on Fri, there is a Ladies Tea. Sat events include the "Street of Rods," where cars are picked for special automobile awards. On Sun street rods chosen for special recognition are on display prior to receiving an award at the 2 p.m. awards ceremony.

In addition to the car activities, there are commercial exhibits, swap meets, and a place for arts and crafts.

Tickets for the event are on sale at the State Fair Park only. Prices are $14 for adults, $12 for seniors 60 and over, $5 for children 6 to 12, and free for children 5 and under. Discounted tickets are available for military personnel with proper identification.

MAY

ARMED FORCES DAY & SHRINERS PARADE
Downtown Del City
(405) 671-2815
www.cityofdelcity.com
This parade started back in 1985. Del City and its chamber work together to organize this event every year. The parade starts at the intersection of I-40 and Sunnylane, goes south to Southeast 29th, then turns east and ends at Linda Lane. The route is about 2 miles long.

Over 100 groups or individuals participate in the parade. In the past, Congresswoman Mary Fallin and the mayor have attended. There is always a large contingent of military officers, shriners, military equipment, classic cars, and community groups and businesses that march in the parade. Dance groups perform. A car show runs in conjunction with the parade.

An estimated 1,000 people attend.

CHUCK WAGON GATHERING & CHILDREN'S COWBOY FESTIVAL
National Cowboy & Western Heritage Museum
1700 NE 63rd St.
(405) 478-2250
www.nationalcowboymuseum.org/events/chuckwagon
First held in 1989, this event has been consistenly successful and continues to grow in popularity and numbers. In 2008, over 8,000 people attended this festival at the National Cowboy & Western Heritage Museum. Every year, people come from 15 to 20 different states to attend the Memorial Day weekend extravaganza. In many cases it is grandparents bringing their

grandchildren to the event. It is a true western festival centered around kids and families.

Children can enjoy stagecoach and covered-wagon rides as well as storytelling, beadwork, weaving, and rope making. Everyone will enjoy the chuckwagon fare. Ten chuck wagons from Texas, New Mexico, and Oklahoma come in and their cooks prepare brisket, sourdough biscuits, beans, corn bread, cobblers, and more for guests to enjoy.

Parking is plentiful and free. Admission is $14 for adults, $12 for seniors, $5 for children 5 to 12, and free for children under 5. Admission gets visitors into the museum and all events. Hours are 10 a.m. to 4 p.m. Sat and Sun.

DOWNTOWN EDMOND ARTS FESTIVAL (EDMOND)
Downtown Edmond
(405) 249-9391
www.downtownedmondok.com
Over 100 artists exhibit at this fine-arts festival held in downtown Edmond. This event has been held since 1979. Guests can visit artists and their booths as well as enjoy delicious food from 20 food vendors. Foods visitors can enjoy are onion blossoms, Indian tacos, catfish, German food, pizza, fried pies, funnel cakes, kettle corn, and onion fried burgers. Those who are interested can enjoy wine tasting from some of the Oklahoma wineries. To read more information about this event, see "The Arts" chapter.

EDMOND JAZZ AND BLUES FESTIVAL
Fifth and Boulevard, Edmond
(405) 830-8902
www.visitedmondok.com/majorevents.htm
For the Edmond Jazz and Blues Festival, guests bring their blankets and lawn chairs to Stephenson Park and settle in to hear some jazz and blues music on Memorial Day weekend. Past performers include Snake Shakers, Chris Hicks Band, the Civilized Tribe, Garrett "Big G" Jacobson, and Pinkie.

While attendees may bring their own picnic suppers and drinks, food vendors are available and sell pizza, cinnamon rolls, funnel cake, Indian

tacos, caramel apples, and more. Arts and crafts vendors display their wares as well. Admission is free.

FESTIVAL OF THE CHILD
2200 S. Holly, Yukon
(405) 350-8937
The Festival of the Child is about and for children. Held at the Yukon City Park it is a full day of activities especially designed for children ages 2 through 13 years old. With over 50 areas of interest, including storytellers, clowns, face painting, arts and crafts, drama and dress-up, a petting zoo, pony rides, a book walk, archery, moon bounces, a super slide, fishing, carnival games, and concessions, every child will find something to enjoy.

Hamburgers and hot dogs are sold at the festival. Parking is free but limited. Tickets are $5 at all park and recreation locations before the event and $7 the day of the festival. In the event of inclement weather, the event is held inside at the Yukon Community Center.

MAY FAIR ARTS FESTIVAL
Andrews Park
201 W. Gray, Norman
(405) 370-1132
www.norman.assistanceleague.org/ps.projects.cfm?id=1620
This festival is hosted by the Assistance League of Norman. May Fair began as a one-day event and evolved into a three-day event several years ago. In 2009, it celebrated its 35th year. Between 70 and 90 local and regional artists exhibit and sell their work. The fine art includes stained and blown glass, jewelry, watercolors, oil paintings, graphics, pottery, photography, turned and sculptured wood. Master craftsmen sell handmade quilts, painted gourds, hair and home accessories, signs, tiles, soaps, birdhouses, and wooden furniture. Each year, the festival highlights an artist. This artist demonstrates his or her painting or sculpture style on Sat afternoon.

There are live performances held throughout the event. Visitors will enjoy local bands, dance troupes, soloists, and more. Food vendors sell such items as homemade sundaes, bratwurst, corn dogs, specialty coffees, kettle corn, gyros, gelato, Indian tacos, and roasted nuts. This festival also holds a food contest.

The May Fair Arts Festival has won several awards, including five Pinnacle Awards given by the International Festivals and Events Association. In 2005, the festival was a winner of the Oklahoma Governor's Redbud Award for the Outstanding Event in Oklahoma, given by the Department of Tourism.

Visitors are allowed to take pictures. Parking is located around the park and is free. Admission is free, however, there is a $5 charge for the children's art yard and for special events programming.

MEMORIAL DAY CEREMONY
45th Infantry Division Museum
2145 NE 36th St.
(405) 424-5313
www.45thdivisionmuseum.com

Memorial Day has been recognized annually at the 45th Infantry Division Museum since 1976. The ceremony starts with a fly over of military aircraft provided by the Oklahoma National Guard. This is followed by a salute fired from the museum's World War II, 37mm antitank gun. Next comes the Massing of the Colors, where color guards from military and patriotic organizations march around the oval on the north side of the museum surrounding the audience. Marshal and patriotic music is provided by the 145th Army Band. A guest speaker makes appropriate remarks and a memorial wreath is laid at the base of the flag as "Taps" is sounded. Following the ceremony, the museum is open for public perusal.

All of Oklahoma City is invited, however only about 400 to 600 people usually attend. The event lasts about an hour and is held outside. In the event of inclement weather, the ceremony is moved indoors and is an abbreviated version of what happens outside. Admission to the event and the museum are free on this day.

OKLAHOMA WRITERS' FEDERATION CONFERENCE
Various locations around Oklahoma City
(405) 282-7230
www.owfi.org

Established in 1968, the Oklahoma Writers' Federation Conference is held the first weekend of May, in locations around Oklahoma City. Writers from across the state and the country come to meet and mingle with other writers, agents, and editors. Hourly workshops are held Fri and Sat to teach want-to-be writers how to get started and to provide established writers with networking opportunities and marketing news. On Fri night, there is a keynote speaker. These speakers are almost always *New York Times* bestselling authors. There is a large writing contest with over 33 categories including poetry, non-fiction book, fantasy, and children's books held in conjunction with this conference. Cash awards are given out at a banquet on Sat night. Conference fee ranges from $125 to $175. See the Oklahoma Writers' Federation Web site for more information about the contest and conference.

OSTRICH EGG BREAKFAST
Oklahoma City Zoo
2101 NE 50th St.
(405) 424-3344
www.okczoo.com

Attend one of the tastiest traditions in Oklahoma City, the Ostrich Egg Breakfast. Hosted by the Oklahoma Zoological Society and the Oklahoma City Zoo, this family-fun breakfast features all-you-can-eat pancakes, sausage, scrambled hens' eggs, waffles, and yes, ostrich-egg omelets cooked to order by professional chefs. There is also live entertainment and free lion show tickets. Reservations are required.

All ages are encouraged to attend. In the past, there have been 3,000 to 3,500 in attendance at this popular event. It is held in the zoo at the Wildcat and Roughneck Pavilions and Devon Energy Picnic Area from 8 to 11 a.m.

Each year, local cartoonist Jim Lange designs a T-shirt for the Ostrich Egg Breakfast. T-shirts are sold in advance online and on the day of the breakfast. This event has been held here since 1986.

PASEO ARTS FESTIVAL
3022 Paseo
(405) 525-2688
www.thepaseo.com/events.paseofestival
.html

This festival was started as a fund-raiser by the Paseo Arts Association in 1976. It is held annually in the historic Paseo Arts District on Memorial Day weekend. It features the work of artists from around the region.

There are over 80 fine artists working in a variety of media; live music on two stages; food, such as corn dogs, burritos, and Indian tacos; performance art; and a children's activity tent. The most notable act is the living Will Rogers' statue.

Approximately 50,000 people attend this event each year. Some areas charge a parking fee. Admission is free. The event goes on, rain or shine.

ZOOLYMPICS
Oklahoma City Zoo
2101 NE 50th St.
(405) 424-3344
www.okczoo.com

"On your mark, get set, go wild" is the mantra for this event. Children 11 and under can go for the gold in Zoolympics as they participate in a variety of events, such as Joey Jump, Roar Like a Lion, and Lily Pad Leap. Each event features educational and interactive elements sure to capture the imagination of any young Zoolympian. There are a total of 10 events in all and each has been designed with consideration toward children with disabilities. Every child is a winner and he or she creates their own medal to wear and take home.

This event is held on the zoo grounds on the same day as the Ostrich Egg Breakfast, but is a separate event. It runs from 10 a.m. to 2 p.m. Zoolympics is free with zoo admission.

JUNE

DEADCENTER FILM FESTIVAL
1015 N. Broadway, Ste. 301
(405) 246-9233
www.deadcenterfilm.org

The name "deadCENTER" refers to the location of this festival—Oklahoma City, which is located in the dead center of the United States. The mission of the festival is to promote independent film arts and it attracts filmmakers from around the world. It is the largest film festival in the state, with hundreds of independent films screened over a five-day period in eight premiere downtown locations. Attendance was nearly 6,000 in 2009. The 10th anniversary of the festival will be in 2010.

Beyond screening world-class films, dead-CENTER Film Festival also hosts a professional panel series and a screenwriting competition for avid film fanatics. The festival opens and closes with two free outdoor screenings. In the event of inclement weather, the screenings are moved to an alternate indoor venue. A variety of merchandise is available, including T-shirts, dated programs, and other commemorative items.

The two outdoor screenings as well as the Kid's Fest—family-friendly short films—are free to the public. All other screenings are $10 per film. A Screening Pass is $50 and allows entry to all film screenings for all five days. The best deal of all is the $100 All-Access Pass, which allows entry into all films, panels, and networking events for the entire five days.

ℹ️ The Oklahoma Native American Basketweavers (www.onab.org) can tell you what the designs in Native American baskets mean and show you how to weave them.

FIBERWORKS
Fiber Artist of Oklahoma
Belle Isle Library
5501 N. Villa
(405) 843-9601
www.fiberartistsok.org

Fiberworks is an annual juried fiber-art exhibit, sponsored by the Fiber Artists of Oklahoma. It features the finest and newest work of Oklahoma fiber artists. Fiberworks accepts pieces primarily constructed of fiber like weaving, basketry, quilting, soft sculpture, handmade felt, handmade paper, knitting, crocheting, and other works.. The show honors original designs or original interpretations of traditional techniques. Visitors can expect to see many different kinds of fiber art here from traditional to experimental.

The first Fiberworks was held in 1978 at the Science Museum in Oklahoma City and was cosponsored by the then Handweavers League of Oklahoma (now called Fiber Artists of Oklahoma). The exhibit has been held every year since, making Fiberworks 2009 the 31st annual show. IFiberworks does not have a permanent home so it is held at a different gallery every year. The dates depend on what dates the chosen gallery has available. Attendance is about 700.

There is no fee to view the exhibit. In the past, there have been no restrictions on taking pictures, however, it's always a good idea to ask first. A majority of the works on display are for sale.

NRHA DERBY SHOW
State Fair Park Arena
Northwest 10th and May Avenue
(405) 946-7400
www.nrha.com/derby.php
The NRHA (National Reining Horse Association) Derby Show runs for one week each summer and showcases the world's best four-, five- and six-year-old reining horses. Thousands of spectators, exhibitors, and horses attend the event each year. The derby is one of two major events presented by the NRHA each year in Oklahoma City and includes a full slate of ancillary reining classes in addition to the derby action.

Pictures for personal use are allowed, but discouraged during the performances so not to interfere with the competition. There is a large amount of free parking. Salads, sandwiches, sweets, Mexican, and American foods are available for purchase. Vendors also sell Western lifestyle, clothing, home decor, gifts, and tack. Tickets are available at the door or ahead of time at www .oktickets.com.

OKLAHOMA FOLKLIFE FESTIVAL
Oklahoma History Center
2401 N. Laird Ave.
(405) 323-9265
www.okhistory.org
The Oklahoma Historical Society and the Oklahoma Folklife Council (OFC) host their annual Oklahoma Folklife Festival, the third Sat in June each year in Oklahoma City at the Oklahoma History Center. It features authentic folk artists and tradition bearers from around the state. Through this event, OFC showcases artists whose works exemplifies the state's rich heritage. Most artists are award winners in their fields or have been recognized nationally as superior examples of living tradition bearers. The range of cultural forms presented includes Native Americans from both eastern and plains tribes, Hispanics, African Americans, and decendents of Europeans heritage, particularly Ireland. Artistic forms include native basket weaving, Native American storytelling, Hispanic traditional dance, Mexican and bluegrass music, cowboy poetry, and American Indian pottery. Family interest and audience appeal are two of the criteria used when selecting artists to perform.

Admission to the performances, demonstrations, and activities is free, as is parking. Food is also available on-site as well as crafts for children and adults.

The National Endowment for the Arts, Oklahoman, Oklahoma Arts Festival, Oklahoma Historical Society, and Oklahoma Humanities Council fund support this event. Audiences are always diverse and have continued to grow in the past few years to where 2,000 visitors have attended the single day event. Picture taking is allowed.

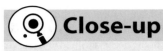 **Close-up**

Red Earth Native American Cultural Festival

Each year more than 1,200 American Indian artists and dancers from throughout North America gather to celebrate the richness and diversity of their heritage at the Red Earth Native American Cultural Festival (held at the Cox Convention Center, 405-427-5228, www.redearth .org) in Oklahoma City. First held in 1986, this festival has matured into one of the most respected visual and performing arts events of its kind. Here, guests get to appreciate the work of the nation's most celebrated Native American artists, with opportunities to purchase contemporary and traditional examples of beadwork, basketry, jewelry, pottery, sculpture, paintings, graphics and cultured attire during the juried art show and market.

On Fri morning, a grand parade through the streets of downtown Oklahoma City opens the festival. Representatives of more than 100 tribes, in full tribal regalia, make the Red Earth Parade one of America's most unique. There is a dance competition and it is one of the rare occasions when dancers from America's Northern and Southern tribes can be seen together. These dancers represent the elite of Native American dance. Live professional performances are also held throughout the festival. Past performers include Arvel Byrd, the American Indian Dance Theatre, and Will Hill. The Art Market opens on Fri. It is a juried art show. All artists must participate in the jury process and meet the standards set by the Red Earth Festival Art Committee. You will find no craft or souvenir vendors here.

In the past, this event has drawn more than 25,000 visitors. This festival has been named Oklahoma's Outstanding Event by the Oklahoma Tourism & Recreation Department, a Top 100 Event in North America by the American Bus Association, and Central Oklahoma's Outstanding Cultural Tourism Event by Frontier Country Marketing.

Admission is $10.00 for adults and $7.50 for seniors and children 6 to 17. Three-day weekend passes are available. Tickets can be purchased at the Ford Center Box Office or online at www .ticketmaster.com. Parking is available in garages for a fee nearby and on the street. Metered spaces are free on weekends. Guests are allowed to take pictures at the festival, however, if you wish to take a photograph of a Native American dancer, it is common courtesy to ask permission.

TASTE OF EDMOND
Festival Market Place, Edmond
(405) 340-2527
www.libertyfest.org/LibertyfestATasteof
Edmond.php

This event is part of Edmond's LibertyFest celebration and it draws thousands of visitors. It is held at the Festival Market Place located west of Broadway on First Street. Filling downtown Edmond with the aroma of tasty foods from various restaurants around the community, this event is a fund-raiser for LibertyFest. Some of the restaurants that have participated are Coach's Restaurant, Othello's of Edmond, Namaste Indian

Cuisine, Ted's Café Escondido, Hideaway Pizza, and Interurban to name a few. Visitors who pay the entrance fee can sample the different kinds of specialties these restaurants have to offer. This is an all-you-can-eat family tradition that began back in 1990. Tickets are $10 for adults and free for children 10 and under.

ZOOBILATION
Oklahoma City Zoo
2101 NE 50th St.
(405) 424-3344
www.okczoo.com

Hosted by the Oklahoma Zoological Society,

Zoobilation is the major fund-raiser for the Oklahoma City Zoo. First held in 1993, this all-adult, casual event is held outdoors, usually on a Fri night from 7 to 11 p.m. and includes food samplings from local restaurants, live entertainment, keeper chats, and a silent auction. Tickets prices are $75 per person and include all food and drink. The event is typically held outside rain or shine. Guests must be at least 21 years old to attend.

ℹ️ The City of Moore is located just south of Oklahoma City. To learn about events happening in Moore, contact the Moore Chamber of Commerce at (405) 794-3400 or visit the Web site at www .moorechamber.com.

JULY

ART IN THE PARK: A CELEBRATION IN THE HEARTLAND
Buck Thomas Park
12th Street, Moore
(405) 793-5000
www.cityofmoore.com

This event is held at Buck Thomas Park in Moore and it offers arts and crafts vendors, food vendors, live entertainment, children's activities, a carnival, and a car show. The City of Moore puts on this event and in 2009, it celebrated its 15th year.

The arts and crafts vendors sell everything from jewelry to T-shirts. The food vendors sell a variety of items, such as Indian tacos, funnel cakes, kettle corn, hot dogs, cowboy tacos, wine, and root beer. Live entertainment performers have included Time Machine, SuperFreak, Banana Seat, and Bad Monkey. A children's tent is available, where kids can do arts and crafts. There is also a magician and a giant sand pit for them to play in.

This event is outdoors, so dress accordingly. Admission and parking are free. Each year, the City of Moore expects around 30,000 people to attend.

FOURTH OF JULY CELEBRATION
Bricktown
(405) 236-8666
www.bricktownokc.org

Called Red, White, and Boom, this two-day event has been celebrated by the community since 1988. Held in the heart of Bricktown at Oklahoma and Sheridan, approximately 50,000 to 60,000 people attend. Outdoor music starts at noon. There is a Kiddie Land for children. It features rides, climbing walls, and blow-up activities. Vendors include face painting and sketch artists. Carnival food, like corn dogs, cheese on a stick, and ribs, are sold outside in the festival area. For those who would like more substantial food, there are plenty of restaurants in the area.

On July 3, the Oklahoma City Philharmonic plays under the stars. Fireworks are shot off immediately following the conclusion of the concert. Then on July 4th, fireworks light up the sky again.

Every other year, the Redhawks baseball team plays a game on the Fourth of July. When they play, they have their own fireworks display. On those years, the Bricktown fireworks follow immediately afterward.

The Bricktown Fourth of July Celebration is free. Upper and lower Bricktown parking is available for a fee.

FREEDOM FEST (YUKON)
Chisholm Trail Park
500 W. Vandament
(405) 350-8937

This event is hosted by the City of Yukon and in 2009, it celebrated its 13th year. Attendance is approximately 25,000 people. Yukon's Freedom Fest includes a children's parade, a children's craft area, family games, and a play area, free swimming, a car show, free watermelon and ice cream, and live music and fireworks at dusk with the Oklahoma City Philharmonic. Past performers include the Irv Wagner Concert Band and the Rodeo Opry Band.

Food vendors sell turkey legs, kettle corn, funnel cakes, and more. The City of Yukon sells glow items as souvenirs.

The event is held outdoors, however, if the weather turns ugly, the concert is held inside the Yukon Fine Arts Auditorium.

All events are free. Parking is free as well, but limited. Because of the size of the crowd, visitors are encouraged to arrive early to claim a parking spot.

LIBERTYFEST
Various locations throughout Edmond
(405) 340-2527
www.libertyfest.org
This event began in 1972, when a handful of Edmond citizens planned park activities and fireworks to celebrate the July 4th. The City of Edmond, the University of Central Oklahoma, area businesses, civic organizations, families, and individuals sponsor and support this festival's events. The festival's purpose is to bring about family-oriented events to celebrate the nation's birthday and Oklahoma's heritage. In 2009, Libertyfest had 11 family-oriented events as part of the festival.

The Car Show kicks off the festival and the fireworks show at the University of Oklahoma ends the celebration. In between visitors can attend a parade, a concert, a rodeo, a kite festival, a road rally, or a food festival. There is so much going on in Edmond the week of the fourth, visitors would be wise to check the Web site before going. Tickets are required for some events and prices vary depending on the event. The fireworks display is free. Edmond expects over 100,000 guests to attend each year.

In 2009, CNN and *USA Today* named Edmond's Libertyfest one of the top 10 places to be in America on July 4th.

MIDSUMMER NIGHT'S FAIR
Lions Park
Flood and Symmes, Norman
(405) 329-4523
www.normanfirehouse.moonfruit.com/#/midsummer-nights-fair/4524980380
This is a free community event that gives people of all ages an opportunity to view, purchase, and learn about the arts in a casual, inviting atmosphere. Held in Lion's Park, which is adjacent to the Firehouse Art Center, the Midsummer Night's Fair has been described by the local newspaper

as one of the six events that "gives Norman character and quality."

There are 40 to 50 artist booths at this event. Visitors can also enjoy live performances. Past performers include Banana Seat, Full Circle, Joe Whitecotton Jazz Quartet, Talk of the Town, and Thomas Anderson. Getting hungry? Seven to 10 food vendors sell hamburgers, Indian tacos, ice cream, funnel cakes, and more.

Summer 2009 drew an estimated 6,000 people. In 2010, this fair will celebrate its 33rd year. Guests may take pictures. There is free street parking available.

AUGUST

BRICKTOWN REGGAE FESTIVAL
Sheridan and Oklahoma Avenue
(405) 236-4143
www.brewerentertainment.com
This festival is held on the corner of Oklahoma Avenue and Sheridan in the parking lot. Huge tents are erected to give some relief from the sun, and both local and nationally known bands come to perform. Past performers include the Ark Band, Mystic Vibe, Kinky Slinky, and Local Hero.

Vendors sell Caribbean foods, beer, soft drinks, hats, tie-dye T-shirts, and more. For live music, food, and fun don't miss this event. Over 40,000 typically attend. Admission is free.

SEPTEMBER

ARTS FESTIVAL OKLAHOMA
7777 S. May Ave.
(405) 682-1611
www.occc.edu/afo
Arts Festival Oklahoma is a three-day event held over the Labor Day weekend each year (Sat–Mon). This arts festival has a wide variety of fine arts, crafts, concessionaires, performing artists, and a children's creative center, where kids can create their own works of art.

In 2009, the festival celebrated its 31st year. The purpose of Arts Festival Oklahoma is to promote and showcase the work of local and out-of-state artists and artisans to provide cultural awareness and opportunities and to present and promote the performing arts. The festival is sponsored by Oklahoma City Community College, the Central Art Association, the South Oklahoma City Chamber of Commerce and Women of the South. For more information about this event, see "The Arts" chapter.

BLACK ARTS FESTIVAL
Edwards Park
1515 North Bryant Avenue
(316) 990-1908
www.blackartsfestivalokc.com

This is an event that creates an awareness of the different kinds of black art that exists. The day begins with opening ceremonies at 10 a.m. and continues until 8 p.m. The festival offers live performances, artwork like painting and sculpture, storytelling, and food.

Past performers include the Sankofa African Percussion Ensemble, the Cailin Rua Irish Dance Company, the Coleman Family Singers, and Aakhu Bastet Sahu. Carnival food is available, such as hot dogs, nachos, sandwiches, chips, and Indian Tacos. The arts and crafts vendors sell things like books, oils, artwork, pottery, and figurines. There is a children's village that offers storytelling, face painting, finger painting, and more.

This free event is held outdoors at Edwards Park and 500 to 800 people typically attend.

DAY OUT WITH THOMAS
Oklahoma Railway Museum
3400 NE Grand Blvd.
(405) 424-8222
www.thomasandfriends.com/use/parents/dowt.html
www.oklahomarailwaymuseum.org

If your child likes Thomas the Tank Engine, head for the Oklahoma Railway Museum in Sept and Oct. Thomas's visit in 2009 is his sixth year visiting the city. Besides rides pulled by the famous engine, there is live entertainment for the children, including Marty the Magician out of Missouri, Ms. Lisa Children's music from Dallas, the Singing Brakeman from Denver, and Mom-O the Clown from Oklahoma City.

This event is held indoors and outdoors and takes place rain or shine. Day out with Thomas tickets can be purchased online and are $18. This price is subject to change. Parking is free. Typically more than 13,000 people attend this event every year.

OKLAHOMA STATE FAIR
3001 General Pershing Blvd.
(405) 948-6700
www.okstatefair.com

For 11 days in Sept, the Oklahoma State Fair takes place at State Fair Park, overtaking 190 acres inside the fence line area. This annual event attracts approximately one million visitors. There are exhibit buildings, a carnival-style midway, concert performances, and Disney on Ice in week one and a rodeo in week two. There are cooking, needlecraft, and livestock competitions and demonstrations and guests will find almost anything they are hungry for from the many food vendors. Visitors will want to visit the Made in Oklahoma building where Oklahoma businesses and products are highlighted. Police patrol the grounds regularly to ensure safety.

i To get your updated schedule of events in Oklahoma City, contact the Oklahoma City Convention and Visitors Bureau at (405) 297-8912, or visit www.okccvb.org.

ROUTE 66 CLASSICS IN THE PARK CAR SHOW & CRAFT FAIR
Hafer Park, Edmond
(405) 341-3554
www.historic66.com/events

Interested in automobiles? At this event, visitors can expect a beautiful park filled with approximately 200 classic automobiles ranging from antique autos to classy Corvettes. Cars are registered to compete in over 26 different categories. Trophies are awarded to the top two vehicles in each category and a cash prize is awarded to the car club with the most preregistered entries. Registration to show a vehicle is $25 per entry. Anyone who registers two weeks prior to the event receives the event T-shirt for free. Additional T-shirts are $10.

There are also approximately 30 craft fair vendors showing and selling their merchandise. There is homemade jewelry to embroidery and woodsy lawn furniture to educational toys for children. Vendors also offer food like grilled burgers and chicken, smoothies, and Indian tacos. No alcohol is served or allowed in the park.

Since this event is held in mid-Sept, the weather usually begins cool in the morning and ends up pretty warm in the afternoon so dress accordingly.

Admission is free. Visitors are allowed to take pictures. Parking is free in designated parking lots.

OCTOBER

AN AFFAIR OF THE HEART
8409 Gateway Terrace
(405) 632-2652
www.aaoth.com

First held in Feb 1985, An Affair of the Heart will celebrate its 25th anniversary in 2010. It is an Oklahoma tradition and people travel from across the United States to attend. Annual attendance is between 40,000 to 50,000 people. Exhibitors come from 25 states and occupy seven large buildings at the State Fair Park in Feb and Oct.

Vendors at the event offer a wide selection of items for sale, including arts, crafts, antiques, collectibles, furniture, decorative items, jewelry, and clothing. If shopping makes you hungry, there are food vendors available selling everything from strudel to strawberries Newport.

Parking is free and trolleys are available to transport guests to and from the parking areas.

There is a one-time admission fee of $6, good for all three days of the show. Tickets can be purchased in advance at the An Affair of the Heart office in Oklahoma City. Children 12 and under are admitted free.

BRICKTOWN'S HAUNTED WAREHOUSE
101 E. California
(405) 236-4143
www.bricktownokc.org

From the first weekend in Oct through Halloween, those who like scary things should visit the Bricktown Haunted Warehouse, located in the heart of historic Bricktown in a three-story warehouse. Here visitors will experience heart pounding, palm sweating, and total disorienting fun. There are vampires, zombies, live scary characters, as well as electronic animated ghouls, smoke, and fog. There is a scare around every corner. In the basement is a 3-D dungeon ride, which takes about 15 to 20 minutes. The Haunted Warehouse itself takes about 30 minutes.

About 40,000 people attend each year. Children under the age of 10 are not allowed. Admission is $12 for the Haunted Warehouse and $17 for both the warehouse and the dungeon ride. Souvenirs like T-shirts, masks, horns, and other Halloween items are available for purchase. Security officers patrol inside and outside of the Haunted Warehouse ensuring that everyone has a safe and fun experience.

CREEPY CONSERVATORY
Myriad Botanical Gardens
301 W. Reno
(405) 297-3995
www.myriadgardens.com/calendar.html

Held at the Myriad Botanical Gardens, the Creepy Conservatory educates the public on conservation. It is a one-day event and is usually held the third or fourth Sat of Oct. Exotic animal displays featuring critter handlers educate children on different species of animals living in the rain forest. There is a tropical "Trick or Treat" trail, arts, crafts and other fun kid activities. Candy is typically handed out. Costumes are encouraged, but not required. Usually 500 to 600 people attend. Creepy Conservatory is included with admission to the Myriad Botanical Gardens.. Admission is $6 for adults, $5 for seniors 62 and over and students 13 to 18 or with valid college ID, $3 for children 4 to 12, and free for children under 12.

FALL PEACE FESTIVAL
Civic Center Music Hall
201 N. Walker Ave.
(405) 524-5577
www.peacehouseok.org

Since 1986, the Fall Peace Festival has taken place, usually on the second Sat in Nov from 10 a.m. to 4 p.m., in the Civic Center Music Hall's Hall of Mirrors. The event showcases some 50 local organizations, artists, and entertainers whose work contributes to social justice, human service, and environmental sustainability.

"Extraordinary holiday shopping opportunities are available at all the tables, including fair trade goods, books, calendars, bumper stickers, buttons, T-shirts, handmade jewelry, candles and soaps, Guatemalan fabrics, Nicaraguan coffee, African carving, American Indian crafts, and the work of local artists and crafts people," says Nathaniel Batchelder, director of the Peace House, which sponsors the festival. "All sales income goes to benefit the groups represented to support their work," he says. "So, bring your check book and shopping lists, and prepare to be amazed by the variety on display."

"The purpose of the Peace Festival is to build awareness and support for local organizations working for the betterment of the human condition," Batchelder said. All the groups make available their bulletins, newsletters, and membership information to engage visitors in how they can become volunteers or supporters.

Represented at the festival are groups such as Amnesty International, Sierra Club, World Neighbors, Mother to Mother, Vegetarians of Oklahoma City, United Nations Association, Esperanza en Accion, RESULTS Hunger & Poverty Lobby, Coalition to Abolish the Death Penalty, Gay/Lesbian Political Caucus, and Human Rights Alliance. Local artisans and crafts people contribute part of their sales to support the festival itself.

A supervised Children's Peace Activities Room includes a story quilt, cooperative games, and arts and crafts opportunities. Art pieces by children are often displayed at the annual Respect Diversity Foundation Symbol Exhibit.

Live entertainment includes local folk singers and dancing by the Aalim School. Refreshments and a variety of snacks, cookies, and confections are offered at many of the tables. Popcorn is prepared by the Closer to Earth Youth Gardens project.

Admission is free, and parking at street meters is free on weekends.

FALL RV SHOW AND CLOSEOUT SALE
State Fair Park
Northwest 10th and May Avenue
(405) 376-3897

The RV Super Show is held at the Oklahoma State Fair Park.It is open to the public and gives those who are interested in owning and RV, or upgrading their existing RV the opportunity to view what's on the market, and what's new in RVing in one location.

There are hundreds of different RV makes and models to see here. Guests can "compare" shop and see which RV would fit into the family budget, be it a Fifth Wheel, Motorhome, or Pop-Up camper. Visitors will find RV displays throughout the grounds and in the Centennial Building, Cox Pavilion, and the Travel and Transportation Building. Besides the RV dealers, RV industry experts will be on hand to answer any questions about RVs and what's right for you.

This event is held mostly indoors but there are some RV displays set up outdoors for visitors to view, weather permitting. There is abundant free parking available. The event averages about 6,000 visitors per show with some recent shows reaching an estimated 12,000. An admission fee is charged.

FRIGHT FEST
Frontier City
11501 NE Expressway
(405) 478-2414
www.frontiercity.com

FrightFest is a Halloween-themed festival that is held at Frontier City in the fall. The park takes on a spooky glow after dark with the presentation of the House of Screams haunted house. Ghouls and monsters come alive throughout the park and join in the fun. For young children, BooVille is a great place to trick-or-treat for candy in a controlled, safe environment.

Ample parking is available in the main parking lot located just north of the park. The park entrance is easily accessible from this area. Parking is $7 per vehicle. Frontier City is wheelchair accessible and offers wheelchairs and wagons for rent.

Tickets may be purchased at the front gate, over the phone, or online at www.frontiercity.com. The price of a one-day general admission ticket is $34.99 plus tax. Admission for seniors, people in wheelchairs and children 48 inches and under is $19.99 plus tax. Children under three are free. Special promotions are offered throughout the season. If you wish to leave the park and return the same day, have your hand stamped at the main entrance and you will be readmitted at no extra charge. However, due to special events, readmission may not always be allowed. Such notice will be posted at the main entrance.

HAUNT THE HARN
Harn Homestead
1721 N. Lincoln Blvd.
(405) 235-4058
www.harnhomestead.com
Since 2005, the Harn has held a safe trick-or-treat event for young children. Besides trick-or-treating, there are many historic games and crafts for the children, such as pumpkin bowling, a ring toss on a witch's hat, roasting marshmallows, listening to ghost stories by the fire, and hayrides.

The event is held both indoors and outdoors. The buildings are heated and provide shelter from the rain. In 2008, 350 children attended. There is ample free parking available. Picture taking is encouraged.

Admission is $3 for children. Adults accompanying a child are free. Currently, tickets can only be purchased upon arrival.

HAUNT THE ZOO
Oklahoma City Zoo
2101 NE 50th St.
(405) 424-3344
www.okczoo.com
The biggest event of its kind in Oklahoma, Haunt the Zoo for Halloween is a safe alternative to trick-or-treating. The event began in 1983 when a group of imaginative animal keepers decided to commemorate Halloween. Participants collect goodies from 21 fantasy-filled booths, venture down a path filled with hundreds of jack-o'-lanterns and props, and enjoy a variety of entertainment, including mascots, clowns, and more.

The event is held at the zoo from 6:30 to 8:30 p.m. for several nights at the end of the month. It is held rain or shine. There are more than 200 multidimensional props decorating the treat path. Over 500 donated pumpkins are carved by the zoo staff each year to line the trail. Nine hundred volunteers and staff are needed to run Haunt the Zoo and they give away around 320,000 pieces of candy. Nearly 40,000 guests attend.

Admission is $6 per child for prepurchased tickets and $7 per child for tickets purchased at the gate. Accompanying adults 18 and over are admitted free. Admission includes an official treat bag.

OKLAHOMA CZECH FESTIVAL
Yukon
www.oklahomaczechfestival.com
OklahomaCzechFestival@Gmail.com
This festival was originally started by two groups of Czechs who wanted to preserve Czech heritage in Oklahoma. They decided to hold the festival after the last fall harvest and before winter set in. Governor Bellmon made Yukon the Czech capital of Oklahoma while he was in office. Yukon is where the festival is held every year on the first Sat in Oct.

The day starts with a 2-hour parade that follows old SR 66 (Main Street). From 9 a.m. until 5 p.m. there is Czech entertainment under a tent on the stage outside the Czech Building located at 5th and Cedar. Czech music, dancers, and singers entertain all afternoon, finishing with the coronation of the royalty. The new Oklahoma Czech queen, junior queen, prince and princess are crowned for the following year. Also under the tent an authentic Czech dinner, consisting of klobasy (sausages), sauerkraut, Czech beans, potatoes, and kolache (a pastry with filling), is served starting at 10 a.m. Of course there is beer that flows all day long.

All the kolaches are handmade in the Czech Building from July to Sept, by Czech members three times a week. The kolaches are sold individually or by the dozen. The vendors do not have any Kolaches made in bakeries. Czech members try very hard to preserve the Czech heritage by doing this. The bakers range in age from 7 to 103. The 103-year-old also attends the festival all day. The klobasy is made here in Oklahoma according to their recipe, by a meat company. The klobasy can only be bought at the festival. Czech vendors sell it cold by the pound to take home or in sandwiches to be eaten at the festival.

Besides the traditional Czech fare there are 35 food vendors that serve Indian tacos, homemade root beer, snow cones, popcorn, hamburgers, hotdogs, and more.

There are almost 200 crafts vendors that sell just about anything you can think of, lots of items are homemade. Many of these vendors have been coming to the festival decades. The Oklahoma Czechs have Czech souvenirs inside the Czech Building, also handmade items made by Czech members. They sell T-shirts about the festival, hand-embroidered tea towels, Czech money, stamps, eggs, dolls, books, cookbooks, and much more. The craft booths outside the Czech Building and across the street are open from 8 a.m. until 5 p.m.

There is a children's carnival that starts on Fri evening and runs all day Sat until 11 p.m. There are inflatables by the craft booths where small children can enjoy themselves, along with face painting and other children's games.

The event is primarily outdoors, however the Czech kolaches, klobasy sandwiches, and souvenirs are inside the Czech Building. The entertainment and Czech dinners are under a huge tent. The festival goes on regardless of the weather.

Estimated attendance 50,000 to 60,000. Visitors are encouraged to take pictures. There is no charge for parking, and parking is where ever you can find it. There is no charge for admission.

STORYBOOK FOREST
Arcadia Lake's Spring Creek Park, Edmond
2.5 miles east of I-35 on 15th Street
(405) 216-7471
www.edmondok.com/parks/arcadialake/
events

Storybook Forest is a safe alternative to traditional trick-or-treating. Kids and parents walk through a winding, well-lit trail in the woods, stopping at scenes along the way. The scenes are from classic stories and nursery rhymes. Kids are given a piece of candy at each one of the scenes and parents/volunteers read a passage from the storybook that depicts the scene. There is also a school carnival–type game area and a hayride. Kids can sit around the campfires, listen to their favorite classic stories being read, and roast hot dogs and marshmallows over the fire. The fires are monitored and a large ring around the actual fire keeps kids back a safe distance.

There are characters roaming the woods, such as Peter Rabbit, Curious George, Raggedy Ann and Andy, Clifford, Spot, and others. Visitors are encouraged to take pictures.

A concession stand is open to the public. Hot dogs, marshmallows, and S'mores packs are available and come with a roasting stick to use at the campfire. The stand also has hot drinks, soda, water, chips, nachos, and candy bars. Glow necklaces are sold as souvenirs. This event is held outdoors, so it could be canceled due to rain. The event does not presell tickets, so no refunds will be given due to weather. Admission is $5 per child. Parents are free. Children are encouraged to wear a Halloween costume, but are not required.

Parking is free. Strollers are encouraged. Attendance is 4,000 to 7,000 visitors.

WORLDFEST
425 E. California Ave.
(405) 752-9700
www.wn.org
Worldfest, celebrating its sixth year in 2009, is Oklahoma's only large fair-trade market and it is hosted by World Neighbors, an international nonprofit organization headquartered in Oklahoma City. Visitors can expect to see fair-trade items offered in all price ranges, including African blankets, Peruvian rugs, Guatemalen textiles, Indian silver, Mexican pottery, and tribal masks. All products come from fair-trade sources, guaranteeing that artisans receive a fair wage for their work.

There are also live performances, including cultural dancers and musicians. Attendees also have the opportunity to try a variety of international cuisine.

Worldfest is an indoor event, held at the Coca Cola Events Center in Bricktown. Admission is $5. There is parking available for a fee. Attendance is typically 3,000 people.

NOVEMBER

CHRISTMAS IN THE PARK
Held in several of city parks in Yukon
(405) 350-8937
Since 1995, the City of Yukon has presented this holiday display in three interconnecting parks—Yukon City Park, Freedom Trail Park, and Chisholm Trail Park. The displays are made up of over one million lights spread over 100 acres and include Christmas characters, music, and animation. There are also live performances, including Irv Wagner's Trombone Quartet and a local dance troop. Special guests include Santa Claus, Jinglesauras, Frosty, and Rudolph.

The lights appear the day after Thanksgiving and operate through Dec. Approximately 60,000 people attend. Hot chocolate is for sale nightly. In case of inclement weather, the lights may be closed. There is no admission fee, but donations are welcome.

NRHA FUTURITY SHOW
State Fair Grounds Arena
(405) 946-7400
www.nrha.com/futurity.php
The National Reining Horse Association (NRHA) recognizes and promotes the sport of reining. The western form of riding is one of the fastest-growing disciplines in the world and showcases its best athletes during the NRHA Futurity & Adequan North American Affiliate Championship Show. In 2009, the NRHA Futurity celebrated its 49th anniversary.

The NRHA Futurity Show is the most elite reining event in the world with more than $1.9 million in cash and prizes. Tens of thousands of horses and spectators come from nearly 20 countries to compete and watch the excitement unfold. The event includes three NRHA/Markel Insurance Horse Sales, the FEI World Reining Masters, the Celebrity Reining benefiting Make-A-Wish of Oklahoma, Invitational Freestyle Reining, an Intercollegiate Judging Contest, a horsemanship clinic, a trade show, and much more. During its 10-day run, the show contributes more than $32 million to the overall Oklahoma City economy.

All performances are live. NRHA million-dollar riders, mlion-dollar owners, and hall of famers can be found at the event competing or having connections to those competing. There are sold out crowd for finals night. More than 1,300 horses and more than 600 riders take part in the event. Picture taking is allowed for personal use. However, taking pictures during the performances is discouraged as it interferes with competition.

ST. ELIJAH'S FOOD FESTIVAL
St. Elijah Antiochian Orthodox Church
15000 N. May
(405) 755-7804
www.stelijahokc.com
Usually held on the first weekend of Nov, this festival features authentic Lebanese cuisine. Falafel, talami, meat pies, baklava, and cabbage rolls are just a few of the items available. Guests can eat here or buy items to take home. A plate costs around $14. Sometimes coupons are available in the local newspaper. There is a small marketplace that sells jewelry and clothing during the event. The *Oklahoma Gazette* typically posts exact dates and times so start looking there in Oct.

VETERANS DAY CEREMONY
45th Infantry Division Museum
2145 NE 36th St.
(405) 424-5313
www.45thdivisionmuseum.com
Veterans Day has been recognized annually at the museum since 1976. The ceremony starts with a fly over of military aircraft provided by the Oklahoma National Guard. This is followed by a salute fired from the museum's World War II, 37mm antitank gun. Next comes the Massing of

the Colors, where color guards from military and patriotic organizations march around the oval on the north side of the museum surrounding the audience. Marshal and patriotic music is provided by the 145th Army Band. A guest speaker makes appropriate remarks and a memorial wreath is laid at the base of the flag as "Taps" is sounded. Following the ceremony, the museum is open for public perusal.

All of Oklahoma City is invited, however only about 400 to 600 people usually attend. The event lasts about an hour and is held outside. In the event of inclement weather, the ceremony is moved indoors and is an abbreviated version of what happens outside. Admission to the event and the museum are free on this day.

DECEMBER

BOYS RANCH TOWN DRIVE THROUGH CHRISTMAS PAGEANT
5100 E. 33rd St., Edmond
(405) 341-3606
www.obhc.org
Between 4,000 and 5,000 people attend this drive-through pageant. It started in 1975 and is always held the first full week of Dec. The pageant is a living nativity complete with children and animals in the care of the Oklahoma Baptist Homes for Children. The pageant depicts the life of Jesus Christ, including his birth, death, and resurrection. The organization believes their event prepares individuals for celebrating the true meaning of Christmas, which is the birth of Jesus Christ.

A drive-through pageant does not need parking, so none is available. Guests line up on 33rd Street to enter the pageant. If it is raining or snowing and road conditions are hazardous, the event is canceled. Visitors are allowed to take pictures. There is no charge for admission, but donations are welcome.

CHRISTMAS TRAIN
Oklahoma Railway Museum
3400 NE Grand Blvd.
(405) 424-8222
www.oklahomarailwaymuseum.org

Since 2002, thousands of people have climbed aboard the Christmas Train. This special event held at the Oklahoma Railroad Museum will put you in the Christmas spirit. A rendition of Chris Van Allsburg's, *Polar Express,* is read by special guests, carolers spread Christmas cheer through songs, and Santa visits. Hot chocolate is available.

Christmas Train tickets are $12 and can only be purchased on-site. Parking is free in a small parking lot.

COWBOY CHRISTMAS PARADE
Stockyards City
(405) 235-7267
www.stockyardscity.org
The Cowboy Christmas Parade is held on the first Sat of Dec each year. It travels from Exchange and Pennsylvania, down Exchange to Agnew, and south on Agnew to 15th Street. It starts off with 100 longhorn cattle, each weighing 1,500 pounds. There are approximately 60 entries in the parade ranging from antique cars, rodeo queens, beauty queens, dog groups, marching bands, drill teams, oxen, lamas, and Indian dancers. Approximately 2,000 spectators come down for the parade and Cowboy Santa, who passes out gifts to the boys and girls at the Opry. There is no charge to attend.

DICKENS WEEKEND
Downtown Edmond
(405) 249-9391
www.downtownedmondok.com/inside DEBA/events.htm
Dickens Weekend is an event held the first weekend in Dec, beginning with the Mayor's Tree Lighting and the lighting of the Christmas tree at the Festival Market Place Plaza. The tradition began in 2002 and is the official beginning of the Christmas season in Edmond. It is sponsored by the Downtown Edmond Business Association. Approximately 3,000 visitors attend the 4-day event.

Activities include carriage rides, music with bands, and a children's choir. The Penn Square Carolers perform every year at this event along with school choirs and a visit from Santa Claus.

Stores in the area stay open until 8 p.m. and some merchants dress in period costumes. Visitors may have pictures taken with Santa at the Karen Moore Studio for a small fee. Street vendors are on hand to sell homemade bread, fudge, and tamales.

This is both an outdoor and indoor event. If the weather is cold and windy there are no carriage rides and most food vendors move inside.

There is ample free parking in the downtown area.

DOWNTOWN IN DECEMBER
210 Park Ave.
(888) OKC-4FUN
www.downtownokc.com

In Oklahoma City, the downtown celebration of the holiday season features events, shopping, holiday lights. and free admission to museums on Sun. If you like to skate, visit the Devon Ice Rink, located in front of the Civic Center Music Hall. For $8, you can skate on the ice with others until you tire out. You can snow tube at Chesapeake Snow Tubing at the Brick at the Bricktown Ballpark for $10 or say hi to Santa as he cruises around on his Segway.

For times and a list of all Dec events held in downtown Oklahoma City, check the Web site.

OKLAHOMA CITY TRAIN SHOW
1313 W. Britton Rd.
(405) 842-4846
www.okctrainshow.com

Held the first weekend in Dec, at the Travel and Transportation Building at the State Fair Park, this is one of the largest model-train related shows west of the Mississippi. In 2008, over 18,000 people attended the two day event. There are 100,000 square feet of nothing but trains, 200 exhibitor booths, and 30,000 square feet for operating model trains for the public to watch. Over 100 vendors, including Custom Trax, Railroad Relics, and Whistle Stop Trains, display and sell their products. In 2008, more than 30 models train sets were given away. Train set manufacturers and distributors donate the train sets given away. Their goal in doing this is to promote interest in trains. Admission is $7.

OPENING NIGHT
Downtown Oklahoma City
(405) 270-4848
www.artscouncilokc.com

Opening Night is 7 p.m. to midnight on Dec 31 every year. It is Oklahoma City's family-friendly New Year's Eve celebration. The heart of downtown Oklahoma City is blocked off to traffic for 10 blocks, so revelers can explore 14 different stages in 10 venues. Nearly 40 performances are held, including reggae, country, rock, Latin, alternative, choirs, jazz, marching bands, and more. There are also clown acts, magicians, hula dancers, and belly dancers. Acoustic guitarist and local celebrity, Edgar Cruz is a staple at this event. In 2009, some performers included Everybody and Their Dog, Lemma, Michael Summers Band, and Sunshine Hahn.

An entire area is dedicated to children's activities and performances. Typically there is face painting, craft making, an inflatable obstacle course, magicians, puppets, and more. This event also has a themed scavenger hunt with clues that lead families through the different venues. At midnight, the Finale Ball rises 15 stories into the sky. When it reaches the top, the fireworks display begins. It is one of the largest in the state.

No alcohol is sold here. City parking lots charge only $5 parking. Other parking includes private lots and street parking. For several years, there have been 65,000 to 75,000 revelers at the Opening Night.

Admission is $8 in advance, sold at various locations in the Oklahoma City metro area, or $10 at the event.

TERRITORIAL CHRISTMAS CELEBRATION
Harn Homestead
(405) 235-4058
www.harnhomestead.com

This celebration is the Harn Homestead's annual holiday open house. Visitors can tour the historic buildings and museum grounds that are adorned with pioneer and Victorian holiday decorations. There is a choir and Santa Claus shows up, too. There are free Polaroid pictures with Santa. Guests may also take their own pictures with

Santa. There are historic crafts and games for the children and hayrides.

In 2008, around 200 guests attended. The Harn Homestead Museum gift shop is open during this event for extended souvenir shopping. It provides hot chocolate, coffee, and hot tea with cookies and candy.

Harn Homestead general admission rates apply. Admission is $5 for adults, $4.00 for senior citizens and military. Children under 3 are free. .This event is held the first Thurs after Thanksgiving from 5:30 to 8:30 p.m. This allows visitors to come after work in the evening to view the holiday displays.

THE ARTS

Oklahoma City has a wide and varied art scene. From its galleries to its wide array of festivals, there is something here for everyone to enjoy.

In this chapter you will find art galleries, such as the Red Earth Gallery which showcases Native American art. Also listed are several organizations, like the Oklahoma Arts Council and the Norman Arts and Humanities Council, that support artists in the community. If your interest lies in museums, by sure to check out the "Attractions" chapter. Museums listed there, like the National Cowboy and Western Heritage Museum, offer art that will excite even the most amateur art lover.

Educational opportunities are available for those who would like to learn about a particular art. The City Arts Center offers classes on a regular basis for adults and children alike. If you are interested in pursuing more in-depth study, check out the University of Central Oklahoma, Oklahoma City University, and the University of Oklahoma. All offer strong art programs.

In this chapter, you will also find several of the larger art festivals listed. While these festivals are covered in the "Annual Events" chapter, they bear repeating here. Be sure to check the "Annual Events" chapter for other art festivals held throughout the year. Artists of all mediums turn out at these events to sell their wares or entertain. You can sit and listen to an artist perform, watch an artist create, or purchase a one-of-a-kind piece of art. At some festivals you may even get the opportunity to watch skilled craftspeople, like weavers, spinners, basket weavers, and potters, demonstrate their craft.

If you get tired of going to several different locations to experience and enjoy art, stop down at the Paseo Arts District. There are galleries, restaurants, and an annual arts festival to enjoy here.

Oklahoma City has several theaters that offer a variety of drama and visual art presentations. If your interests lie in music, you will not be disappointed by the offerings at the Civic Center Music Hall and at the Zoo Amphitheatre. With all the art that Oklahoma City and the surrounding areas have to offer, art lovers will be pleasantly surprised.

ALLIED ARTS
One N. Hudson Ave., #140
(405) 278-8944
www.alliedartsokc.com
This organization is Oklahoma's only United Arts Fund. Founded in 1971 by corporate, community, and cultural leaders, it strives to generate awareness of the importance of art throughout the community. Since its founding, it has raised more than $37 million to further the arts. More than 3.8 million people, including over 368,000 school-children, have been affected by this group's advancement and support of theatrical produc-

tions, visual arts exhibits, dance performances, and art venues.

Allied Arts has 20 member agencies. Through the year, this organization raises money and then disperses it into the community through marketing their member agencies, educational programs, and small grants.

CANTERBURY CHORAL SOCIETY
428 W. California Ave., #100
(405) 232-7464
www.canterburyokc.com
The Canterbury Choral Society's concerts are held

at the Civic Center Music Hall. They hold four concerts a year along with public appearances. Those presentations are held from Oct to May. Performances include, but are not limited to great master works, jazz, and Broadway music. The Society was originally founded at the All Souls Episcopal Church in May 1969 and had 60 singers.

Today, the 125-member adult choir is the largest in the state and the 7th largest volunteer choral organization in the United States. Even though the singers are volunteer, they must still audition to win their place in the choir. Most have musical training and have done some stage work. They come from all across the state.

The adult chorus collaborates with the Oklahoma City Philharmonic and Oklahoma City Ballet to put on performances. The chorus has performed in three of England's cathedrals, at the Capitol dome dedication in 2002, and at Oklahoma's Centennial celebration.

Besides the adult choir, there are two youth choirs that belong to this organization. The Canterbury Youth Chorus ranges from grades 2 through 8. These young people must audition just like the adults and perform in three concerts per year.

The average ticket price ranges from $20 to $45.

CARPENTER SQUARE THEATRE
400 W. Sheridan Ave.
(405) 232-6500
www.carpentersquare.com
Carpenter Square Theatre is a nonprofit community theater group that has been producing plays since 1985. Those who perform in the productions are from the community and are not professional actors. Auditions are held for every show and then rehearsals follow. Those actors who make the cut receive a small stipend and complimentary tickets as way of thanks for their participation. Performances in the past have included *Rehearsal for Murder, The Glass Menagerie,* and *The Chosen.*

The theater group performs in the Stage Center performing arts complex in downtown

Oklahoma City. Tickets range from $18 to $20 depending on the play. Season tickets and multiple discount tickets are available.

ℹ **Are you interested in writing poetry, fiction, or nonfiction? Check out the Oklahoma City Writers at http://okcwriters .toogroagency.com. The organization holds monthly meetings with speakers who discuss topics such as marketing and writing techniques.**

FINE ARTS INSTITUTE OF EDMOND
27 E. Edwards
(405) 340-4481
www.edmondfinearts.com
Located downtown across from the post office on the north side of Edwards, the Fine Arts Institute of Edmond offers art classes for all ages. Classes include drawing, painting, clay, pottery, theater arts, mixed media, print making, jewelry design, and seasonal art. Classes are kept to a 12 to 1 ratio, so students can receive the individual attention they may need or want.

The institute has been part of the Edmond community since 1986. It has its own 8,000-square-foot-facility in which to hold classes. In the 2007–2008 season over 3,300 students participated in art sessions here.

Price and class schedules vary. Check the Web site or call for a list of available class openings.

IAO GALLERY (INDIVIDUAL ARTISTS OF OKLAHOMA GALLERY)
706 West Sheridan
(405) 232-6060
www.iaogallery.org
Does art make you think? Do you look at a piece of art and wonder how the artist came up with his idea for the piece? Individual Artists of Oklahoma (IAO) mission is to support and encourage the artist who think and work outside the traditional, experiment and push the boundaries of art, be it with topic or method. Founded in 1979, the IAO Gallery presents original works by Oklahoma artists in all mediums, including visual art,

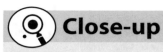 **Close-up**

Civic Center Music Hall

The Civic Center Music Hall (201 N. Walker Ave., 405-297-2584, www.okcciviccenter.org) is not only a beautiful structure with its art-deco design, but a building that has through renovation become nationally known for its "near perfect accoustics." Originally called the Municipal Building, the building was part of President Franklin D. Roosevelt's New Deal Program and was completed in 1937. At the time, it could seat 6,000 people and was used for numerous events like conventions, sporting events (boxing and basketball) and performing arts.

In 1966, the hall went through a renovation and its name was changed to the Civic Center Music Hall. The size of the main auditorium was decreased by 3,200 seats and the walls were brought in to improve the acoustics.

Beginning in 1998, the hall went through a second major renovation. The renovation included gutting the interior of the 1937 structure and building a new, modern performing arts hall within the existing building. Since the building is owned by Oklahoma City, it was to benefit from the 1993 tax-based initiative known as MAPS (Metropolitan Area Projects). Then in Sept 2001, three years later, the $52.4 million newly renovated 2,500-seat Civic Center Music Hall reopened its doors. The new hall is striking and stylish. In 2006, a study was done and the Music Hall was rated "one of the top 3 acoustic halls in the United States.

Today, the Canterbury Choral Society, Lyric Theatre and Academy, Oklahoma City Ballet Company and Oklahoma City Philharmonic make their home here. Nationally known singers, musicians and artists like Mikhail Baryshnikov, Michael Buble, Placido Domingo, The Gaithers, and Itzhak Perlman have performed here,

There is street-level parking around the building, both on the street side and in municipal lots. Metered parking spaces are free after 6 p.m. Fees vary for the lots but generally range from $6 to $8 per space. Admission prices vary for each performance. Individual tickets for season performances and special limited engagements can be purchased from the box office in person at 201 N. Walker Ave. The box office is open Mon through Fri from 9 a.m. to 5 p.m. and for two hours before each show time. Tickets may also be purchased by phone (405-297-2264 or 800-364-7111) or online (www.okcciviccenter.com or www.myticketoffice.com). Season tickets for any of the civic center's resident arts companies can be purchased by contacting the individual group.

poetry, creative writing, theater, improvisational comedy, film, and video.

Programming at IAO is very diverse. They recognize artists of all ages, levels of accomplishment, race, sex, knowledge, and culture. The IAO Programming Committee chooses to exhibit an artist's work or performance based on quality and the relevance of the work to society, rather than on the likelihood of sales. Artists exhibiting at IAO are largely, although not exclusively, from Oklahoma and the surrounding region.

The IAO Gallery offers monthly exhibits, poetry readings, and several regularly occurring events and exhibitions. One such exhibit, the biennial 24 Works on Paper exhibit, has a 20-year history of traveling to venues throughout the state. In its 20th year in , the annual 2009 EdgeArtNow exhibit brought together the most experimental art and artists from across Oklahoma for a multimedia show that never fails to surprise. Biting the Apple is the gallery's annual erotic art exhibition and largest fund-raiser. Since

1990 this perpetually controversial exhibit, brings together many art disciplines to explore sexuality and erotica in our culture.

The gallery publishes a free monthly newsletter online, titled *ArtZone*. You can subscribe to it on the gallery's Web site.

ISTVAN GALLERY
1218 N. Western Gallery
(405) 831-2874
http://istvangallery.com
At this art gallery visitors can expect to see a variety of artwork by local artists, including sculpturs, glass, oil, acrylic, watercolor, and other mediums. There are quarterly exhibits throughout the year which feature a different artist and his or her artwork.

Istvan Gallery believes art comes in every form, so it hosts monthly story slams, film and video viewings, poetry readings, and other community events. Story slams are events where people get together to tell stories that revolve around a set topic. These events are free.

Visitors are allowed to take pictures. The gallery welcomes casual wear and is wheelchair accessible. There is no gift shop, but the artwork on display is for sale. Admission to the gallery is free. On-site parking is free. The gallery is open Tues and Thurs from 1:30 to 5 p.m., Sat and Sun from 1 to 5 p.m., and by appointment.

JRBART AT THE ELMS
2810 N. Walker
(405) 528-6336
www.jrbartgallery.com
JRBArt started with a smaller gallery back in 1999. Today, this gallery has 4,500 square feet of exhibition space and was opened in 2002. It is located in the historic Paseo Art District and fits in well with the community. Paintings, drawings, sculpture, fiber work, and photography from selected artists are exhibited at the gallery. for sale. Gallery sales have doubled every year since its opening. The gallery has a large space and it rotates exhibits monthly. It welcomes the community to come in and enjoy the artwork and encourages dialogue about the exhibits.

The gallery holds six major exhibitions a year and four smaller solo and group shows every year. It has a mailing list of 4,600, an e-mail distribution of 3,000 and an active customer base of 350 individual and corporate clients.

Admission to the gallery is free. Hours are Mon through Sat from 10 a.m. to 6 p.m. and Sun from 1 to 5 p.m.

LYRIC THEATRE
(405) 524-9310
www.lyrictheatreokc.com
The Lyric Theatre is Oklahoma's premiere professional theater company, founded in 1963. It hires professional actors, designers, and directors directly from Broadway and blends them with the best of Oklahoma talent to providestellar productions that are on par with Broadway itself.

The Lyric Theatre performs two series of productions at two different venues throughout the year. The Lyric at the Civic Center series takes place during the summer, while the Lyric at the Plaza series takes place during the fall, winter, and spring months. The size difference in the venues allows the Lyric to offer audiences both big, splashy Broadway productions and smaller, more intimate shows.

Lyric at the Civic Center takes place at the Civic Center Music Hall in downtown Oklahoma City. The Lyric began its summer series there in 2002. Its productions take place in the Thelma Gaylord Performing Arts Theater within the Civic Center, which seats 2,500 people. The theatre company performs big musicals like "The Producers," "Music Man," and "Joseph and the Amazing Technicolor Dream Coat" here over the summer. Ticket prices range from $28.00 to $50.00.

Lyric at the Plaza takes place at the Plaza Theatre in Oklahoma City, in a historical neighborhood known as the Plaza District. The Lyric moved into the neighborhood in 2000, joining a citywide effort to revitalize this once thriving historical district. The Lyric raised the money necessary to renovate the Plaza Theatre, a former 1930s movie house that had been abandoned. Now the permanent home of the Lyric's productions and the Lyric Academy training program for young performers, Lyric's Plaza Theatre is an intimate venue which seats 281 people. Here the company performs smaller scale musicals, new works and plays like "Greater Tuna," the "Rocky Horror Show," and "Steel Magnolias." Tickets are $40.00 for a single ticket.

Limited free street parking is available at the Civic Center Music Hall. Pay lots are available for about $8 per car. Free parking is available at the Plaza Theatre on the street and in the two lots owned by Lyric within easy walking distance of the theater.

Tickets to all Lyric Theatre productions can be purchased from the ticket office at (405) 524-9312 or on the theater's Web site.

NORMAN ARTS AND HUMANITIES COUNCIL (NORMAN)
220 E. Main St.
(405) 360-1162
www.normanarts.org
The Norman Arts and Humanities Council is a nonprofit organization set in the heart of Norman. Its purpose is to aid the local art organizations, artists, and galleries to thrive and grow. The council promotes and supports the arts throughout Norman by initiating art and cultural activities that enhance economic growth. The NAC has a grant program that benefits dozens of nonprofit organizations in Norman. It also cofounded Jazz in June and with the City of Norman, created the Arts District, the Art in Public Places Program, and the Norman Music Festival. The NAC Arts-in-Education programs benefit over 13,000 public school children in Norman. Some of the programs are Get the Lead Out Festival for Young Authors and Artists, the Readers and Writers Program, the Visiting Artist Program, and Creative Problem Solving through the Arts.

NORMAN FIREHOUSE ART CENTER
444 S. Flood Ave., Norman
(405) 329-4523
www.normanfirehouse.com
In the spring of 2007, the Norman Firehouse Art Center remodeled its exhibition gallery to achieve a professional exhibition space. The Art Center displays paintings, sculptures, jewelry, and weaving exhibits. It holds one man shows, themed shows, and hosts traveling exhibits. In 2009 the center was awarded the Readers Choice Award by the *Norman Transcript*.

Art classes are held here for all ages from age 5, teenagers, and adults. Individuals can learn about everything from artists to a specific art discipline. Tuition fees for classes vary.

During the winter holidays, the center holds a special event called the Holiday Gift Gallery. The gift gallery offers over 75 different artists presenting their art for sale. It is a wonderful opportunity to purchase unique gift items for the holidays. The Holiday Gift Gallery is held from Nov 13 through Jan 7. The Center also sponsors the Chocolate Festival and Midsummer Night's Fair.

The center also has a gift store featuring handmade fine art and high craft works created by Oklahoma artists. Items include jewelry, ceramics, painting, sculpture, and glass works.

Admission to the Norman Firehouse Art Center is free. Visitors are allowed to take pictures. Casual attire is recommended. The center is wheelchair accessible and the hours are Mon through Fri from 9:30 a.m. to 5:30 p.m. and Sat from 10 a.m. to 4 p.m.

OKLAHOMA ARTS COUNCIL
2101 N. Lincoln Blvd., #640
(405) 521-2931
www.arts.ok.gov
In 2009, the Oklahoma Arts Council celebrated its 44th anniversary of service to Oklahoma citizens. The Council's headquarters is located in Oklahoma City just south of the Capitol Building. "For over 40 years, the Oklahoma Arts Council has supported Oklahoma's vibrant nonprofit arts industry," said Suzanne Tate, executive director of the Council. "Created by the Oklahoma Legislature to encourage and stimulate all forms of artistic endeavors, the Oklahoma Arts Council is responsible for increasing the access Oklahomans have to the arts and represents the institutional infrastructure that is now a part of the cultural fabric of the state."

Thousands of matching grants have been

given to cultural organizations, local governments and schools since the Oklahoma Arts Council was formed. Those grants are funded through State Legislature and National Endowment for the Arts allocations. Over 1,000 organizations that create and bring about community art and educational programs have benefited from these grants. Today, with the convenience of the Internet, organization can get on the Council's website and download a grant application.

The Oklahoma Arts Council Sponsors the Governor's Arts Awards. Nominees for these awards come from across the state of Oklahoma. Awards, given in seven categories are given annually to artists, businesses and organizations that show support and valuable contribution to the success of art in the state of Oklahoma. The awards are handed out in Oct. To read about current winners, visit www.arts.ok.gov/about/gaa .html.

OKLAHOMA ARTS INSTITUTE
2600 Van Buren St., #2606
(405) 321-9000
www.oaiquartz.org
The Oklahoma Arts Institute (OAI) is headquartered in Norman, Oklahoma. Since 1977, this organization has been educating young people and adults through its intensive art workshops. The teaching staff of these workshops is well qualified as they include Academy, Emmy, Grammy, Pulitzer Prize, and Tony Award winners. The workshops are held in Lone Wolf, Oklahoma at the Quartz Mountain Arts and Conference Center.

One of the workshops, the Oklahoma Summer Arts Institute is a two week long concentrated workshop for high school students. The young people study such disciplines as acting, ballet, chorus, creative writing, drawing/painting, film/video, modern dance, orchestra, and photography. Students who attend are chosen through an audition process.

The second workshop, the Oklahoma Fall Arts Institute is a series of four day weekend workshops held in Oct and Nov for adults over 21.

Amateur artists, educators, and professional artists attend these weekend events. There is a variety of workshops offered in literary, performing arts, and visual disciplines. The fall 2009 schedule has classes for writing, painting, print making and dance to name a few.

The Oklahoma Arts Institute is a private non-profit organization. Funding for its programs is provided by private donations and then matched by dollars from the Oklahoma Arts Council, the Oklahoma State Department of Education, and the Oklahoma Department of Tourism and Recreation.

Free concerts and performances are offered to the community during the workshops. Visit the Oklahoma Arts Institute's Web site for more information.

OKLAHOMA CHILDREN'S THEATRE
2501 N. Blackwelder Ave.
(405) 606-7003
www.oklahomachildrenstheatre.org
Nationally recognized for its educational live theater experiences for young children, this organization holds school-year productions; summer, winter, fall, and spring break camps; and after-school creative drama programs for school-age children. Over 1000 children participated in the camps in 2009. Besides serving children in the public school system, the theater also offers a homeschool program as well as a preschool program. Some of the skills students learn in the classes are basic theater skills, stage direction, theater terminology, voice projection, and controlled movement.

Tuition for classes is $80 and camps run from $100 to $400.

OKLAHOMA CITY ARTS CENTER
3000 General Pershing Blvd.
(405) 951-0000
www.cityartscenter.org
The Oklahoma City Arts Center is located on the east side of the Oklahoma State Fair Park. It began back in 1961 as the Oklahoma Science and Arts Foundation. The foundation offered science and visual arts education to children and adults. The

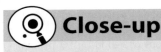 **Close-up**

Oklahoma Visual Arts Coalition

The Oklahoma Visual Arts Coalition (OVAC) (730 West Wilshire, Suite 104, 405-879-2400, www .ovac-ok.org), a statewide, non-profit organization, believes that "art is essential and that artists are worthy of support." OVAC was founded in 1988 by John McNeese. All of OVAC's programs and events are centered around creating an environment that allows artists not only to survive, but also to thrive. . Through publications, education, exhibitions, and Oklahoma's largest online gallery this organization promotes public interest in the arts and supports visual artists living and working in the state.

OVAC creates opportunities, connects resources and catalyzes motivation for Oklahoma artists. Through a variety of programs, OVAC provides professional development workshops, exhibition opportunities, awards and grants to individual artists to help them and their art thrive. Artists who benefit work in all visual art disciplines including painting, drawing, sculpture, fiber, photography, installation, film/video and more.

Some of the regular events that OVAC holds includes Momentum, an annual exhibition that features Oklahoma artists 30 years of age and younger working in all mediums, including 2-D and 3-D art, film, installations, and performance. The exhibition is held each year in Oklahoma City in Mar and in Tulsa in Oct. The 12x12 Art Show and Sale is the OVAC's only fund-raiser. It features 150 of Oklahoma's finest artists, live music, delectable food and fun. Each artist creates an artwork to measure no more than 12inches by 12 inches and each piece is sold through a silent and blind auction. Bid prices start at $168. 24 Works on Paper is a collaboration between OVAC and the Individual Artists of Oklahoma. It is an exhibition of 24 individual artworks on paper created by Oklahoma artists. The juried exhibition opens in July at the IAO Gallery in Oklahoma City and then travels the state for one year.

OVAC exhibitions are on a rotating schedule, with one happening nearly every year. They are held in a Tulsa and Oklahoma City each time and feature Oklahoma artists. Art 365 is held every third year, offering artist's time, money and curatorial input to create new installations or bodies of work for the exhibition. Admission is free to these exhibitions.

planetarium was originally located here, but it became so popular, it relocated to what is now the Science Museum.

After the planetarium was moved, the building became known as the Arts Annex. It continued its arts and dance class scheduling, but a slow period followed. In 1987, it was decided to breathe new life back into and reopen the Arts Annex Program. In 1988, the City Arts Center was born as a non-profit organization.

Today, several art organizations use the building for classes, demonstrations, meetings, and more. Classes for adults include drawing, painting, photography, pottery, and weaving. During session, these classes are held every week.

They have four sessions a year: Winter, Spring, Summer, and Fall. Class costs right now vary from $112 to $142 per class.

Camps and workshops are offered for children ages five to twelve. As these programs change frequently, check the Web site to see what is being offered.

The Arts Center does have a gallery with different exhibits held at various times through the year. Their gallery is always free to the public.

i Interested in or appreciate wood carving? Check out the Oklahoma Woodcarvers (405-731-2888; www.okcarver.org). They hold monthly meetings and yearly art shows featuring artistry in wood.

OKLAHOMA CITY BALLET
7421 N. Classen Blvd.
(405) 843-9898
www.balletoklahoma.com

The Oklahoma City Ballet is a professional company dedicated to producing artistically exciting, educational programs while it works to make its community more artistically aware. The organization began in 1967. The ballet has 18 dancers who present a complete range of balletic choreography from the classics to contemporary works choreographed by the best artists working today. There are ballets without sets and ballets with huge sets. There are at least 17 public performances scheduled in the 2009–2010 season. These public performances are held in the Civic Center Music Hall and the Plaza Theatre in Oklahoma City as well as any place the company may be booked for touring engagement within the state of Oklahoma. In addition to public performances, the ballet presents 335 performances for schools plus various community performances annually.

Robert Mills, the new artistic director coming aboard in Aug 2008, is working to build its repertory and to make it a strong, regional ballet. The Oklahoma City Philharmonic plays for the ballet when its schedule permits. The ballet company has received two Governor Arts Awards, a Oklahoma City Community College Spring Fest Award, and a number of state arts grants.

Ticket prices range from $28 to $45 per performance. Visit the ballet's Web site to view a performance schedule and to check ticket prices.

OKLAHOMA CITY MUSEUM OF ART
415 Couch Dr.
(405) 236-3100
www.okcmoa.com

The Oklahoma City Museum of Art offers visitors more than three floors exhibiting fine works of art. The museum's Special Exhibitions Gallery, located on the ground floor, presents national and international traveling exhibits. The second and third floor galleries display works from the museum's permanent collection. The museum is home to the world's most comprehensive Dave Chihuly collection of glassworks and also has the tallest glass tower in the world at 55 feet. The museum also offers films and arts education.

The Museum Store is located on the ground floor. It offers a wide variety of merchandise, including books on key artists, music, decorative objects, and jewelry. It also has a children's section and a section dedicated to Dave Chihuly.

The Museum Café serves lunch, dinner, and Sun brunch. It is located on the ground floor of the museum as well. The cafe's metropolitan ambience, superb cuisine, and exceptional service bring a taste of Chicago, San Francisco, and London to Oklahoma City. The full-service restaurant offers fine dining with a French flair. Patio tables are available for seasonal dining along with an array of coffees, teas, espressos, cappuccino, and a full bar. Dinner and Sun brunch reservations are suggested. Call (405) 235-6262.

The museum is located downtown. On weekdays parking is $1 for two hours at a meter or $8 in a parking lot north of the museum. On weekends, meters are free. The museum is wheelchair accessible and it provides wheelchairs as well as strollers free of charge.

Admission is $12 for adults, $10 for seniors and students, and free for children under five and museum members.

OKLAHOMA CITY PHILHARMONIC
428 W. California Ave., #210
(405) 232-7575
www.okcphilharmonic.org

Music lovers of all ages enjoy the performances of the Oklahoma City Philharmonic, a professional, full symphony orchestra. Top musicians from around the world join the philharmonic for concerts of both traditional classical music as well as contemporary orchestral Pops. The philharmonic also offers family concerts that introduce orchestral music to youngsters.

The Oklahoma City Philharmonic continues a long tradition of classical music performances in Oklahoma that began before statehood. It was founded by a group of dedicated community members in 1989. Founding conductor Joel

Levine continues his successful tenure as music director. In 1995, they were asked to perform at the memorial service for the victims of the Oklahoma City bombing. This services was broadcast worldwide on CNN, FOX, MSNBC, and other news stations. In Nov 2007, the philharmonic was part of the Oklahoma Centennial Spectacular that was broadcast on OETA, Oklahoma's Educational Television channel, throughout the state. Other notable performances featured opera superstar Reneé Fleming in 2007, cellist Yo-Yo Ma in 2003, R&B legend Ray Charles in 2001, and Van Cliburn in 1996. In addition to their work with the orchestra, many of the musicians of the Oklahoma City Philharmonic hold positions in music education at all levels throughout the community. Several members of the orchestra are primarily employed teaching at various schools and colleges like Norman Public Schools, the University of Central Oklahoma, and the University of Oklahoma.

The Oklahoma City Philharmonic offers a regular concert season from Sept to May with holiday performances to celebrate Independence Day, Labor Day, and Christmas. These concerts include the Classics, eight concerts where classical music compositions are performed; Pops, six concerts a year with two performances per concert featuring more modern music and a celebrity guest; and finally the Discovery Family series, which includes three concerts a year. The concerts are aimed toward children ages 4 to 13. The philharmonic also performs with the Oklahoma City Ballet and the Canterbury Choral Society.

Each year, the philharmonic can be seen in more than 50 performances. The majority of the performances are held at the Thelma Gaylord Performing Arts Theater in Civic Center Music Hall. Others are held at various locations around the community and in surrounding cities and towns. Classics and pops concerts are priced from $12 to $75. Family concerts are $9 with all seating as general admission.

OKLAHOMA OPRY
404 SW 25th St.
(405) 632-8322
www.okopry.com

The Oklahoma Opry has been in operation since 1977. It is located in the historic Capitol Hill District at Southwest 25th and Walker Avenue. The Oklahoma Opry is one of the longest running country and gospel shows in Oklahoma. It is a live show with a variety of entertainment, including singers, comedians, and gospel groups. Performers come from Oklahoma, Texas, Missouri, Kansas, Arkansas, and some even come from other countries.

The Oklahoma Opry also holds the Oklahoma Opry Rising Star Competition several times a year to help students from in and around the state show off their talents.

Most shows are held Sat evenings, except holidays and special events. Tickets are $12 for adults and $7 for children 12 and under. Special show prices vary.

PASEO ARTS DISTRICT
28th and North Walker to 30th and North Dewey
3022 Paseo
(405) 525-2688
www.thepaseo.com

The Paseo, which curves south of Northwest 30th Street, near Dewey Avenue, was built in 1929 and was intended to be a miniature version of the Country Club Plaza in Kansas City. The district's dress shops, laundries, and other businesses were built in the Spanish and Mission style, finished with glazed ceramic-tile entries, red-tile roofs, and wrought iron.

As the neighborhood around the shopping center shifted, so did the building's tenants, and by the 1960s, artists had staked out the territory for their own. Always interesting, the street has lately attracted established artists and the area is flourishing. A pottery studio, a handful of artists' cooperatives, and gift shops are sprinkled in among individual artists' studios. In the summer, a farmers' market sells fresh produce every Sat from 9 a.m. to 4 p.m. The Paseo Arts Festival, held each Memorial Day, features 100 or so artists and three days of local music.

RED EARTH MUSEUM

Located inside the Science Museum

2100 NE 52nd St.

(405) 427-5228

www.redearth.org

Casual attire and comfortable shoes are recommended for visits to this museum. It houses over 1400 items of detailed beadwork, textiles, incredible baskets, potter, and fine art in its permanent collection. The Red Earth Museum has the only collection of Bative American totem poles in the region. It is also home to the renowned Deupree Cradleboard Collection. This exclusive collection is one of the best in North America.

Since the museum is located inside Science Museum Oklahoma, admission to the Red Earth Museum is free with paid admission into the science museum. There is a gift shop inside the museum complex. Hours are Mon through Fri from 9 a.m. to 5 p.m., Sat from 9 a.m. to 6 p.m., and Sun from 11 a.m. to 6 p.m.

SHAKESPEARE IN THE PARK

400 W. Sheridan Ave.

(405) 235-3700

www.oklahomashakespeare.com

If you like Shakespeare, then be sure to check out Shakespeare in the Park. During the summer season, there are three or four outdoor productions and there is one indoor spring production. Three productions are offered for tour in Oklahoma throughout the year.

The performances began in Edmond in 1985. The crowds were small at first, but by the end of that first summer, over 6,000 guests had attended. In the third season, a record-breaking 8,500 people attended and audiences continued to grow.

Spring productions are held at Stage Center or Oklahoma City University while summer productions are held at the Myriad Gardens Water Stage. Tickets average $10 per person. Dress casually and be sure to bring food and beverages.

STAGE CENTER

400 W. Sheridan

(405) 270-4800

www.artscouncilokc.com/stage-center

Stage Center opened in 1970 as the Mummers Theatre. The building was originally designed by John Johansen, an internationally known architect. His design for the building won the American Institute of Architects Honors Award. Up until 1986, when the theater closed, several theater companies made their home here. Then in 1987, the building was bought by the Arts Council of Oklahoma City. They hired architect Rand Elliott for a renovation project on the structure. In the end the project cost $2 million.

In 1992, Stage Center reopened. Anyone who sees the multi-colored modern building knows why students, architects, and those who love art have to stop and study its design. Steel tunnels connect three pods. It is always brightly painted and the building has been described as strange and beautiful in the same sentence. There are two theatres here, one that seats 210 people and one that seats 550.

Carpenter Square Theatre is a resident theater company that presents year-round productions in the smaller Arena Theater and various other theater companies, dance groups, and community organizations present programs in the larger Tolbert Theater. In addition, Carpenter Square Theatre, Metropolitan School of Dance, and Oklahoma Shakespeare in the Park have the offices at Stage Center.

Parking is available just south of Stage Center in the Arts Council parking lot. Most of the time parking is free, but during certain events, there may be a fee. There are also Metro Parking garages located directly northwest and northeast of Stage Center. Tickets to many events can be purchased through the Civic Center Box Office or at the door.

FESTIVALS

ARTS FESTIVAL OKLAHOMA

7777 S. May Ave.

(405) 682-1611

www.occc.edu/afo

Arts Festival Oklahoma is a three-day event held over the Labor Day weekend each year (Sat–Mon). This arts festival has a wide variety of

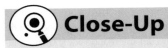 # Close-Up

Untitled [Artspace]

Untitled [Artspace] (1 Northeast 3rd, 405-815-9995, www.1ne3.org) is located in a historic part of downtown Oklahoma City-the Deep Deuce district. During the 20s and 30s, this area was alive with the sounds from the black jazz community. Many of the buildings began to fall in to disrepair in the 1960s and were torn down. However, one of those buildings survived. It was an old industrial warehouse purchased in 1996 by Laura Warriner. She refurbished the old warehouse and turned it into an art gallery. Originally it was called Untitled Gallery, but in 2003, the name was changed to [Artspace] at Untitled.

The gallery's goal is to bring contemporary art to the state. Artspace wants to expand people's ideas about what they think about art. They want to encourage public debate about art to expand the community's perception of what art is. The gallery is a non-profit organization.

The gallery has four main programs: Art Forums, Exhibitions, Untitled [Press], and Visiting Artists. The exhibitions draw artists not only from Oklahoma, but from all over the world. Through the gallery's Art Forums they hold lectures, performances, and panel discussions and through Visiting Artists and Untitled [Press], they offer the community public talks and workshops. No memberships are available here. They work with artists on a one to one basis. A catalogue is produced for the exhibitions.

Untitled [Artspace] holds six exhibitions a year featuring artists from our region, nationally, and internationally. Of these six, there are two biannual events. Roots and Ties feature Oklahoma artists who were born, raised, and educated in the state, but whose work has expanded beyond Oklahoma's borders. Function and Design is their cutting edge exhibition. Local and regional artists get to show off their work that is cutting edge in design. This exhibit looks at the long lasting, "green," and serviceable issues of the art design.

The gallery is open Tues through Fri from 10 a.m. to 6 p.m. and Sat from 10 a.m. to 4 p.m. It is closed Sun and Mon. Admission to the gallery is free.

fine arts, crafts, concessionaires, and performing artists.

In 2009, the festival celebrated its 31st year. The purpose of the Arts Festival Oklahoma is to promote and showcase the work of local and out-of-state artists and artisans to provide cultural awareness and opportunities and to present and promote the performing arts. The festival is sponsored by Oklahoma City Community College, the Central Art Association, the South Oklahoma City Chamber of Commerce, and Women of the South.

Both daytime and evening entertainment is offered. The daytime entertainment typically showcases Oklahoma performing artists, like Edgar Cruz, Debbie Henning, Full Circle, the Jewish Dancers, Mike Black & the Stingrays, just to name a few. Headliners perform in the evenings and these have included: BJ Thomas, Ballet Folkloric-Mexico, the Bellamy Brothers, Ray Price, Shenandoah, Texas Swing legend Red Steagall, the Kingston Trio, the Lettermen, the Platters, Three Dog Night, Ty England, and Western swing revivalists Bob Wills' Texas Playboys.

Food concessionaires are a big part of the festival, too. Some of the food that is available includes Indian tacos, roasted corn on the cob, gyros, pizza, hamburgers, cheeseburgers, hot dogs, funnel cake, kettle corn, fried green tomatoes, baked potatoes (with or without meat), strawberry New Orleans, corn dogs, turkey legs,

BBQ brisket sandwiches, curly fries, nachos, fruit smoothies, and waffle sundaes.

The Children's Creative Center has a wide variety of activities that are planned for children each year. Children can also create their own works of art. The cost is $1 per child.

The arts festival is an outdoor event, so prepare for the weather by listening to the forecast and wearing or bringing appropriate clothing. Admission to the festival is free. There is a $3 charge for parking. Attendance in years past has been between 15,000 and 50,000 people.

DOWNTOWN EDMOND ARTS FESTIVAL
Downtown Edmond
(405) 249-9391
www.downtownedmondok.com
Over 100 artists exhibit at this fine arts festival held in downtown Edmond. This event has been held annually since 1979. Guests can visit artists and their booths as well as enjoy delicious food from 20 food vendors. The foods visitors can enjoy are onion blossoms, Indian tacos, catfish, German food, pizza, fried pies, funnel cakes, kettle corn, and onion fried burgers. Wine tasting is also offered by some of Oklahoma's wineries.

There is live entertainment at the Festival Market Place Plaza. Artists who have performed in the past are Edgar Cruz, a local favorite; Stephanie Jackson; and the 145th Army Jazz Trio. A children's area offers face painting, pony rides, a giant slide, a moon walk, and a climbing rock wall.

During the festival, downtown Edmond streets are closed from Second and Broadway north to Hurd. First Street is closed west to the railroad tracks and east to the alley. Main Street is closed both east and west.

No animals are allowed at this event. Admission is free. Parking is ample throughout town and is free.

FESTIVAL OF THE ARTS
Downtown Oklahoma City
(405) 270-4848
www.artscouncilokc.com/festival-of-the-arts
This annual festival is produced by the Arts Council of Oklahoma City. In 2009, it enjoyed its 43rd year. It is held on Hudson Avenue, Festival Plaza, and Myriad Gardens and Stage Center grounds in downtown Oklahoma City. It is known as Oklahoma City's rite of Spring and has garnered national attention as a premier event. Locally, it's known as a great place to stop, get a bite to eat, and enjoy the sounds of free music and the sites of downtown.

This is a six-day event that combines visual, performing, and culinary arts. There are 144 fine artists, nearly 200 performing artists, and more than 30 unique food vendors. There are opportunities to admire art, buy art, and observe art being made. The food along International Food Row includes Greek, Indian, and Asian food and fair favorites, like Indian tacos, strawberry Newport, and pizza.

The main souvenir, a collectible item itself, is the festival gift poster. It costs $40. Every year, a commissioned artist creates the art for the poster. There is also a kids-only shopping area at the Young-at-Art Mart, where kids can purchase art for $5 or less.

The Festival of the Arts is held outdoors. All artists are housed in tents to keep patrons dry if it rains. In 2009, over 700,000 attended the six day event.

DAY TRIPS AND WEEKEND GETAWAYS

Even though there are enough things to do in Oklahoma City to keep you busy, sometimes it's nice to escape the hustle and bustle and see and do something a little different. All of the locations listed in this chapter can be reached by car in about an hour, two at the most. Getting out of town is easy. You can travel south or north on I-35 or east or west on I-40. These main arteries will take you to smaller highways that will get you to your place of interest.

Some places will only take a day to see. For others you'll want to take a few days. If you head down to the southwest part of the state, you can learn about the American Indians that came to Oklahoma before it was a state. If you head northeast to Ponca City, you can learn about the early settlers. In the east and southeast are numerous forests and lakes to visit.

I've put 11 destinations in this chapter, almost one for each month of the year. All are located within Oklahoma. For those hearty explorers and the more adventurous, Dallas, Branson, Tulsa, Wichita, or Amarillo can be reached in half a day's drive time. If you're interested in flying, you can reach Dallas/Fort Worth International Airport in 30 minutes.

For any of the destinations here, contact the area's chamber of commerce a week or two in advance to learn more about what's going on there. If there is a festival, tournament, or community activity taking place, then you may have to make hotel reservations weeks in advance. If you are going to an area for a specific event, checking with the chamber to see if the event is still happening is another good idea. You don't want to drive for an hour only to be disappointed.

Whichever destination you choose, I'd like to offer a piece of advice. Plan to take your time. Oklahoma has a lot of interesting things along the way that could not be listed here. If you are driving to a destination and something catches your eye, stop and check it out. By being flexible and taking your time, you will discover your own favorite places and enjoy your trip even more.

ANADARKO

ANADARKO CHAMBER OF COMMERCE
516 W. Kentucky
(405) 247-6651
www.anadarko.org

About an hour's drive southwest of Oklahoma City, you will find Anadarko, "the Indian Capital of the Nation." Today's Anadarko was built just south of the old Anadarko. It is well worth taking a day to go down and see what the town has to offer. To get to Anadarko from Oklahoma City, take the H.E. Bailey Turnpike south and then exit to Chickasha on US 62. Anadarko is straight west of Chickasha.

With so much to do, a good place to start is the Anadarko Visitor Center. It is located at the National Hall of Fame for Famous American Indians (405-247-5555) at the intersection of US 62 and OK 8. Immediately west of the outdoor sculpture garden is the Southern Plains Indian Museum and Crafts Center (405-247-6221).

While here, you'll want to stop in the Anadarko Post Office building and see the murals painted there. Three artists, Stephen Mopope, James Auchiah, and Spencer Asah, were commissioned by the federal government in the 1930s to paint them. The Anadarko Philomathic Pioneer Museum sits at 311 E. Main. It was founded in 1935 by a women's study circle called the Philomathic Club. Don't leave town without visiting the Indian City USA Cultural Center, located 2.5 miles south of Anadarko on OK 8. At this center, visitors learn what life was really like in an Indian village. Check the Web site at www.indiancityusa.com to see what's new.

The third week in Aug, the American Indian Exposition is held at the Caddo County Fairgrounds. It is a festival filled with Native American dancing and foods, a rodeo, arts and crafts, and a historical pageant.

If you find there is too much activity to take in on a single day and want to spend the night, Anadarko has several hotels. The Anadarko Executive Suites (405-247-2538) and Best Value Southern Plains Inn (405-247-3100), are two suggestions. If you find you are hungry, Melton's Drug and Soda Fountain Eatery serves sandwiches, sodas, and limeades. K.I.G. Que smokes beef and pork and Nicoli's Italian Restaurant is a place you might want to try if you have hearty appetite.

i Red Carpet Country is the tourism info center in northwest Oklahoma. Call (800) 447-2698 or visit www.redcarpetcountry.com for the Red Carpet Country Visitor's Guide.

ARBUCKLE MOUNTAIN AREA

DAVIS CHAMBER OF COMMERCE
100 E. Main St.
(580) 369-2402
www.davisok.org

Seventy-five miles south of Oklahoma City, just off I-35, you will find the Arbuckle Mountain area a perfect place for a day trip. The little town of Davis can serve as your base as you begin to explore the area.

On Main Street, visitors will want to check out the Main Street Restaurant, and the Arbuckle Historical Museum.

The museum is open from 10 a.m. to 4 p.m. Donations of $1 are requested. Call (580) 369-2518 for more information.

Davis' claim to fame is nearby Turner Falls Park (580-369-2988). It has a 77-foot waterfall, the largest waterfall in Oklahoma. Admission to the park is $10 per person.

The falls are at the very heart of the Arbuckle Mountains, which run east and west. A recommended loop through the Arbuckle Mountains follows OK 77D, which heads south from OK 7 between Davis and Turner Falls Park.

The Arbuckle Wilderness Exotic Animal Theme Park, (580) 369-3383 makes its home in this area and was awarded Oklahoma's Outstanding Tourist Attraction for 2005 by the Oklahoma Department of Tourism.

Call the park office at (580) 369-3383 for more information.

If you decide to spend the night, a unique place to stay is the Gingerbread House (www.the-gingerbreadhouse.com), a bed-and-breakfast located in downtown Davis Prices range from $75 to $95 depending on the season. Call (580) 369-7862 for more information.

GRAND LAKE OF THE CHEROKEES

GRAND LAKE ASSOCIATION
9630 US 59 N.
(866) 588-4726
www.grandlakefun.com

Located in the upper northwest part of the state, you'll want to make this a weekend trip. From Oklahoma City, hop on I-44, or as the locals call it, the Turner Turnpike. Go through Tulsa and hook up with the Will Rogers Turnpike on the east side. You'll want to take the Afton/Grove exit and head south until you reach OK 10. The straight road begins to wind itself into curves the closer you come to Grand Lake O' the Cherokees (918-588-4726 or 866-LUV-GRAND; www.grandlakefun.com), the place where northeastern Oklahoma residents go to unwind.

A quiet and affordable place to enjoy Grand Lake and its natural beauty is Reflections Bed & Breakfast (www.grandnorthstar.com/REF). John and Pam request advance notice, so call (918) 787-7727 for information.

Activity on the north end of the lake centers in Grove (918-786-9079; www.groveok.org) once a little farming community but now a sprawling hub for recreation. The new Grove is found at places like Rheingarten Restaurant, 911 South Main Street, (918-786-8737), a German restaurant located in a cozy house. Hours are Wed through Sat, 11 a.m. to 9 p.m.

Lendonwood Gardens is a botanical garden featuring Japanese-style cascading pools, a shade garden, an English terrace garden, a bonsai collection, and rare varieties of flowers and trees. The garden is at 1308 W. 13th Street. The gardens are open from dawn to dusk. Call (918) 786-2938 or go to www.lendonwood.org.

A little farther down Har-Ber Road is its namesake, Har-Ber Village, (918) 786-3488) www .har-bervillage.com, a reconstructed early 20th-century frontier town. The village takes about three hours to tour. To get to the village, travel along Har-Ber Road for 3.5 miles west of Grove. There's a big sign marking a turn south. Follow that road south and then back west to Har-Ber Village. Har-Ber Village is open Mon through Sat from 9 a.m. to 6 p.m. and Sun from 12:30 p.m. to 6 p.m. from Mar through Nov.

Within walking distance of Har-Ber Village is the Candlewyck Cove Resort, a lakefront cluster of suites on a little peninsula.

For reservations call (918) 786-3636 or visit www.candlewyckcove.com.

There's a little cluster of entertainment just east of Sailboat Bridge on US 59 west of Grove. Ninety-minute cruises depart daily from May through Sept aboard the *Cherokee Queen II*, a diesel-powered replica of a paddle wheel. For reservations call (918) 786-4272.

Down the road is Shebang, a sprawling pink-and-gray restaurant that caters to both families and couples. Pasta is a specialty, but the restaurant also serves ribs, prime rib, and seafood. Call (918) 257-5569.

GREAT SALT PLAINS AREA

GREAT SALT PLAINS RECREATIONAL DEVELOPMENT ASSOCIATION
111 S. Grand
(580) 596-3053
www.greatsaltplains.com

From Enid, take US 81 north to where it intersects with US 64; then take US 64 west to Jet. Drive north from Jet along OK 38 to the entrance to Salt Plains National Wildlife Refuge. The Refuge is a grat place for bird enthusiasts to see birds as the area is a stopover for birds migrating from Canada to South America.

An estimated 250 species of bird have been spotted at Great Salt Plains State Park (www.great saltplains.com), on the east side of the reservoir and also off OK 38. The park has cabins, 90 campsites, picnic areas, a nature trail, and showers.

About 20 miles south on OK 8, south of the little town of Aline, is the Sod House Museum (580-463-2441). The museum is open Tues through Fri from 9 a.m. to 5 p.m. and Sat and Sun from 2 to 5 p.m.

Not far from the sod house is another distinctive, even odd, structure, the Heritage Manor Bed and Breakfast (www.1aj.org), a rambling, 20-room Victorian-style dwelling. There are four guest rooms, a dining room where breakfast, lunch, and dinner are available (innkeepers Carolyn and A. J. Rexroat used to run a restaurant), and a 5,000-volume library. For reservations call (580) 463-2563.

i If you are looking to get away, but not too far away, look no farther than 90 minutes up the Turner Turnpike to Tulsa, Oklahoma's second-largest city. It's another short trip with big rewards. Contact the Tulsa Convention and Visitors Bureau at (918) 585-1201, visit www.visittulsa.com, or pick up *Insiders' Guide to Tulsa.*

GUTHRIE

GUTHRIE CHAMBER OF COMMERCE
212 W. Oklahoma Ave.
(405) 282-1947
www.guthrieok.com

If you are interested in history and would like to step back in time, hop on I-35 and head north. About 30 minutes and 20 to 25 miles from Oklahoma City sits Guthrie, Oklahoma's territorial capital. The downtown area of this town is listed on the National Register of Historic Places.

Visitors will find an abundance of things to do in Guthrie. If driving up for a day, there are several museums to see. The Oklahoma Territorial Museum and Carnegie Library, located at 406 E. Oklahoma is a must. The Oklahoma Publishing Museum at 301 W. Harrison holds both early newspaper and town history. One block north is the Oklahoma Frontier Pharmacy Museum, 214 W. Oklahoma. and farther west, on the south side of the street is the Oklahoma Sports Museum (www .oklahomasportsmuseum.com). In the middle of town, on the north side of Harrison, you'll find the Pollard Theatre (www.thepollard.org) and on the east side of town is the Double Stop Fiddle Shop and Music Hall (www.doublestop.com). Don't go to Guthrie without visiting the Scottish Rite Masonic Temple. It sits on top of a hill at 900 E. Oklahoma. Guthrie has many events that take place through the year. In Apr the 89er's Celebration (www.89erdays.com) commemorates the Land Run of 1889 and the birth of Guthrie. In Mar and Nov, the Guthrie Art Walk is held and in Oct the Oklahoma International Bluegrass Festival (www.oibf.com) takes over the town. At the end of the year, in Dec, Guthrie is turned in to a Victorian wonderland for the Territorial Christmas Celebration.

If you are planning an extended stay, you will not have a difficult time finding accommodations. With its 15 bed-and-breakfasts, Guthrie is considered the bed-and-breakfast capital of Oklahoma.

If a bed-and-breakfast isn't your cup of tea, Guthrie has several hotels to accommodate you. Along I-35 and OK 33, you'll find several new hotels being built, so check Guthrie's Web site before you plan to travel there for an overnight stay.

Guthrie is filled with quaint little places to eat. The Blue Bell Saloon at 224 W. Harrison in a local favorite. Granny Had One (www.grannyhadone .biz) is located right up the street.. Miss Carolyn's Territorial House, Oklahoma's Most Famous Barbeque, R&R Restaurant, Stables Café, and the Victorian Tea Room are also places visitors can find great meals. Finally to top off your visit, stop in at Winans' Fine Chocolate and Coffee (www .winansofguthrie.com), 109 W. Oklahoma.

LAKE TEXOMA

LAKE TEXOMA ASSOCIATION
(580) 564-2334
www.laketexomaonline.com
If you are ready for a day at the lake, head south out of Oklahoma City on I-35 to US 70. Go east about 30 miles to Lake Texoma.

Texoma is a big lake, so striper guide services flourish. You can pick up a list of guides at the Lake Texoma Association (580-564-2334; www.laketexomaonline.com); offices are at Lake Texoma State Park, 10 miles east of Kingston.

In the winter, the park naturalist conducts waterfowl tours on a pontoon boat every Sat There's a $10 fee for the tour, which includes lunch. Fish lovers (eating, not fishing) should detour across I-35 and follow OK 32 along the Red River. About 4 miles west, signs direct travelers down a zigzagging series of gravel roads to McGeehee's Catfish Restaurant.

The restaurant is open weekdays from 5 to 8:30 p.m. and on weekends from 1 to 8:30 p.m. and is closed Wed. Call (580) 276-2751 for information.

After a day of water activities, you might want to explore a small town. Just east and south on OK 78, is Durant, an agricultural center since the railroad went through in 1882.

Ten blocks east, at the corner of Fourth and Main, is the Three Valley Museum. The museum is open Mon through Fri, from 1 to 5 p.m.; admission is free. For more information call (580) 920-1907.

Feeling lucky? The Choctaw Indian High Stakes Bingo Palace and Casino is on US 69 south of downtown Durant. Call (580) 920-0160 for information.

LAWTON FORT SILL DISCOVERY TRAIL

LAWTON CHAMBER OF COMMERCE
607 East Ave.
(580) 355-3541
www.lawtonfortsillchamber.com
About two hours from Oklahoma City is the Lawton-Fort Sill Discovery Trail, your passport to adventure.

> **i** While in the Lawton area, check out the Fort Sill Military Reservation. To get there take I-44 to the Key Gate entrance. History can be found in the Guardhouse, along the Cannon Walk, and in the museum. For information, call (580) 442-5123.

Lawton (www.lawtonfortsillchamber.com) is Oklahoma's fourth-largest city. It was settled by a lottery of the Kiowa, Comanche, Wichita, Caddo, and Apache.

The Mattie Beal House, (580) 678-3156, www .lawtonheritage.com, is a place you'll want to visit while in town. The house, which has stained-glass windows depicting the nearby Wichita Mountains, is open for tours the second Sun afternoon of each month or by appointment. It is located at 1006 SW Fifth St. Admission is $4.

Also in Lawton is the newly expanded Museum of the Great Plains, dedicated to the cultural and natural history of the plains. The museum, at 601 Ferris Ave., is open Mon through Sat from 10 a.m. to 5 p.m. and Sun 1 to 5 p.m.; the museum stays open an hour later during the summer. Call (580) 581-3460 or visit www .museumgreatplains.org.

Behind the McMahon Auditorium, at 701 NW Ferris Ave., is the Comanche National Museum and Cultural Center (580-353-0404; www.coman chemuseum.com).

Hours of operation are Mon through Fri, 8 a.m. to 5 p.m. and Sat, 10 a.m. to 2 p.m. It is closed on Sun. Admission is free and tour groups are welcome.

Pick up OK 19 and travel east to OK 115, which takes visitors to the north entrance to the Wichita Mountains Wildlife Refuge (580-429-3222; www.fws.gov/southwest/refuges/oklahoma/ wichitamountains).

A visitor center at the intersection of OK 49 and OK 115 is a worthwhile stop.

On the west side of the refuge is the Charon's Garden Wilderness Area, a 5,000-acre preserve that offers hiking through canyons and past waterfalls. Backcountry camping is allowed in the area by permit, which can be reserved by writing to the Department of the Interior, U.S. Fish and Wildlife Service, R.R. No. 1, Box 448, Indiahoma, OK 73552.

Only 10 overnight camping permits are issued each day; reservations are taken one month in advance.

The Holy City of the Wichitas (580-429-3361; www.theholycitylawton.com) is located in this neck of the woods. It has 20 interesting buildings and a stone amphitheatre where the Passion Play is acted out every Easter.

If you are hungry, you'll need to head a little out of your way. OK 115 takes travelers to Meers, on the northern edge of the refuge, or, more accurately, to Meers Store (580-429-8051; www .meersstore.com), formerly a general store, but now a restaurant.

> **i** You can learn a lot more about what there is to do in northeastern Oklahoma by contacting Green Country (800-922-2118; www.greencountryok.com). Ask for the *Great Green Getaways* book.

OUACHITA FOREST AREA

CHOCTAW RANGER DISTRICT
HC 64, Box 3467
(918) 653-2991
www.southernregion.fs.fed.us/ouachita
For nature lovers, there is no better place to go than southeast Oklahoma. Hours away from the metro area, you'll want to pack a bag for this trip as you'll be spending the night. Camping, hiking, horseback riding, and scenic drives can keep you busy for a day, for a weekend, or for a week.

The Ouachita Forest sits on the border of Oklahoma and Arkansas. It is the oldest national forest in the South. Cedar Lake Campground (918-653-2991) is a good camping base from which to explore the forest.

Cedar Lake Campground is a trailhead for the Ouachita Trail. Maps to the trail are available at the Ouachita National Forest West End Information Center (918-567-3434) in Talihina, also the gateway to the Talimena Scenic Byway. The Talimena Scenic Byway (www.talimenascenicdrive

Great Plains Trails

If you have a day and feel like a drive, why not check out one of the 13 driving loops designated in western Oklahoma to showcase some of its wildlife? The **Oklahoma Wildlife and Prairie Heritage Alliance** (www.owpha.org), with its partners and volunteers, has unveiled the Great Plains Trails of Oklahoma. These trails consist of 13 loops that cover 1,777 miles and include 33 counties. Travelers can view some of Oklahoma's unique and diverse wildlife species, including prairie chickens, horny toads, scissor-tailed flycatchers, and elk plus experience some of the state's small-town hospitality. To get your free Great Plains Trails of Oklahoma map call (800) 652-6552 or visit www.wildlifedepartment.com/wildlifetrails.htm.

.com) is an adventure everyone should take at least once. It is a 56.5 mile drive with beautiful vistas. Whether you believe Bigfoot exists or not, you might want to check out the Annual Bigfoot Festival (www.oklahomabigfoot.org) before passing final judgment.

The Robert S. Kerr Nature Center Arboretum, 2 miles west of the junction of Talimena Drive and US 259, was created in an 8,000-acre natural botanical area between the Winding Stair Mountains and the Rich Mountains. If camping isn't really your idea of a good time, don't worry. There are places within 50 miles where you can find a place to spend the night. Poteau, located north up US 259, has the Best Western Trader's Inn (918-647-4001) and the Kerr Conference Center (918-647-8221). In Wilburton, west of the park, visitors can reserve rooms at the Belle Starr View Lodge (918-465-2565). A little farther west is McAlester. There you will find many more options.

If you are traveling to southeastern Oklahoma, call (800) 722-8180 or visit www.kiamichicountry.com for a Kiamichi Country travel guide.

PONCA CITY

PONCA CITY TOURISM
420 E. Grand Ave.
(580) 765-4400
www.poncacitytourism.com

About an hour and a half away from Oklahoma City, north up I-35, is the booming little town of Ponca City, a typical pioneer town until after statehood when oil was discovered.

Pioneer Woman, a 17-foot-high bronze statue, stands on Monument Avenue, near the intersection of US 77 and Lake Road. Adjacent to the statue is the Pioneer Woman Museum (www.pioneerwomanmuseum.com). Visitors who travel up this way won't want to miss the Marland Estate (www.marlandmansion.com). Marland's biggest legacy, also on the estate grounds, is the Marland Estate Mansion (www.marlandmansion.com).

The Conoco Museum, located at 501 W. South Ave. in Ponca City, offers insight into its namesake's history and development. Admission is free. The museum is open Mon through Sat from 10 a.m. to 5 p.m. and Sun from 1 to 5 p.m. It is closed holidays. Guided tours are available upon request. To learn more, visit www.conocomuseum.com.

The Poncan Theatre (www.poncantheatre.org) is another landmark in the city. The theater is located at First and Grand.

For visitors who plan to spend the night, check out www.poncacitylodging.com. While there are seven hotels and motels listed, like Motel 6, Econo Lodge, Comfort Inn and Suites, and Holiday Inn Express, for a special treat, visitors might want to check out the Rose Stone Inn. Visitors who have come this far will want to visit Kaw Lake (www.kawlake.com), just east of Ponca City. The lake is over 25 miles long and 90 feet deep in areas.

TAHLEQUAH

TAHLEQUAH CHAMBER OF COMMERCE
123 E. Delaware
(918) 456-3742
www.tourtahlequah.com

Tahlequah (800-850-0348; www.tourtahlequah .com) is the 160-year-old capital of the Cherokee Nation and a picture-book small town. Visitors can pick up a brochure for a tour of historic sites at the Tahlequah Visitor Center at the corner of Water and Delaware Streets. The Morgan Bakery (918-456-3731), on Muskogee Street, sells sugar cookies, old-fashioned pastries, and wholewheat bagels. The bakery is open Tues through Fri from 7:30 a.m. to 5 p.m. and Sat from 7:30 a.m. to 2 p.m.

Cherokee history is apparent right across the street, at the Old Cherokee National Capitol Building.

Across the square, at the corner of Keetoowah Street and Water Avenue, is the 1845 Cherokee Supreme Court Building. Up the street, is the Iguana Café. It is open Mon through Fri from 9 a.m. to 9 p.m. and Sat from 10 a.m. to 3 p.m. The Iguana Cafe (918-458-0044) is at 500A Muskogee.

While in Tahlequah, tour the historic Thompson House, on the corner of College and Choctaw. Admission is $3 per person. To schedule a guided tour, call (918) 456-3554 or (918) 458-9035.

A stop at the Cherokee Heritage Center, (888-999-6007; www.cherokeeheritage.org) three miles south of Tahlequah, is a must for anyone interested in Cherokee or Native American history. Behind the museum is the Tsa-La-Gi Ancient Village.

Adams Rural Village, next to the ancient village, demonstrates Cherokee life after their arrival in Indian Territory.

The Cherokee Heritage Center is east of OK 62 on Willis Road. The museum is open Mon through Sat 10 a.m. to 5 p.m. and Sun from 1 to 5 p.m. It is closed in Jan. Admission is $8.50 for adults, $7.50 for seniors 55 and over, and $5 for children. Call (918) 456-6007 for information.

Not far from the heritage center is the Murrell Home. The Murrell Home is 1 mile east of OK 82 on Murrell Road. It is open Wed through Sat from 10 a.m. to 5 p.m. and Sun from 1 to 5 p.m. The museum is closed on Tues during the winter. Admission is free; call (918) 456-2751 for information.

ALABASTER CAVERNS STATE PARK AREA
OK 50 & OK 50 A (Freedom Oklahoma)
(580) 621-3381
www.oklahomaparks.com

If you seek adventure, pack your sleeping bag and head northwest out of the Oklahoma City area. About a three-hour drive away, you will find a great place to cool off in the summer-Alabaster Caverns State Park. Daily guided tours of the cave are available on the hour. The tour takes about an hour and covers approximately 1 mile. The route is not demanding. There is a fee.

Another cave in the area is the Selman Bat Cave. North of the state park, this cave is a bat nursery. Half a million migratory Mexican free-tailed bats come to the cave each spring to give birth. If you plan to attend this event, call (405-424-0099) in mid-May to make your reservation as spaces are usually filled by June. Only 75 people are accepted for each watch. Plan to wear sturdy shoes and long pants to protect your legs from brush and snakes.

Since you are hours from the metro, you will probably want to spend the night. The park has 20 campsites and if you have your mind set on camping and those places are full, check out Boling Springs State Park (580-256-7664) just south. If you'd rather stay in more modern accommodations, the town of Freedom (580-621-3583) is only 6 miles from the caves. The Cedar Canyon Lodge (www.cedarcanyonlodge.com) has six rooms visitors can stay in and the Sage & Saddle Bed & Breakfast (580-621-3338; www.sageand saddle.com) has five rooms.

While in the area, go exploring in Freedom. If Freedom accommodations are full, you can go about 35 miles southwest to Woodward (www

.woodwardok.com). It is northwest Oklahoma's second-largest metropolitan area. Places to stay include Days Inn (580-256-1546), Super 8 Motel (580-254-2964), Olde Holiday Inn Bed and Breakfast (580-254-2242), and Neely's Inn at the Park (580-254-3830).

Before leaving town, even if you aren't a history buff, you should consider stopping at the Plains Indians and Pioneers Museum (www.pipml.org).

RELOCATION

Oklahoma City has many housing options, from apartments to historic mansions. The interstate system that runs around and through Oklahoma City allows you to get from one side of town to the other in about 30 minutes. Want to live in Edmond? You can hop on the Broadway Extension or I-35 and be downtown in about 40 minutes on a busy traffic morning.

No matter where you choose to live, you will have access to hospitals, colleges, and shopping opportunities. On the south side of the city, in Del City or Moore, residents have easy access to the University of Oklahoma in Norman and to Crossroads Mall. On the north side, there are the University of Central Oklahoma, Quail Springs Mall, and hospitals, like Integris Baptist and Mercy. Centrally located are Penn Square Mall, 50 Penn Place, St. Anthony's Hospital, and Oklahoma City University.

Included in this chapter is a list of the area's chambers of commerce. These chambers can give you demographics of their cities and provide information about schools and business districts. Many have relocation packages that can be mailed you. Others will direct you to their Web sites where you can peruse information on your own.

In this chapter you will also find a short list of real estate agents. Real estate is doing very well here so there are a number of agencies at your disposal. No matter what your budget is, you will be able to find a home that is right for you. Edmond and Norman are pricier than other locations. Del City, Midwest City, Bethany, Warr Acres, and Yukon have nice homes for families and couples just starting out. Moore has been rebuilt since the tornado of 1999, so if you're looking for a house around 10 years old, check out this area. Nichols Hills' prices are higher, but this area has large older homes and they rarely go on the market. You will also find apartment-hunting information in this chapter and some details about what there is in the way of lofts, town houses, and apartments available downtown.

Also in this chapter you will find information on how to apply for a driver's license and car tags, register to vote, and find a library in your area.

You will find the people who live here friendly; the economy is one of the best in the country; and the city continues to thrive, grow, and expand. As such, let me be the first to welcome you to our city.

CHAMBERS OF COMMERCE

If you are planning a move to Oklahoma City and you're not sure where to start, contact any of the Chamber of Commerce offices below and request a relocation packet or guide. Relocation packets typically include information on housing, education, businesses, and entertainment.

DEL CITY CHAMBER OF COMMERCE
4505 SE 15th St.
(405) 677-1910
www.cityofdelcity.com

EDMOND CHAMBER OF COMMERCE
825 E. Second St.
(405) 341-2808
www.edmondchamber.com

GREATER OKLAHOMA CITY CHAMBER OF COMMERCE
123 Park Ave.
(405) 297-8900
www.okcchamber.com

GREATER OKLAHOMA CITY HISPANIC CHAMBER OF COMMERCE
4316 S. Walker
(405) 616-5031
www.okchispanicchamber.com

MIDWEST CITY CHAMBER OF COMMERCE
5905 Trosper Rd.
(405) 733-3801
www.midwestcityok.com

MOORE CHAMBER OF COMMERCE
305 W. Main
(405) 794-3400
www.moorechamber.com

NORMAN CHAMBER OF COMMERCE
115 E. Gray St.
(405) 321-7260
www.normanok.org

NORTHWEST CHAMBER OF COMMERCE
7440 NW 39th Expressway
(405) 789-1256
www.thenorthwestchamber.com

SOUTH OKLAHOMA CITY CHAMBER OF COMMERCE
701 SW 74th
(405) 634-1436
www.southokc.com

YUKON CHAMBER OF COMMERCE
510 Elm St.
(405) 354-3567
www.yukoncc.com

MOTOR VEHICLE INFORMATION

Driver's License

OKLAHOMA DEPARTMENT OF PUBLIC SAFETY
3600 N. Martin Luther King Ave.
(405) 425-2424
www.dps.state.ok.us

To obtain an Oklahoma driver's license, contact the Oklahoma Department of Public Safety. To qualify for a license, you must be a legal resident of Oklahoma, meet the age requirement, pass a vision test, have acceptable identification and a Driver's Education Completion Certificate, and pass a written test and a driving test.

Applicants will want to find a Driver's License Exam Station in their area. At these stations, applicants can take the written and driving tests. You can find those locations from the Web site.

Every applicant must provide two forms of identification. There is a list of acceptable documents listed on the Web site.

Vehicle Registration and Car Tags

OKLAHOMA TAX COMMISSION
Motor Vehicle Division
2501 N. Lincoln Blvd.
(405) 521-3221
www.tax.ok.gov/motveh.html

This agency is responsible for the titling and registration of vehicles, including boats and motor homes. It has over 300 agents around the state who can process any vehicle title and or registration transaction. Locating one of these agents in your local community will save you time. You can find these agents by going to the commission's Web site and clicking on "Find a Tag Agent/Office" or calling the number listed above. The Web site also provides answers to most vehicle-registration and car-tag questions.

If you have purchased a new vehicle and want to know what you will owe for tag, title, and tax, contact the commission or any tag agency with the vehicle identification number, purchase price and date, and registration classification.

VOTER REGISTRATION

OKLAHOMA STATE ELECTION BOARD

2300 N. Lincoln

(405) 521-2391

www.ok.gov/~elections

To register to vote in Oklahoma, you must be at least 18 years of age, a United States citizen, and a resident of Oklahoma. There are some restrictions to becoming a registered voter, so visit the Web site to see if any apply to you.

When you are ready to register, you must fill out an application form. These are available at the County Election Board, post offices, tag agencies, libraries, and many other public locations. You will be offered a voter registration application when you get your driver's license. You may also download an application from the election board's Web site or request that one be mailed to you.

The form asks for your name and address, political affiliation, birth date, driver's license number, and the last four digits of your Social Security number. You must also sign and date the oath on the form.

You may submit your application at any time. However, voter identification cards cannot be issued during the 24 days prior to an election. So, if you submit your application just before or during those 24 days, you will not receive your card until after the election.

For more information on voting and voter registration call the Oklahoma State Election Board or visit the Web site.

i To obtain a Handicap Parking Permit, contact the Oklahoma Department of Public Safety by calling (405) 425-2290 or visiting www.dps.state.ok.us.

REAL ESTATE OFFICES

If you are interested in moving to Oklahoma City, you will find an army of real estate agents ready to help you find a new home. Some of the major agencies are listed below.

Quick Utility Contacts

Electricity:
Edmond Electric (405) 359-4541
Oklahoma Electric Coop (Norman) (405) 321-2024
Oklahoma Gas & Electric (OG&E) (405) 272-9741

Water and Sewer:
Oklahoma City Department of Utilities (405) 297-2833
Bethany (405) 789-2146
Edmond (405) 359-4541
Nichols Hills (405) 843-6637
Norman (405) 366-5320

Cable:
Cox Digital Cable (405) 600-8282

Trash Services:
All American Waste Control (405) 745-4141
Waste Management (405) 949-2121
Bethany (405) 789-1193
Del City (405) 671-2872
Edmond (405) 359-4626
Midwest City (405) 739-1370
Moore (405) 793-5072
Nichols Hills (405) 843-6637
Norman (405) 329-1023
The Village (405) 751-4933

Natural Gas:
OG&E (405) 272-0888
Oklahoma Natural Gas (ONG) (405) 551-4000
ONG Emergency (405) 458-4251

Telephone:
AT&T (800) 222-0300
AT&T Telephone (800) 464-7928
Cox Communications (405) 600-8282

OKLAHOMA REAL ESTATE COMMISSION (STATE AGENCY)

2401 NW 23rd

(405) 521-3387

www.ok.gov/orec

If you have a question, complaint, or compliment about any Oklahoma real estate agency, this is the place to report it. This commission oversees and sets standards for the real estate community across the state. Its mission is to safeguard the public interest, provide resources, and assist the public in resolving real estate issues in an accurate and timely manner.

i **Want to verify that your real estate agent is truly licensed? Want to access real estate laws? Visit www.arello.org to get all this information and more.**

Real Estate Agencies

CENTURY 21 GOLD CREST REALTY

8220 S. Pennsylvania

(405) 680-9200

www.c21goldcrest.com

This office can assist you with a search for homes located in the Oklahoma City metropolitan area, Edmond, Moore, and Norman. It handles residential, new homes, resale, luxury homes, condos, town houses, and lots. This office can also direct you to other Century 21 offices around the city.

COLDWELL BANKER MIKE JONES COMPANY

1300 E. 15th

(405) 340-4224

www.cbmikejonescompany.com

Even though this is primarily a real estate agency, it also offers a relocation service. The agency also offers individual counseling and area tours and has over 35 sales associates ready to serve buyers and sellers.

GOSCOUT HOMES OKLAHOMA CITY

6301 Waterford Blvd., Ste. 305

(405) 286-5500

www.goscouthomes.tv

This is a local television channel offered by Cox Cable that shows real estate offered in the area. Here you will find house and property listings of all sizes. Visit the Web site or turn to Cox Cable channel 22 and watch the listings as they rotate on the screen. Don't worry; you will have plenty of time to take notes as a description of each property is given.

KELLER WILLIAMS REALTY

1624 SW 122nd

(405) 691-2556

www.kw.com

This agency has 10 offices in the Oklahoma City area. It also has offices in Yukon, Midwest City, and Guthrie. Keller Williams was originally founded in 1983. In 2009, the agency was the third-largest residential real estate firm in the United States.

NORTHWEST OKLAHOMA CITY OFFICE

4101 NW 122nd

(405) 755-9052

www.denisewhitehead.com

Located in the northern part of Oklahoma City, this office serves the metro area as well as Edmond, Midwest City, Moore, and Nichols Hills.

OKLAHOMA CITY METROPOLITAN ASSOCIATION OF REALTORS

3131 NW Expressway

(405) 840-1493

www.okcrealtors.com

This is a professional association for real estate agents. Its Web site offers access to the MLS (Multiple Listing Service), which offers listings of properties for sale. Select the city you want to investigate and prepare to spend some time looking at listings. You can narrow your search by keying in particular specifics, like the number of bedrooms or bathrooms or a price range.

OKLAHOMA INDEPENDENT REAL ESTATE AGENTS

(405) 759-3737

www.okagents.com

This is a co-op of 55 real estate agents. They started this organization in late 2008. Through this co-op, these Oklahoma agencies advertise about the properties they sell. They service all of central Oklahoma.

PRUDENTIAL ALLIANCE REALTY
www.pruhomequest.com
Prudential has offices throughout the central part of the state, including Edmond, Del City, and Oklahoma City.

REMAX PREFERRED PROPERTIES
3705 W. Memorial Rd., Ste. 1310
(405) 751-4848
www.mlsokc.com
Over 35 associates work here and service clients all across the metro Oklahoma City area.

SOUTH OKLAHOMA CITY OFFICE
1500 SW 104th
(405) 378-4442
www.realestateokc.com
This agency provides real estate services to home buyers and sellers in Del City, Edmond, Oklahoma City, Midwest City, Moore, Norman, and Yukon.

RELOCATION SERVICES

BEKINS RELOCATION SERVICES
3501 N. Santa Fe Ave., #B
(405) 521- 8000
www.bekins.com
Bekins has been around for over 100 years. Its Web site offers moving guides, moving check-lists, and a packing guide. You can also get an estimate on how much it will cost to use Bekins. They help clients locate locally, nationally, or internationally. Bekins is a full service company. They will pack, load, deliver, unload, and unpack. Want to move yourself? Bekins sells boxes, paper, tape, and pads so you can move on your own. Summer months are the busiest move times so contact your local Bekins agent 30 to 45 days in advance of your move date.

APARTMENT LIVING AND OTHER RENTALS

APARTMENT GUIDE GREATER OKLAHOMA CITY
5400 N. Grand Blvd.
(405) 947-2626
Once a month, this free magazine hits the stands. It advertises apartments available in the Oklahoma City metro area. The magazine can be found at all 7-Eleven convenience stores and other businesses across the city or you can call to have an issue sent to you.

HOUSES FOR RENT OF OKC
2545 SW 59th
(405) 605-5477
www.buyahouseinoklahoma.com
This company is not associated with any real estate agency. The individual owner owns all the houses shown in his listings. If you are looking for property to buy, rent, or rent to own, this company has homes for you to see and consider. While most homes are located in Oklahoma City, there are a few in Edmond, Del City, and surrounding areas.

i Looking for an apartment? Look no further than the Apartment Finder (http://oklahomacity.apartmentfinder .com). On the Web site you can search by size, price range, and location. If you tire of looking online, you can order a hard-copy for your area. You can also find this publication at certain restaurants and other places of business.

Downtown Living
BLOCK 42
824 N. Broadway
(405) 228-1000
www.block42.com
This high-end, modern urban complex is located near museums, restaurants, and shopping. If you work or plan on working downtown, Block 42 will allow you the convenience of walking to work. However, if you want or need to drive, access to I-235 and I-35 is just minutes away.

Home seekers will find 42 unique units located here—one bedrooms, two bedrooms, flats, and town houses. There is a green space located at the heart of the community with cascading fountains and a centerpiece water element, and there is a rooftop deck.

The homes here are LEED certified, meaning they are green homes, good for residents and good for the environment. They offer low maintenance and features include Jenn-Air stainless steel ovens, cook-tops, dishwashers, stone counters, hardwood floors, and private garages.

Square footage and prices vary so check the Web site or call to learn more. Floor plans are available on the Web site.

DEEP DEUCE
314 NE 2nd
(405) 228-0922
www.deepdeucebricktown.com
Located just northeast of downtown off Second Street, these apartments are near restaurants, clubs, parks, schools, and the Harkins movie theatre. Community amenities include a fitness center, swimming pool, limited access gates, and attached garages. Apartment features are ceiling fans, double stainless-steel sinks, and garden bathtubs. Select apartment homes have wood-burning fireplaces, stackable washer/dryers, and kitchen pantries.

Square footage ranges from 500 square feet to over 1,200 square feet. Rent starts at $650 and goes up to $1,200. Check with the leasing office about availability before you get your hopes up.

GARAGE LOFT APARTMENTS
113 NW 13th
(405) 605-0825
www.garageloftokc.com
In the 1930s, the Garage Loft Apartments building was a 60,000-square-foot Buick showroom. The Norton-Johnson Buick Company had their business located here along Dealership Row. After decades of neglect, Nick Preftakes and Mark Ruffin decided to renovate the building in 1995 and turn it into loft-type apartments.

Today, there are 24 units located in this three-story building, ranging from 800 to 2,600 square feet. Each unit features a security system, full-size kitchen, washer and dryer, and lots of windows. The building's historic charm is retained by the galvanized metal lining the interior walls and the exposed original interior brick. The developers also retained the car ramps so residents can drive in and park right in front of the unit.

THE LOFTS AT MAYWOOD PARK
Triangle Development
415 N. Broadway, Ste. 100
(405) 605-1000
www.theloftsatmaywoodpark.com
The Lofts offer modern one- to two-bedroom flats. The complex is within walking distance of Bricktown and the central Oklahoma City business district. A few of the features include reserved underground parking, individual storage facilities, a rooftop patio, and a top-floor lounge.

Square footage ranges from 578 square feet to over 1,300 square feet, costing an average of $230 per square foot. You can view floor plans on the Web site.

WIRED LOFT APARTMENTS
Hefner & Broadway Extension
(405) 990-8400
www.wiredlofts.com
Eight miles north of downtown, Wired Loft Apartments sit on the east side of the Broadway Extension. These are modern apartments, decorated with metallic and wood finishes throughout. Each unit has two living areas, two bedrooms, two baths, and a little over 1,100 square feet. Considered high tech, they also have a cable outlet in each room, high-speed Internet service, and an intrusion alarm. Features include a vegetable sink, a full-size washer and dryer, a large refrigerator with ice maker, a foyer with storage, and a two-car attached garage. Some units have wood-burning fireplaces. Concierge service is available for errands and pet service. Monthly rent runs just under $1,200.

RELOCATION

LIBRARIES

Need to do research? Interested in reading for fun? Head down to your local library. Below you will find the main branch address and its Web site. On the Web site, you can find information on all the other branches around Oklahoma City. It also provides a map of how to get to each branch. They all have free wireless Internet available and hold different types of classes for children and adults.

To get a library card, take two current forms of identification and proof of residency in Oklahoma County to any library location.

If you do not live in Oklahoma County, but still would like to borrow library materials, you may use the Annual Fee and Cash Deposit Service for $40 per year. Please see the library's Web site for more information about this service.

METROPOLITAN LIBRARY SYSTEM
Downtown location
300 Park Ave.
(405) 231-8650
www.mls.lib.ok.us

BELLE ISLE LIBRARY
5501 N. Villa
(405) 843-9601

BETHANY LIBRARY
3510 N. Mueller
(405) 789-8363

CAPITOL HILL LIBRARY
334 SW 26th
(405) 634-6308

DEL CITY
4509 SE 15th
(405) 672-1377

EDMOND LIBRARY
10 South Blvd.
(405) 341-9282

MIDWEST CITY
8143 E. Reno
(405) 732-4828

RALPH ELLISON LIBRARY
1918 NE 23rd
(405) 424-1437

SOUTHERN OAKS LIBRARY
6900 S. Walker
(405) 631-4468

THE VILLAGE
10307 N. Pennsylvania Ave.
(405) 755-0710

WARR ACRES
5901 NW 63rd
(405) 721-2616

HEALTH CARE AND WELLNESS

Besides its more than 15 medical and surgical hospitals, Oklahoma City has specialized hospitals and federal medical installations. In the past, Oklahoma and Oklahoma City concentrated on treatment of illnesses, but lately the focus has turned to education and prevention. Today, alternative medicine is a grassroots movement and health-food stores and holistic, chiropractic, and eastern arts clinics are becoming known throughout the community.

A 2007 health report for Oklahoma County shows heart disease and cancer are still the leading causes of death. Oklahoma is ranked as the 8th most obese state in the Union, as the 5th most inactive state, and as the 50th in the consumption of fruits and vegetables. Oklahoma's smoking rate has dropped to a historic low of 25 percent. Public officials feel this drop is due not only to recent smoking legislation but also to the education of the public by health professionals.

In an effort to bring down the obese rate, many programs have been created to get the public fit and healthy. None has been more popular than Oklahoma City mayor Mick Cornett's OKC Million Program (www.thiscityisgoingonadiet.com). On Dec 31, 2007, he announced a million-pound loss as a collective goal for the residents of Oklahoma City. His goal is to inspire citizens to become healthier and lose weight. People can join the program for free on the program's Web site and then log on to learn about nutrition, exercise, and how to set realistic weight loss goals; track their weight loss; and contribute to the total weight-loss goal. Since the program's inception, 29,298 people have registered. There is an average of 13.02 pounds lost per person and total pounds lost as of June 2009 was 368,501.

This chapter lists health departments, hospitals, resources for health care, health-food stores, and some of the alternative health-care options available. It is by no means a complete list and just because an establishment is listed, does not mean it is recommended. Please consider this chapter a place to start.

i Oklahoma City and its surrounding suburbs have instituted the 911 Emergency Services System. If you have an emergency, dial 911 to receive emergency assistance.

HEALTH DEPARTMENTS

OKLAHOMA CITY-COUNTY HEALTH DEPARTMENT
921 NE 23rd St.
(405) 427-8651
www.cchdoc.com
This public health agency was formed in 1954. It has many divisions that aid and assist the community to promote health, protect citizens, and prevent illnesses. It conducts inspections and licenses eating establishments, child-care centers and group homes, pools and spas, food warehouses, and manufacturing plants. It also inspects barbershops, hotels and motels, and trash and septic haulers. It investigates complaints regarding single and multidwelling housing, food, kennels, illegal dumping and discharges, and any situation that threatens public health. The agency also operates an adult health clinic and immunization clinics, and issues vouchers for the Women, Infants and Children (WIC) Program. Its laboratory conducts water testing. Representatives from this agency also go into the community and offer presentations on smoking, tobacco, keeping chil-

dren healthy, and other health-related topics.

To find all the services, visit the Web site or call for more information.

OKLAHOMA STATE DEPARTMENT OF HEALTH

1100 NE 10th St.

(405) 271-5600

www.health.state.ok.us

Formed in 1907, the Oklahoma State Department of Health is Oklahoma's health watch dog agency. Its purpose is to safeguard and further advance the health of Oklahoma citizens. By preventing disease and injuries, they make sure Oklahomans are as healthy as they can be. The organization is overseen by the State Board of Health and has nine members. The Governor appoints these members and then the Senate confirms them. The Board of Health appoints the commissioner of health.

The central office in Oklahoma City provides technical and administrative guidance, as well as fiscal support, to 68 organized county health departments. At its administrative offices in Oklahoma City, the Oklahoma State Department of Health monitors nearly 70 diseases, conditions, and injuries that are reported to the agency. It performs thousands of laboratory examinations annually to confirm infectious, chronic, or genetic diseases. It also licenses several trades and professions such as nurses, construction workers, and food handlers, and it licenses and certifies long-term care facilities like nursing homes for participation in Medicare and Medicaid. More than 300,000 birth and death records are issued by the department each year.

To learn about all the services and programs that the Oklahoma State Department of Health provides, visit the Web site.

WIC PROGRAM

2401 NW 23rd St.

(405) 271-4676

www.ok.gov/health (click on "Child and Family Health")

The Women, Infants and Children Supplemental Nutrition Program (WIC Program) provides nutritional education and supplemental foods to Oklahoma infants, children under age five, and women who are pregnant, breastfeeding, and or have recently given birth. The program is a federally funded program by the USDA. There are seven Oklahoma City sites that assist mothers and children. They are listed below.

921 NE 23rd St., (405) 425-4384

210 SW 25th St., (405) 230-1942

3450 SW 29th St., (405) 419-4053

6912 E. Reno, (405) 419-4116

4330 NW 10th St., (405) 419-4182

720 N. Dewey, (405) 425-4384

1911 N. Classen, (405) 425-4345

HOSPITALS

The Big Six

DEACONESS HOSPITAL

5501 N. Portland

(405) 604-6100

www.deaconessokc.com

Located on the west side of Portland, Deaconess Hospital has been serving residents of northwest Oklahoma City since 1900. It is a full-service, acute-care facility and has 313 licensed beds and 200 active physicians in its network. There are 13 physician clinics, including seven family practice clinics, one internal medicine clinic, and two otolaryngology clinics. Cardiology, hematology, neurology, pain management, and sleep studies are just 5 of the 36 specialties this hospital offers. Services include nutrition counseling, a cancer center, a critical care unit, labor and delivery, and pediatrics with a nine-bed, level-two Neonatal Intensive Care Unit. Prenatal classes are available monthly. Breastfeeding, Sibling, and Baby Boot Camp are just a few of the classes offered.

In Oct 2008, Deaconess Hospital completed an $80-million expansion and renovation project.

MERCY HEALTH CENTER

4300 W. Memorial Rd.

(405) 755-1515

www.mercyok.net/mhc

Mercy Health Center is located northwest of

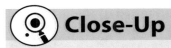 **Close-Up**

INTEGRIS Baptist Medical Center

Located on the northwest side of Oklahoma City, INTEGRIS Baptist Medical Center (3300 NW Expressway, 405-949-3011, www.integris-health.com) sits on the southwest corner of the Hefner Parkway and the Northwest Expressway. You can reach the main entrance of the Medical Center by turning off NW 50th onto Independence Avenue and going north or turning south at the stop light at Independence and the Northwest Expressway. As you travel east on the Northwest Expressway, you can also turn in to the entrance on the north side of the hospital complex. This entrance will take you to the Emergency Room entrance, which is on the northwest side of the hospital. There are four doctors' office buildings around the office complex. Plenty of parking is available here-five parking garages, a small parking area on the northwest corner and a large parking area on the east side of Independence Avenue. Valet parking is available at some entrances.

This hospital is owned by INTEGRIS Health, Oklahoma's largest state-owned health care company. This corporation was formed when Oklahoma Health System and the Oklahoma City Southwest Medical Center merged in 1995. As a result, this company runs 13 hospitals across the state in areas like Blackwell, Clinton, Enid, Grove, Madill, Miami, Pryor, Seminole, Spencer, and Southwest Oklahoma City. Its corporate headquarters is located at the Oklahoma City INTEGRIS Baptist Health Center campus.

INTERGRIS opened in 1959 with 200 beds. Today, it is licensed for more than 500. Services offered range from heart disease treatment through the Heart Hospital to hearing restoration at the Hough Ear Institute. Need help sleeping? Visit the Sleep Disorder Center. Other INTEGRIS centers available to patients at INTEGRIS Baptist and its sister hospital, INTEGRIS Southwest Medical Center, 4401 South Western, are the Henry G. Bennett Jr. Fertility Institute, Jim Thorpe Rehabilitation Network, MDA/ALS Neuromuscular Center, Mental Health Services, Nazih Zuhdi Transplant Institute, Oncology Services, Paul Silberstein Burn Center, Stroke Center of Oklahoma, and INTEGRIS Women's and Children's Services.

downtown Oklahoma City. It sits on the south side of the Kilpatrick Turnpike, off Memorial Road and east of Meridian Avenue. There are doctor's offices located to the east and northeast of the hospital itself. While the largest parking lot is on the north side of the building, there is a parking lot on the east and on the south side where the Emergency Room entrance is located.

Mercy was started by the Sisters of Mercy, who has their roots in Ireland, in 1947 when they began their health care ministry in Oklahoma. They had originally arrived in Indian Territory in 1884 and concentrated on education. In 1974, the Sisters moved the health care facility to its present location and began expanding.

Today, Mercy has more than 2400 employees, 900 physicians, and 70 areas of expertise in areas like stroke treatment, women's health at the Mercy Women's Center, cardiovascular care through the Oklahoma Heart Hospital, neurological care in Mercy's NeuroScience Institute, and neonatal care in Mercy's Level III Neonatal Intensive Care Unit.

OKLAHOMA CITY VA MEDICAL CENTER
921 Northeast 13
(405) 270-0501
www.oklahoma.va.gov

The Oklahoma City VA Medical Center opened its doors on Sept 14, 1953, as a 488-bed hospital. Since that time, the hospital has grown to nearly 1 million square feet with 168 private and semiprivate rooms. It receives referrals from around the state and serves 48 Oklahoma counties and two north central Texas counties with a veteran population of over 225,000. The VA is located on the University of Oklahoma Health Sciences Center campus.

The VA recently developed an animal therapy program to assist stroke patients as well as other patients. It also successfully completed its first cochlear implant, a surgically implanted electronic device that provides a sense of sound to a person who is profoundly deaf.

In 2008, the Oklahoma City VA Medical Center treated 6,516 inpatients and 441,322 outpatients. Overall, they treated 49,694 unique patients, which means if a patient came for several visits, he or she was only counted once.

The VA is a teaching hospital, providing a full range of patient-care services, with state-of-the-art technology as well as education and research. It offers many educational classes for patients in all treatment areas and it occasionally offers seminars and workshops that are promoted within the hospital and through the Web site.

OU MEDICAL CENTER
700 Northeast 13th St.
(405) 271-4700
www.oumedical.com
The OU Medical Center has 697 licensed beds and in 2008, it treated over 26,000 inpatients and over 199,000 outpatients. This hospital has the state's only level-one trauma center and the state's only freestanding children's hospital. It also offers comprehensive cancer care, three Medi Flight air ambulances, a fully integrated women's center inside the Children's Hospital, pediatric urology, and pediatric and adult bone marrow transplant units.

OU Medical Center was one of the five initial medical facilities in the world to purchase the da Vinci-Si surgical-assisted robot.

Classes, workshops, and screenings are offered here on a regular basis. Some regular events include prenatal classes, car-seat safety inspections, cancer screenings, and urology patient seminars.

ST. ANTHONY HOSPITAL
1000 N. Lee Ave.
(405) 231-8866
www.saintsok.com
St. Anthony Hospital was founded by a small order of Franciscan sisters who originally journeyed from Maryville, Missouri, to Oklahoma City in the spring of 1898 to ask for contributions for their local hospital. When they approached Father D. I. Lanslots of St. Joseph's Church for funds, he agreed to help raise funds, but he asked that the funds be used to open a hospital in Oklahoma City instead. At that time there was no hospital in Oklahoma City or Oklahoma Territory and one was badly needed. Sister Beata Vinson and Sister Clara Schaff returned to Maryville to ask their order to establish a hospital in Oklahoma City. In July 1898, four Sisters of St. Francis returned to Oklahoma City and rented two houses at 219 NW 4th St. One structure served as the Sisters' residence and the other was used for the hospital. On Aug 1, 1898, St. Anthony's opened with Mother Augustine's mandate that no one be turned away.

Today, the hospital has 686 beds and in 2008 cared for over 17,000 inpatients. It provides general, acute care services, including cardiology, oncology, neuroscience, behavioral medicine, surgery, kidney transplantation, and a variety of other disciplines. Besides the Hospital, people looking for health care will find Saints Heart & Vascular Institute, St. Anthony Behavioral Medicine Program, Frank C. Love Cancer Institute, Cyberknife, a painless non-invasive radiosurgery that treats non-operable tumors, Surgical Services, St. Anthony Breast Center, and the St. Anthony SCORE program, a comprehensive wellness exam, formerly called the executive physical.

St. Anthony's also offers childbirth classes; an Annual Celebrity Chef event, focusing on heart healthy cooking; the Annual Stroke of Courage, a stroke educational event; and a variety of other timely topics for both professionals and the public.

Specialty Hospitals

BONE AND JOINT HOSPITAL

1111 N. Dewey
(405) 272-9671
www.boneandjoint.com

The Bone and Joint Hospital opened in 1926 and has 85 beds. It has been one of the top orthopedic hospitals in the United States for years. Hand, hip, knee, shoulder, and spine procedures are conducted here. Services include same-day surgery, patient education, and research.

In 2003, *Money* magazine named the Bone and Joint Hospital one of the top orthopedic hospitals in the region, and AARP ranked it as one of the top 10 orthopedic hospitals in the nation.

LAKESIDE WOMEN'S HOSPITAL

11200 North Portland
(405) 936-1500
www.lakeside-wh.com

Lakeside Women's Hospital of Oklahoma City was established in 1997 by a group of female OB/GYN physicians who wanted to offer women a more comprehensive and personal kind of health care. Currently the hospital has 23 beds. It provides health-care services for women of all ages, including gynecology, obstetrics, robotic, general and plastic surgery, endoscopy, cardiac and cancer evaluations, ultrasound, digital mammography, bone density testing, and sleep disorder treatment.

The physicians here are board certified and the hospital is accredited by the Joint Commission for Accreditation of Hospital Organizations.

McBRIDE CLINIC ORTHOPEDIC HOSPITAL

9600 Broadway Extension
(405) 486-2100
www.mcboh.com

For more than 85 years, the McBride Clinic has provided orthopedics and arthritis care to Oklahomans. In Aug 2005 the McBride Clinic opened the McBride Clinic Orthopedic Hospital, a state-of-the-art orthopedic facility providing a full range of orthopedic surgical services, physical and occupa-

tional therapy, and a level IV emergency room that is open 24 hours, 365 days a year.

Licensed as an acute-care hospital, the McBride Clinic Orthopedic Hospital has 64 acute care beds, 14 rehabilitation beds, and 29 physicians, specializing in orthopedics, rheumatology, physical medicine and rehabilitation, primary care, sports medicine, occupational health, and podiatry. It also has a Radiology Department, a laboratory, a pharmacy, and a dietary department with a cafeteria.

Since its first year of eligibility in 2008, McBride Clinic Orthopedic Hospital has received the Specialty Excellence Award for Overall Orthopedics twice from HealthGrades, a leading independent health-care company. McBride also has ranked number one in Oklahoma two years in a row for overall orthopedic services. In 2009, McBride Clinic Orthopedic Hospital received five-star ratings in overall orthopedic services, joint replacement, total knee replacement, total hip replacement, hip fracture repair, spine surgery, and back and neck surgery.

OKLAHOMA CHILDREN'S HOSPITAL

1200 N. Everett Dr.
(405) 271-4700
www.oumedical.com

The Oklahoma Children's Hospital is the only freestanding children's hospital in the state of Oklahoma. It is a full-service hospital with two Pediatric Intensive Care Units, an 88-bed Neonatal Intensive Care Unit, and Oklahoma's only pediatric Bone Marrow Transplant Unit. In addition, hospital has pediatric specific operating rooms, pediatric dialysis, and areas sponsored by the Troy Aikman Foundation, Ali's House (a charity spearheaded by country singer Toby Keith), and the Ronald McDonald House.

Other Hospitals and Medical Care Units

COMMUNITY HOSPITAL

3100 SW 89th St.
(405) 601-8100

DEAN McGEE EYE INSTITUTE
1000 N. Lincoln Blvd.
(405) 232-8696
www.dmei.org

EDMOND MEDICAL CENTER
1 S. Bryant
(405) 341-6100
www.edmondhospital.com

MIDWEST REGIONAL MEDICAL CENTER
2825 Parklawn Dr., Midwest City
(405) 610-4411
www.midwestregional.com

MOORE MEDICAL CENTER
700 S. Telephone Rd., Moore
(405) 793-9355

NORMAN REGIONAL HEALTH SYSTEM
901 N. Porter, Norman
(405) 307-1000
www.normanregional.com

OKLAHOMA HEART HOSPITAL
4050 W. Memorial Rd.
(405) 608-3200
www.okheart.com

OKLAHOMA PHYSICIANS HOSPITAL
3100 SW 89th
(405) 378-3755 or 602-8202

OKLAHOMA SPINE HOSPITAL
14101 Parkway Commons Dr.
(405) 749-2700
www.oklahomaspine.com

SURGERY CENTER OF OKLAHOMA
9500 Broadway Extension
(405) 475-0600

WALK-IN CLINICS

BEST CARE MEDICAL CENTER
1265 E. 33rd St.
(405) 216-5565
www.bestcaremedicalcenter.com
Located on 33rd St. just west of Bryant, this urgent care was formed in 2007 by Medhat Michael, a certified family physician. For many years, Dr. Michael worked as an emergency room physician and he wanted to offer the community an alternative to an emergency room.

The Best Care Medical Center specializes in urgent care and emergency health care for injuries and illnesses. It treats colds and flu, cuts and stitches, insect bites, and upper respiratory and urinary tract infections. The center also conducts sports physicals, drug screening, and blood-type testing.

The Best Care Medical Urgent Center is open seven days a week. Hours are Mon through Fri from 8 a.m. to 8 p.m. and Sat and Sun from noon to 5 p.m. No appointment needed. The center accepts all major health insurance, including Medicaid and Medicare.

CONCENTRA URGENT CARE
200 Quadrum Dr., (405) 942-8767
36 W. Memorial Rd., Ste. C3, (405) 755-3110
6101 W. Reno, Ste. 800, (405) 495-3085
7100 S. I-35 Service Rd., Ste. 7, (405) 632-1002
This urgent care has four locations. Each can treat minor illnesses, like colds and flu, and injuries, like sprains and fractures. Each office is open Mon through Fri from 8 a.m. to 5 p.m. No appointment is needed.

FIRST MED
4510 NW 39th Expressway, (405) 495-5841
13420 N. Pennsylvania, (405) 478-0633
7807 S. Walker, (405) 636-0767
805 W. Covell, Ste. 200, Edmond, (405) 844-1633

First Med treats nonlife threatening injuries and illnesses. It also conducts wellness exams and gives immunizations. An on-site laboratory and X-ray services are available here. First Med is open seven days a week from 8 a.m. to 7:30 p.m. On Easter, July 4th, Thanksgiving, Christmas Eve, and Christmas Day, it has reduced hours.

HEALTH INFORMATION & REFERRAL SERVICES

BLUE CROSS AND BLUE SHIELD OF OKLAHOMA
3401 NW 63rd
(405) 841-9525
www.bcbsok.com

Blue Cross and Blue Shield of Oklahoma is the state's oldest and largest private-health insurer. Founded in 1943, it continues to serve families and businesses across the state. The company has a network of over 8,000 health providers and insures over 835,000 Oklahomans. The insurance company offers individual and group plans, dental plans, pharmacy programs, and Medicare supplement insurance.

Members can check the status of their benefits and coverage on the Web site. Information about insurance legislation and a list of health-care providers are also available on the Web site.

CENTRAL OKLAHOMA INTEGRATED NETWORK SYSTEM (COINS)
3816 N. Santa Fe Ave.
(405) 557-1100
www.coinsaccess.org

Formed in 1997, the Central Oklahoma Integrated Network System (COINS) is a 501c health-care network that serves underinsured and uninsured people in central Oklahoma. Applicants must meet certain guidelines to participate in the program. Representatives are available to help member find primary-care providers and hospital providers. This organization is overseen by a community board of directors and its mission is to improve access to health care for those with low incomes and those who are uninsured. COINS is a United Partner Agency.

To be considered call the number listed above.

ALTERNATIVE MEDICINE

CHIROPRACTIC ASSOCIATION OF OKLAHOMA
(405) 682-3527

This association is an information and referral service for individuals interested in chiropractic care. It promotes prevention and wellness and educates chiropractors across the state through seminars. Each year over 500 attend the educational programs offered by this organization.

EASTERN HEALING ARTS
1117 NW 50th
(405) 401-6380
www.easthealingarts.com

This clinic's focus is on traditional Chinese medicine. It offers acupuncture, Chinese herbal medicine, auriculo therapy, moxabustion, cupping, and gua-sha. Health and wellness programs include antiaging, emotional wellness, men's and women's health, and pain management.

Gardner Singleton, a graduate of the American College of Traditional Chinese Medicine and board certified in acupuncture and Chinese herbal medicine by the National Certification Commission for Acupuncture and Oriental Medicine (NCCAOM), has been seeing clients since 1993. He prescribes programs for individuals based on their health needs. These programs may include massage, meditation, herbs, or lifestyle changes. Eastern Healing Arts also offers classes, workshops, and retreats. Check the Web site for what is being offered now.

In addition to the Oklahoma City office, Singleton maintains an office in Norman at 905 North Flood Ave. He is in Oklahoma City two days a week and then is in Norman several days a week. To arrange an appointment, call the number above.

OKLAHOMA HEALING ARTS INSTITUTE
1715 NW 16th St.
(405) 524-4000
www.okhealingarts.com

This wellness center takes a holistic approach to health care. It offers acupuncture, aromatherapy, reflexology, massage therapy, and Chinese herbs. Each client gets a complete evaluation before any therapy is recommended.

The ACU College (www.acucollege.org) is the Institute's acupuncture college and is located on its grounds. It is licensed by Oklahoma's Board of Private Vocational Schools. It trains students to reach a level of proficiency in the basic Chinese healing arts of acupuncture and Chinese herbal medicine.

The institute specializes in deep-tissue and hot-stone massage, shiatsu massage, and Swedish, and connective tissue release. Massage appointments are available Mon through Sat.

FULL CIRCLE HEALTH CLINIC
3601 S. Broadway Extension
(405) 753-9355
www.starrwalker.com/clinic.htm

Practitioners at the Full Circle Health Clinic believe that people are made in the image of God and when toxins are removed and proper nutrients are consumed, the body heals itself.

Mary Shrick, a board certified naturopath with a Ph.D. in nutritional science, sees patients at the clinic. After facing several health problems herself, she began looking for information and products to resolve those problems. She realized that the quality of products was an important issue in the recovery process and began manufacturing her own. She soon wanted to help others take control of their own health and in 1998 she started her own radio program. Today, thousands of listeners tune in to her show daily on KTLR 890 AM.

Besides consultations, the Full Circle Health Clinic offers various therapeutic programs, including ion foot cleanses, IV therapy, acupuncture, massage, and colon-hydro-therapy. Prices vary depending on the service. Packages are available. A full line of natural supplements is also available.

Educational health seminars are held throughout the year. Call to find out about upcoming events or check the Web site.

i If you are looking for a chiropractor, there are over 20 listed in the Oklahoma City phone book. The online Chiropractic Directory (www.chirodirectory.com/dir/ok/oklahomacity) offers many more. It also lists each doctor's education and specialties.

HEALTH FOOD AND NUTRITIONAL SUPPLEMENT STORES

AKIN'S NATURAL FOODS MARKET
Mayfair Shopping Center
63rd and North May Avenue
(405) 843-3033
www.akins.com

There are two Akin's markets in Oklahoma City. The Mayfair Shopping Center location is the original store. The other store is located in the Quail Springs Marketplace at 2370 W. Memorial Rd., on the south side of the Kilpatrick Turnpike across from Quail Springs Mall.

Shoppers will find a large variety of organic fruits and vegetables here. All produce is certified as organically grown and Akin's guarantees it. There are vitamins and minerals, homeopathic products, body care, essential oils, sports supplements, pet care, and more. Food items include, cheeses, meats, chips, crackers, dried beans, and frozen dinners. Along the south and east walls, consumers will find cold boxes loaded with dried fruits, milk, organic eggs, frozen pizzas, and burritos.

Big Sky Bread, a local bakery, sells its bread products here. Big Sky breads contain no preservatives. Also available is Big Sky's granola. It is simply the best found anywhere.

Hours for both Akin's locations are Mon through Sat from 8 a.m. to 9 p.m. and Sun from 9 a.m. to 9 p.m.

DOORWAY TO HEALTH
6401 NW Expressway
(405) 621-2273
www.starrwalker.com/doorwaytohealth.htm

This store, sitting on the north side of the Northwest Expressway in the Courtyard Plaza Shopping Center, opened in 2001. It offers oxygen treatments, holistic balanced supplements, and more. Events, like the Test, Don't Guess Health Fair, are held here every two or three months. Participants can have their blood tested to get a view of what their body looks like on the inside. Classes like Liquid for Life are held here too. Class times vary so call or check the Web site.

The store is open six days a week, Mon through Fri from 10 a.m. to 6 p.m. and Sat from 9 a.m. to 4 p.m.

EDMOND HEALTH FOODS
1530 South Blvd.
(405) 341-6443
South of 15th Street, just off Boulevard to the east, you will find Edmond Health Foods. This small 1,000-square-foot establishment has been in this location since 1976. It is a second-generation family-owned business. The current owner's father opened the store after visiting a chiropractor and learning about nutrition and nutritional supplements. Inside you will find supplements in half of the store and food items in the other half. Nature's Plus, Twin Labs, and Garden of Life are a few of the brand-name supplements in stock. In the food section, the store has chips and quite a selection of wheat and gluten-free products, like bread, donuts, muffins, ice creams, and a few organic meats. There is also a small bookrack.

HEALTH FOOD CENTER
7301 S. Pennsylvania Ave.
(405) 681-6060
http://shop.thehealthfoodcenter.net
This 20,000-square-foot, natural-food store has frozen and refrigerated products, fresh organic produce, pet products, nutrition bars, beverages, snacks, vegetarian items, and more. The meats here are organic, free range, antibiotic, and hormone free. The store carries health and beauty products, including soaps, fresheners, shampoos, cleaning supplies, laundry supplies, and pet products.

If you get hungry while shopping, stop by the Coconut Hut Juice Bar. Located in the store,

the juice bar serves fruit smoothies, hot panini sandwiches, espresso, iced coffees, and more.

Events are held regularly here. Check the Web site or call for the schedule.

MERIDIAN AVENUE NUTRITION
1321 N. Meridian
(405) 943-6000
The current owner has operated this nutritional supplement center since 2005. She carries herbs, vitamin products, and nutritional supplements from such manufacturers as NOW, Shaklee, Blue Bonnet, Nature's Way, Nature's Plus, Seagate, Water Oz, and Nordic Natural.

Special events are held here regularly. Biofeedback treatments can be scheduled for Mon or Tues. Call to see what's going on or to ask about your favorite supplement.

NUTRITIONAL FOOD CENTER
1024 N. Classen Blvd.
(405) 232-8404
www.nutritionalfoodcenter.com
Located on the southeast corner of 10th and Classen, this store has been in business since 1954. It claims to have the largest selection of natural foods in Oklahoma. The store carries herbs, nutritional supplements, books, organic fruits and vegetables, goats' milk, grains, flour, body care products, and homeopathic remedies. It also has gluten-free products and protein powders.

No classes or workshops are offered here because space is limited. There is lots of parking to the south of the building. Hours are Mon through Sat from 8 a.m. to 6 p.m.

OKC ORGANICS
12401 N. May Ave.
(405) 842-3412
This store offers organic fruits and vegetables, free-range meats, vitamins, and nutritional supplements. It encourages customers to eat 70 percent raw fruits and vegetables and encourages stir-fries and salads. Workshops and seminars are offered occasionally. Seminars are typically on detoxifying the body. Nutritional counseling is also offered.

Emergency and Information Numbers

Emergencies: fire, police, ambulance	911
Nonemergency health, social, and community services	211
Al-Anon	(405) 767-9071
Alcohol Anonymous (Oklahoma County)	(405) 947-3834
American Cancer Society	(405) 841-5800
American Diabetes Association	(405) 840-3881
American Heart Association	(405) 948-2142
American Lung Association	(405) 748-4674
American Red Cross	(405) 228-9500
Arthritis Foundation (Oklahoma chapter)	(405) 521-0066
Crisis Referral Center	(405) 525-2525
Cystic Fibrosis Foundation	(405) 787-0056
Emergency Management Agency	(405) 521-2481
Leukemia and Lymphoma Society	(405) 943-8888
Lupus Association of Oklahoma	(405) 427-8787
Muscular Dystrophy Association	(405) 722-8001
Narcotics Anonymous	(405) 524-7068
OG&E Electric emergencies	(800) 522-6870 or (405) 272-9595
Oklahoma Department of Health	(405) 271-6225
ONG Gas emergencies	(800) 458-4251
Overeaters Anonymous	(405) 942-0577
Parkinson Foundation of the Heartland	(405) 810-0695
Poison Control Center	(405) 271-5454
Oklahoma Blood Institute	(405) 297-5700
Social Security Administration	(800) 772-1213
Women, Infants and Children Supplemental Nutrition (WIC) Program	(405) 237-1203 or (405) 271-4676

EDUCATION

Since before the turn of the 20th century, Oklahoma City residents have been determined to make the city an educational center. Today it has more than a half-dozen institutions of higher learning, including a major university located 30 minutes south of the city limits.

About a month after the Land Run of 1889, Mrs. L. H. North started a subscription school in a tent in the new downtown area. This was the city's first primary school. Seats consisted of boards on nail kegs. No desks were available. The number of students reportedly ranged from 20 to 70. Class fees started at $1.50 a month and went up.

The first public school opened on Mar 1, 1890, after the Oklahoma Territory Congress set aside $50,000 for schools. The first school graduated six students. In 1890, the first legislature also gave the small city of Stillwater a college named A & M College, which later became Oklahoma State University. Edmond received a state teacher's school and the territorial university went to Norman.

Today, whether you are looking for early education for your children or want to learn how to become a farrier, Oklahoma City and its surrounding suburbs has a school for you. There are Vocational and technical schools and four-year colleges within easy driving distance from all areas of the city.

This chapter gives an overview of the Oklahoma City public school system. The suburbs have their own systems. This chapter also briefly discusses private schools and homeschooling. Included, too, is information on the larger colleges and a list of smaller ones.

This chapter is not all-inclusive, but it is a place to start. You will find basic information that will help you narrow your search. Most colleges have Web sites that can be investigated. Those that don't have Web sites will gladly mail information.

OKLAHOMA CITY PUBLIC SCHOOL SYSTEM

OKLAHOMA CITY PUBLIC SCHOOLS
900 N. Klein
(405) 587-0000
www.okcps.org

Oklahoma City's school district educates over 40,000 students a year. It is responsible for 57 elementary schools, 7 middle schools, 10 high schools, 5 alternative schools, and 12 charter schools. The average class size is around 20 and the district employs 4,500 people.

Three of the largest schools in the district are Putnam City North High School, Moore High School, and Westmoore High School. Putnam City North (www.putnamcityschools.org) is

located on the northwest side of Oklahoma City off north Rockwell. It has over 2,300 students in grades 9 through 12. Moore High School (www.mooreschools.com) sits on the south side of the city on North Eastern. Its grade levels are 10 through 12 and the school has over 2,000 students. Westmoore High School (www.moore schools.com) is also located on the south side of Oklahoma City, but is located on South Western. It educates nearly 2,000 students a year in grades 10 through 12.

Always looking for ways to improve education, the way children learn, and the places they learn in, Oklahoma City presented an ambitious project to the public. On Nov 13, 2001, voters approved MAPS (Metropolitan Area Projects) for Kids. This was a temporary one-cent sales tax that would be collected for seven years. It would bring in about $500 million. Seventy percent of the money would go to District I-89, the Oklahoma City School District. Thirty percent would go to the suburban districts for improvement to their school systems.

One of the things MAPS money in District I-89 is to be used for is renovation, expansion, or rebuilding of schools. There are more than 100 projects on its construction program. Projects are scheduled to be completed in 2012. The money has also been used to provide fire alarms, new roofs, over 4,300 new computers, telephones, network and library technology, and new school buses. The MAPS for Kids is overseen by the OCMAPS Trust, made up of seven members who are in charge of sales tax funds and management of bond projects. These members are appointed by the Oklahoma City Council and the Oklahoma City School District.

The Oklahoma City School District has a bright future. Its citizens are a driving force in improving the educational engine that helps its children learn and excel.

OKLAHOMA CITY PRIVATE SCHOOLS

Oklahoma City has over 80 private schools. Enrollment in these schools ranges from 20 to over 800 students. There are 34 elementary schools, 30 middle schools, and 18 high schools. Several schools offer elementary through high school grades, but many focus on specific grade levels. Most middle and high schools offer music, sports, physical education, and other activities.

The four largest private schools in the Oklahoma City area are: **Heritage Hall,** 1800 NW 122nd St., (405) 749-3001, www.heritagehall.com, pre-K through 12, over 800 students enrolled.; **Casady,** 9500 N. Pennsylvania, (405) 749-3100, www.casady.org, first grade through 12, over 800 students enrolled; **Oklahoma Christian School,** 4680 E. 2nd St., Edmond, (405) 341-2265, www.ocssaints.org., pre-K through 12, over 800 students enrolled; **Bishop McGuinness High School,** 801 NW 50th St., (405) 842-6638, www.bmchs.org, grades 9 through 12, over 700 students enrolled.

HOMESCHOOLING

For many years, Oklahoma parents have been choosing to homeschool their children. According to the Home Educator's Resource Organization of Oklahoma, Oklahoma is the only state in the United States where homeschooling is provided for in its constitution (Oklahoma Constitution, Article XIII). Parents who choose to homeschool must adhere to 180 days of six hours of teaching and teach their students the basics—math, English, history, science, and other subjects. Parents are able to choose their own curriculum and have numerous choices for study from hands-on to computer-based learning.

Oklahoma City and its surrounding suburbs have many resources for homeschoolers. Most every community has smaller homeschool groups that participate in field trips, sports, theater, music, and more. The two sources below can direct parents to these groups in their area.

HOME EDUCATOR'S RESOURCE ORGANIZATION OF OKLAHOMA (HERO) OF OKLAHOMA CITY AND EDMOND
917 Richmond Road, Edmond
(405) 359-7328
www.oklahomahomeschooling.org

OKLAHOMA CHRISTIAN HOME EDUCATOR'S CONSOCIATION (OCHEC)
3801 NW 63rd St.
(405) 810-0386
www.ochec.com

programs available in nursing, music, art and design, premed, and biblical studies. Students can participate in 13 different sports here, including basketball, baseball, golf, softball, and soccer.

Education Resources

The Foundation for Oklahoma City Public Schools
5225 N. Shartel Ave., #201
(405) 879-2007
www.okckids.com

Home Educator's Resource Organization of Oklahoma (HERO) of Oklahoma City and Edmond
917 Richmond Road
(405) 359-7328
www.oklahomahomeschooling.org

Oklahoma Christian Home Educator's Consociation (OCHEC)
3801 NW 63rd St.
(405) 810-0386
www.ochec.com

Oklahoma City Public Schools
900 N. Klein
(405) 587-0000
www.okcps.org

Oklahoma State Department of Education
2500 N. Lincoln Blvd.
(405) 521-6205
www.sde.state.ok.us

HIGHER EDUCATION

OKLAHOMA CHRISTIAN UNIVERSITY
2501 E. Memorial Rd.
(405) 425-5000
www.oc.edu

This university originally opened in Sept 1950 in Bartlesville, Oklahoma. It moved to Oklahoma City in 1956 and in 1958 classes were finally held at the Oklahoma City campus on Memorial, 11 miles north of downtown on a 240-acre location. This college is affiliated with the Churches of Christ.

Over 2,000 students a year attend this university. It has an undergraduate student to teacher ratio of 15 to 1. Eighty percent of students live on campus. This is a four-year university with

OKLAHOMA CITY UNIVERSITY
2501 N. Blackwelder
(405) 208-5000
www.okcu.edu

Oklahoma City University is a 104-acre campus located in the Midtown District of Oklahoma City. It sits north of Northwest 23rd Street, between the major streets of North Pennsylvania and North Classen. *U.S. News & World Report* listed this college at the top of their regional, master's level university college and is listed as a 2008–2009 college of distinction.

The university was established in 1904 and is a United Methodist university. Over 3,500 students attend a year. The student to faculty ratio is 11 to 1. The university offers 60 undergraduate majors, 12 graduate degrees, and a bachelor of arts or a bachelor of sciencein the Adult Studies Program.

OKLAHOMA STATE UNIVERSITY– OKLAHOMA CITY (OSU–OKC)
900 N. Portland
(405) 947-4421
www.osuokc.edu

Oklahoma State University–Oklahoma City (OSU–OKC) was founded as Oklahoma State University Technical Institute, a branch campus of Oklahoma State University–Stillwater in 1961. The North Central Association accredited the institute separately from OSU Stillwater in 1975. In 1990, the institute changed its name to Oklahoma State University–Oklahoma City.

OSU–OKC offers 5 certificates, 7 associate degrees, 33 associate of applied science degrees, and a four-year bachelor of technology degree. The campus spans more than 80 acres and graduates over 600 students a year. Enrollment is approximately 6,000 students of which 67 percent attend part-time. Average age of the student body is 28 years. Many of OSU–OKC's students work full time in addition to taking college

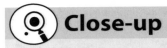

Rose State College

Rose State College (6420 SE 15th St., 405-733-7311, www.rose.edu) is located in Midwest City, a suburb east of Oklahoma City. Students can reach the campus by exiting off I-40 onto South Sooner Road. Go north to Southeast 15th Street and then turn east. Its 21 buildings sit on 116 acres. The college enrolls around 12,000 students per year.

In Sept 1970, the college opened for its first set of classes. After it was approved by the College Board of Trustees, it joined the Oklahoma State System of Higher Education in Dec 1973. Many of the longtime residents remember the college when it was Oscar Rose Junior College. The college was changed to Rose State College in 1983.

Rose State College offers associate degrees in business and information technology, engineering and science, health science, humanities, and social science. Their most popular degrees are in the health sciences in the areas of nursing and dental hygiene and dental assisting. Other health science degrees offered are health information technology, clinical laboratory technology, radiologic technology, and respiratory therapist.

This college has many advantages according to the students who have attended and graduated from here. First, they like the small class size. They feel it makes them able to approach their professors more easily and they feel more comfortable entering college. Second, they like the family like atmosphere here.

Something few people hear about because it's not discussed much is the 1400 seat performing arts theatre at Rose State. There is a campus sponsored performing arts series held here. The theatre is also rented out for performances ranging from dance to comics to music concerts.

classes, and many are transitioning to second careers or are returning to the workforce.

Students choose from six divisions of study: agriculture technologies, business technologies, arts and science, science and engineering, health services, and human services. OSU–OKC's four-year bachelor of technology in emergency responder administration is specially designed for police, fire, and EMT professionals who want to advance in their career fields. In 2008 OSU–OKC was approved to offer the state's first associate degree in wind turbine technology.

OSU–OKC is the only university in the state to offer a bachelor's degree in emergency responder administration; an associate of science in alcohol and substance abuse counseling, and public service; associate of applied science degrees in crime victim/survivor services, electrical power technology, police science, turfgrass

management, technical Spanish/translation and interpretation, and wind turbine technology; and a certificate of mastery in early care education administration.

i Financial aid and scholarships are available at most colleges and universities. Be sure to ask about financial assistance when you are looking at your school of choice.

SOUTHERN NAZARENE UNIVERSITY
6729 NW 39th Expressway
(405) 789-6400
www.snu.edu

Southern Nazarene University (SNU), is located in Bethany, a suburb in northwest Oklahoma City. The campus sits on approximately 80 acres on the north side of Northwest 39th Expressway, also known as historic Route 66. North MacArthur Boulevard borders the east side and North Rockwell is on the west. The campus is and has always been easy to reach. Early in the 20th Century, the Interurban Bethany Depot sat across the street from the campus. The Interurban commuter train ran down what is now Northwest Expressway.

Southern Nazarene University was originally founded in 1899, in Peniel, Texas. This liberal arts college moved to Bethany in 1909. The college celebrated its 100 year Anniversary in this location in 2009. The university is owned and affiliated with the Church of the Nazarene. The college feels its mission is to transform lives by educating in a Christ-centered environment. Holding true to this goal, Southern Nazarene University offers undergraduate and graduate degrees in more than 70 academic majors. Academic areas for undergraduate students are biology/pre-med, business, music, and nursing. Business administration and management, counseling, curriculum and instruction, educational leadership, nursing, and theology are offered at graduate level for masters degrees.

There are 21,000 students who study on the Bethany campus and at Tulsa and Del City facilities. The university is a member of the Council for Christian Colleges and Universities and is the Church of the Nazarene's representative in higher education for the south central United States region.

Many talented student athletes are involved in the university's Crimson Storm athletic program. They compete in the NAIA Division I, the Sooner Athletic Conference, and in equestrian events and many place in national tournaments annually. For more than 35 years, the university has operated the Southern Nazarene University School for Children (kindergarten to fifth grade). This school helps students who are preparing to become teachers. The university is kind enough to offer the community access to its library on campus, the R.T. Williams Library. The college also has a School of Music, which offers concerts and recitals to the community. If you can make it, don't miss the annual musical performed by the Southern Nazarene University students.

SOUTHWESTERN CHRISTIAN UNIVERSITY (BETHANY)
7210 NW 39th Expressway
(405) 789-7661
www.swcu.edu

Located in Bethany on a wooded campus northwest of downtown Oklahoma City, this university was founded in 1946 by the International Pentecostal Holiness Church. It is a four-year university, granting degrees in religion. Always evolving the university includes business courses and continues to offer its pastoral ministry and youth ministry courses. The student to teacher ratio is 14 to 1. The univeristy's ongoing goal is to be a place where men and women can expand and broaden their personal Christian growth.

UNIVERSITY OF CENTRAL OKLAHOMA
100 N. University Dr., Edmond
(405) 974-2000
www.uco.edu

The University of Central Oklahoma (UCO) is located north of 2nd Street between N. Bryant and Boulevard in Edmond. Edmond is a northern suburb of Oklahoma City. The largest parking area is on the east side of the campus. The football stadium and home to the UCO Bronchos football team is located on the north side of the campus. This beautiful campus sits on 210 acres.

This university was established in 1890 when the first territorial legislature met. George Gardenhire, first Senate President, suggested Edmond get the state's teachers' school. Today, it is Oklahoma's third largest school with an enrollment of 16,000. Forty one percent of its students are 21 to 25 years of age, 12 percent are 26 to 30, 15 percent are 31 years old and over. About 92 percent of the students studying here are from Oklahoma, which speaks to this school's popularity in-state.

The college has 112 undergraduate majors and 54 graduate programs. It offers bachelor's degrees in actuarial science, creative writing, dance education, and humanities. Jazz studies and athletic training students can receive a master's. The University of Central Oklahoma is the only college in Oklahoma to offer these.

The college also offers programs in forensic science, mass communications, music theatre, and nursing.

Following the nation's green initiative, the University is working on its own "green" status. Currently, it is utilizing 100 percent wind power, has its own campus wide recycling program, and is turning used cooking oil in to biodiesel fuel in its own manufacturing facility. It has been nationally recognized for its efforts.

UNIVERSITY OF OKLAHOMA (OU) (NORMAN)
1000 Asp
(405) 325-2251
www.ou.edu

The University of Oklahoma (OU) was one of three colleges created in 1890 by the first Territorial Legislature of Oklahoma. It was designated the "territorial university." This college is located in Norman, about a thirty minute drive south from downtown Oklahoma City.

The campus covers 3000 acres and is bordered to the north by Boyd Street, the south by Timberdell Road, the east by Jenkins Avenue, and the west by Chautauqua Avenue. Lindsey Street cuts the campus in half. On the north side of Lindsey, along Jenkins, is the Gaylord Family–Oklahoma Memorial Stadium. This football stadium seats over 82,000 people. The Lloyd Noble Center is located off South Jenkins Avenue. It hosts basketball games, concerts, and other events. It seats over 11,000 people. On the south side of Lindsey Street across from the football stadium, guests will find student dormitories and apartments.

Enrollment at this college is 30,000 students. There are 2,400 full-time faculty, 350 student organizations, and 40 national fraternities and sororities. The college offers baccalaureate, masters, doctorate and major degrees. Anyone interested in research must visit the Bizzell Memorial Library. It sits in the middle of the campus and is the largest research library in Oklahoma. It has 4.7 million book volumes, over 1.5 million maps, 31,000 periodicals, 1.6 million photographs, and more.

Two museums are also located on the University of Oklahoma campus—the Fred Jones Jr. Museum of Art and the Sam Noble Oklahoma Museum of Natural History. For more information on these two museums, look in the "attractions" section of this book.

COMMUNITY COLLEGE

OKLAHOMA CITY COMMUNITY COLLEGE
7777 S. May
(405) 682-1611
www.occc.edu

Oklahoma City Community College started with a desire to have a junior college in the area in 1969. In 1971, ground was broken for the college and in 1972 the building started going up. When construction was complete and the college held its first classes on Sept 25, 1972, it was called South Oklahoma City Junior College. The name was changed to Oklahoma City Community College, also called OCCC, in 1983.

This college sits on 143 acres on the southwest corner of I-240 and South May Avenue. It is the fifth largest college in the state and has approximately 20,000 students enrolled annually.

This is a two-year college with almost 50 associate degree programs available to students in areas like business, education, liberal studies, pre-medicine, psychology, and more. The associates degree two-year programs help students prepare to transfer to four-year colleges and step into baccalaureate programs. There are also a number of certificate and degree programs that will help students step into the work field in a variety of areas. Classroom teacher/student ratio is 20 to 1.

Besides the degree programs, this college offers conferences, continuing education courses, festivals, seminars, and workshops. If you are busy or live too far away to drive to class everyday, check out the Oklahoma City Community College's online classes.

i Looking for a college? Go to www.collegefind.com. Here you will find links to college courses online, colleges that offer bachelor's degrees, and more.

VO-TECHS

Vocational and technical schools around the Oklahoma City area offer everything from vehicle maintenance training to a medical education. High school students as well as adults can attend these schools and learn new skills in their field of study or interest.

FRANCIS TUTTLE VO-TECH (MAIN CAMPUS)
12777 N. Rockwell Ave.
(405) 717-7799
www.francistuttle.com

METRO TECH HEALTH CAREERS CENTER
1720 Springlake Dr.
(405) 424-8324
www.metrotech.org

METRO TECH SOUTH BRYANT CAMPUS
4901 S. Bryant
(405) 424-8324
www.metrotech.org

MOORE NORMAN TECHNOLOGY CENTER
4701 12th Ave. NW
(405) 364-5763
www.mntechnology.com

OKLAHOMA TECHNOLOGY INSTITUTE
9801 Broadway Extension
(405) 842-9400
www.oti-okc.edu

SPECIALTY SCHOOLS

ACADEMY OF RECORDING ARTS
305 SW 25th
(405) 632-0993

AMERICAN BROADCASTING SCHOOL
4511 SE 29th, Del City
(405) 672-6511
www.radioschool.com

CC'S COSMETOLOGY COLLEGE
4439 NW 50th St.
(405) 943-2300
www.ccscosmetologycollege.org

CENTRAL STATE BEAUTY ACADEMY
8494 NW Expressway
(405) 722-4499
www.centralstatebeautyacademy.net

ITT TECHNICAL INSTITUTE
50 Penn Place
(405) 810-4100
http://itt-tech.edu/

KISS INSTITUTE OF PRACTICAL ROBOTICS
1818 W. Lindsey
(405) 579-4609
www.kipr.org

OKLAHOMA HORSESHOEING SCHOOL
26446 Horseshoe Circle
(800) 538-1383
www.horseshoes.net/school

PLATT COLLEGE
2727 W. Memorial Rd.
(405) 749-2433
www.plattcolleges.edu/campuses/
okc-north-campus

UNIVERSITY OF PHOENIX
6501 Broadway Extension
(405) 842-8007
www.phoenix.edu

WRIGHT CAREER COLLEGE
2219 SW 74th St.
(405) 681-2300
www.wrightcareercollege.com

CHILD CARE

Oklahoma City has numerous child-care options for parents who need or want them. There is everything from day-care centers to in-home care and preschools. You will find church-operated and privately run centers in the area.

When looking for child care, the best place to start is by making a list of what you are looking for in child care and then talk with other parents who have their children in day care. Do you need a service that stays open late or opens early? What kind of safety and developmental standards are you looking for? What is a satisfactory child to provider ratio?

If you are looking for referrals or child-care resources, contact **Rainbow Fleet Childcare Resources and Referral** (405-525-3111; www.rainbowfleet.org) or the **Oklahoma Child Care Resource Referral Association** (405-942-5001; www.oklahomachildcare.org). These organizations can help you find the child-care center that is perfect for your family.

You might also want to contact the **Oklahoma Department of Human Services** (405-521-3646; www.okdhs.org/childcare). It offers child-care assistance and child-support services for families who need it. On the Web site you will find a child-care locator. Here you can view information about child-care facilities.

Among the child-care chains operating in Oklahoma City are **KinderCare Learning Centers** (405-722-0541; www.kindercare.com), **La Petite Academy,** (405-722-5448; www.lapetite.com), and **Childtime Learning Centers** (405-751-6930; www.childtime.com).

The key to finding quality day care is take your time, do your research, and make sure you are comfortable with where you leave your child.

WORSHIP

Since its earliest days, Oklahoma City has had deep religious roots. Six days after the Land Run of 1889, a service was held in downtown Oklahoma City by a Presbyterian minister. Two weeks later, a Methodist Sun School was organized. Four weeks after the Land Run, on May 19, the first Catholic service was held on Main Street between Robinson and Harvey at Indiana House. The First Methodist Episcopal Church Society was not far behind for on June 23, they organized their society with 17 charter members. The Baptists met and organized on July 21, 1889.

Today, worshippers of any religion can find a place to worship here. Look in the local phone book and you will find page after page of churches. If you are looking for a church, synagogue, temple, or mosque, then not only check the phone book but also ask friends, coworkers, and neighbors for suggestions. Searching on the Internet is also a good idea.

In this chapter, you will find five churches with large and growing congregations. Each of these churches is unique in that each embraces technology or offers programs beyond worship, a message, and prayer. Also in this chapter are two historic churches that have been a part of Oklahoma City since its founding.

Oklahoma City has many Christian and religious organizations, like Proactive Faith Ministries, Feed the Children, and the Oklahoma Conference of Churches. Over 70 organizations can be found listed in the yellow pages. Some are connected to religions and others are faith based, but all are community oriented. Denominations like the Nazarenes, Church of Christ, and Methodists have colleges in the Oklahoma City area. Oklahoma Christian College (www.oc .edu) is a four-year, private, co-ed college located in Edmond. The Southern Nazarene College (www.snu.edu) was founded in 1899 and is located in Bethany on a 40-acre campus. A second, smaller college, Southwest Christian University (www.swcu.edu) is also located in Bethany, a little west of the Nazarene College. Finally, following the United Methodist tradition is the Wimberly School of Religion and Graduate Theological Center (www.okcu.edu/religion) located at Oklahoma City University.

Oklahoma City has plenty of worship centers for all its residents. They welcome anyone who wants to worship.

FIVE HAPPENING CHURCHES

CHURCH OF THE SERVANT
14343 N. MacArthur Blvd.
(405) 721-4141
www.churchoftheservant.com

Located on the west side of MacArthur just north of the Kilpatrick Turnpike, this church continues to grow and expand. First organized in 1968, the church grew steadily and on August 2, 1970, held its first service in the current building. Today, it has over 6,800 members.

Part of the United Methodist congregation, an organization with over eight million people, Church of the Servant is a connectional church, which means each church is autonomous and is governed by its own board of directors, or trustees. This church is a family of faith with members from different walks of faith. It has a blend of contemporary and traditional worship. There is nursery care, a children's ministry, and a student's ministry for young people. Sun services begin at

8:15 a.m., 9:15 a.m., and 10:45 a.m. Once a month a 6 p.m. Sun-night service is held.

The church has community outreach programs, such as discovery classes. These classes range from personal writing experiences to yoga to Bible studies. The church also has two bookstores. The Servant Bookstore sells Bibles, reference books, and other study materials. The Earthglow Gift Shop sells decorations, greeting cards, and gifts, like candles, room sprays, and more. Profits from the gift shop are donated to selected missions each year.

CHURCH ON THE ROCK
1780 W. Memorial Rd.
(405) 943-2484
www.cotr.tv

Church on the Rock was founded in 1991 in Oklahoma City by Dr. John Benefiel and his wife, Judith. Its vision is to see "all Oklahomans saved." Large services are held on Sun morning at 9 a.m. and 11 a.m. and Wed at 7 p.m. Rock groups, small home fellowship groups ranging from 5 to 15 people, typically meet on Sun evening, but some groups meet at other times through the week. These groups have worship, discussion of Bible scripture, and prayer.

The church has a children's ministry, a student ministry, and a prison ministry, and they support missionaries in Peru through their COTRPeru ministry. On the Web site, you can read not only about these programs, but also about what the church stands for, its vision, and its goals.

The church is in the process of building a new sanctuary. Current plans are to have it seat from 750 to 1,000 people. It also wants a new children's facility and a large foyer for fellowship. All these plans depend on the building fund, which continues to increase.

HENDERSON HILLS BAPTIST CHURCH
1200 E. I-35 Frontage Rd.
(877) 901-4639
www.hhbc.com

Started in 1964, this church is a community of believers who are committed to God and each other. Their mission is to be a biblical church and to help people improve their relationship with each other and God. The church used to hold services on 33rd and Boulevard in Edmond before it grew and moved to its present location, merging with the church that was already on-site. Today, Henderson Hills Baptist Church is a large complex, which sits on the northeast corner of 15th St. and I-35 east of Edmond.

There are discovery classes for those new to the church. The church also has ministries for children, teens, young adults, adult small groups, women, and men. For those interested in music and the arts, this church has a massive worship and arts program. There is music, dance, drama, and an instrumental ministry.

Services are held Sat at 5:30 p.m., Sun 9 a.m. and 10:45 a.m., and Wed at 6:30 p.m. There is a calendar on the Web site that lets members and visitors alike know what's going on.

LIFE CHURCH TV
2001 NW 178th St.
(405) 478-5433
www.okc.lifechurch.tv

Part of the Evangelical Covenant Church, this multiethnic denominational church has people from all walks of life attending their services. Its mission is to help individuals become devoted followers of Christ and to reach others through His love and His people.

Life Church TV started in 1996. Its leaders embraced technology. Today, the church has satellite broadcasts that connect all 13 of its locations across six states. Through its broadcasts, the church reaches 21,000 people weekly through 49 worship services.

For those who want to attend, there are several services to choose from. Sat services start at 5 p.m. and 6:30 p.m. and Sun services begin at 8:30 a.m., 10 a.m., 11:30 a.m., and 1 p.m. Life Church has programs for all age groups. There is Lifegroups for those who want to get to know others in the church on a more personal level. Lifegroups are small groups of adults who meet regularly in homes, coffee shops, and parks. LifeKIDS is a program for children up to the fourth grade. Youth programs are available for children in grades 6 to 12.

If you can't make it to services at the church, you can watch a live podcast of the service online. Go the Life Church's Web site and click on the "LIVE in" link in the upper-right-hand corner of the page.

Spend some time checking out all this church has to offer online. One Web site to investigate is www.youversion.com. It is a free online Bible with assigned Bible readings or you can choose your own. This site allows you to offer comments on scripture, see pictures and videos, post blogs, write journal entries, and more.

ST. ELIJAH'S ANTIOCHIAN ORTHODOX CHRISTIAN CHURCH
15000 N. May Ave.
(405) 755-7804
www.stelijahokc.com
West of Quail Springs Mall and north of the Kilpatrick Turnpike on May Avenue, you will find this beautiful church. St. Elijah's is part of the Diocese of Wichita and Mid-America. It sees it mission as telling the world about salvation through Jesus Christ. The archdiocese refers to this church as "the Spiritual center of the Southwest."

A nursery is available as are many programs, like adult fellowship, choir, cultural committee, Ladies Guild, and Parish Counsel. The college outreach, Orthodox Christian Fellowship, meets every Tues at 9 p.m. in Norman. It is the students' connection to their church on campus. St. Elijah's also offers a vacation Bible school over the summer here for children.

Vespers is held on Sat at 5 p.m. Orthros and Sun school are at 9:30 a.m. Sun morning and divine liturgy is at 10:30 a.m. On the church's Web site is a calendar listing dates and times of all activities. Check it often to see which ones fit your schedule.

HISTORIC CHURCHES

FIRST PRESBYTERIAN CHURCH
1001 NW 25th St.
(405) 525-6584
www.fpcokc.org
The first church service held in Oklahoma City was on Sun, Apr 28, 1889, a few days after the Land Run. Presbyterian minister reverend Charles C. Hembree preached a sermon on Christian warfare at a water well at the intersection of Main Street and Broadway. This was the beginning of the First Presbyterian Church.

From its humble beginnings, the church has continued to grow and flourish. Services have been held in several buildings over the years due to its growth. In the mid-1950s the congregation decided to build the church they inhabit now. The church has a Gothic exterior and beautiful stained-glass windows created by Willet Stained Glass Studios of Philadelphia.

Always seeking "to share God's love from the heart of Oklahoma City" First Presbyterian Church has many programs to achieve its goal. There is an infant child care, a preschool, and a kindergarten afterschool program, plus a prayer chain, music opportunities, and more. Sun school meets at 9:30 a.m. each Sun, but summer and winter church service hours vary, so check the Web site for more information. Sun worship times are at 8:30 a.m. and 11:00 a.m.

ST. PAUL'S CATHEDRAL
127 NW 7th St.
(405) 235-3436
http://stpaulsokc.org
This cathedral was built in 1903 and is listed on the National Register of Historic Places. On Apr 19, 1995, it was damaged when the Alfred P. Murrah Federal Building was bombed. The blast was so powerful, it did extensive damage to the church and shattered the stone Celtic cross on the top of the church. The church had to close for two years. It took five more years and over seven million dollars for the facility to be rebuilt.

Today, the church is fully functional again. Services are held and the four gardens on parish grounds are visited regularly. Some of the programs available here are Sun school, Christian education, and a summer camp.

Worship times are Sun at 8 a.m., 9 a.m., 10:10 a.m., 11 a.m. and when announced at 5 p.m. Thurs at 12:10 p.m. Holy Eucharist and Healing is held. Check the Web site for Holy Days and Lent worship times.

ℹ️ On your computer, you can listen to liturgical music, plus prayers, readings, lectures, and interviews on Ancient Faith Radio at www.ancientradio.com. You can also get music or talk from on-demand podcasts and streaming audio programming.

RADIO STATIONS

If you want more than a Sun morning or Wed night worship service, Oklahoma City has several radio stations you can turn to that have Bible teaching and gospel music.

KOKF 90.9 FM (www.air1.com) launched in 1995. This station plays music for the young at heart. Its purpose is to get the message of Jesus out through music. KTLV 1220 AM (www.ktlv1220.com) is gospel talk, where listeners can hear programs from Joyce Meyers, Francis Chandler, and Charles Capp. On KQCV 800 AM and 95.1 FM (www.bottradionetwork.com) you'll find more bible teaching and Christian news. Such notables as Phyllis Schlafly, Jay Sekulow, and Tony Perkins broadcast from this station. KYLV 88.9 FM (www.klove.com) also known as "K-Love" goes on the air with a simple message "to be positive and encouraging." This channel plays Christian music and offers a prayer line that is open whenever you need prayer.

If you like to watch television, TBN Channel 14 (www.tbn.org) is the local Christian station in Oklahoma City. Programs like Praise the Lord, Joel Osteen Ministries, and Believer's Voice of Victory can be seen here.

RETIREMENT

Those who are looking to retire in Oklahoma City will find a favorable location not only for its number of retirees already here, but also its services and low cost of living. There are a number of services available here for seniors on the federal, state, and city level. Employment and volunteer opportunities can be found by contacting a few agencies. Everything from independent living to nursing homes is offered across the area.

This chapter includes resources to get seniors or those who care for seniors started toward retirement and personal care. While there is no way to list all the services available, this chapter will point readers in the right direction. There are Web sites to check out as well as phone numbers to call as the search begins. Readers will find a number of retirement communities and living areas for seniors. These communities invite people to come in for tours of their facilities. Keep in mind that communities offer different services and amenities. When checking out senior services and facilities, be sure to ask questions. A good rule of thumb is to write down questions well in advance. Ask for references and check with state organizations to see if any complaints have been filed.

The Areawide Aging Agency, 3200 NW 48th (405-943-4344), is a good source for all areas of senior care. It has a wide range of services and programs available to seniors from home delivered meals to caregiver support. It publishes the book, *Survival Kit for Seniors* every year and the content is available online at http://areawide.ok.networkofcare.org/aging/resource/find/cfm.

SENIOR SERVICES

Federal

MEDICARE SERVICES
701 NW 63rd St., Ste. 300
(800) 633-4227
If you are having a problem with your Medicare payments or aren't sure what services Medicare covers, call the number above to get your questions answered.

SOCIAL SECURITY AND MEDICARE
Located in Shepherd Mall
2615 Villa Prom
(405) 605-3000
www.ssa.gov
This office helps individuals who have questions about their Social Security benefits, disability

benefits, or Medicare. They can also help with lost or stolen cards. Hours are Mon through Fri from 9 a.m. to 4 p.m. The TDD number for Oklahoma City is (405) 605-3001, extension 3020.

State

ADULT PROTECTIVE SERVICES
(800) 522-3511 (statewide 24/7 abuse hotline)
This agency protects and is an advocate for senior citizens. You can also look in the blue pages of the phone book for local county offices. These offices are listed by zip code.
Quick Numbers
In-Home Personal Care Unit, (405) 521-4165
Long Term Care Ombudsman, (405) 521-6734
Special Unit on Aging, (405) 521-2281
Support Services Unit, (405) 521-4214

OKLAHOMA DEPARTMENT OF HUMAN SERVICES AGING SERVICES DIVISION

2401 NW 23rd St., Ste. 40
(405) 521-2281
www.okdhs.org/divisionsoffices/visd/asd
www.okdhs.org/programsandservices/aging

The Oklahoma Department of Human Services Aging Services Division provides information and leadership concerning issues which may concern or affect senior citizens living in Oklahoma. It develops community-based systems that assist, support, and protect older citizens. This division has many service arms, such as Adult Protective Services, which investigates abuse of vulnerable adults and arrange services to stop the abuse from continuing; In-Home Personal Care, which helps those who need it with their daily living activities at home; Long Term Care Ombudsman, which serves residents in long-term care facilities; the Special Unit on Aging, which provides policy, monitoring, and technical assistance to 11 area agencies who are receiving federal and state funds; and the Support Services Unit, which develops, manages, and coordinates activities for Adult Day Services, Disabled Transportation programs, Oklahoma Senior Corps Programs, and more.

DEPARTMENT OF HUMAN SERVICES HOME MAINTENANCE AND PERSONAL CARE

Oklahoma County, North
2801 NW 50th St., (405) 601-5700

Oklahoma County, North
2409 N. Kelley, (405) 522-5818

Oklahoma County, Southeast
9901 SE 29th St., (405) 739-8000

Oklahoma County, Southeast
1115 SE 66th St., (405) 604-8800

Oklahoma County, Southeast
401 W. Commerce, (405) 644-5700

County

OKLAHOMA COUNTY SENIOR SERVICES

7401 Northeast 23rd St.
(405) 713-1893
www.oklahomacounty.org (click on "Senior Services")

This county division provides information and services to Oklahoma County seniors. There are many services available like adult day care, nutrition, home-repair assistance, in-home assistance, and more. You can also find information on affordable housing, Alzheimer's support, and prescription drug assistance. It can also direct seniors to volunteer opportunities in the community.

Private

AARP, OKLAHOMA STATE OFFICE

126 N. Bryant
(405) 715-4462
www.aarp.org/states/ok

AARP is a nonprofit organization that provides information and education to senior citizens and is an advocate for issues relating to senior citizens 50 year of age or older, such as health care, housing, transportation, and retirement planning.

CARE PLUS HOME HEALTH

9828 Northeast 23rd St.
(405) 769-2551
www.careplusathome.com

This is an Oklahoma State licensed home health agency. Whether you need assistance for three hours or 24 hours a day, this service can provide it. It offers everything from meal preparation to medication reminders to personal care assistance with things like bathing. There is also a sitter service. Call or visit ther Web site to see all the services offered.

SENIOR LAW RESOURCE CENTER

1200 NW 22nd
(405) 528-0858
www.oklahomaseniorlaw.org

This center is a nonprofit organization which educates and supports Oklahoma senior citizens and their caregivers. It offers assistance with wills, trusts, probates, powers of attorney, diminished capacity, Medicare, and health care and more. To learn more about the services the center provides or to read up on issues you may be concerned about visit the Web site. You can also request information by phone.

MEALS

MOBILE MEALS OF OKLAHOMA COUNTY
6051 N. Brookline Ave., Ste. 123
(405) 607-2314
Made possible through area churches and non-profit agencies, this program delivers hot meals to homebound seniors in Oklahoma County. You must fill out an application. Call and one will be mailed to you. There may be a waiting list.

OKLAHOMA COUNTY SENIOR NUTRITION PROGRAM
5016 NW 10th St.
(405) 949-2709
www.oklahomacounty.org (click on "Senior Services")
This areawide aging agency funded program provides hot meals to 32 sites across the community. Seniors transport themselves or be picked up by Congregate Meal Transportation. The program also offers meal delivery to homebound seniors. You must fill out an application, so call as soon as you think you may need this service. Sometimes there is a waiting list. You can also get a list of all the places where this program serves meals by calling the number above.

EMPLOYMENT

For seniors who enjoy working and are looking for a place to work, the three sources listed below will help them in their search. Seniors need to call for an appointment.

AARP FOUNDATION WORK SEARCH
2200 NW 50th St., Ste. 109E
(405) 879-3899

EXPERIENCE WORKS
7401 NE 23rd St.
(405) 713-6502

OKLAHOMA COUNTY
Career Connection Center
7401 NE 23rd St.
(405) 713-1890

VOLUNTEER OPPORTUNITIES

Seniors who are looking for a rewarding volunteer experience will find help from the organizations listed below. These sources can place seniors in a position of their interest from working with children to being companions to older citizens. Seniors will need to fill out an application and their competency will be evaluated.

FOSTER GRANDPARENT PROGRAM
1025 Straka Terrace
(405) 632-6688, extension 257

RETIRED AND SENIOR VOLUNTEER PROGRAM (RSVP)
500 N. Broadway, Ste. 50
(405) 605-3110

SENIOR COMPANION PROGRAM
Through Sunbeam Family Services
616 NW 21st St.
(405) 943-4344

SENIOR CENTERS

Oklahoma City and the surrounding areas have many centers available to seniors. These centers host a number of activities, including dance classes; exercise programs; yoga; games, like cards and dominos; and quilting. Each center offers different programs. For instance Woodson Park has a weight-lifting program where Will Rogers offers defensive driving classes. Each center sets its own schedule so call to find out what programs are available and the hours they are open. Ask about meals too as most centers have a meal program. A partial list of centers is below.

EDMOND SENIOR CITIZENS CENTER
2733 Marilyn Williams Dr. (at Mitch Park)
(405) 216-7600

LINCOLN SENIOR CENTER
4712 Martin Luther King
(405) 427-0862

MIDWEST CITY SENIOR CENTER
8251 E. Reno
(405) 737-7611

MOORE SENIOR CITIZENS CENTER
501 E. Main
(405) 799-3130

WARR ACRES SENIOR CENTER
4301 N. Ann Arbor
(405) 789-9892

WILL ROGERS SENIOR CITIZENS CENTER
3501 Pat Murphy Dr.
(405) 942-4339

WOODSON PARK SENIOR ACTIVITY CENTER
3401 S. May Ave.
(405) 681-3266

i The *Survival Kit for Seniors* is published regularly by the Senior Connection office of the Areawide Aging Agency. It is a full of vital information for senior citizens and includes topics, like dental care, pet care, nutrition programs, utilities, and health services. To get your copy, call (405) 943-4344.

HOUSING

Independent Living

CONCORDIA SENIOR LIVING
7707 W. Britton Rd.
(405) 720-7200
www.concordiaseniorliving.com
Concordia is owned by the Lutheran Senior Citizens. It is a nonprofit corporation that was formed

in 1959 for the purpose of providing senior housing and other services to Oklahoma City. Seniors can choose from apartment or patio homes. All residences include a washer and dryer, a walk-in closet, and a full-size, electric kitchen. There is on-site assisted-living nursing care, a mail room, a library and business center, a health center, restaurant-style dining, scheduled transportation, 24-hour security, and weekly and biweekly housekeeping. Activities include exercise like chair exercise and strength training , cards, bingo, movies, and shopping and dining-out trips.

EPWORTH VILLA
14901 N. Pennsylvania Ave.
(405) 752-1200
www.epworthvilla.com
Located on 40 acres in northwest Oklahoma City, this senior living community is located near shopping and restaurants. Epworth Villa's beautiful grounds welcome visitors and residents alike as they enter the property.

The community offers 11 styles of apartments from 405 to over 1,400 square feet and 8 duplex-style cottages ranging from 1,400 to over 2,000 square feet. Community amenities include a heated swimming pool with whirlpool, exercise equipment, exercise classes and regularly scheduled transportation that transports residents to shopping areas, museums and more. Activities, such as cards, arts and crafts, and gardening are also offered. Nursing care is available if needed.

Check the Web site or call for more information. Management is always available to give tours.

STATESMAN CLUB RETIREMENT COMMUNITY
10401 Vineyard Blvd.
(405) 775-9009
www.statesmanclubret.com
This retirement community sits between North May and Pennsylvania, south of West Hefner Road. Studios to two bedroom living spaces are offered and the price ranges from $1,700 to $3,500 a month. The community is always 97 to 100 percent full so those who would like to live

here sometimes find themselves on a waiting list. There are 137 units here and the building is three stories with stairs and an elevator. The age range of seniors living here is 60 to 100.

Meals are served daily. There is a beauty shop, library, and pool on the premises. Activities include regularly planned outings for shopping or to visit museums, gardening, exercise classes, in-house movies, and arts and crafts.

SUPERBIA RETIREMENT VILLAGE
9720 Stacy Court (two blocks east of North-west Expressway and Council)
(405) 721-5656
www.superbiaretirementvillage.com
Efficiency and one-bedroom apartments and one-bedroom and efficiency cottages are available here for a total of 194 units. There is no buy-in, just rental. There is a variety of affordable options and HUD/Section 8 rental assistance is offered for the efficiency apartments. Water, gas, trash, and electric services are provided to apartment residents at no cost in the two manor buildings. Water and trash service is paid in cottages, but residents must arrange and pay for their own electric and gas service independently.

Housekeeping service is available. Residents may eat in the cafeteria or order lunch delivery. Bible studies, Sun worship services, shopping trips, bingo, cards, and other activities are offered. Pets are allowed here.

For those who are considering living here, you can call for a tour of the village or call for more information. You can also visit the Web site.

THE WELLINGTON
12525 N. Pennsylvania Ave.
(405) 755-3200
www.thewellington.org
Whether you are looking for a small apartment (450 square feet) or something larger (1,000 square feet), you will find it at the Wellington. Rental prices range from around $1,500 to $2,400 a month. Pets and smoking are allowed, but there is a fee charged for allowing pets and smoking in rooms. Pets must meet admission criteria, and smoking is only allowed in a designated area

like in specific residents rooms. However, most residents who smoke do so outside. There are benches in the front parking lot under some trees where they are allowed to gather.

Restaurant-style dining where residents can eat with other residents, is offered as well as private dining, where residents can eat alone or with their families. There is a beauty and barber salon, an enclosed courtyard and patio, a game room with card tables, laundry rooms, a library, and more. A 24-hour emergency response system is also available.

If you are interested, call and set up an appointment for a tour. Walk-ins are welcome as well.

Assisted Living

OKLAHOMA ASSISTED LIVING ASSOCIATION
3800 E. 2nd St.
(405) 235-5000
www.okala.org
The Oklahoma Assisted Living Association is a nonprofit organization. It helps seniors and their families decide which living option is best for them and can offer assisted-living choices. You can call to talk to a representative or visit the Web site. On the Web site you will find articles, forums, and advice on what you should look for in a quality residence. A directory of assisted living communities is also available on the site that can help with your search for the perfect assisted living center for you or your loved one.

EMERALD SQUARE ASSISTED LIVING
701 N. Council Rd.
(405) 787-4466
www.emeraldsquarealf.com
Located on the west side of Oklahoma City, this assisted-living center offers month-to-month apartment rentals. Potential residents are assessed prior to moving in to see what kind of services they may need. Additional charges may apply based on the assessment. Three meals are served per day. Apartment maintenance and weekly housekeeping is provided and is included

in rent fee as are all utilities. . Activities include exercise classes, gardening, arts and crafts, bingo, card games, and scheduled outings.

THE FOUNTAINS AT CANTERBURY
1404 NW 122nd St.
(405) 751-3600
www.thefountains.com
Situated on 38 acres, this senior community offers all levels of assisted care. There are 272 living spaces, including one to two bedroom apartments, patio homes, duplexes, and cottages. There is an Alzheimer's care unit where Alzheimer's residents live located toward the back of the property.

The community also offers dining services, health and wellness services, beauty and barber services, and private transportation.

Conveniently located just northwest of downtown Oklahoma City, the Fountains at Canterbury provides easy access to theaters, museums, golf courses, and shopping.

i Want to live alone or know someone who wants to live alone? There are three companies that offer personal response systems: Lifefone (800-882-2280), Lifeline (800-543-3546), and Link-to-Life (800-848-9399). These companies sell a device that you can wear. If you get hurt or find yourself in trouble, all you have to do is press a button on the device and help will come. Call to find out prices and all the services these companies offer.

TRANSPORTATION

There are several senior transportation programs available throughout Oklahoma City. The Community Action Agency (405-232-0199) has two locations and devotes seven vehicles for senior services. Metro Lift (405-235-7433), Congregate Meal Transportation (405-297-2583), and STEP-Shopping Shuttle (405-297-2583) also provide transportation. These services are all coordinated through the METRO Transit system. Visit www.gometro.org and click on "Special Services and Programs" to learn about the senior services available.

HANDICAPPED PARKING PERMIT
3600 N. Martin Luther King
(405) 425-2290
www.dps.state.ok.us/dls/pub/HPA.pdf
Seniors can apply for a handicapped parking permit from the Department of Public Safety Division. The Web site offers a form that seniors can fill out and mail. Be aware that the application must be signed by the applicant and his or her doctor to be accepted.

PUBLICATIONS

OKLAHOMA SENIOR JOURNAL
841 NW 34th St.
(405) 558-9878
www.okseniorjournal.com
The *Oklahoma Senior Journal* is a free publication for seniors that can be found in over 450 locations in the 405 area code. It has been in business since 1993 and offers articles on senior living, coupons, and a resource of over 5,000 phone numbers for senior-related items and services. The journal is published every six months, but is distributed monthly with a 95 to 100 percent pick-up rate. For the computer savvy, articles are available on the journal's Web site.

SEASONED READER
8101 NW 10th St.
(405) 470-4276
www.seasonedreader.com
Directed at the 55 and over age group, this tabloid-type newspaper can be found on racks across Oklahoma City. It is a free publication that focuses on information for seniors.

i For those seniors who are computer savvy, check out the Web site Senior Magazine Online at www.seniormag.com. There is no subscription fee and you can just click and read whatever topic you are interested in.

LIBRARIES

OKLAHOMA LIBRARY FOR THE BLIND AND PHYSICALLY HANDICAPPED

300 NE 18th St.
(405) 521-3514
(405) 521-4672 TDD

This library loans reading material in Braille and on audio cassette. It also loans listening machines. Individuals may visit the library in person or order materials over the phone. To get started, one must fill out an application. Once service is established, all it takes is a phone call to receive materials. Materials are sent by mail and returned the same way. This service is for not only the blind, but also for severely handicapped individuals and those people who can't hold a book. There is no charge for this service.

Volunteers come in and narrate books of all types on tape for patrons. If someone requests a book that's not available on cassette, a volunteer will record the book so it can be sent to the patron. Everything from biographies to mysteries is available.

RONALD J. NORICK DOWNTOWN LIBRARY

300 Park Ave.
(405) 231-8650
www.mls.lib.ok.us

There are programs for seniors available from the downtown library and its branches through its Outreach Division. For those seniors who are unable to get to the library, they can still enjoy library services through the Books by Mail program. It is available free to Oklahoma County residents 65 and over or to homebound seniors. The program has over 800 customers. To get started, seniors can call (405) 606-3295. If a requested book is already checked out, the senior will have to wait for it just like any other library patron. No movies can be ordered through the program, only books. Books need to be returned or rechecked within three weeks.

i A Place for Mom (www.aplaceformom .com) is a Web site that offers information for seniors and those who care for them.

Health Associations and Foundations

Alzheimer's Association (Central Oklahoma Regional Center)
3555 NW 58th St., Ste. 220
(405) 319-0780

American Diabetes Association
3000 United Founders Blvd., Ste. 108
(405) 840-3881

Arthritis Foundation (Oklahoma chapter)
3232 W. Britton Rd., Ste. 200
(405) 936-3366

Lupus Foundation of America (Oklahoma chapter)
4100 N. Lincoln, Ste. 208
(405) 427-8787

Oklahoma Health Care Authority
(405) 522-7300

Parkinson Foundation of the Heartland
1000 W. Wilshire, Ste. 364
(405) 810-0695

MEDIA

Oklahoma City has no shortage of media outlets for news and entertainment. As a matter-of-fact, one could make an argument for media gluttony. There is a wide range of publications this chapter is unable to include, like college, business, politics, current affairs, history and culture, entertainment and leisure, sports and outdoors, religion, and professional and trade publications.

Many of Oklahoma City's newspapers have been around since before statehood. It has large newspapers and small newspapers, large television and radio affiliates and small home-grown stations. Most newspapers large and small can be found in racks around the city. Subscription services are available with online viewing added as a bonus.

Television newscasts have a range of personalities who have become like family to viewers because of their longevity and staying power on their particular television networks. Oklahoma City's radio stations offer everything from news and sports talk to gospel contemporary music. When cable became an option for Oklahoma City residents, many chose Cox Cable. Cox Cable is the largest digital cable company in the city and offers residents not only cable television, but also Internet and telephone services.

If you are a visitor to Oklahoma City and want to learn about its residents, turn on one of its radio stations or pick up one of its cultural publications. Any information you need, be it sports, weather, local or national news, health care, education, arts, or science can be found through some media outlet in Oklahoma City. The *Oklahoma Gazette* is a good place to start.

While I have included newsstand prices and some subscription fees, remember these are always subject to change.

DAILIES

EDMOND SUN
123 S. Broadway, Edmond
(405) 341-2121
www.edmondsun.com
Located on the northwest corner of Broadway and 2nd Street, this newspaper has been serving the Edmond area for over 100 years. Started as a weekly in Oklahoma Territory, it published its first issue on July 18, 1889. Today, it boasts over 74,000 subscribers. The paper offers local news, sports, community events, seasonal content, and obituaries. The daily edition is printed Tues through Sat and can be purchased for 50 cents. The *Edmond Sun Weekender* is delivered on Sat and is $1.50 per issue. Subscription rates vary, but readers who want to try the paper can get two weeks of home delivery free.

JOURNAL RECORD
101 N. Robinson, Ste. 101
(405) 235-3100
www.journalrecord.com
If you want to know what's happening businesswise in Oklahoma City, pick up the *Journal Record*. Since 1903, this newspaper has been providing daily general business and legal news to residents. The articles range from local business trends to in-depth stories about Oklahoma City and Tulsa's business communities. Stories can include topics about drive-ins, commercial real estate, energy, health care or any other subject that affects Oklahoma City's economy. The price for a six-month print and online subscription (26 weeks) is $95.

ℹ️ If you are interested in knowing about all the media opportunities and contact information, check out the Oklahoma Press Association (405-499-0020; www.okpress.com). It prints public notices, puts out a press directory, and assists in digital clipping.

NORMAN TRANSCRIPT

215 E. Comanche St., Norman
(405) 321-1800
www.normantranscript.com

Founded in 1889, this newspaper is Norman's oldest business. The first issue came off the press on July 13, 1889, three and a half weeks after the Land Run of 1889. This daily newspaper's goal is to provide a unique identity for Norman, Cleveland, and McClain Counties in south-central Oklahoma. They do this by covering local news, community events, sports, and more for these areas. The paper has features on food and fashion and it makes wedding, engagement, and anniversary announcements. It also provides TV listings, classified ads, and more. Its circulation runs a little over 12,500.

Readers can pick up the paper off a rack around town for 50 cents for the daily edition and $1 for the Sun edition. Home delivery subscriptions cost $8.95 per month.

OKLAHOMAN

9000 N. Broadway
(405) 475-3311
www.newsok.com

The *Oklahoman* is the largest daily newspaper in Oklahoma and the only newspaper that covers the entire Oklahoma City area. It was started in 1889 by Reverend Sam Small, an evangelist and reformed drinker, who later sold it to Roy Stafford. In 1903, Stafford sold interests in the paper to Edward K. Gaylord, R. M. McClintock, and Ray Dickinson. Gaylord continued to run the paper and today, his heirs own it.

The *Oklahoman* provides national and local news, sports, weather, comics and classified ads. Its Sun edition offers expanded coverage and includes a large number of coupons.

Readers can find this newspaper in local bookstores or on racks around the metro. Subscriptions are available as well. The paper costs 75 cents and the Sun edition costs $2. A 13-week subscription of the Sun edition only costs $19.29 and a 13-week daily subscription costs $36.22. Circulation is over 250,000.

WEEKLIES

BLACK CHRONICLE

1528 Northeast 23rd St.
(405) 424-4695
www.blackchronicle.com

Started in 1979 by Russel M. Perry, this weekly periodical provides interesting and unique news and feature articles for Oklahoma City's African-American population. Readers will find stories on politics, sports, religion, crime, community events, and entertainment. Subscription prices start at $20.

CAPITOL HILL BEACON

124 W. Commerce
(405) 232-4151

This newspaper covers Oklahoma City's southern communities. It has a circulation of around 2,000 and features articles of local interest like community events, politics, education, sports, and more. Readers can subscribe for $25.00 a year or pick up a single paper for 50 cents.

CITY SENTINEL

1111 N. Hudson Ave.
(405) 605-6062
www.city-sentinel.com

Serving downtown and central and northwestern parts of Oklahoma City, this newspaper features news items covering government, health, business, education, and Oklahoma City news. It also prints community news and says it is the "premiere source for news straight from the heart of Oklahoma City" on its Web site. Subscription rates vary so call or check the Web site. A subscription includes home delivery weekly by mail and online access.

MIDWEST CITY SUN
351 N. Air Depot Blvd., Midwest City
(405) 737-3050
www.mwcsun.com
The *Midwest City Sun* is eastern Oklahoma County's source for news and information. The paper serves Midwest City, Del City, Jones, Spencer, Luther, Harrah, and Choctaw. It prints articles on local news and sports, community events, education,health and wellness and is published twice a week. Circulation is around 3,000. Readers can find the paper on Wed and Sun. For subscribers the Sun paper is delivered on Sat. The price of a single paper is 50 cents at the newstand and a subscription is $18 for 16 months.

OKLAHOMA CITY FRI
10801 N. Quail Plaza Dr.
(405) 755-3311
www.okcFri.com
This community newspaper focuses on northwest and north-central Oklahoma City. It prints columns, editorials, school news, local sports news, wedding and engagement announcements, and more. A subscription is $25 a year for Oklahoma City residents.

TRIBUNE
7300 NW 23rd, Bethany
(405) 787-1964
www.bethanytribune.net
Since 1923, this newspaper has been serving the communities of Bethany, Warr Acres, and northwest Oklahoma City. It publishes local news and sports, community issues and events, a church directory, senior news, book reviews, and crossword puzzles. The price is 75 cents at the newstand or residents in Oklahoma County can subscribe for $25.00 a year.

MAGAZINES AND OTHER PUBLICATIONS

ART FOCUS OKLAHOMA
730 W. Wilshire Blvd., Ste. 104
(405) 232-6991
www.ovac-ok.org

This magazine is published by the Oklahoma Visual Arts Coalition (OVAC). It is home delivered to members of the coalition to keep them up to date on artists' activities around the state. Individuals who are not members can pick up a copy at various galleries and other locations around the Oklahoma City area. In each issue readers will find OVAC news, artist profiles, reviews and previews of art activities around the state, features, and a gallery guide.

CHRONICLES OF OKLAHOMA
2401 N. Laird Ave.
(405) 522-4860
www.okhistory.org/publications
Published by the Oklahoma Historical Society (OHS), this publication is mailed to OHS members and subscribers quarterly. Each issue has book reviews, notes, documents, minutes of the quarterly OHS Board of Directors meeting, and four articles on historical Oklahoma subjects, like Indians, railroads, or notable people. The OHS also publishes an eight-page monthly newsletter titled *Mistletoe Leaves,* which informs members of activities of the organization and what is happening in the historical community of the state. Membership in OHS ranges from $35 to $1,000.

EDMOND LIFE & LEISURE
107 S. Broadway, Edmond
(405) 340-3311
www.edmondpaper.com
Edmond's culture and community resource, this publication covers local businesses, sports, education, entertainment, politics, health and fitness, and more. Printed in color and black and white, this approximately 36-page weekly is a free publication and can be found at 250 rack locations around Edmond.

METROFAMILY
306 S. Bryant, Ste. C152
(405) 340-1404
www.metrofamilymagazine.com
Since 1998, this free monthly periodical has been helping parents become more successful in raising their children and pointing them to things and places where they can have fun with their families.

Each issue has articles on family and relationships and a calendar of family events. Articles, like "Taming the Spirited Child" and family-fun topics, like "Exploring the Arts" and "Natural Wonders," offer parents insight and guidance as to what to do with their children. *MetroFamily* magazine has over 450 distribution sites. The oversize publication can be found in public libraries, restaurants, retail stores, and hospitals. Be sure to check out *MetroFamily's* Web site as Sarah Taylor, the publisher, is always adding bonuses there for parents.

OKLAHOMA GAZETTE
3701 N. Shartel
(405) 528-6000
www.okgazette.com
This weekly publication is Oklahoma City's cultural and social-scene magazine. It has articles on social needs and entertainment opportunities and features pieces on film, music, the arts, restaurants, and more.

Over the summer, the *Gazette* holds its Best of OKC readers poll. The *Gazette* prints up a ballot of nominees and readers vote on who they consider the best in the area.

Readers can find this paper in various locations throughout Oklahoma City, like bookstores, libraries, restaurants, and museums.

OKLAHOMA TODAY
120 N. Robinson Ave., 6th Floor
(405) 230-8450
www.oklahomatoday.com
Considered the state's magazine, this slick bimonthly publication features stories about people, places, events, and things from across the state. Readers will find interesting articles on everything from hound dogs to art at the Oklahoma State Capitol. The price is $4.95 for a single issue and $24.95 for a one-year subscription, which includes six issues.

OKLAHOMA WOMAN AND OKLAHOMA MEN
500 N. Meridian
(405) 917-9662
www.okwomanmag.com
From people profiles to health issues, readers will find interesting topics covered in both these publications. *Oklahoma Woman's* mission is to provide its female readership with informative and interesting articles and news. It is published monthly.

Oklahoma Men is published in July and Dec and includes articles that its male readership will find interesting and informative. Readers might find people profiles, golf info, safety tips, health or history features in any given issue.

Issues of both magazines are free and can be found in racks at restaurants, businesses, and libraries.

OUTDOOR OKLAHOMA
1801 N. Lincoln
(405) 521-3851
www.wildlifedepartment.com/outdoor oklahoma.htm
Published by the Oklahoma Department of Wildlife Conservation, this full-color bimonthly magazine features articles on hunting, fishing, camping, conservation, wildlife, and more. In each issue readers will find fine examples of outdoor photography. Single copies are $4 by mail or $3 at the newsstand. A subscriptions is $10 a year for six issues.

PERSIMMON HILL MAGAZINE
1700 Northeast 63rd St.
(405) 478-2250
www.nationalcowboymuseum.org
Persimmon Hill is the National Cowboy and Western Heritage Museum's award-winning, glossy, full-color magazine. Since 1970, it has provided readers with informative and interesting articles on the West. Well-known authors, such as Laura Ingalls Wilder, John Steinbeck, and Louie L'Amour, have been published in the magazine. Roy Rogers, John Wayne, and other notable westerners have been profiled here. The price is $11 for a single copy and $30 for a one-year subscription. The magazine is published quarterly.

PREVIEW MAGAZINE
5601 NW 72nd St., Ste. 178-G
(405) 728-1990
www.previewokc.com
Want to know what's happening around Okla-

homa City? Check out the city's monthly art and entertainment magazine. Articles on real estate, personal finance, shopping, dining, and events and interviews of Oklahoma City's movers and shakers are included in each issue. Twelve issues (a one-year subscription) costs $21.95.

RADIO

Oklahoma City

KOKC, 1520 AM
(405) 478-5104
www.1520kokc.com
This is a news talk station. Listeners can also hear Gary England's forecast and weather alerts. Follow Oklahoma Sooner sports here as well.

KMGL, 104.1 FM
(405) 478-5104
www.magic104.com
Adult contemporary

KQOB, 96.9 FM
(405) 848-0100
www.969bobfm.com
Classic rock

KRMP, 1140 AM
(405) 427-5877
www.perry-pub-broadcasting.com/krmp
Urban AC

KRXO, 107.7 FM
(405) 478-5104
www.krxo.com
Classic rock

KTLR, 890 AM
(405) 616-5000
www.ktlr.com
Community talk

KTLV, 1220 AM
(405) 672-3886
www.ktlv1220.com
Black gospel

KTOK, 1000 AM
(405) 840-5271
www.ktok.com
Find out all the latest news and talk about it here.

KTST, 101.9 FM (THE TWISTER)
(405) 840-5271
www.thetwister.com
Plays country hits. The 4Warn Storm Team broadcasts weather and weather alerts from this station.

KTUZ, 106.7 FM
(405) 616-9900
www.ktuz.com
Regional Mexican

KVSP, 103.5 FM
(405) 427-5877
www.kvsp.com
Urban

KXY, 96.1 FM
(405) 858-1400
www.kxy.com
Plays country hits. Just one of the many stations Mike Morgan and the 4Warn Storm Team broadcast weather information and alerts from.

KYIS, 98.9 FM
(405) 848-0100
www.kyis.com
Adult contemporary

WKY, 930 AM
(405) 840-0100
http://newsok.com/?radio
WKY is the oldest radio station in Oklahoma and was the first radio station west of the Mississippi River. It has seen many formats in its existence, from country to news talk. Today, it is a regional Mexican station.

WWLS, 640 AM AND 97.9 FM THE SPORTS ANIMAL
405) 840-0100
www.thesportsanimal.com

Anyone interested in sports will want to tune in to this channel. This sports talk station is nothing but sports talk 24 hours a day. Listeners express their opinion and all sports from golf to Oklahoma Sooner football are covered.

Edmond

KCSC, 90.1 FM
(405) 974-2414
www.kcscfm.com
Classical music is played from this station, located on the campus of the University of Central Oklahoma.

KUCO, 99 FM
(405) 974-2589
www.kuco.fm
On the air for 24 hours a day, this is the student broadcast network at the University of Central Oklahoma. It plays today's hit music for the college crowd.

Moore

KMSI, 88.1 FM
(405) 794-5674
www.oasisnetwork.org
Southern gospel music, Bible teaching, and Christian contemporary

Norman

KGOU, 105.7 FM
(405) 325-3388
www.kgou.org
Located on the University of Oklahoma campus, this station broadcasts National Public Radio (NPR).

KREF, 1400 AM
(405) 321-1400
www.kref.com
Sports talk

TELEVISION

Oklahoma City

KAUT, CHANNEL 43
444 E. Britton Rd.
(405) 516-4300
www.ok43.com
If waiting around until 10 p.m. to catch the nightly news doesn't working for you, you can catch a 9 p.m. newscast on this channel. A daily schedule line-up is located on the Web site.

KFOR, CHANNEL 4
444 E. Britton Rd.
(405) 424-4444
www.kfor.com
This station, formerly WKY-TV, was Oklahoma City's first television station and it went on the air in June 1949. The second-most viewed channel in Oklahoma City, this National Broadcasting Company (NBC) affiliate has shows like *Dateline, The Office, Heroes, Law & Order,* and *America's Got Talent.*

Viewers who watch the news cast on this channel feel like they are welcoming family into their homes. Many of the anchors have been with the channel for years. Linda Cavanaugh, who is the principal anchor at 6 and 10 p.m., joined the station in 1978. Kevin and Kent Ogle, sons of broadcast journalist legend, Jack Ogle, both work here. Kevin is coanchor at 6 and 10 p.m. with Cavanaugh and Kent is coanchor for the morning news and principal anchor at noon.

KFOR has chopper 4 with pilot James Garner. He heads to the sky to cover breaking news and severe weather. Channel 4 also has the most powerful Doppler radar in Oklahoma at 1 million watts of power.

KOCB, CHANNEL 34
1228 E. Wilshire Blvd.
(405) 843-2525
www.kocb.com
A local station owned by the Sinclair Broadcasting Group, this channel provides news, weather, and comedy and drama shows.

KOCO, CHANNEL 5
1300 E. Britton Rd.
(405) 478-3000
www.channeloklahoma.com

KOCO, the American Broadcast Company (ABC) network channel, continues to grow in popularity in the Oklahoma City market. Shows like *Lost, Grey's Anatomy, Dancing with the Stars*, and *The Bachelorette* can be seen on this station. Weather meteorologist, Rick Mitchell has been with the station since 1994. He brings consistency to the local newscast.

KOKH, CHANNEL 25
1228 E. Wilshire
(405) 475-9100
www.okcfox.com

This FOX affiliate station has a morning show that focuses on community events and a prime-time news show. It covers weather, sports, local and national news, and more. Viewers can watch their favorite FOX shows like the *Simpsons* here as well.

KSBI, CHANNEL 52
1350 SE 82nd St.
(405) 631-7335
www.ksbitv.com

Viewers like this station because of its commitment to quality family-friendly programming. It is owned by the Family Broadcasting Group, headed by founder and President Brady M. Brus. Show topics include drama, news, reality, sports, and travel.

KTBO, CHANNEL 14; DIGITAL 15 TBN
1600 E. Hefner Rd.
(405) 848-1414
www.tbn.org

For viewers interested in religious programming, this channel fits the bill. Owned by the Trinity Broadcast Network (TBN), this station launched on Mar 6, 1981. TBN is the largest religious network and most-watched faith network in America. It presents drama, variety, health, and inspirational music programs and programs for teens, young adults, and children. Rod Pars-

ley, Kenneth Copeland, Joyce Meyers, and Joel Osteen have programs on this channel.

KWTV, CHANNEL 9
7401 N. Kelley
(405) 843-6641
www.news9.com

A Central Broadcasting System (CBS) affiliate, this station carries all the shows from CBS, like *CSI, NCIS, 60 Minutes, Two and a Half Men*, and the *Late Show with David Letterman*. It has prime-time, daytime, and late-night viewing. Gary England is the chief meteorologist here and has been for a number of years. He warns residents about impending dangerous weather. Also on this channel's newscast is Kelly Ogle, son of legendary broadcast journalist, Jack Ogle. Watch to see his opinion segment, "My 2 Cents."

OETA, CHANNEL 13
7401 N. Kelley
(405) 848-8501
www.oeta.onenet.net

The Oklahoma Educational Television Authority (OETA) is Oklahoma's public television station. It provides educational and public television programming to the entire state. Television topics here include art, music, travel, history, education, science, and more. Shows include *NOVA, Sesame Street, This Old House, Oklahoma News Report*, and *NewsHour with Jim Lehre*.

Edmond

KUCO-TV, CHANNEL 6
100 N. University Dr., Rm. 196
Edmond
(405) 974-2589
www.kuco.tv

Located on the University of Central Oklahoma campus, this station presents local news and entertainment. Their slogan is "Where News Comes First." This is a student's cable channel and is on the Cox Digital.

INDEX

ABOUT THE AUTHOR

Deborah Bouziden was born in Oklahoma and has lived there all her life. Since 1985, she has had hundreds of articles published in not only Oklahoma publications but also in national magazines, such as Writer's Digest and Woman's Day. She is also the author of eleven books including *Off the Beaten Path: Oklahoma* (Globe Pequot Press). Check out her website at www.deborahbouziden.com where you can sign up for Twitter updates, read her blog, or join her on Facebook.

Travel Like a Pro

gpp
travel

e Cheap Bastard's Guide® to
NEW YORK CITY
MORE THAN 1,000 FREE LISTINGS

100
BEST
Resorts of the Caribbean

OFF THE BEATEN PATH®
VIRGINIA A GUIDE TO UNIQUE PLACES →

The Luxury Guide to
Walt Disney World® Resort Second Edition
How to Get the Most Out of the
Best Disney Has to Offer

shifra stein's
day trips®

from kansas city
fifteenth edition

JOHN HOWELL S ▦
NINTH EDITION
CHOOSE COSTA RICA
FOR RETIREMENT

Hundreds
of Ideas FOR
Day Trips
WITH THE
Kids
UN WITH THE FAMILY

Connecticut

INSIDERS' GUIDE
Florida Keys
and Key West

SCENIC DRIVING
COLORADO
STEWART M. GREEN